KIERKEGAARD ON SELF, ETHICS, AND RELIGION

Many of Søren Kierkegaard's most controversial and influential ideas are more relevant than ever to contemporary debates on ethics, philosophy of religion, and selfhood. Kierkegaard develops an original argument according to which wholeheartedness requires both moral and religious commitment. In this book, Roe Fremstedal provides a compelling reconstruction of how Kierkegaard develops wholeheartedness in the context of his views on moral psychology, metaethics, and the ethics of religious belief. He shows that Kierkegaard's influential account of despair, selfhood, ethics, and religion belong to a larger intellectual context in which German philosophers such as Kant and Fichte play crucial roles. Moreover, Fremstedal makes a solid case for the controversial claim that religion supports ethics, instead of contradicting it. His book offers a novel and comprehensive reading of Kierkegaard, drawing on important sources that are little known.

ROE FREMSTEDAL is Professor of Philosophy in the Department of Philosophy and Religious Studies at NTNU, Trondheim. He is the author of *Kierkegaard and Kant on Radical Evil and the Highest Good* (2014), and has published extensively on German philosophy, existentialism, ethics, and religion.

KIERKEGAARD ON SELF, ETHICS, AND RELIGION

Purity or Despair

ROE FREMSTEDAL

Norwegian University of Science and Technology

Shaftesbury Road, Cambridge CB2 8EA, United Kingdom

One Liberty Plaza, 20th Floor, New York, NY 10006, USA

477 Williamstown Road, Port Melbourne, VIC 3207, Australia

314–321, 3rd Floor, Plot 3, Splendor Forum, Jasola District Centre, New Delhi – 110025, India

103 Penang Road, #05–06/07, Visioncrest Commercial, Singapore 238467

Cambridge University Press is part of Cambridge University Press & Assessment, a department of the University of Cambridge.

We share the University's mission to contribute to society through the pursuit of education, learning and research at the highest international levels of excellence.

www.cambridge.org
Information on this title: www.cambridge.org/9781009074735

DOI: 10.1017/9781009076005

First published 2022
First paperback edition 2023

A catalogue record for this publication is available from the British Library

Library of Congress Cataloging-in-Publication data
NAMES: Fremstedal, Roe, 1977– author.
TITLE: Kierkegaard on self, ethics, and religion : purity or despair / Roe Fremstedal, Norwegian University of Science and Technology, Trondheim.
DESCRIPTION: Cambridge, United Kingdom ; New York, NY, USA : Cambridge University Press, 2022. | Includes index.
IDENTIFIERS: LCCN 2021042054 (print) | LCCN 2021042055 (ebook) | ISBN 9781316513767 (hardback) | ISBN 9781009074735 (paperback) | ISBN 9781009076005 (ebook)
SUBJECTS: LCSH: Kierkegaard, Søren, 1813–1855. | BISAC: PHILOSOPHY / History&Surveys / Modern
CLASSIFICATION: LCC B4377 .F74 2022 (print) | LCC B4377 (ebook) | DDC 198/.9–dc23
LC record available at https://lccn.loc.gov/2021042054
LC ebook record available at https://lccn.loc.gov/2021042055

ISBN 978-1-316-51376-7 Hardback
ISBN 978-1-009-07473-5 Paperback

To Johan and Oskar

Contents

PART IV FAITH AND REASON

Figures and Tables

Figure

Table

Acknowledgments

Parts of the present book have been presented to audiences in Antwerp, Bergen, Bologna, Clermont-Ferrand, Copenhagen, Frankfurt am Main, Oslo, Tromsø, and Trondheim. I am grateful to the audiences at these locations for comments on earlier versions of different book chapters. In addition, I want to thank the following persons in particular: the anonymous reviewers who contributed greatly to this book as well as Anthony Aumann, Adam Buben, Rob Compaijen, Jörg Disse, Kristine Farstad, Rick Anthony Furtak, Hilary Gaskin, Erik Hanson, Eleanor Helms, Beatrix Himmelmann, Timothy P. Jackson, Robert Louden, Melissa Fox-Muraton, Rene Rosfort, Gerhard Schreiber, Heiko Schulz, Jon Stewart, and Patrick Stokes. Thanks are also due to the following institutions and groups: The Department of Philosophy and Religious Studies, Norwegian University of Science and Technology, Trondheim; the Ethics Research Group and the Department of Philosophy, University of Tromsø – the Arctic University of Norway; the Faculty of Protestant Theology and the Institute of Philosophy, Goethe University, Frankfurt am Main; NordForsk.

Chapters 1–3 and 8–11 of the present work are partially based on earlier articles that have been heavily reworked and developed specifically for this book. In more detail:

Chapter 1 draws on Roe Fremstedal (2019a) "Kierkegaard's Post-Kantian Approach to Anthropology and Selfhood," in Patrick Stokes, Eleanor Helms, and Adam Buben (eds.), *The Kierkegaardian Mind*, London: Routledge (Routledge Philosophical Minds), 319–30.

Chapters 1–3 and 10 contain excerpts from Roe Fremstedal (2015a) "Kierkegaard's Use of German Philosophy: Leibniz to Fichte," in Jon Stewart (ed.), *A Companion to Kierkegaard*, Oxford: Wiley-Blackwell (Blackwell Companions to Philosophy, vol. LVIII), 36–49.

Chapters 1–3 contain excerpts from Roe Fremstedal (2015b) "Kierkegaard's Views on Normative Ethics, Moral Agency, and Metaethics," in Jon Stewart (ed.), *A Companion to Kierkegaard*, Oxford: Wiley-Blackwell (Blackwell Companions to Philosophy, vol. LVIII), 113–25.

Chapters 2–3 contain excerpts from Roe Fremstedal (2015c) "Why Be Moral? A Kierkegaardian Approach," in Beatrix Himmelmann and Robert B. Louden (eds.), *Why Be Moral?*, Berlin: Walter de Gruyter 2015, 173–97.

Chapter 3 contains excerpts from Roe Fremstedal (2019b) "Demonic Despair under the Guise of the Good? Kierkegaard and Anscombe vs. Velleman," *Inquiry: An Interdisciplinary Journal of Philosophy*, 1–21, DOI:10.1080/0020174X.2019.1610047.

Chapters 8–9 contain excerpts from Roe Fremstedal (2019c) "Hidden Inwardness and 'Subjectivity Is Truth': Kant and Kierkegaard on Moral Psychology and Religious Pragmatism," in Lee C. Barrett and Peter Sajda (eds.), *Kierkegaard in Context: A Festschrift for Jon Stewart*, Macon, GA: Mercer University Press (Mercer Kierkegaard Series), 112–29.

Chapter 10 contains excerpts from Roe Fremstedal (2020a) "Kant and Existentialism: Inescapable Freedom and Self-Deception," in Jon Stewart (ed.), *The Palgrave Handbook of German Idealism and Existentialism*, Basingstoke: Palgrave Macmillan (Palgrave Handbooks in German Idealism), 51–75, reproduced with permission of Palgrave Macmillan.

Chapter 11 contains excerpts from Roe Fremstedal (2017) "Eiríksson's Critique of Kierkegaard and Kierkegaard's (Drafted) Response: Religious Faith, Absurdity, and Rationality," in Gerhard Schreiber and Jon Stewart (eds.), *Magnús Eiríksson: A Forgotten Contemporary of Kierkegaard*, Copenhagen: Museum Tusculanum Press (Danish Golden Age Studies, vol. x), 145–66.

Abbreviations

Works by Kant

Except for *Critique of Pure Reason*, references to Kant use the pagination in the German Academy edition of Kant's works, specifying volume and page number (e.g., Ak 2:268). I quote the translations in the *Cambridge Edition of the Works of Immanuel Kant* (15 vols., ed. by Paul Guyer and Allen Wood, Cambridge: Cambridge University Press 1992–2012). The following abbreviations are used:

A	*Anthropology from a Pragmatic Point of View*, in *Anthropology, History, and Education*, ed. by Günter Zöller and Robert Louden, transl. by Mary Gregor, Paul Guyer, Robert Louden, et al., Cambridge: Cambridge University Press, 2009.
A/B	*Critique of Pure Reason*, ed. and transl. by Paul Guyer and Allen Wood, Cambridge: Cambridge University Press, 2007 (references are to the A and B editions).
Ak	*Gesammelte Schriften*, 29 vols., Berlin: Reimer, later de Gruyter, 1900–.
CF	*The Conflict of the Faculties*, in *Religion and Rational Theology*, ed. and transl. by Allen Wood and George Di Giovanni, Cambridge: Cambridge University Press, 2001.
CPR	*Critique of Practical Reason*, in *Practical Philosophy*, ed. and transl. by Mary Gregor, Cambridge: Cambridge University Press, 1999.
G	*Groundwork of the Metaphysics of Morals*, in *Practical Philosophy*.
LE	*Lectures on Ethics*, ed. by Peter Heath and J. B. Schneewind, transl. by Peter Heath, Cambridge: Cambridge University Press, 2001.

LL *Lectures on Logic*, ed. and transl. by J. M. Young, Cambridge: Cambridge University Press, 2004.
LPDR *Lectures on the Philosophical Doctrine of Religion*, in *Religion and Rational Theology*.
MM *The Metaphysics of Morals*, in *Practical Philosophy*.
O "What Does It Mean to Orient Oneself in Thinking?" in *Religion and Rational Theology*.
R *Religion within the Boundaries of Bare Reason*, in *Religion and Rational Theology*.
WE "An Answer to the Question: What Is Enlightenment," in *Practical Philosophy*.

Works by Kierkegaard

References to *Søren Kierkegaards Skrifter* use volume and page number (e.g., SKS 1, 61). References to *Søren Kierkegaards Papirer* use volume and tome number, entry category and number, and page number where appropriate (e.g., Pap. X–6, B68, 73). When the relevant text is translated into English, I also refer to *Kierkegaard's Writings* and *Journals and Papers* (both transl. by Howard Hong and Edna Hong), alternatively to *Kierkegaard's Journals and Notebooks*.

I use the following standard abbreviations:

BA *The Book on Adler*, Princeton: Princeton University Press, 2009.
B&A *Breve og Aktstykker vedrørende Søren Kierkegaard*, ed. by Niels Thulstrup, 2 vols., Copenhagen: Munksgaard, 1953–54.
CA *The Concept of Anxiety*, Princeton: Princeton University Press, 1980.
CD *Christian Discourses*, Princeton: Princeton University Press, 2009.
CI *The Concept of Irony*, Princeton: Princeton University Press, 1989.
CUP1 *Concluding Unscientific Postscript to Philosophical Fragments*, Princeton: Princeton University Press, 1992, vol. 1.
EO1 *Either/Or, Part I*, Princeton: Princeton University Press, 1987.
EO2 *Either/Or, Part II*, Princeton: Princeton University Press, 1990.
EUD *Eighteen Upbuilding Discourses*, Princeton: Princeton University Press, 1990.

FSE	*For Self-Examination*, Princeton: Princeton University Press, 1990.
FT	*Fear and Trembling*, Princeton: Princeton University Press, 1983.
JC	*Johannes Climacus, or De Omnibus Dubitandum Est*, Princeton: Princeton University Press, 1987.
JFY	*Judge for Yourself!*, Princeton: Princeton University Press, 1990.
JP	*Søren Kierkegaard's Journals and Papers*, 7 vols., Bloomington: Indiana University Press, 1967–78 (references are to the numbering of the passages, unless otherwise stated).
KJN	*Kierkegaard's Journals and Notebooks*, ed. by N. J. Cappelørn, A. Hannay, B. Kirmmse, et al., 11 vols., Princeton: Princeton University Press, 2007–20.
LD	*Letters and Documents*, Princeton: Princeton University Press, 1978.
M	*The Moment and Late Writings*, Princeton: Princeton University Press, 1998.
Pap.	*Søren Kierkegaards Papirer*, 2nd expanded ed., ed. by Niels Thulstrup, 16 vols., Copenhagen: Gyldendal, 1909–48, 1968–78.
PC	*Practice in Christianity*, Princeton: Princeton University Press, 1991.
PF	*Philosophical Fragments*, Princeton: Princeton University Press, 1987.
PV	*The Point of View*, Princeton: Princeton University Press, 1998.
SKS	*Søren Kierkegaards Skrifter*, ed. by N. J. Cappelørn, J. Garff, J. Kondrup, et al., 55 vols. (SKS 1–28, K1–K28), Copenhagen: Gad, 1997–2013.
SLW	*Stages on Life's Way*, Princeton: Princeton University Press, 1988.
SUD	*The Sickness unto Death*, Princeton: Princeton University Press, 1983.
TA	*Two Ages*, Princeton: Princeton University Press, 1978.
TD	*Three Discourses on Imagined Occasions*, Princeton: Princeton University Press, 2009.
UD	*Upbuilding Discourses in Various Spirits*, Princeton: Princeton University Press, 2009.
WA	*Without Authority*, Princeton: Princeton University Press, 1997.
WL	*Works of Love*, Princeton: Princeton University Press, 1998.

Introduction

Main Theses and Ideas Summarized

The present work reexamines the importance of the Danish philosopher and theologian Søren Kierkegaard (1813–55). It argues that many of Kierkegaard's most controversial and influential ideas are more relevant than ever. Specifically, it shows how we can make good sense of ideas such as subjective truth, "the leap" into faith, and "the teleological suspension of the ethical." When properly understood, none of these ideas are as problematic as commentators have long assumed.

This book shows that Kierkegaard offers a novel account of wholeheartedness that is relevant to discussions of personal identity, truth, ethics, and religion (particularly after Frankfurt, MacIntyre, C. Taylor, and Williams). *Concluding Unscientific Postscript,* notably, describes wholeheartedness as subjective truth, and despair as subjective untruth. This account involves an original, adverbial theory of truth in which agents, rather than propositions, are the basic truth bearers (Watts 2018). For Kierkegaard, wholeheartedness requires living truly by having a coherent personal identity (something he also describes as "purity of heart"). Despair, by contrast, involve an incoherent (or double-minded) identity, which fails to be true to itself.

Objective truth is quite different and involves an idealized third-person perspective that is objective by being fully informed yet disinterested, detached, and impartial. As such, it belongs to an idealized spectator, or epistemic agent, who sees an object from all perspectives simultaneously. Kierkegaard's emphasis on subjective truth underlines a duality in our concept of truth. Truth concerns not only that which agrees with facts or reality but also truthfulness, faithfulness, fidelity, loyalty, and veracity. Truthfulness, in particular, involves not only accuracy but also sincerity and authenticity, which is true to itself (Williams 2004). For Kierkegaard, the latter requires wholeheartedness.

This focus on wholeheartedness allows Kierkegaard to develop original critiques of amoralism and eudaimonism that remain relevant to moral psychology. Specifically, he argues in some detail that amoralism is incoherent, since wholeheartedness requires not just full commitment but also morality. Moreover, he radicalizes a Kantian critique of eudaimonism, which claims that eudaimonism involves an objectionable egoism and instrumentalism concerning virtue, by developing a modern account of *alterity*, in which morality is essentially other-regarding. Both here and elsewhere, he offers an interesting synthesis of Kantianism and virtue ethics (while criticizing consequentialism).

However, many scholars and readers of Kierkegaard prefer either his aesthetic or his religious works to the ethicist Judge William (and the ethical in *Fear and Trembling* and the non-Christian ethics in *The Concept of Anxiety*). Both tendencies are problematic, however. The former tends to ignore Kierkegaard's Hegelian critique of Romanticism and to downplay reasons for being moral, by opting for amoralism. The latter, by contrast, downplays the decisive roles played by ethics, rationality, and human effort for religion; despite appearances, Kierkegaard does not claim that human reason is worthless, or that all human volitional efforts are futile due to original sin (cf. Davenport 2017: 171).

Both approaches, by overlooking the ethical, are equally wrong since ethics is the key not only to religion but also to coherent selfhood and a meaningful life for Kierkegaard. Without moral commitment, neither wholeheartedness nor meaning nor faith is possible (which is not to say that morality is all that matters). Against both approaches, this book thus stresses the decisive importance of Judge William and ethics – and religion – that is not specifically Christian. Kierkegaard not only develops non-Christian ethics; he also reintroduces natural religion after Kant in a highly interesting manner by viewing the moral God as essentially hidden. Three examples of such natural religion are immanent religiousness in *Concluding Unscientific Postscript*, the Socratic hypothesis in *Philosophical Fragments*, and the ethical in *Fear and Trembling*.

Kierkegaard's relevance is therefore not limited to Christian ethics and theology. Instead, his contribution concerns non-Christian and Christian approaches to both ethics and religion. Indeed, it concerns the very relation between ethics *and* religion as well as the very relation between philosophy *and* theology.

Kierkegaard posits a close relationship between the ethical and the religious. Despite appearances, the notorious "teleological suspension of the ethical" and Abraham's sacrifice of Isaac do not concern conflict between ethics and religion (as such). There is strong textual evidence ruling out such conflict, and Kierkegaard's account does not even provide conceptual room for it, since he *identifies* the good and the divine. Instead, the "teleological suspension" concerns a transition from one interpretation of the ethico-religious to another one. Typically, it involves a leap from natural to supernaturally revealed standards, or a transition from law to grace. It thus concerns how ethics is supported theologically by divine power and intervention. Instead of suspending ethics, Kierkegaard therefore stresses the overriding nature of morality, seeing what we ought to do all-things-considered as a specifically ethico-religious question.

As a direct result, his position is much more defensible than commonly thought. Indeed, Kierkegaard is explicit that it would have been "an error" on Abraham's part if he were to kill Isaac (SKS 24, 375, NB24:89 / KJN 8, 379). Moreover, Abraham's sacrifice of Isaac represents a special case that cannot possibly be imitated by others. Indeed, Kierkegaard rules out religion that conflicts with morality or lays claim to possess privileged insight and truth. *Two Ethical-Religious Essays*, notably, clearly deny that moral obligations can be overridden by any claim to possess a higher truth.

Kierkegaard interprets ethics in religious terms, by ruling out secular ethics. He therefore sees ethics and religion, the good and the divine, as each implying the other. This is missed by secular readings of the ethical in *Either/Or* and later writings. Since the 1990s, scholars have rightly emphasized Kierkegaard's Christian ethics. But the operative assumption is still that only part of religion is moral since religion must have some autonomy from ethics. However, the present book shows that Kierkegaard clearly denies such autonomy, since he *moralizes* religion completely. Despite appearances and long-standing interpretative traditions, it is not Kant but Kierkegaard who reduces religion to ethics, by viewing it as a moral way of life that is supported theologically. Yet Kierkegaard's famous existential interpretation of religion is a development of Kant's moral interpretation of religion. In short, "existential" is a new term for "practical" and "moral," which is exactly why the introduction of the term in *Concluding Unscientific Postscript* invokes Socrates, who introduced moral philosophy. Therefore, *Either/Or* identifies the existential choice of oneself with the choice of the ethical.[1]

[1] Still, the traditional, Aristotelian, contrast between theoretical and practical concerns may not be exhaustive, insofar as there are questions about how we should feel that concerns *evaluative* reasons that are neither practical nor theoretical. Although existential issues typically concern practical and moral issues for Kierkegaard, it nevertheless seems possible to include such evaluative issues as part of existential issues in a broad sense. For evaluative reasons and concerns, see Skorupski 2012: 36.

Kierkegaard constantly contrasts existential concerns with theoretical speculation. But instead of denying theoretical speculation (which is concerned with thinking), Kierkegaard follows Kant in viewing it as *secondary* to practical concerns (which are concerned with action). Like Kant and William James, he maintains that belief can be justified practically if epistemic evidence is lacking. Kierkegaard is therefore a pragmatist – not an evidentialist – concerning belief.

He is relevant to discussions of the ethics of belief in philosophy of religion and epistemology for two different reasons. First, he sketches a practical argument for belief, according to which nonbelief involves despair, which deserves more attention both historically and systematically. Second, he potentially sheds new light on the debate on pragmatism versus fideism concerning belief (in which pragmatism provides practical reasons for belief, something fideism does not do). Like recent scholarship on fideism, this book indicates that the fideist label is problematic, insofar as it is used pejoratively and anachronistically to criticize views that contrast faith and reason in highly different ways. The dominating fideist reading of Kierkegaard particularly ignores pragmatist elements in his thinking that are decisive for assessing whether religious belief is supported by practical reasons or not.

Although Kierkegaard often contrasts faith and reason, this hardly supports fideism or irrationalism. Faith can be above reason in one sense yet rational in another sense. It can defy complete conceptual understanding yet be rationally defensible. At least, this is what Kierkegaard suggests, developing a nuanced hybrid account, in which faith is partially above conceptual understanding yet supported by practical reasons. Although Christian revelation transcends reason as a natural faculty, faith is only against reason if viewed from the perspective of nonbelievers who take offense at it. Faith cannot be irrational or absurd for believers, as the irrationalist reading indicates. But this fact is often ignored since key texts are still not translated into English or made readily available (cf. Pap. X–6, B68–B82). The widespread irrationalist reading of Kierkegaard is shown to be untenable, unless viewed as a form of normative pluralism that emphasizes leaps between different normative standards.

Although Kierkegaard never speaks of a "leap of faith," he nevertheless introduces a leap into faith relevant to contemporary normative pluralism and philosophy of religion. This leap involves both general transitions between different normative standards and religious conversions in particular. Even when different standards diverge and conflict, such leaps need not be blind or irrational, if one abandons standards that collapse internally and the new standards hold up. Therefore, leaps can be rational and justifiable. Here Kierkegaard sketches a weak form of normative pluralism, which avoids blind leaps, whims, or plumbs, while justifying existential leaps that avoid despair or double-mindedness.

Kierkegaard is motivated by traditional Christian faith that was endangered by "contemporary culture, philosophy and theology"; but "in trying to reassert" Christianity, he "developed a language that was later to be used, contrary to anything he would have ever imagined, to undermine them instead."[2] Rather than championing radical choice, decisionism, or irrationalism, Kierkegaard is a Christian Platonist who argues that moral goodness is divine and inescapable. However, the widespread reading of Kierkegaard as the father of existentialism tends to neglect this fact. Still, the case of Kierkegaard shows strong continuity between existentialism and the history of philosophy. Specifically, his attempt to reassert Christianity in modernity is interesting because it makes creative and constructive use of Enlightenment philosophy, German Romanticism, and idealism as well as liberal theology. Kierkegaard is not so much dismissive toward classical German philosophy as a selective reader who uses ideas for his own purposes. Lore Hühn and Philip Schwab comment:

> There is no doubt that, philosophically, German Idealism constitutes the background and point of departure for Kierkegaard's thinking. Essential concepts, ideas, and moves in Kierkegaard's oeuvre are indebted to impulses from Fichte, Schelling, and Hegel and are, in the first instance, to be understood by reference back to classical German philosophy. (2013: 62)

This is a valid point which holds more generally for classical German philosophy from Leibniz to Hegelianism. Indeed, Paul Ricoeur (1998: 16) suggests that "in a sense, Kierkegaard can be regarded as part of the move in philosophy after 1840 generally known [as] a 'return to Kant.'" Alison Assiter comments:

> [I]n a sense the whole of Kierkegaard's thought could be seen to be a response to Kant. No doubt it is also a reaction to Schelling and others, but the response to Kant seems to me to be particularly important. Kierkegaard's response to Kant is a criticism of his ethics. (2009: 71)

This book shows the relevance of Kant and idealism for Kierkegaard studies. But the focus on Kierkegaard's polemics against Hegelianism in earlier scholarship risks obscuring Kierkegaard's constructive and creative

[2] Di Giovanni and Livieri (2018: Part v). The formulation of this point is heavily indebted to Giovanni and Livieri, who make essentially the same point in very similar terms about Jacobi.

use of German philosophy from Leibniz to idealism. The importance of Leibniz, Lessing, Kant, Hamann, Jacobi, Fichte, and Schelling are still somewhat underappreciated in the Kierkegaard literature, although it is decisive for understanding his accounts of selfhood, ethics, and religion.[3]

The present work particularly sheds light on Kierkegaard's relations to Kant and – to a lesser extent – Fichte, both historically and conceptually. Specifically, it is shown that Kierkegaard's influential account of despair, selfhood, ethics, and religion belongs to a larger intellectual context in which Kant and Fichte played crucial roles. Historically, this book therefore shows the importance and relevance of classic German philosophy for Kierkegaard studies. German philosophy is decisive not only for Kierkegaard's intellectual development but for our understanding of him and his relevance to philosophy and theology – both past and present.

Still, Kierkegaard goes beyond his predecessors by moralizing both religion and selfhood. Without moral commitment, neither faith nor wholeheartedness is possible since moral normativity is constitutive of coherent selfhood and authentic religion. But Kierkegaard is not a Stoic who thinks that only morality matters. Instead, he is a noneudaimonist and normative pluralist who thinks that morality requires personal sacrifice, since morality and prudence conflict. Still, our final end – the highest good – synthetizes both by conditioning prudence on morality. The latter is not only an eschatological idea but also a regulative idea that we should strive toward in this life.

Chapter Outlines

Part I of the present monograph deals with selfhood, despair, and wholeheartedness. Chapter 1 deals with Kierkegaard's influential account of selfhood and anthropology. This account is decisive for understanding his importance for theories of personal identity and human nature as well as action theory. In addition, it provides the necessary conceptual and historical background for understanding his contribution to truth theory, ethics, and religion on the one hand and existentialism and continental philosophy on the other. Finally, it sheds light on the relation between philosophical and theological anthropology.

[3] Note that Kierkegaard only seems to have studied Hegel's texts thoroughly in the 1841–43 period, although there is no evidence that he studied Hegel's *Lectures on the Philosophy of Religion*. See Stewart 2003: 598–605.

Chapters 2 and 3 both discuss the relation between selfhood, agency, and ethics. Specifically, both examine Kierkegaard's claim that wholehearted or coherent selfhood and agency requires full moral commitment. Both argue that *Either/Or* develops an original critique of amoralism and practical moral skepticism that escapes a difficult dilemma associated with justifications of morality. According to this dilemma, any such justification must either offer moral or nonmoral (prudential) reasons for being moral. But the former seems circular and question-begging, whereas the latter seems like the wrong kind of reasons, which could only support legality and rational egoism rather than morality and altruism. However, Kierkegaard develops three different argumentative strategies that all escape this dilemma, offering a powerful response to amoralism that is relevant to contemporary concerns, while being rooted in historical discussions of Kantianism, German Romanticism, and idealism.

Part II deals with the relation between morality, prudence, and religion. Chapters 4 and 5 discuss systematically Kierkegaard's elusive critique of ethical eudaimonism. It is shown that Kierkegaard develops and radicalizes an influential Kantian critique of eudaimonism, according to which ethical eudaimonism entails egoism and instrumentalism concerning virtue that make morality second to self-interest. In the late twentieth century, discussions of this familiar critique have been renewed by the reemergence of virtue ethics and eudaimonism. However, many still share the concern that eudaimonism involves an objectionable egoism and instrumentalism concerning virtue. Chapters 4 and 5 both show Kierkegaard's relevance to this ongoing discussion, emphasizing how he develops and radicalizes a Kantian critique of ethical eudaimonism by combining a modern account of alterity, in which morality is essentially other-regarding, with the idea that morality is Christocentric, since it concerns imitating Christ *and* serving the neighbor.

Although controversial and more successful against hedonistic eudaimonism (Epicureanism) than Stoicism or Aristotelianism, Kierkegaard's critique of eudaimonism is still largely defensible. At least, reconstructions indicate that genuine (noninstrumental) other-regard is incompatible with eudaimonism's focus on personal happiness as the highest good. Still, Chapter 5 shows that Kierkegaard is not an antieudaimonist, who dismisses legitimate self-interest, personal happiness, or salvation. Instead, he develops a noneudaimonistic ethics and theology, in which morality overrides prudence in cases of conflict. Yet, the "highest good" nevertheless involves a synthesis of morality and prudence, in which happiness is conditioned on moral virtue.

Chapters 6 and 7 both examine the relation between ethics and religion by discussing "the teleological suspension of the ethical" and Abraham's sacrifice of Isaac in *Fear and Trembling*. It is shown that – despite appearances – religion cannot possibly conflict with ethics. Apart from strong textual evidence precluding such conflict, more principled reasons show that there is no conceptual room for any such conflict within Kierkegaard's Platonico-Christian framework. The implication is that for Kierkegaard ethics entails religion and *vice versa*, although we must distinguish between Christian and non-Christian ethics *and* religion. I argue that the non-Christian ethics has (temporal and conceptual) priority over Christian ethics. Specifically, it represents "the first ethics" that provide the default position that Christian ethics must presuppose. Still, Kierkegaard suggests that Christian ethics overrides non-Christian ethics to some extent, although there is no break with ethics (as such). Instead of suspending ethics, Kierkegaard stresses its overridingness, seeing what we ought to do all-things-considered as a specifically ethico-religious question.

Part III discusses the relation between subjectivity, inwardness, and truth. Chapter 8 reconstructs Kierkegaard's concept of inwardness and his ignored critique of consequentialism in ethics. It is argued that both morality and religion require not only good intentions but also a good character. However, since moral character itself is not directly accessible, but only shown indirectly by words and deeds, Kierkegaard describes it as "hidden inwardness," which is only seen by God. Pace Mulder (2000: 317), such inwardness neither entails a hidden, private domain nor "negative outwardness," which "confines itself (in order not to be seen for what it is)." Nor does it entail enclosing reserve or uncommunicativeness (*Indesluttethed*), which is inwardness in deadlock. Rather, it represents an inwardness that strives to express itself in words and deeds.

Chapter 9 examines different readings of the notorious thesis that "subjectivity, inwardness, is truth" in *Concluding Unscientific Postscript*. It is argued that, instead of involving (objectionable) subjectivism, subjective truth involves an original, adverbial theory of truth that is relatively unexplored. Specifically, subjective truth concerns living truly by being wholehearted (as argued by Watts [2018]). In addition, it is closely associated with subjective, practical justifications of religious belief found in pragmatism concerning religious belief; these justifications of belief need not involve subjectivism or fideism, since faith could be supported by practical reasons that are objective.

Part IV systematically discusses the relation between Christian faith and reason. Chapter 10 deals with the category of the leap, which concerns both

Christian conversions and more general transitions between different paradigms or normative domains. It is shown that – by responding to Kant, Jacobi, and Lessing – Kierkegaard develops an original account of the leap, which is relevant both to philosophy of religion and more general debates concerning rationality, incommensurability, and noncommensurability in value theory and theories of rationality. Finally, Kierkegaard uses Leibniz, Jacobi, Kant, and Schelling to develop the famous distinction between thought and being and he sketches a *reductio ad absurdum* argument for faith that seems Kantian.

By examining little-known primary sources that are largely untranslated, Chapter 11 shows that Kierkegaard clearly denies that Christian (and Jewish) faith is absurd or irrational. Still, faith does seem absurd to nonbelievers since it provokes and scandalizes our understanding. However, faith overcomes this absurdity since it is not offended by divine revelation. Chapter 12 then shows that Kierkegaard is a suprarationalist, who takes faith to be above reason, not against it. Still, his nonreligious pseudonyms contrast faith and reason in order to counteract theological views which are overly rationalistic and scientific. Indeed, Kierkegaard criticizes the Augustinian idea of faith seeking understanding. Although not promoting blind faith, he attacks intellectualist and rationalist accounts of faith that do not do justice to the mysteries of divine revelation and the incarnation. Faith cannot be reduced to conceptual understanding, but it must nevertheless both involve and seek practical understanding.

The final chapter shows that Kierkegaard discusses the ethics of belief, that is the normativity that governs the formation, maintenance, and relinquishment of beliefs. Kierkegaard is a clear nonevidentialist concerning religious belief, since he denies that justified religious belief requires sufficient epistemic evidence (indeed, such evidence is impossible to obtain due to human finitude). However, the widespread fideist reading of Kierkegaard, which takes belief to involve a self-constituting leap of faith, is challenged by a pragmatist reading, which takes belief to be justified by normative practical reasons instead. By examining different interpretations and different primary sources, the chapter concludes that the pragmatist reading is highly promising both textually and philosophically. Despite appearances, Kierkegaard offers justificatory practical reasons for religious belief. Still, his account of divine revelation involves an element of fideist self-constitution, although it does not amount to any blind leap of faith.

The reason for ordering the topics in this manner are roughly the following: I believe that it is best to start (in Chapter 1) with

Kierkegaard's account of *wholehearted* agency and selfhood, since this account provides the conceptual basis for his interrelated accounts of ethics, religion, and truth. Specifically, Chapters 2 to 4 argue that wholeheartedness requires noneudaimonistic *ethics*. Moreover, Chapters 4 and 5 indicate that ethics involves *theological commitments*, while Chapters 6 and 7 argue that religion support ethics instead of contradicting it. Chapters 6 and 7 particularly build on the concept of eternal happiness (highest good) introduced in Chapters 4 and 5. In light of this ethico-religious background, Chapters 8 and 9 then discuss the thesis "subjectivity, inwardness, is truth," denying that it entails either subjectivism or a hidden, private domain. This discussion of subjective truth then prepares the ground for the examination of faith and reason in Chapters 10 to 13.

Methodology and Kierkegaard's Pseudonyms

The different chapters of this monograph combine historical and systematical considerations. On the one hand, the book indicates Kierkegaard's relevancy to contemporary discussions of selfhood, ethics, and religion. On the other, it sheds new light on Kierkegaard historically, by emphasizing his creative use of German philosophy. It thus combines historical and systematical approaches by using historical texts in contemporary discussions. My methodology here corresponds largely to what Gary Hatfield describes as being

> aware of the need for historical context to gain better access to past texts while still wanting to use those texts primarily as a source of raw material for solutions or answers to present philosophical problems. This would be historically sensitive reading in the service of fixed-upper ends. (2005: 91)

This book therefore focuses on some of Kierkegaard's ideas that are still relevant to contemporary debates. It does not deny that some ideas are problematic or objectionable. But it maintains that Kierkegaard remains relevant to ongoing debates on selfhood, ethics, and religion. As a result of this methodology, I thus seek to use contemporary terminology rather than working with Kierkegaard's Danish and the Golden Age Denmark context.

But to make sense of Kierkegaard's contribution I nevertheless include historical background that helps us to understand his theory, particularly with regard to points that are still relevant and that can enrich contemporary discussions. This book therefore brings Kierkegaard's ideas, and contemporary versions of them, into contact with modern thinkers such as

Elizabeth Anscombe, Harry Frankfurt, Jürgen Habermas, John E. Hare, Alasdair MacIntyre, and Charles Taylor. To facilitate this, I include Kierkegaard's pseudonymous writings, which are significant for discussions of selfhood, ethics, and religion – independently of whether these writings can be attributed to Kierkegaard or not.

Kierkegaard indicates two reasons for using pseudonyms: First, he can avoid a straightforward public attack on personal acquaintances (Pap. VII–1, B88–B92; Pap. X–6, B128 / JP 6, 6596). He can distance himself from the persons involved and avoid unnecessary offense and embarrassment in a small-town context where the leading figures are all personally acquainted (Stewart 2003: 42; Schreiber 2018: 88). Second, the different pseudonyms speak from different *perspectives* (SKS 23, 182–3, NB17:28 / KJN 7, 185). Specifically, Johannes de silentio (in *Fear and Trembling*) and Johannes Climacus (in *Philosophical Fragments* and *Concluding Unscientific Postscript*) are nonbelievers. By contrast, Kierkegaard and Anti-Climacus (in *The Sickness unto Death* and *Practice in Christianity*) typically speak as Christian believers (see SKS 16, 17, 64–5n / PV, 31–2, 85–6n; Pap. X–6, B68–B82 / JP 1, 10–12 and JP 6, 6598–601). The two former both see faith as absurd and offensive, while the latter two do not. We will see in Chapter 11 that Kierkegaard has theological and philosophical reasons for using this *perspectival* approach to faith and reason.

Kierkegaard indicates that he shares Anti-Climacus' views and ideals, without living up to them (SKS 22, 130, NB11:209 / KJN 6, 127; cf. Theunissen 2005: 122n), since they are highly demanding morally. But for the sake of clarity, I generally specify the pseudonym author to clarify the relevant perspectival viewpoint. Although he distances himself from his pseudonyms (SKS 7, 571 / CUP1, 627), Kierkegaard nevertheless suggest that the pseudonyms often agree with each other and repeat each other. He therefore writes:

> [...] I would be glad to have another pseudonym, one who does not like Johannes de Silentio say he does not have faith, but plainly, positively says he has faith – Anti-Climacus – repeat what, as a matter of fact, is stated in the pseudonymous writings. (Pap. X–6, B82, 88 / JP 6, 6601)

In this monograph, we will see many cases where the pseudonymous writings overlap and repeat each other, just as they overlap with and repeat (or anticipate) Kierkegaard's signed (nonpseudonymous) works. Specifically, we will see substantial overlap and consistency concerning selfhood and agency, as well as ethics, truth, and religion. It is then difficult to see why we cannot attribute pseudonymous views to Kierkegaard in these cases. But not everything depends on how we approach the pseudonyms, since I make extensive use of Kierkegaard's signed writings and specify the pseudonymous authors. Finally, there is nothing that prevents us from engaging with and benefiting from the pseudonymous texts, irrespectively of whether they fit into a larger framework or not.

PART I

Self, Despair, and Wholeheartedness

CHAPTER 1

Selfhood and Anthropology

The Historical Background: Anthropology and Self after Kant

This chapter relates Kierkegaard's views on selfhood and anthropology to Kantian and post-Kantian philosophical anthropology. It focuses on Kierkegaard's contribution to debates on selfhood and anthropology and discusses the relation between philosophical and theological anthropology in Kierkegaard. The chapter gives a synopsis of these issues by focusing on *The Sickness unto Death*, although important elements of this work are anticipated by *Either/Or*, *The Concept of Anxiety*, and *Concluding Unscientific Postscript*. After an historical introduction and brief remarks on Kierkegaard's method, the chapter moves to human nature, selfhood, and despair in *The Sickness unto Death*. We will see that human nature is interpreted as a synthesis of opposites, and that selfhood requires self-consciousness and higher-order volition (i.e., volition concerning volition, or a will to change lower-order volition).

The term "anthropology" refers both to various views regarding human nature, and to different academic disciplines. The first of these has a very long history, although the term "anthropology" first appeared in 1501. Regarding the second, anthropology first became an academic discipline in the late eighteenth century, and gradually became institutionalized in the first half of the nineteenth.[1] From its inception, the discipline of

[1] The term "anthropology" is more established in Kantianism and continental philosophy than in analytic philosophy. In the early twentieth century, anthropology was reestablished as a philosophical discipline in Germany, something that lead to theoretical controversies regarding vagueness, empiricism, scientism, reductionism, and reification (see Marquard 1971; Orth 1997; Honenberger 2015). It is beyond the scope of this chapter to discuss these controversies in great depth. Nevertheless, I will say that Kierkegaard's existential approach to anthropology and selfhood cannot be easily dismissed, since it deals with central questions regarding our very existence, identity, and self-understanding (see Grøn 1997; Rudd 2012). In this respect, Kierkegaard's anthropology differs strongly from scientific studies of man as an object. Still, one may ask whether Kierkegaard's work is best described in terms

anthropology was divided into two very different fields of study. Contemporary physical anthropology (biological anthropology) goes back to the physiological anthropology of Ernst Platner of the late eighteenth century – a discipline that included not only anatomy but also ethnography and empirical psychology (including the relation between mind and body – a topic that was also relevant to philosophical anthropology).

Kant's pragmatic anthropology was a second distinct field of study, which contributed to the philosophical anthropologies of the nineteenth century as well as to the existential and phenomenological anthropologies of the twentieth (Louden 2011: 67, 81). Kant describes the difference between (Platner's) physiological anthropology and his own pragmatic anthropology by claiming that the former concerns "what *nature* makes out of the human being," whereas pragmatic anthropology concerns what *man* "as a free-acting being makes of himself, or can and should make of himself" (A 7:119). The former sees human beings as objects shaped by nature, whereas the latter emphasizes (1) what we *actually* make out of ourselves, (2) what we can *potentially* make out of ourselves, and (3) what we *ought* to make out of ourselves.

Philosophical anthropology in the nineteenth century is not only concerned with the study of human nature, in general (and the relation between mind and body, in particular); it is also concerned with the evolution of humanity.[2] In addition, it discusses the relation between different academic disciplines extensively, particularly the relation between the humanities and natural sciences (Marquard 1971; Orth 1997): Like the German "*Wissenschaft*," the Danish term "*Videnskab*" covers not only natural science but also the humanities and anthropology.

Kierkegaard argues that science essentially differs from ethics and religion. Science concerns explanatory and descriptive questions, whereas ethics and religion concern practical normative questions in the wide

of anthropology, psychology, or selfhood. To a great extent, this will probably depend on the relevant context and on theoretical preferences, although the different approaches may enrich each other reciprocally.

2 Still, philosophical anthropology not only concerns knowledge of human nature (as one topic among others), but it also sees human beings as the locus of *all* possible understanding, including the understanding of nature in science. Nineteenth-century philosophical anthropology therefore focuses not only on the experience of the human being but also on how all science, and other human activities, rely on human experience. Instead of merely focusing on the nature of man, anthropology focuses on the problem of experience in general, our total "encounter with and understanding of the world" (Orth 1997: 522). For Kierkegaard's view of human experience and consciousness, see Stokes 2010: chs. 2–4.

sense of how we should live our lives (SKS 25, 187, NB27:72 / KJN 9, 187–8).[3] Kierkegaard assumes that Christian theology goes beyond philosophy and science by relying on divine revelation. Specifically, Christian anthropology differs from philosophical anthropology by presupposing divine revelation and central dogmas of faith (cf. SKS 18, 125–6, HH:3 / KJN 2, 117, 120). Still, both theological and philosophical anthropology include both descriptive *and* normative elements since both concern both human facts *and* ideals (Compaijen 2018: 91).

Kierkegaard can be seen as contributing to the nineteenth-century discourse on anthropology by distinguishing between philosophical and theological anthropology on the one hand, and between science, ethics, and religion on the other.[4] His influential account of human nature and selfhood is also reminiscent of nineteenth-century anthropology. Kierkegaard develops an existential approach to anthropology that focuses on what it means to be an embodied human being and to become a self. Unlike later cultural anthropology, he is concerned with what is common to all humans, at least potentially, rather than what is idiosyncratic to different individuals, groups, or historical epochs.

In the nineteenth-century context, these issues belong to philosophical (and theological) anthropology. Even though Kierkegaard rarely uses the term "anthropology," he is familiar with both nineteenth-century philosophical and theological anthropology, and frequently deals with anthropological issues in his work.[5] For these reasons, I will follow earlier scholarship in referring to Kierkegaard's anthropology, while acknowledging that this anthropology is closely related to debates on selfhood and philosophical and theological psychology (cf. Theunissen 2005).

[3] Even if *Videnskab* includes normative legal theory, political theory, and economics, it may still not include ethical normativity. Nevertheless, *The Concept of Anxiety* describes ethics as a *Videnskab*, something that is untypical for Kierkegaard (see SKS 4, 323–5 / CA, 16–17).

[4] In addition, the "Interlude" of *Philosophical Fragments* argues that contingent truths, in historical and empirical disciplines, differ essentially from necessary truths (e.g., 2 + 2 = 4). See Chapter 10 of the present monograph.

[5] "Anthropology" is spelled both with and without the letter "h" by Kierkegaard. There are sixty-two occurrences in the Danish electronic edition (which covers almost Kierkegaard's entire corpus), although fifty-one of these are from the commentaries. It is often the case that some important terms and names occur more frequently in the commentaries than in the primary sources, however, partially because the latter presuppose context. Important material can therefore be implicit and somewhat hidden to modern readers. Nevertheless, Kierkegaard's familiarity with the nineteenth-century discourse on anthropology is indicated not only by his own account but also by his references to anthropology. For different overviews, see JP 1, 22–37; JP 7, page 6; "Search results for: ant*ropologi*," *Søren Kierkegaards Skrifter*, electronic version 1.8, 2013, accessed on February 22, 2021, http://sks.dk/zoom/search.aspx?zoom_sort=1&zoom_xml=0&zoom_query=ant*ropologi*.

The Sickness unto Death approaches selfhood and anthropology negatively by focusing on despair – a double-minded or incoherent form of selfhood and agency. Kierkegaard argues that despair can only be overcome by ethico-religious wholeheartedness. Whereas Part I of *The Sickness unto Death* provides a philosophical anthropology that distinguishes between inauthentic (nonconscious) and authentic (conscious) despair, Part II develops a theological anthropology that focuses on despair before God. Part I largely analyses and criticizes various forms of despair on their own terms, whereas Part II identifies despair with sin in a Christian sense. Still, the Christian analysis of Part II is anticipated by the title, preface, and introduction of *The Sickness unto Death* (Grøn 1997: 299–300).

Overall, *The Sickness unto Death* provides a systematic analysis of despair that has been influential in continental philosophy and theology. However, it is also relevant to discussions of personal identity in Anglophone philosophy after Frankfurt, MacIntyre, and Taylor. Due to its typology and negative phenomenology, *The Sickness unto Death* is a fascinating contribution to anthropology and theories of selfhood. On the one hand, the analysis of nonconscious despair provides an intriguing account of self-deception, facticity, and freedom. On the other, the analysis of demonic despair – which does evil because it is evil (at least in some instances) – appears to challenge the widespread idea that all intentional action is prompted by something that appears good.

Method: Phenomenology, Dialectics, Negativism

Part I of *The Sickness unto Death* gives a phenomenological account of despair that is reminiscent of the account given in Hegel's *Phenomenology of Spirit*, while also anticipating twentieth-century phenomenology. Like Hegel, Kierkegaard (Anti-Climacus) describes, analyses, and criticizes various forms of consciousness (or self-experience) on their own terms in a dialectical and teleological progression. Like Heidegger and Sartre, he not only emphasizes historicity and the relational nature of the self (Welz 2013: 447), but also views consciousness as always being mine, since it is characterized by immediate (prereflexive) self-referentiality (*Jemeinigkeit*, mineness). At the same time, however, he introduces a normative ideal for selfhood that breaks with twentieth-century phenomenology (Stokes 2010: 55–60). Although Kierkegaard (Anti-Climacus) does not claim to be scientific, he nonetheless provides a systematic analysis of despair. Despair and related phenomena are described from the first-person perspective in a reflective, methodical, and systematic manner that partially anticipates twentieth-century hermeneutic phenomenology (cf. Welz 2013).

Part II of *The Sickness unto Death* goes beyond the philosophical anthropology of Part I by analyzing the kind of despair and sense of selfhood that we experience when we become conscious of existing before God. Whereas Part I largely criticizes various forms of despair on their own terms, Part II criticizes them on Christian grounds instead (Grøn 1997). Perhaps the most original element in Kierkegaard's (Anti-Climacus') account lies in his *negative* approach to selfhood. *The Sickness unto Death* indicates that we only understand selfhood negatively through its failure, through despair. Indeed, a wholehearted self must constantly overcome despair. And to understand the self, we must therefore approach it indirectly by focusing on despair and how to overcome it (Grøn 1997; Theunissen 2005).

Human Nature as a Synthesis

Following earlier works such as *The Concept of Anxiety*, *The Sickness unto Death* views human nature as a *synthesis of opposites*. These opposites are described as soul and body, freedom and necessity, infinitude and finitude, eternity and temporality. In general terms, the first pole of the synthesis deals with our possibilities and our ability to be free by transcending limitations. The second pole, by contrast, deals with constraints that limit freedom. However, both poles are constitutive of human nature; therefore, we cannot identify exclusively with either our freedom or our given character (Rudd 2012: 31–4).

Kierkegaard introduces the concept "facticity" (Danish, *Facticitet*) as that which not only limits freedom but also makes it possible. This concept together with the related idea of choosing oneself represents one of Kierkegaard's most important contributions to modern European philosophy.[6] Facticity involves always already being situated in a specific situation. We are always already particular embodied human beings, with specific histories, who are born into – and entangled in – specific traditions and communities. Facticity then refers to the very limits – and possibility – of human freedom, as represented by embodiment and an inescapable historical and social context (SKS 8, 75, 91 / TA, 77–8, 96; SKS 20, 90, NB:129 / KJN 4, 90; cf. SKS 1, 316 / CI, 281; SKS 11, 152 / SUD, 36).

The concept of facticity (German, *Faktizität*) was coined by J. G. Fichte in his middle phase around 1800 and developed further by Kierkegaard and

[6] Fremstedal 2014a: ch. 3, referencing Arne Grøn and others.

Heidegger, eventually becoming one of the key concepts of twentieth-century continental philosophy. While Fichte suggests that the subject projects or throws the world, Kierkegaard anticipates the Heideggerian idea that the subject itself is thrown (cf. Kisiel 2008: 61–2). Still, even Fichte uses "facticity" to describe facts that resist complete theoretical construction (Breazeale and Zöller 2005: ix). Kierkegaard, however, uses it for facts (i.e., a historical and social context or situation) that resist, or limit, our freedom. For both, however, the subject is confronted with something it has not created (Hoeltzel 2020: 82–3).[7]

Kierkegaard's use of "facticity" seems sporadic and unsystematic, although he (Anti-Climacus) uses the related terms "finitude" and "necessity" systematically. Both pseudonymous and signed writings emphasize that one receives oneself as a specific self that is always already situated in a particular historical and social context (SKS 3, 207, 172 / EO2, 215–16, 176; SKS 5, 167 / EUD, 168; SKS 8, 49 / TA, 49–50). We are finite, historical, and social beings who have to relate to something that is always already given, something that makes self-creation impossible.

Kierkegaard thus emphasizes the *interplay* between freedom and facticity (whereas earlier philosophical anthropology focused on activity and passivity in human beings). Facticity constrains and limits our freedom by situating it in specific contexts. As a result, there is a fundamental *tension* between facticity and freedom, which is *constitutive* of our human nature. This tension will develop into despair that exaggerates either facticity or freedom unless facticity and freedom are actively reconciled (Rudd 2012: 48–9). What makes Kierkegaard's account so interesting then is not just his highly modern account of facticity but also the *interplay* between what is given and chosen in this account. Anthony Rudd writes:

> It was Kierkegaard more than any other author who helped me to understand the relation between the sense that we are responsible for shaping and authoring our lives, and the sense that there is something distinct and

[7] Kierkegaard had high regard for Fichte, describing him as "a man whom I have always venerated, old Fichte, a man in the great sense, a character in the elevated sense, a thinker in the noble Greek sense" (SKS 15, 91 / BA, 226). This is high praise coming from Kierkegaard. Still, his relation to Fichte is generally ambiguous, involving both admiration and critique. Fichte was one of the most referenced and discussed philosophers of the early nineteenth century. He was known not only for the idealism of the *Wissenschaftslehre*, but also for his reworking of Kantian ethics in *The System of Ethics* and for popular writings such as *The Vocation of Man* and *The Way Towards the Blessed Life*. Although Kierkegaard owned several of Fichte's works and many secondary sources that discuss Fichte, he rarely refers to Fichte's texts except for a few references to *The Vocation of Man*, *The Way Towards the Blessed Life*, and Hegelian criticisms of Fichte. See Kangas 2007: 75–7; Hühn and Schwab 2013: 62–4, 81–2, 88–9; Wood 2019: 340–9.

> definite about ourselves that has to be accepted as simply given. For Kierkegaard, we do not need to choose between these views, but should see the tension between them positively, as a *creative* tension – one which is actually constitutive of the self. (2012: 3)

Inauthentic (Nonconscious) Despair and Self-Deception

Kierkegaard (Anti-Climacus) approaches human self-realization *negatively* by studying despair, understood as a double-minded form of selfhood and agency. He distinguishes between two basic types of despair that need not be recognized consciously. However, both of these come in two variants (which are very similar though). Specifically, the "despair of necessity" lacks possibility (SKS 11, 153–7 / SUD, 37–42), just as the closely related variant "despair of finitude" lacks infinity (SKS 11, 149–51 / SUD, 33–5). Together these two variants represent the first main type of basic despair, which denies that it is free or capable of transcending facticity. For example, a person could give up the hope of breaking a self-destructive pattern of behavior such as excessive drinking. This basic type of despair gives up on life and takes a fatalistic and careless attitude toward existence. It views itself as a suffering victim, entirely in the hands of fortune. It does not try to realize itself, since it lacks the proper awareness of itself and what is involved in the task of becoming a self. It is unwilling to accept the freedom and responsibility that necessarily comes with human existence.

By contrast, the "despair of possibility" lacks necessity (SKS 11, 151–3 / SUD, 35–7), just as the closely related "despair of infinitude" lacks finitude (SKS 11, 146–8 / SUD, 30–3). Together these variants represent the second main type of basic despair, which overemphasizes freedom and self-creation. It regards facticity as a mere hindrance to freedom, not as something that makes freedom possible. It absolutizes freedom, understood negatively as freedom from limitations. As a result, freedom itself becomes abstract, fantastic, and empty, since it is disconnected from the situation in which it finds itself and does not allow positive freedom to realize anything specific or concrete. Nor does it allow criteria for choosing between different possibilities or alternatives, which means that it results in arbitrariness, since all possibilities are equally valid *and* invalid. Both variants of the second type of despair want to *create itself* without any restrictions, in order to get rid of the constraints of the present situation (including moral constraints). This implies, however, wanting to be someone else than the person one in fact, is (Grøn 1997: 119–22). The agent is therefore *double-minded* or in despair since he is split between who he is (actuality) and who he wants to be (ideals). He is stuck in a hopeless situation in which ideals and reality cannot be reconciled, something that epitomizes despair more generally (cf. SKS 11, 133–4 / SUD, 18).

The despair of possibility (futilely) wants possibility without necessity, whereas the despair of necessity (futilely) wants necessity without possibility. Both entail *double-mindedness* – divided between what it wants and what it tries futilely to escape. Kierkegaard describes such double-mindedness as despair (SKS 8, 144 / UD, 30), since the Danish word for despair, *Fortvivlelse*, is based on the numeral two (*tvi*), just like the German word for despair, *Verzweiflung*, is based on two (*zwei*).

Taken together, these forms of despair represent the basic forms of *inauthentic* despair (SKS 11, 145–57 / SUD, 29–42), a novel type of despair introduced by Kierkegaard (Anti-Climacus) in order to explain self-deception or bad faith. This type of despair is controversial because it need not be consciously experienced as despair by the person who is (supposedly) in despair, although it can be diagnosed from outside. While Kierkegaard (Anti-Climacus) says that it is not authentic despair, Theunissen (2005: 15) questions whether it is despair at all. I believe, however, that incoherence in the human synthesis does give ground for a despair that differs from the subjective experience of despair. At least, this is the case if despair and selfhood are subject to formal and objective constraints that go beyond subjective experience, just as *eudaimonia* involves such constraints. Not all forms of happiness qualify as *eudaimonia*: we can feel happy without being *eudaimon* as a result of lacking the necessary virtues or external goods. Similarly, we might feel happy and show no sign of authentic despair yet be in inauthentic despair. Where eudaimonists see virtue as constitutive of *eudaimonia,* Kierkegaard sees *wholeheartedness* (or purity of heart) *as constitutive of coherent (ideal) selfhood.* An agent without wholeheartedness is therefore double-minded or in despair, even if he fails to realize it. Since despair can be hidden or unacknowledged, Kierkegaard (Anti-Climacus) thinks that it is much more widespread than is usually assumed. Indeed, he thinks it is universally self-inflicted (yet possible to overcome, as is evident in Part 11 of *The Sickness unto Death*).

Thus, despair is not just a psychological phenomenon or something we can experience or suffer (e.g., a feeling of hopelessness). It is also an objective, ontological misrelation, a double-mindedness, because of a failure to reconcile facticity and freedom. As such, it differs from the subjective (phenomenological) experience of despair, and can be characterized as inauthentic despair.[8] But inauthentic and authentic despair seem to be *ideal types* that actual cases of despair resemble to varying degrees. Although despair generally involves some opacity or self-deception, there is normally some level of self-awareness involved as well. This means that very often the despairing person has at least a dim idea of his or her state.[9] Nevertheless, Kierkegaard (Anti-Climacus) tells us he deals with inauthentic despair "abstractly, as if it were not the despair of any person," whereas authentic despair concerns various actual cases of despair (Pap. VIII–2, B151 / SUD, 151 [Supplement]).

Authentic (Conscious) Despair and Selfhood

Kierkegaard does not identify selfhood with our freedom or soul as such. Nor does he identify it with the synthesis of facticity and freedom or the synthesis of soul and body (like substance dualists do). However, he does identify this synthesis structure with the human being:

> A human being is a synthesis of the infinite and finite, of the temporal and eternal, of freedom and necessity, in short a synthesis. A synthesis is a relation between two. Considered in this way, a human being is still not a self. (SKS 11, 129 / SUD, 13)

For Kierkegaard (Anti-Climacus), the self is not a substance but a self-relating process, in which I relate both to the human synthesis and to the divine and human other (Stokes 2015: 145). The self is therefore conceived

[8] However, Grøn argues that despair always involves an act whereby we actively despair by giving up hope and courage. We typically suffer a loss or despair over an event, and then attribute infinite significance to it (1997: 153). Still, the person in despair may or may not be consciously aware of giving up hope and courage. Inauthentic despair normally refers to a form of consciousness that speaks about itself and claims to be free of despair, typically by claiming to be safe and content (Grøn 1997: 127–32). There is a conflict between what this form of consciousness says and what it shows, between what it intends and what it achieves, that makes it possible for the observer to conclude that it misinterprets the situation. This misinterpretation results from a complex interplay between cognition and volition, in which we tend to deny problems to ourselves, so that we do not even realize our state of despair. For these reasons, inauthentic despair implies self-deception and a volitional failure rather than a mere cognitive one. Although all forms of despair involve some self-deception, inauthentic despair involves a particularly strong form of it that denies its state of despair and its need to be improved or cured (Grøn 1997: 125–32).

[9] Westphal 2014: 243. Wood says that "the states with which despair is involved, such as doubt or hope, are not only states of consciousness but dispositional states, which can be manifested in behavior without the subject's admitting their presence. No doubt some form of denial or self-deception has to be involved whenever someone is in despair without being conscious of it, but that is precisely Kierkegaard's point" (Wood 2019: 345).

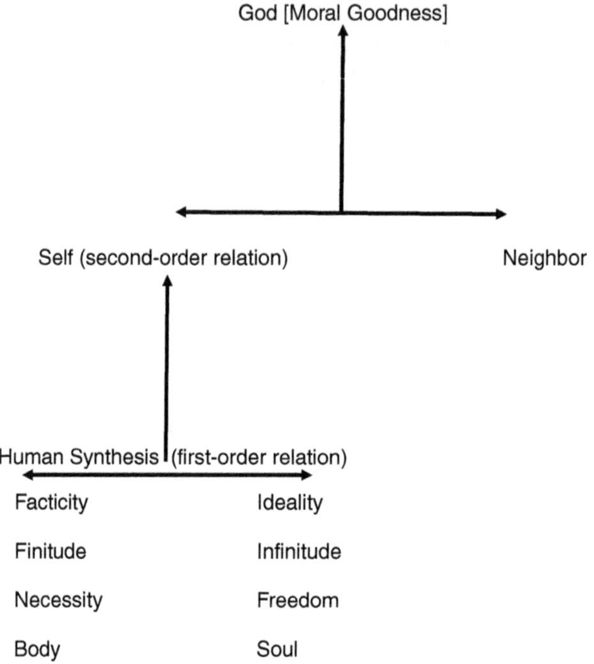

Figure 1.1 The self and alterity

of in *relational* and intersubjective terms. My self-relation is (at least implicitly) intertwined with my relation to God and other human beings, so that "a discord in any" relation "prevents the others from taking their proper form" (Davenport 2013: 239n; cf. Lippitt 2013: 96, 102, 109, 136, 182). Becoming myself, therefore, requires not only the right self-relation but also a proper relation to God and one's neighbor (see Figure 1.1).

The Sickness unto Death distinguishes selfhood from human nature. On its own, human nature represents a plurality without unity. The self, by contrast, is capable of unifying the plurality represented by human nature (SKS 11, 129 / SUD, 13; Blattberg 2020: 54–5). Human nature has a latent *potential* for selfhood, but the actualized self is neither the human synthesis nor one of its poles such as the soul (SKS 11, 129 / SUD, 13). Instead, the self is a reflexive self-relation that relates actively to the human synthesis by forming *second-order* (or higher-order) *volitions*.[10] Specifically, selfhood

[10] See Davenport (2013: 234–5), who notes that Kierkegaard's (Anti-Climacus') account of human nature seems either to be a form of broadly Aristotelian hylomorphism or a two-aspect account of body and mind.

requires not only self-consciousness but volitional identification with some first-order motives and alienation from other motives (Davenport 2012: 117). For instance, I identify with my desire to take care of my son and alienate myself from my desire to oversleep. The self is then only a self insofar as it presides over itself, or exercises self-relation, by forming higher-order volitions (see Westphal 2014: 238; Wood 2019: 344). Instead of being something given or something that creates itself, the self is therefore "something that exists in and though the shaping of itself and in constantly negotiating the limits of what it can and cannot alter" (Rudd 2012: 43).

On this account, selfhood entails *hierarchical* agency, in which higher-order motives reinforce and weaken lower-order motives. Thus, selfhood requires *self-evaluation* that shapes agency for practical purposes (Rudd 2012: ch. 4). Although Kierkegaard asks for a "valid reason [*fornuftig Grund*]" for acting (SKS 15, 182, 207 / BA, 59, my transl.), he is less explicit whether selfhood entails *autonomous* agency that evaluates (or values) motives as normative reasons for action. However, it is exactly such autonomous agency that seems necessary to avoid agency that is akratic, self-deceived, conflicted, wanton, or coerced (Davenport 2012: 6). And it is precisely such agency that seems necessary for understanding the normativity and reasons of the ideal self we should try to become. I will therefore follow commentators who take Kierkegaard to accept autonomous agency, although this involves a rational reconstruction of his account.[11]

In any case, the "imperfect" "actual self" differs from the "ideal self" (SKS 3, 246–7 / EO2, 259; cf. SKS 12, 186 / PC, 187). The latter is identified with spirit and actively overcomes despair at every instant. This is the wholehearted self we are supposed to become, something that represents a never-ending task that is highly demanding (more on this later). The actual self, by contrast, despairs consciously.[12] Indeed, one only becomes a self by relating to oneself, recognizing that one is in despair, and by forming second-order volitions. Whereas inauthentic despair recognizes neither selfhood nor despair (as problems or tasks to be dealt with), authentic despair is aware of both. As we will see, overcoming despair requires a wholehearted, ideal self that accepts itself fully without any self-estrangement. However, this does

[11] For the view that we can act for normative reasons, according to Kierkegaard, see Evans 2006b: 324; Irwin 2011: vol. III, 299–300; Davenport 2012; Rudd 2012; Compaijen 2018: 181; Stokes 2019: 278; McDaniel 2020.

[12] Stokes (2015) argues that the self only exists in the present, whereas the human being is temporarily extended. He also discusses the relation between practical and metaphysical identity in this connection. Unlike metaphysical identity, "practical identity" is understood in *normative* terms as "a description under which you find your life to be worth living and your actions to be worth undertaking" (Korsgaard 1996a: 101).

not require actual perfection as much as it requires hope of improvement, which reconciles ideals with reality.

Part II of *The Sickness unto Death* deals not only with religious faith that overcomes despair but also with despair that is conscious of existing before God, which I will examine in further detail below. *The Sickness unto Death* thus provides a *typology* of despair. Allen Wood comments:

> Kierkegaard follows the German idealist tradition in developing a concept systematically by beginning with the immediate, reflecting on it, and developing new determinations of it through each successive reflection, as Fichte proposes to do in his *Wissenschaftslehre*, Schelling in his *System of Transcendental Idealism*, or Hegel in his *Phenomenology of Spirit*. (2019: 345)

Kierkegaard (Anti-Climacus) describes a dialectical progression of various forms of conscious despair that involve more and more self-consciousness, selfhood, and volition. The self is intertwined with self-consciousness and volition, so that intensified (second-order) volition goes together with intensified self-consciousness and selfhood. Except for the ideal self, this process of intensification also involves an intensification of despair that moves increasingly further from faith (SKS 11, 213 / SUD, 101). At its most extreme, despair does not seek help, or forgiveness, but it wants to remain as despair even when it is aware of existing before God (SKS 11, 220–2 / SUD, 108–10).

Kierkegaard (Anti-Climacus) takes all despair to be dominated by either weakness or defiance, that is, either by passivity or activity (SKS 11, 162 / SUD, 49; see also Table 1.1). The "despair in weakness" does not want to be

Table 1.1 *Types of despair*

Dominating attitude ↓	Objective/ inauthentic (nonconscious) despair: incoherence in human synthesis	Subjective/authentic (conscious) despair: incoherent (nonideal) selfhood	
		The human self without divine revelation	The theological self before God
Passivity or weakness	Despair of finitude; despair of necessity	Despair in weakness; despair over (a) something earthly, (b) the earthly, or (c) oneself	Despairing over one's sin; despairing over the forgiveness of sin (offense)
Activity or defiance	Despair of infinitude; despair of possibility	Defiance – demonic despair	In despair to dismiss Christianity

itself, whereas "defiance" desperately wants to be itself. The former despairs over a loss or a misfortune, something that is described as "despair over something earthly" (SKS 11, 165–75 / SUD, 50–60). This despair can develop into despair over "the earthly" in general, if one does not cope with the loss, but sees it as fatal by attributing decisive importance, or infinite value, to it (SKS 11, 175 / SUD, 60). One then despairs over life in general, not just one part of it. But such universalized despair entails despairing over oneself, as someone too weak to cope with the relevant loss. Then one is stuck in a desperate situation in which one neither copes with the loss nor realizes oneself (SKS 11, 175–81 / SUD, 60–7). The problem, though, is not so much the initial loss or misfortune as the response toward it, which relinquish all hope and courage (Grøn 1997: 153).[13]

At the other extreme, we have the "defiant," or "demonic," who desperately wants to be himself (SKS 11, 184–7 / SUD, 71–4). He initially strives to be himself by creating himself – something that he fails to do – which, in turn, leads him to conscious despair. In this situation, the defiant, or demonic, gives up hope that despair can be overcome, because he thinks that it is too late for any improvement. He rejects all help to overcome despair and takes pride in despair and victimhood by identifying with it. He is highly conscious of despair, focusing all his attention on it, while refusing to share or communicate this problem with anyone (the state of "enclosing reserve," *Indesluttethed*).

The defiant, or demonic, feels offended by existence, hates it, and rebels against it with rage and malice. He sees himself as the big typo in God's creation which demonstrates just how bad an author God is (SKS 11, 187 / SUD, 73–4). Still, scholars disagree over whether he pursues evil only because it is evil, or because he has a perverse understanding of the good. This is not only an exegetical question, but also a question of whether despair and *acedie* represent counterexamples to the influential view that intentional action is always prompted by something that appears good in some respect.[14]

Nevertheless, even defiance involves some weakness and vice versa. Accordingly, Kierkegaard (Anti-Climacus) clams that weakness and

[13] Kierkegaard's (Anti-Climacus') analysis of despair here seems anticipated by Fichte's account of "despair over oneself [*Verzweiflung an sich selbst*]"; see Fichte 2005: 303 [IV, 319]; Wood 2019: 340.

[14] Elsewhere, I argue that for Kierkegaard (Anti-Climacus) demonic defiance and *acedie* must *presuppose* the guise of the good thesis (Fremstedal 2019b). Hühn and Schwab (2013: 83) argue that Kierkegaard's interpretation of defiance is reminiscent of Schelling's interpretation of evil as defiance. See also Wood 2019: 347.

defiance, passivity and activity, are both involved in all forms of despair (SKS 11, 135–6, 164 / SUD, 20, 49; see also Table 1.1).[15] The "despair of weakness" does not want to be the actual self it is, whereas the defiant "desperately wants to be . . . a self that he is not (for the will to be the self that he is in truth is the very opposite of despair)" (SKS 11, 136 / SUD, 20). The "despair of weakness" is estranged from its actual identity, while the defiant wants an identity he cannot have (e.g., being Caesar). Neither accept themselves fully. Neither want wholeheartedly to be themselves, since both value – or identify with – what they are not.[16] And neither hope to overcome despair. Therefore, both find themselves stuck in intolerable situations (cf. SKS 11, 133–4, 153 / SUD, 18, 37).

Overcoming Despair – Wholeheartedness, Ethics, Religion

There is always a tension in the human synthesis between our freedom and its limits, between activity and passivity, defiance and weakness. This tension results in despair (double-mindedness) unless I manage to shape my (practical) identity in a coherent manner. In order to reconcile freedom and facticity, I need not only second-order volitions, but also something that shapes and *unifies* selfhood.

Kierkegaard (Anti-Climacus) describes the process of shaping one's identity dialectically as a process of breaking with *and* returning to finitude or facticity (as alienation and reconciliation). It involves both negative freedom (from first-order states) and positive freedom (realized in an ideal self). He writes: "the progress of becoming [oneself] must be an infinitely moving away from oneself in the infinitizing of the self, and an infinitely coming back to itself in the finitizing process" (SKS 11, 146 / SUD, 30).

First, one has a specific (traditional or conventional) identity by virtue of being a specific individual in a specific historical and social context. Second, the self distances itself completely from this identity by being free in a negative way and by imagining different possibilities and ideals. This is the much-discussed "naked abstract self [*nøgne, abstrakte Selv*]" (SKS 11, 170 /

[15] Davenport (2013: 238n) says that "the way one wills to be oneself or not is . . . also a way of willing to be what God created one to be or not." All despair misrelates to God, as the normative standard (of success) for selfhood. Similarly, all love relates to God, either in an adequate way or not (cf. SKS 9, 64 / WL, 57–8).

[16] Fichte anticipates much of this by claiming that those who despair "are divided [*entzweit*] from everything good only because they are divided from themselves" (2005: 302 [IV, 318]; cf. Wood 2019: 341). Partially because of this Wood (2019: 340–9) argues that Kierkegaard's (Anti-Climacus') view of despair is based on Fichte.

SUD, 55).[17] Finally, it returns to finitude by realizing ideals (cf. SKS 12, 189 / PC, 190). Instead of just contemplating different possibilities, the self acts in the world by being fully committed to one project. In doing this, the self both breaks with its given (traditional or conventional) identity and returns to it, by taking it over and reforming it based on its commitments.

One of the few instances where Kierkegaard (Anti-Climacus) references J. G. Fichte is in a discussion of imagination as the capacity *instar omnium* (SKS 11, 147 / SUD, 31).[18] He suggests that imagination is not one capacity among other capacities that the self uses, but rather *the* capacity thorough which there is a self at all – the capacity of capacity. Specifically, productive imagination makes it possible to separate oneself from one's givenness or facticity, by projecting different possibilities (Kangas 2007: 75–7). Imagination makes it possible to infinitely move away from oneself, transcending one's given self or identity by imagining new possibilities and ideals (SKS 11, 146–7 / SUD, 29–30; cf. SKS 7, 180–1 / CUP1, 197). However, the existential task of becoming oneself also requires that one continually use freedom and imagination to return to finitude. One does this by trying to express or actualize (ethical) ideals *in* reality by viewing them as tasks to be realized.[19] It is exactly this that represents moral imagination (Stokes 2010: ch. 5).

17 This "naked abstract self," (SKS 11, 170 / SUD, 55) "clearly evokes the Fichtean idea of a self as an 'I = I' capable of conceiving of itself in abstraction from, and as independent of, anything other than its own relation to itself" (James 2011: 595). It need not be a minimal self (as suggested by Stokes 2015: 23–4). Rather, it involves an extremely abstract, reflective self.

18 Scholars disagree on whether this use of imagination represents a substantive engagement with Fichte or not (Kangas 2007: 77 referencing Schmidinger). For a Kantian approach to Kierkegaard's concept of imagination, see Helms 2020.

19 Existing scholarship points to strong structural overlap between the accounts of selfhood in Fichte and Kierkegaard. For Kierkegaard, the main structural features of the self are: (1) the human synthesis; (2) a self-relation, which (3) involves infinite striving and self-realization, based on (4) higher-order volition, and (5) imagination, which, in turn, (6) abstracts from anything but its own self-relation, yet (7) relates to other human beings as well as (8) the power that posited it (God).

Fichte anticipates all but the last feature. Wood (2019: 344) says that (2) "[t]he relation that relates itself to itself," "is [4] a *volitional* relation: it is the self-volition through which Fichte claims that the I posits itself." Kangas (2007: 75 –7), on the other hand, takes (2) the self to be a relation to itself that projects itself by making use of imagination (5). Yet, Kierkegaard is generally critical of Fichte's idealism, complaining about how abstract and contentless the Fichtean ego is. But we have seen that even Kierkegaard introduces (6), a "naked abstract self" (SKS 11, 170 / SUD, 55), which resembles the Fichtean "I = I," abstracting from anything but its own self-relation (James 2011: 595). In addition, the relation to others (7) is reminiscent of the dialectics of recognition in Fichte and Hegel. However, the God-relation (8) conflicts with the Fichtean account of self-positing. Fichte stresses the act of self-creation, suggesting that the subject grounds itself, whereas Kierkegaard portrays the self as posited by the divine Other. The latter involves an element of givenness that differs from Fichte's self-positing self (Kangas 2007: 87; James 2011: 592). In Kierkegaard, the self is not grounded in the sense that we can account fully for its conditions. This is related to the fact that Kierkegaard is more concerned with passivity and negativity than Fichte is, focusing on despair, anxiety, and suffering (cf. Grøn 1997). Still, Fichte seems to help Kierkegaard to break with an ontological

However, some read Kierkegaard as a subjectivist who thinks that unconditional commitment to any cause will do (e.g., Dreyfus 2008: 16–17). But not just any unconditional commitment will do. Although some aspects of life can be morally insignificant or indifferent (by representing *adiaphora*), Kierkegaard denies that our characters or basic attitudes toward life can escape morality insofar as we are free and responsible beings. As we will see in the following chapters, he connects selfhood and agency to objective moral standards. Therefore *Either/Or, Part II* presents the existential choice of oneself as *identical* to the choice of the ethical (cf. SKS 3, 170–3, 236–9 / EO2, 174–8, 247–51). Later writings which focus on Christian ethics also see selfhood as based on moral normativity. The basic idea in all these writing is that only morality allows wholeheartedness or purity of heart, although it has religious implications, since Kierkegaard identifies the good and the divine. This is something we will examine in greater detail in all the following chapters.

Theological and Philosophical Anthropology (and Selfhood)

Philosophical anthropology differs from theological anthropology (SKS 18, 125–6, HH:3 / KJN 2, 117, 120) insofar as the former relies on human experience and (unaided) reason, whereas the latter presupposes divine revelation. Like other Christian anthropologists, Kierkegaard here emphasizes the dogma of original sin and that man is created in the image of God.[20] He rejects Ludwig Feuerbach's claim that "theology is anthropology" (SKS K7, 363), because it implies a reduction of theology (and theological anthropology) to philosophical anthropology. Feuerbach thinks God is created in the image of man, whereas Kierkegaard assumes the opposite (cf. SKS 26, 285, NB33:43 / KJN 10, 291–2).

Part II of *The Sickness unto Death* develops a Christian anthropology that focuses on the *theological self* that is aware of itself as existing before God. For Kierkegaard (Anti-Climacus) this self requires not just divine revelation but also sin-consciousness. Indeed, he identifies despair with sin

description of the subject by focusing on subjectivity, including self-consciousness, reflection, act, will, and freedom. Kierkegaard went beyond Fichte by developing the category of existence and by stressing the situatedness and finitude of the existing subject (Kangas 2007). Indeed, Hühn and Schwab (2013: 88–9) argue that Kierkegaard takes over the later Fichte's self-criticism and that Kierkegaard's ethical vocabulary resembles Fichte's use of the term seriousness or earnestness (German, *Ernst*; Danish, *Alvor*). See also Hoeltzel 2020: 77–8 (esp. on ##1–3).

20 See, e.g., Kierkegaard's notes on Christian anthropology from H. N. Clausen's lectures (SKS 19, 23–84, Not1:6–9 / KJN 3, 18–82). For Kierkegaard's views on original sin and *imago Dei*, see Manis 2009b; Welz 2016: 39–40, 127–8.

and interprets it as an unwillingness to be oneself before God (that involves self-deception). Despair before God takes three forms (see Table 1.1):

1. The sin of despairing over one's sin
2. The sin of despairing over the forgiveness of sin (offense)
3. The sin of dismissing Christianity

The first gives up hope and courage because of his own sin (SKS 11, 221–4 / SUD, 109–12). The second gives up hope and courage by taking offense at divine forgiveness, since he thinks he is beyond forgiveness (SKS 11, 225–36 / SUD, 113–24). Both represent Christian variants of despair over oneself (cf. SKS 11, 175 / SUD, 60). But the third differs from both by defiantly denying the incarnation. As such, it represents a Christian variant of demonic despair (SKS 11, 236–42, cf. 184–7 / SUD, 125–31, cf. 71–4).

These three forms involve increasing sinfulness and despair, insofar as they move increasingly further away from faith by breaking more explicitly and defiantly with Christianity (SKS 11, 213 / SUD, 101). But instead of providing an independent analysis of Christian despair, Part II is largely based on Part I, which it *reiterates* by sketching Christian counterparts to human despair (cf. Grøn 1997: ch. 7). Since the content clearly overlaps substantially, the Christian content of Part II therefore seems supported by reasons that are independent of faith. At least, any valid critique of the pagan variants of despair would also hold for the Christian variants, since the latter reiterates the former (cf. Table 1.1).

Still, Kierkegaard (Anti-Climacus) takes the self to be established by God, so that any conflict in the human synthesis reflects itself (implicitly) in the relation to God. Despair is contrasted with Christian faith, which involves an unconditional (higher-order) will to be oneself before God in which "the self rests transparently in the power that established it" (SKS 11, 242 / SUD, 131). However, resting transparently in God is interpreted as a moral conscience scrutinized by God (SKS 11, 235 / SUD, 124). As Merold Westphal (2014: ch. 12) argues, this appears to involve an openness to God and other human beings that is aware of the relational nature of the self, and that affirms it by being unconditionally committed toward Christian ethics, while recognizing the human tendency toward sin, despair, and self-deception. The Christian believer humbly accepts himself as a sinner who is forgiven by God.

Still, we could ask whether the theological anthropology in Part II of *The Sickness unto Death* is implicit in the philosophical anthropology of Part I. The concept of infinitude, for instance, may resemble divine infinitude. Yet, *The Sickness unto Death* interprets infinitude in the human synthesis only as the unlimited (Greek, *ápeiron*) that is dialectically dependent upon finitude as its opposite (SKS 11, 151 / SUD, 35). The attempt to abstract infinitude from finitude therefore leads to the "despair of infinitude."

However, *The Sickness unto Death* seems to presuppose that God creates us. But Part I only assumes that defiance, the phenomenon of desperately wanting to be oneself, indicates that the self does not constitute itself normatively (SKS 11, 130 / SUD, 14). The self despairs because it is confronted with constraints on selfhood that are not self-imposed (e.g., facticity and moral facts). These constraints are external to the will, so the agent cannot set all the rules of its existence autonomously, nor the rules for setting the rules (SKS 11, 182–3 / SUD, 68–9).

In *The Sickness unto Death*, the philosophical anthropology of Part I results in despair that prepares the transition to Christian anthropology in Part II. Similarly, *Concluding Unscientific Postscript* suggests that philosophy can help us to "seek the leap as a desperate way out" (SKS 7, 103 / CUP1, 106) because Christianity fits human subjectivity completely (SKS 7, 210 / CUP1, 230). Christian faith solves the pre-Christian problem of despair, but it cannot be reduced to philosophical anthropology, since it has its own perspectives and language. Indeed, pre-Christian philosophical standards (e.g., non-Christian ethics) are valid, yet insufficient, since they state some but not all conditions for avoiding despair.

Despair is then only overcome by Christian faith in a wide sense that appears to include hope and charity. Christian hope takes the form of "hope against hope," as hope in a (humanly) hopeless situation (SKS 13, 102–4 / FSE, 81–3). Indeed, Christian hope only becomes an extant possibility when everything breaks down because of despair (Pap. VI, B53, 13 / JP 2, 1668). Christian hope is a divine gift that, if accepted, overcomes human (pre-Christian) despair. It expects the possibility of good for oneself and one's neighbor alike (SKS 9, 249 / WL, 249, 260). Without a God that makes everything possible (SKS 11, 185 / SUD, 71), there is nothing that secures hope or prevents despair.

Conclusion

Like Kant, Kierkegaard is a forerunner of twentieth-century existential and phenomenological anthropology. Kierkegaard's approach to anthropology shares some basic features with Kant's pragmatic anthropology. First, both sketch a normative nonnaturalistic anthropology that includes ethics, religion, and teleology. Second, both emphasize what is common to all humans, rather than what is specific to various groups and nationalities. Specifically, both are concerned with human actuality, possibilities, and (objective) ideals. For Kierkegaard, the past seems to represent the actual, the future the possibilities, and the present the moment in which the self relates to the whole by taking full responsibility for itself (cf. Stokes 2015: 163).

In the nineteenth-century context, Kierkegaard's analysis of historicity and contingency is reminiscent of the German historicism that was part of the nineteenth-century discourse on anthropology after Herder. It is particularly by introducing the concept of facticity and richer notions of historicity and selfhood that he goes beyond Kant's anthropology and Fichte's idealism, offering an account that anticipates twentieth-century phenomenology and existentialism.

The Sickness unto Death represents perhaps Kierkegaard's (Anti-Climacus') most important contribution to anthropology, moral psychology, and theories of selfhood. Kierkegaard's (Anti-Climacus') approach is original particularly because it involves a negative phenomenology (Grøn 1997) and a typology of despair that covers everything from nonconscious despair to demonic despair. His views on anthropology and selfhood have been highly influential, particularly in continental philosophy and theology. But they are also relevant to debates on personal identity and ethics in Anglophone philosophy after MacIntyre and Frankfurt, as shown by Rudd (2012), Davenport (2012), and Stokes (2015).

CHAPTER 2

Why Be Moral? The Critique of Amoralism

The Dilemma of Justifying Morality: Circularity or Wrong Reasons

The fact that the question "why be moral?" has been discussed many times suggests that the question is meaningful, even if a fully moral agent may not contemplate it seriously in the sense that he actively considers being immoral.[1] Still, Hallvard Fossheim (2015: 66) points out that even a moral person can ask the "why be moral?" question, since he can "see and feel a pull from other, non-moral options and alternatives." A reflection about *reasons* for being moral is therefore relevant not only for someone who tries to become moral but also for someone who continues to be committed toward morality, while still seeing and feeling the "pull from non-moral options and alternatives."

The "why be moral?" question asks whether it is rational or irrational to be moral and whether it is rational or irrational to be amoral or even immoral (Sinnott-Armstrong 2019). H. A. Prichard, F. H. Bradley, and others point out that justifications of morality face a difficult dilemma:[2] Should one be moral for moral reasons *or* for nonmoral reasons?

The first horn of the dilemma seems circular and question-begging, since it presupposes what it seeks to prove. Any reference to moral reasons presupposes that one is already committed toward morality, or somehow feels morally responsible, but this is exactly what the amoralist questions. Indeed, amoralism (i.e., practical moral skepticism concerning reasons for action) can easily be motivated by pointing to this circularity (Sinnott-Armstrong 2019).

[1] Hare 2002a: 95. It is often assumed that the "why be moral?" question is raised by someone who is either alienated from morality or at least not committed towards it. See Louden 2015a: 45; Schaber 2015: 33–4.

[2] See Schaber (2015: 31–2) on Pritchard. A similar point was made by F. H. Bradley; see Louden 2015a: 45.

Still, it is not clear if such circularity is avoidable or not, or whether it is vicious or not.

The second horn offers nonmoral reasons for being moral. Typically, one argues that being moral is prudent (or that it has clear religious, legal, social, or aesthetic advantages, independently of morality and prudence). But as we will see, any such argument at best supports *legality* instead of morality (at worst, it could pay off to be immoral). Morality requires not only that we perform the right actions – legality – but also that we act for moral reasons, or with the right motivation, intention, or will. Thus, helping someone (e.g., a refugee) just because it pays off hardly seems moral. Rather, it involves acting for the *wrong kind of reason*, or with an inappropriate motive, intention, or will. As such, it lacks moral worth, indicating that morality cannot be justified in nonmoral terms, since moral normativity cannot be justified by, or derived from, nonmoral normativity. Morality cannot be justified in terms of anything more basic; it therefore needs to be recognized on its own terms (Rudd 2012: 121).

However, different ethical theories diverge here. Kantians and virtue ethicists agree that the reasons and motives we act on matter morally. Consequentialists, by contrast, evaluate moral actions based on consequences, not motives and reasons for acting. Still, motives and reasons do matter if we evaluate whether *an agent*, as opposed to an action, is moral or not. To evaluate the agent's character, we must consider his motives. John Stuart Mill writes:

> [T]he motive has nothing to do with the morality of the action, though much with the worth of the agent . . . the motive, that is, the feeling which makes him will so to do, when it makes no difference in the act, makes none in the morality [of the act]; though it makes a great difference in our moral estimation of the agent. (1969: 219–20)

Much the same point is made later by G. E. Moore. As Michael Zimmerman explains, Moore "insists that motives have no bearing on whether an action is morally right or wrong, although they may well be relevant to other moral judgments, such as the judgment that someone is to be praised or blamed."[3]

Thus, even consequentialists could agree that morality requires more than legality.[4] Morality concerns not only actions but also (local and

[3] Zimmerman (2015: 18) referencing G. E. Moore (2005 [1912]), *Ethics*, Oxford: Clarendon Press, 95–.

[4] Martin makes a similar point, saying that "motives matter" since "[t]hey are important in understanding character, which concerns desires and commitments just as much as conduct" (Martin 2012: 108).

global) character traits. This is decisive since the question "why be moral?" concerns not only why we should *act* morally but also why we should be moral *persons* (Sinnott-Armstrong 2019). Indeed, the existential choice of the ethical in *Either/Or* precisely concerns the choice to become a moral person, not the choice of specific actions. It concerns moral character and the general attitude toward morality, in which we take responsibility for our characters and accept our lives (Davenport 2017: 177–8).

Like Kant, Kierkegaard sees different actions and choices as grounded in our character or fundamental attitude toward life. The approaches of both thinkers resemble character-based ethics that focuses on life as a whole, rather than modern ethics that focuses on specific actions, choices, and situations as well as different rules and procedures.[5] Kierkegaard is concerned with ethics not just in the narrow sense, which concerns moral duties, but also in the wide sense, which concerns authentic selfhood, the proper use of freedom, living well, and living in a meaningful and valuable manner.[6]

Indeed, Kierkegaard's ethicist – Judge William – sees the ethical task as the human task, arguing that the existential choice of oneself is *identical* to the choice of the ethical. Unless this account is to be circular, we must assume that there is some nonmoral *content* to the self that a person should become (Evans 2006a: 97). We need to distinguish between the moral *form* of the self and its material content. The aesthetic or sensuous elements of the self are not to be eradicated but merely given a moral form. Personal happiness and prudence must then be a matter of *secondary* importance if they conflict with strict moral duties.

This is exactly what Kierkegaard and Kant hold. Both refuse to justify morality prudentially, since morality entails noninstrumental other-regard that cannot be justified by mere self-interest.[7] Both therefore dismiss ethical eudaimonism. As *noneudaimonists*, they hold that morality can be justified without appeal to prudence, so that "we have sufficient reason to pursue [morality] above all other goods or advantages even if it conflicts with [prudence] or it does not affect it either way"; still, prudence is important for morality in other respects, since it can provide

[5] Fremstedal 2014a: chs. 2–3; cf. Vos 2016. Rudd (2012: ch. 3) defends a Kierkegaardian notion of character against skepticism concerning character.

[6] For ethics in a narrow and wide sense, see Wood 2016: 125.

[7] See Lippitt (2013: 96, 102, 109, 136, 182) for an extended discussion of how morality involves both other-regard and self-regard. By focusing on love, Lippitt shows that self-regarding and other-regarding moral concern are intertwined. But this seems to largely leave the issues of amoralism, eudaimonism, and normative conflict, which the present book discusses.

practical reasons and a second defense of morality (Irwin 2011: vol. 1, 289).

But the dismissal of eudaimonism makes the justification of morality quite demanding. For morality requires noninstrumental other-regard, which cannot be justified egoistically outside of an eudaimonistic framework (or objective list theories of happiness that see personal happiness as constituted by moral virtue).[8] Still, Kierkegaard offers a sophisticated response to the "why be moral?" question that goes far beyond Kant and is directly relevant to contemporary discussions of amoralism. This response arose historically as a reaction to German Romanticism, which is influenced by Kant and German idealism.

The Argumentative Structure of *Either/Or*

Kierkegaard offers (and combines) several argumentative strategies that escape the dilemma above. The first strategy criticizes amoralism (or practical moral skepticism)[9] on its own terms. Kierkegaard argues that the amoralism of aesthetes collapses internally due to despair or double-mindedness (an incoherent personal identity). If successful, this argument supports morality indirectly by showing that there is no rational alternative to morality. This argument can be successful unless morality also collapses internally; specifically, morality must facilitate wholeheartedness or a coherent personal (practical) identity.

A second, closely related but more specific strategy argues that amoralism collapses internally because morality is *inescapable*. This is a view that Kierkegaard develops particularly in "Purity of Heart," Part 1 of *Upbuilding Discourses in Various Spirits*. But even *Either/Or* portrays the ethical as inescapable, so that we can speak of the intrusion of the ethical (cf. Grøn 1997: 261–2; Evans 2009: 87–9). However, this strategy involves circularity, something that seems defensible if it is nonvicious and if morality does turn out to be inescapable in some sense (something that may require an additional argument).[10]

8 See Chapters 4 and 5 on eudaimonism.

9 "Moral skepticism" could refer both to *practical* moral skepticism about *reasons for action* and to *epistemological* moral skepticism about *reasons for belief.* I only discuss the former variant of moral skepticism here.

10 Like the previous strategy, this strategy undermines amoralism but not necessarily skepticism concerning whether morality overrides other reasons and concerns. For Kierkegaard's view of the latter, see Chapters 4–7.

A third strategy argues that the dilemma between circularity and legality is false or at least overly simplistic since *mixed motives* escape the dilemma. Specifically, we can have two different reasons or motives for being moral that are both operative simultaneously.[11] We can be moral *both* because morality (on its own) requires it *and* because it is supported by nonmoral reasons. However, the latter should be of strong normative importance to the moral agent. Prudential reasons are then particularly relevant (Dorsey 2016), especially if we include existential meaning and practical identity.[12] At best, morality is then supported by nonmoral normativity, making it rational, all things considered, to be moral. Still, such mixed motives transcend legality if the agent acts on moral reasons. But morality should not be second to nonmoral (e.g., prudential) motives and reasons. Rather, morality must dethrone other considerations in cases of conflict. Yet, these considerations add substantial support to morality in many other cases.

As suggested by the title of Judge William's letter "The Balance between the Esthetic and the Ethical in the Development of the Personality," the ethicist introduces mixed motives and argues for morality on both aesthetic and moral grounds. One example of this dual strategy is the claim that love needs moral obligations to endure; another is that the ethicist gains aesthetically by disciplining his desires. Instead of merely condemning the aesthete on moral grounds – something that appears moralistic and unhelpful – the ethicist thus sketches an internal critique: On the one hand, the aesthetic stage fails on its own terms, and on the other it is preserved (yet dethroned) in the ethical stage (Ferreira 2009: 90–2). This argument involves a Hegelian *Aufhebung* of the aesthetic stage, where the aesthetic is partially negated because it is self-defeating, and partially recontextualized or lifted up to the ethical. Thus, apart from an external (transcending) critique of the aesthete on ethical grounds, the ethicist sketches an internal (immanent) critique that involves negative arguments as well as correctives.

These argumentative strategies are only successful if they show that amoralism is more problematic than moral commitment. An answer to the "why be moral?" question therefore requires a *comparative judgment* about the merits of moral commitment over amoralism. *Either/Or* (and later pseudonymous works) involves a comparison and dialogue between various aesthetes (notably the pseudonym "A") and the ethicist (the

11 Martin (2012: 112) writes that "we have evolved as creatures with mixed motives that constantly dovetail, with only occasional severe conflict." See also Irwin 2011: vol. II, 814–15.

12 Regarding meaning, see Martin 2012: esp. ch. 7. Regarding meaning and practical identity, see Davenport 2012; Rudd 2012.

pseudonym "Judge William" or "B" for short) that shed light on why we should be moral. Kierkegaard's pseudonymous writings develop the ethical position, or the ethical stage, by engaging in dialogue and comparison with the aesthetic stage. The different pseudonyms are used to describe different positions from within the first-person perspective. It is precisely this dialogical and comparative approach that makes Kierkegaard's pseudonymous writings literary interesting and philosophically relevant for discussing amoralism. Thus, *Either/Or* gives an extremely vivid literary portrayal of an amoralist instead of the colorless placeholder for a position of theoretical interest usually found in philosophical texts (Rudd 2005: 68; cf. Compaijen 2018: ch. 5). Rudd elaborates:

> *Either/Or* as a whole challenges us to compare the self-portrait of the aesthete in [Part] 1, with the description of him that emerges from Judge William's letters [to him] in [Part] 2, and consider whether the Judge's account enables us to gain a better understanding of [the aesthete] "A" as he had appeared in his own writings. Within the work itself, the Judge challenges "A" to consider whether the ethical perspective will enable him to articulate more adequately what he already feels about his own life. (2001: 144–5)

Rudd seems to suggest that the argument here takes an abductive form, since the ethical offers a better explanation than amoralism does (2001: 144–5). In any case, the ethicist William is not just portraying the aesthetic and ethical forms of life but he argues against the aesthete.[13] His first letter to A is called "The Esthetic Validity of Marriage" and his second letter is called "The Balance between the Esthetic and the Ethical in the Development of the Personality" (SKS 3, 13–151, 153–314 / EO2, 3–154, 155–334). These two letters focus on the central and shared importance of *love, selfhood, freedom, and meaning* for the aesthete *and* the ethicist. Thus, Judge William indicates that the aesthete has protomoral reasons for being moral, since only morality sustains love, selfhood, freedom, and meaning – which are all normatively significant to the aesthete. Roughly, the idea is that without ethical commitment, life lacks meaning, love is episodic (lacking continuity and importance), while selfhood is incoherent, and freedom is negative, empty, and arbitrary. Thus, the ethical seems to succeed better than the aesthetic, even on the latter's terms.

This is important, since *reasons internalism* implies that an agent only has reason to become moral if these reasons are based on his subjective (internal)

[13] I agree with Rudd (2012: 70) who says: "I do think that Kierkegaard means to endorse Judge William's critique of the aesthetic stance, though he doesn't want to endorse all the Judge's positive views."

motivational set. Still, it seems that a sound deliberative process can *enlarge* the actual motivational set by articulating and discovering new normative reasons.[14] For example, the aesthete's reason to pursue erotic love could be enlarged or even cultivated to include other forms of love as well (more on this later). In any case, reasons to be moral must at the very least be recognizable to the aesthete.

This chapter compares the ethicist and aesthete, largely abstracting from the religious perspective developed in Kierkegaard's writings (including "Ultimatum" in *Either/Or, Part II*). Thus, I will focus on what is traditionally known as the aesthetic and ethical stages, not the religious stage. I do not deny that there are problems with the ethical stage and that the aesthetic and religious stages may avoid some of these problems. But we still seem to have reason to be moral despite these problems.

As we will see in Chapters 4–7, religion entails and supports morality. Still, some readings tend to deny this, either by favoring aesthetic amoralism or a religious suspension of morality.[15] My reading, by contrast, focuses on the reasons and motives Kierkegaard offers for being moral. Both this chapter and later ones show that he argues that moral concerns *override* prudential ones, whereas religion is interpreted in moral terms.

The *aesthete* is an *amoralist* who lives *premorally* since he is not fundamentally committed to morality. In what follows, I will focus on Kierkegaard's reflective aesthete (rather than the immediate or prereflective aesthete), since the reflective aesthete represents and concretizes amoralism. Unlike the immediate aesthete, he is capable of higher-order motives and acting for normative reasons.[16] Still, the reflective aesthete only allows ethical considerations insofar as these considerations are second to prudential considerations (in a *wide* sense).[17]

Put in Kantian terms, the aesthete gives priority to empirical (material) principles over moral (formal) principles. He is not ruled by moral incentives

[14] See Wietzke 2011: 422–3; Compaijen 2018: 42–3, 180–6, referencing Bernard Williams, Ryan Kemp, and Walter Wietzke. Compaijen, Kemp, and Wietzke defend internalist readings of Kierkegaard, which Davenport (2017) rejects.

[15] Georg Brandes, who popularized the aesthetic, ethical, and religious stages, argues that Kierkegaard only allows two fundamentally different ways of life, namely aesthetic hedonism and religious asceticism (1877: 155). Ethics, by contrast, is but a short-lived transition to religion for Kierkegaard, Brandes contends (1877: 185).

[16] As seen in the previous chapter, I follow commentators who assume that we can act for normative reasons. Examples of immediate aesthetes, who lack this ability, include Don Giovanni in *Either/Or, Part I* and infants who are not yet capable of distinguishing between themselves and their surroundings (SKS 2, 55–80 / EO1, 47–75; SKS 17, 117, BB:25 / KJN 1, 111).

[17] See particularly "Rotation of Crops: A Venture in a Theory of Social Prudence" in *Either/Or, Part I* (SKS 2, 271–89 / EO1, 281–300).

but by competing incentives and principles. Like Kant, Kierkegaard describes these competing incentives in terms of sensuousness, egoism, self-interest, and happiness (Knappe 2004: 54–5, 94–7). The aesthete, then, is someone who is ruled by sensuousness, so that rationality and reflection serve sensuousness rather than morality. This intimate connection between the aesthete and sensuousness can be partially explained from the fact that Kierkegaard takes the aesthetic in the original Greek sense of *aisthesis*, as perception from the senses – although he associates it with sensation, sensibility, and sensuousness (cf. SKS 3, 29–30 / EO2, 21–2; Furtak 2005: 54).

By definition, the aesthete lacks moral character. He may act morally occasionally, but he is not categorically committed toward morality. Instead, morality serves self-interest in the broad sense of sensuousness and inclinations. Some aesthetes seem to be *hedonists* concerning happiness and value, whereas others seem to be *desire-satisfactionists* or *preferentialists* instead as in the case of aesthete A. A writes:

> Real enjoyment [*Den egentlige nydelse*] consists not in what one enjoys [*nyder*] but in the idea [*Forestillingen*]. If I had in my service a submissive jinni who, when I asked for a glass of water, would bring me the world's most expensive wines, deliciously blended, in a goblet, I would dismiss him until he learned that the pleasure [*Nydelsen*] consists not in what I enjoy [*nyder*] but in getting my own way [*faae min Villie*]. (SKS 2, 40 / EO1, 31)

For A *Nydelse*, which can be translated as either enjoyment or pleasure, consists in the second-order desire to always get one's first-order desire, irrespectively of what it consists in. As such, it does not respect any moral restrictions.

More generally, plausible variants of amoralism rest on two assumptions, namely that all normative practical reasons are prudential (i.e., rational egoism) and that there is conflict between prudence and morality. Undermining any of these assumptions would make amoralism much less plausible (cf. Sinnott-Armstrong 2019). Kierkegaard's approach here is to criticize rational egoism rather than denying conflict between morality and prudence.

The Internal Critique of the Aesthete: The Argument from Despair

Kierkegaard develops a *via negativa* approach to ethics in which we only understand the ethical through the experience of moral failure, through guilt, sin, and despair.[18] This approach denies that we first have the ethical

[18] In German and Danish scholarship, this methodology is currently referred to as methodological negativism (Grøn 1997; Theunissen 2005).

and then only afterwards have the possibility of failure. Rather, the normative task of being ethical, or becoming oneself, can only be understood against the background of failure (Grøn 1997: 227, 261–2, 277). And the case of failure represents the rule rather than the exception insofar as ordinary human beings are concerned. In order to understand ethics, we therefore need to approach it indirectly by focusing on amoralism, immorality, and despair. This is related to the fact that ordinary humans have character flaws that prevent moral perfection (or the unity of the virtues). The latter is not only Kierkegaard's view but also a widely held view in moral psychology.

In *Either/Or, Part II* the ethicist develops a negative argument against the aesthete that I will refer to as the argument from despair. This argument tries to reduce the position of the aesthete *ad absurdum*. (The absurdity, however, need not involve a logical contradiction but rather involves a practical absurdity in the form of existential despair and not merely something immoral.)[19] The central idea is that *to avoid despair*, one must transcend the aesthetic by choosing oneself, something that is *identical* to choosing the ethical. The ethicist thus offers a *motive and reason* for transcending the aesthetic (Compaijen 2018: ch. 5; cf. Lübcke 1991: 97). This analysis of despair is sketched in *Either/Or* and developed further in *Concluding Unscientific Postscript*, "Purity of Heart," and *The Sickness unto Death*.

The ethicist argues that

> it is manifest that every esthetic life-view [*Livs-Anskuelse*] is despair, and that everyone who live esthetically is in despair, whether he knows it or not. But when one knows this . . . then a higher form of existence is an imperative [*uafviselig* – inescapable] requirement. (SKS 3, 186 / EO2, 192)

Despair is only overcome by categorical moral commitment, which is not contingent on anything. But many aesthetes are *not* sufficiently aware of this fact since they simply do not care enough about their problems (cf. Wietzke 2011: 425). As a result, they are not yet ready to embrace morality. Still, the ethicist tries to prepare them for morality by recommending that they despair over their whole lives (Rudd 2001: 144). Still, to become moral represents an inescapable requirement that holds *categorically*. It is not an instrumental requirement, contingent on avoiding despair. As we will see (in Chapter 4), Kierkegaard therefore contrasts the choice of oneself with instrumentalism concerning morality (cf. Pap. IV, A246 / JP 5, 5636). He

[19] For practical *reductio ad absurdum* arguments, see Wood 1970: 29–34; Skirbekk 1994: 49–72.

(Judge William) also denies that marriage – the paradigm case for the ethical stage – is a means to build character, to have children, or to have a home (SKS 3, 69–71, 73–84 / EO2, 64–6, 68–80). Indeed, morality must be pursued for its own sake (SKS 19:403, Not13:39 / KJN 3, 401). But doing so allows not just significant side effects but also meaningful social relations, love, freedom, and coherent selfhood.[20]

Either/Or, Part I describes the aesthetic stage from within, giving several indications of despair, particularly in the chapter "The Unhappiest One" (SKS 2, 211–23; EO1, 217–30). It is more difficult, however, to show that the different aesthetic views all imply despair. To succeed in this, the ethicist must distinguish between despair that is conscious and nonconscious, authentic and inauthentic, as *The Sickness unto Death* does. Thus, the *aesthete has to be in despair*, even if he is not aware of it.[21]

As we have seen, despair involves double-mindedness, or an incoherent identity, which need not be recognized by the agent it belongs to (cf. SKS 11, 157–62, cf. 136 / SUD, 43–7, cf. 20). Given that selfhood is characterized both by freedom and facticity, neither can be done away with since both are constitutive of human nature; therefore, we cannot just identify with our given character or only with freedom. Since freedom and facticity are both constitutive of human nature, any attempt to identify with only one of them is self-defeating and will result in double-mindedness. Still, we tend to *exaggerate* either freedom or facticity, since freedom and facticity stand in a *tense* relation to each other because our freedom is always situated in a specific situation or context that limits it. But it is only by actively reconciling freedom and facticity that we can become coherent selves who overcome despair (Rudd 2012: 48–9). Indeed, the (ideal) self unifies the duality (or plurality) represented by human nature (SKS 11, 127 / SUD, 13).

The ethicist argues that the solution to the problems posed by despair lies in getting continuity or coherence in one's existence by appropriating facticity. He stresses that one's history is not solely a product of one's own free acts, but something closely related to the history of mankind as a whole (SKS 3, 171 / EO2, 175). Hence, one's life can only have continuity if one relates to other human beings, both the living and the dead (SKS 3, 239 / EO2, 250–1). By appreciating this historical and social reality, one sees

20 For a related point, see Davenport 2007: 163–8, 211–84.

21 I agree with Kosch (2006a: 142, 152–5), Rudd (2012: 40, 70), and Compaijen (2018: 176) who argue for a strong connection between the notion of despair in *Either/Or* and in later works such as *The Sickness unto Death*.

oneself in a *historical* and *social* context. Here, the ethicist stresses that the self should be seen as socially mediated:

> [T]he self that is the objective . . . is a concrete self in living interaction with these specific surroundings, the life conditions, this order of things. The self that is the objective is not only a personal self but a social, a civic [*borgerligt*] self. (SKS 3, 250 / EO2, 262)

As we will see, one cannot become a self, which synthetizes freedom and facticity, without moral and social commitment (cf. SKS 3, 243–4, 249–50, 261 / EO2, 255–6, 262–3, 274–5). Without such commitment, the self *either* lapses into an unbalanced stress on restrictions and givenness *or* an equally unbalanced stress on freedom and voluntarism (Rudd 2012: 70, 104).

Wholeheartedness Requires Morality

Claudia Welz (2019: 288) points out that "the good is not defined in terms of content. Kierkegaard is not telling us what is good, but only gives us an indication of the formal features of the good: it is that which does not contradict itself." Or rather, the good has the unique feature that it does not involve any incoherence or double-mindedness. Thus, it offers the self a moral *form.*

On the one hand, selfhood could be fragmented into different projects and roles that are not integrated as parts of a single life. Such a life would lack coherence and unity, but it need not be contradictory. On the other, we may pursue projects and roles that are incompatible with each other, either in principle or in fact. This allows role conflicts and conflicts of interest (e.g., my job as an ethicist conflicts with my financial interests).

But a fundamental orientation toward good would prevent all these problems by being a *metaproject* that shapes, unifies, and coordinates all our other projects and roles. As such, it underlies all the different projects and roles that we engage in (Rudd 2012: 45–6, 139–40, 187–8; Davenport 2012). However, not just any commitment to a project or cause will prevent double-mindedness. Rather, we need a *normative standard* that allows the shaping and unification of our entire identity.

First, wholeheartedness requires *unconditional* commitment. The agent cannot shape and unify his whole identity in all circumstances if he is only instrumentally, occasionally, or partially committed to coherent self-shaping. He cannot, for instance, only commit when he feels like it, or when it serves some external end (e.g., maximization of pleasure). The development of a coherent identity cannot be conditioned on, and limited by, anything external to it; for this would entail double-mindedness divided between self-shaping and something else (e.g., pleasure). But this cannot support self-shaping in cases which does not serve this external end. To avoid double-mindedness completely, the shaping and unification of selfhood therefore requires categorical commitment that is not a mere means to something else.

Second, wholeheartedness requires normativity that is *ubiquitous and basic* to autonomous agency and human selfhood. This normativity cannot be unique to each individual but must rather be *shared*, since our self-relation is fundamentally intertwined with our relation to others. As we saw, Kierkegaard sees the self as social and relational, since it relates both to the human synthesis and to others (see Figure 1.1). A proper self-relation therefore requires a proper relation to others and vice versa since these relations are interdependent.

The Judge distinguishes between personal virtues (courage, valor, temperance, and moderation) that are necessary for self-development and civic virtues (notably justice) that are necessary for participation in social life. He argues that these virtues are interdependent, so that I cannot have any personal virtues without also having civic or social virtues (SKS 3, 249 / EO2, 262). He thus presents the task of becoming oneself as the task of cultivating oneself by functioning in, and contributing to, society (SKS 3, 249–50, 261 / EO2, 262–3, 274–5).

Here and elsewhere, Kierkegaard appears to rely on the broadly Hegelian idea that self-consciousness requires intersubjectivity, and that our self-relation is mediated by others (cf. Grøn 1997: ch. 5; Furtak 2005: 74, 99).[22] However, we will see (in the next chapter) that also our rationality depends on others, since reasoning requires dialogue. It is not only reasoning, narratives, and language that require social relations, however. Even gestures, emotions, affects, bodily attunement, and synchronic movements require such relations.[23]

Kierkegaard maintains that both our self-relation and our relation to others involve a shared normative standard for success, which he *identifies* with the morally good and the divine (SKS 9, 111–24 / WL, 107–21; cf.

[22] There are elements in Kierkegaard that resemble Hegelian ethics (itself a synthesis of Aristotelianism and Kantianism). *Either/Or, Part II* and *Works of Love* in particular give an account of love and human agency as fundamentally intersubjective that is reminiscent of Hegel's (and Fichte's) ethics of recognition. Like Hegel, these writings portray our self-consciousness and self-relation as interdependent with our relation to others. But while Hegel conceives of (true) recognition as reciprocal, Kierkegaard presents the relation between self and other as asymmetrical. *Works of Love* presents the other as transcending my representation of him, stressing the unconditional and one-sided duty to love the other independently of whom she is or what she does. Cf. Grøn 1997: chs. 5–6.

[23] Indeed, these relations seem constitutive not only of narrative selfhood but even of prereflective, embodied being with others. See Kyselo 2020.

Lippitt 2013: 56–7, 121–2). To become a wholehearted self therefore requires ethics that is other-regarding and altruistic rather than self-regarding or egoistic (cf. SKS 7, 121–33, 385–95 / CUP1, 129–42, 423–34; Pap. IV, A246 / JP 5, 5636). Indeed, *Philosophical Fragments* claims that self-love is sublated by love of another (SKS 4, 252 / PF, 47–8). Self-love is both negated and confirmed when it is recontextualized or *aufgehoben* by love of another. As egoistic or self-serving, love is negated (or rather *dethroned*, cf. Lippitt 2013: 75), whereas it is transformed and preserved as unselfish love for the other. In line with this, *Works of Love* claims that justified self-love requires neighbor-love, while justified hope for oneself requires hope for all others (SKS 9, 227–62 / WL, 225–63 / SKS 10, 127–32 / CD, 116–22).

Kierkegaard argues that hope without neighbor-love is false, so that the real alternative to neighbor-love is despair. He proceeds by discussing a case where I hope for myself while giving up others by viewing them as hopeless (SKS 9, 253–6 / WL, 254–6). However, hoping only for myself involves conceiving of hope and the good as something private that does not concern my relationship to others, as if I have a future of my own without others, or as if what is good for me differs from the good for others. Kierkegaard argues convincingly that by hoping in this way I fail to appreciate the extent to which I am dependent upon others. If there is no hope for others, then there cannot be any hope for me either since I am dependent upon others. If they are trapped in hopelessness, this must also hold for me, even if I do not realize it myself. In this sense, I can be trapped in despair or hopelessness without realizing it.

The point is that hoping for oneself must involve hoping for others, hoping for society (SKS 9, 253–4, 248 / WL, 253–4, 248). Kierkegaard writes:

> [L]ove is . . . the middle term: without love, no hope for oneself; with love, hope for all others – and to the same degree one hopes for oneself, to the same degree one hopes for others, since to the same degree one is loving. (SKS 9, 259 / WL, 260)

Love thus connects hope for oneself with hope for others, transforming the object of hope into something universal – arguably an ethical commonwealth or invisible church.[24] The upshot is not only that goods must be shared but also that one is trapped in despair without neighbor-love.

[24] See Fremstedal 2014a: 108–10. One may object that one is not dependent on all human beings but only on some. However, whom I depend upon in different contexts seems contingent. There does not seem to be a principal reason that prevents me from being or becoming dependent on anyone in particular. Still, Kierkegaard's point is not mainly that I may find myself being dependent upon

Rudd's Reconstruction of the Argument from Despair

Recently, Rudd reconstructed the argument from despair, arguing that Judge William's ethical views are defensible and relevant to contemporary debates about morality.[25] Rudd summarizes his reconstruction as follows:

1. One can only avoid the necessity of judging one's life in moral terms by evading long-term commitments.
2. But to live such a life is to be in despair; for a life without commitments is one without purpose, and hence is one that makes it impossible to develop a coherent personal identity. (2005: 69)

But why does long-term commitment involve specific moral normativity? Rudd argues that a meaningful and fulfilled life requires a stable sense of self, something that

> can only be achieved through commitment to social roles and relationships which carry with them objective standards of assessment. One must become a participant in communities and the traditions which define them, and must develop the virtues necessary for such participation. The failure to do this will render one's life quite literally pointless. Without any unifying *telos*, one's life collapses into a series of disconnected moments, and to live in this way . . . is to live in despair. (2001: 139)

Here personal identity or selfhood is not something simply given but rather something that must be achieved through moral commitment over time that synthetizes facticity and freedom.[26] Specifically, Rudd follows Bernard

a stranger or an enemy. Put in the terms of Apel and Habermas, Kierkegaard is concerned rather with how actual discourses (performatively) presuppose an ideal discourse. The Kantian parallel seems to be Kant's claim, in Book III of *Religion within the Boundaries of Mere Reason*, that individual struggle against moral evil requires an ethical commonwealth (or kingdom of God) that makes the victory of the good principle over the evil one possible. Hare explains: "His argument is that we will have ends which require the help of others if we are going to reach them . . . We are linked together by our needs and abilities into a single unit, or kingdom, which we must be prepared to will into existence as a whole. It contains our needs (for even in the true church we will be creatures of need), and it contains other people with the developed abilities to meet our needs; but it also contains the needs of others, and our developed abilities to meet their needs" (2002b: 265).

[25] Like Davenport (2012), Rudd (2012) is particularly concerned with the contemporary debate over whether nonmoral caring involves implicit rational commitment to ethical values.

[26] Cf. Rudd 2005: 84. Rudd (2012) and Davenport (2012) argue that both actions and practical identity involve a narrative structure. Intelligible actions are purposive, involving (at least ideally) a decision, an act, and the attainment of a goal (Rudd 2005: 84–5). Practical identity, on the other hand, requires not just single actions but also projects consisting of a pattern of purposive action. And it is only when our actions and identity belong to a larger narrative that they are intelligible and meaningful (cf. Davenport 2012). Rudd and Davenport thus connect moral agency to the narrative ideal, something that is controversial. John Kekes (2013) recently criticizes the narrative ideal (as put forward by Alasdair MacIntyre) by making the case that narratives are not necessary for a meaningful life. However, Rudd

Williams in arguing that our most fundamental projects, our "ground projects," give meaning to life and continuity to our characters.[27] Such projects are necessary if we are to develop a coherent personal identity (Rudd 2005: 92–3).

Like others, Rudd focuses on practical identity here. In the words of Korsgaard (1996a: 101), "practical identity" is essentially normative since it concerns "a description under which you find your life to be worth living and your actions to be worth undertaking." Rudd argues that developing a coherent practical identity, or achieving purity of heart, requires shaping oneself by having ground projects (or final ends). However, these projects or ends must be cared about for their own sake, and not just as a means to something else. Rudd explains: "I may adopt a project because I feel a need for something to give my life meaning [and coherence], but it will only do so if I come to care about the project for itself" (2012: 45).

Furtak (2005: 105) makes a related point by arguing that when one loves nothing unselfishly, one must also "suffer the unbearable emptiness of a life in which there are no final ends, because nothing is cared about for its own sake." A similar Butlerian point about satisfaction is made by Korsgaard (2013: 55), who says that "you cannot get any satisfaction from the fulfilment of your desire for an object, unless you want the desired object itself for its own sake." Instrumental value is *derived* from noninstrumental value. It is therefore only when you are interested in something (notably activities, practices) for its own sake that it becomes "a major contributor to human good" (Adams 2006: 87). Indeed, many forms of satisfaction are by-products of goods and activities that must be pursued for their own sake (Davenport 2007: 145–6, 155, 163–8, 211–31). Otherwise, such by-product satisfaction is impossible.

However, Rudd proceeds by arguing that the ground projects we pursue for their own sake must involve developing and exercising moral virtues.[28] He follows Peter Geach in arguing that

(2012: 214–27) and Davenport (2012: 197) both respond to various objections against the narrative ideal, including objections developed by Kekes in his earlier publications. For present purposes, it seems unnecessary, and perhaps unfeasible, to discuss the narrative ideal thoroughly. Still, it could be mentioned that Kekes' criticism concerns meaning in life rather than why we should be moral and that Kekes targets MacIntyre, not Rudd, Davenport, or Kierkegaard. Kekes argues that only an elite would be able to live according to the narrative ideal, whereas Rudd seem to hold that purposive action and participation in moral practices suffices for basic meaning in life. Kekes (2013: 71) sees narratives as contingent human constructions, something Rudd and Davenport deny by connecting narratives to objective meaning and moral realism. See also Stokes (2015: chs. 7–9) for a critical discussion of narrative and minimal selfhood in Kierkegaard.

[27] Rudd 2005: 86. Rudd (2012: 44–5) also makes use of Frankfurt's notion of "final ends" that one cares about for their own sake.

[28] Rudd's reconstruction of Judge William's argument for the ethical relies on moral virtues without the traditional idea of life having a final end (*eudaimonia*) that all human beings share (2005: 78–80, 99–105; cf. Kosch 2006a: 146–7). Rudd (2005: 94) follows William's distinction between personal

> [w]e need prudence and practical wisdom for any large-scale planning. We need justice to secure cooperation and mutual trust among men . . . We need temperance in order not to be deflected from our long-term and large-scale goals by seeking short-term satisfactions. And we need courage in order to persevere in face of setbacks, weariness, difficulties, and dangers.[29]

The argument can be summarized as follows:

> Whatever projects one undertakes, one will need the virtues of courage, self-control, and practical wisdom, and also the virtue of honest perception [of oneself] . . . In so far as one is committed to living in a society . . . one will also need the virtues of justice and benevolence, in some measure anyway . . . the ethical task of developing the virtues is the same for everybody . . . The need to cultivate the virtues derives from the need to engage in projects, and this derives from the need to live a coherent and meaningful life.[30]

On this view, there is a very close connection between the objectivity of moral values and the idea of meaning in life (Rudd 2012: 149). Specifically, a

1. coherent and meaningful life requires
2. significant projects, something that in turn involves
3. social interaction and practices, which again
4. presuppose moral norms.

The aesthetic stage necessarily involves despair (or ennui) in the sense of one's life lacking point and purpose. Since the aesthete does not want to commit fully to any projects for its own sake, his life is pointless and without purpose. The aesthete A writes:

> My life is utterly meaningless. When I consider its various epochs, my life is like the word *Schnur* in the dictionary, which first of all means a string, and second a daughter-in-law. All that is lacking is that in the third place the word *Schnur* means a camel, in the fourth a whisk broom. (SKS 2, 45 / EO1, 36)

Without something that gives meaning to his life, the aesthete lacks something to unify the different parts of his life, something that makes it

virtues (courage, valor, temperance, and moderation) that are necessary for self-development and civic virtues (notably justice) that are necessary for participation in social life.

[29] Geach 1979: 16. Rudd (2005: 101) follows Iris Murdoch in stressing the importance of honesty with oneself.

[30] Rudd 2005: 108–9, cf. 87. Virtue is described as "a disposition . . . giv[ing] constancy and stability to my character" (Rudd 2005: 108). Rudd does not think that Geach or classical virtue ethics succeeds completely in justifying the virtue of justice. Even though justice is necessary in order to secure cooperation and mutual trust among men, this hardly explains why I need to be just (Rudd 2005: 101–2). Rudd concludes that justice remains problematic within the ethical stage, but not within the religious stage (2005: 115), something that seems questionable – at least exegetically.

into a coherent whole with a clear practical identity. As a result, his life is nothing but a mere series of moments or episodes without meaning or a unifying structure. His life is ruled by a multiplicity of moods and situations, unlike the ethicist who relies on the unifying power of personality (Rudd 2001: 138–9 and 2005: 75, 79).[31]

It is important, however, that meaning is connected to social roles and commitments that the aesthetes cannot accept. Therefore, *Either/Or* describes the aesthetes as refraining from promises and obligations, and as warning against entering into friendship, marriage, and the acceptance of official positions (SKS 2, 284–7, 356 / EO1, 295–8, 367). This, however, indicates a certain respect for the ethical (SKS 2, 356 / EO1, 367). The idea is that one must avoid getting seriously involved with others; one must avoid commitment if one is to live aesthetically; otherwise, one will be trapped into social morality. One must therefore be able to avoid relationships, or to break them off by a sheer act of will (SKS 2, 286 / EO1, 297).

To the aesthete, morality is strict, harsh, boring, and rigid (*kantet*; see SKS 2, 145, 356 / EO1, 145, 367), since moral duties are opposed to our inclinations (SKS 3, 144 / EO2, 146). It is not coincidental that this view resembles Schillerian criticism of Kantian ethics, since Kierkegaard's aesthete is heavily influenced by German (Jena) Romanticism.[32] To a great extent, Kierkegaard relies on a Hegelian and Fichtean critique of Romanticism that is fundamentally incompatible with aesthetic amoralism (or mere irony as infinite absolute negativity). His detailed use of this *Romantikkritik* indicates that he is highly critical of aesthetic amoralism (but this does not prevent him from appreciating other aspects of Romanticism).[33]

[31] Still, the connection between morality and meaning is perhaps not quite as tight as Rudd assumes. Even amoralists may have nonmoral projects and experience some minimal meaning, even if they must treat others merely instrumentally. But it is still the case that the moral life seems more meaningful than the amoral life (Landau 2015). It therefore seems that existential meaning favors morality. But the argument from existential meaning is perhaps better seen as a weak argument for morality that is neither exclusively prudential nor moral. Existential meaning seems distinct from both morality and prudence, although it is interwoven with both in many different ways (see Martin 2012: 6–7, 183). Strong arguments aim to show that morality is necessary, and not optional, for us. Weak arguments, by contrast, only aim to show that morality is favored, but not required.

[32] For Schillerian criticism of Kantian ethics and its influence on Hegel and Kierkegaard, see Stern 2012: ch. 4 and 193–9. For Kierkegaard and German Romanticism, see Bohrer 1989: 62–72, 153–7, 161; Behler 1997; Stewart 2003: 170–81; Tjønneland 2004: esp. ch. 2.

[33] The best candidate for a historical model for Kierkegaard's ethicist is probably J. G. Fichte. Fichte and the ethicist share the following features: (1) The general idea that marriage is a step on the path to become an ethically developed person and that the love relation is nature's way of overcoming itself and pushing us toward becoming ethical beings. Marriage is therefore considered a duty (something Kant denies). (2) Individual conscience, or subjective conviction, is taken to have ultimate

Concluding Discussion: In Defense of Ethics

Rudd's central idea is that any project significant enough to give life purpose and meaning involves social interaction, practices, and institutions.[34] However, these social practices and institutions always come with standards of assessment that are not only intersubjective, non-instrumental, and nonarbitrary, but also moral. Thus, significant projects involve sustaining noninstrumental personal relationships that require recognition of authoritative moral norms and ideals (Rudd 2005: 95, 115).

A similar point is made by Rick Furtak (2005: 76) who argues that to "accept the roles of husband, judge, and friend (or mother, author, and confidante) is to accept certain beliefs about what is of value." Social roles and relationships involve intersubjective standards of behavior that are not merely dependent on my will, emotions, or subjectivity. Without such moral standards of assessment, I would lack something that makes it possible for me to assess whether significant actions and projects are objectively better or worse (Rudd 2005: 71–2 and 2012: 110).

Rudd (2012: 91) proceeds by arguing that there are good reasons for endorsing Harry Frankfurt's view that full selfhood requires evaluation of my desires, dispositions, cares, and loves. However, this need for evaluation also involves an attempt to get things right (or get closer to being right); as evaluative beings, we cannot suppose that our evaluative judgments are incapable of being objectively correct or better (Rudd 2012: 95). We can only shape our identity as part of a rational, nonarbitrary process if we are able to make ourselves better or worse, judged by standards independent of our will.

normative authority and to be the final arbiter of truth. (3) Conscience is seen as beginning from concrete circumstances rather than general principles like the categorical imperative. Conscience is therefore seen as exercising reflecting rather than determining judgment. (4) Moral failure is interpreted in terms of laziness, inertia, and a lack of energy; it is not seen as a result of original sin. Although willing with utmost energy does not directly guarantee that we make the right choice, it nevertheless guarantees apprehension of the correct thing to do, and that in turn guarantees the right choice (Kosch 2006b: 270–3).

However, Kierkegaard's religious writings break not only with the last point but probably also the first point. This means that even if Kierkegaard used Fichte as a model for the ethicist, Kierkegaard's religious position breaks with Fichte's views on evil and marriage. Kosch argues that there was a quite general consensus among Kierkegaard's contemporaries that Fichte's ethics was Kantian ethics in its most perfect form or even that it was the best example of philosophical normative ethics available. Although Fichte's ethics is obscure today, *The System of Ethics* nevertheless represented a central ethical work in Kierkegaard's historical context (Kosch 2015a and 2015b). For Hegelian elements, see Stewart 2003: chs. 3–4; 2007: ch. 5.

[34] Rudd 2005: 94. Rudd uses MacIntyre's definition of practice here. A slightly different approach is represented by Hare (2001: 42–6) who argues for the necessity of assuming that what other people evaluate as good to pursue is at least roughly consistent with what I evaluate as good to pursue, since many of the goods I am likely to pursue depend for their achievement on the cooperation of others.

Rudd therefore concludes that

> I have to ask, "Do *I* consider this, or that good?" And this is why I think that the idea of *the* Good is unavoidable, if only as a regulative ideal. It is what my moral deliberation has to be constantly moving towards. (2012: 141)

Rational agency therefore presupposes the possibility of rational examination of our higher-order cares and commitments in light of the idea of something objectively good (or at least better or worse in a realist sense). Without this possibility, the irrationality (or rather arationality) of our cares and commitments would cascade down the levels, and we would have no basis for thinking of ourselves as more than instrumentally rational agents (Rudd 2012: 112).[35]

On this line of interpretation, Kierkegaard is concerned with autonomous agency that allows us to take responsibility for ourselves as agents who shape our ends and priorities. John Davenport comments:

> Formal autonomy involves volitional identification with some first-order motives and alienation of others . . . Caring about first-order ends rationally commits us to [second-order caring] that the putative values to which we respond in our central commitments, relationships, and life goals are objectively or intersubjectively sound . . . [and] mutually consistent. (2012: 117)

This involves the idea of wholehearted agency as a regulative ideal that evaluates and sustains first-order motives based on putative objective values. Like Rudd, Davenport here introduces the objective good as a regulative idea. By its very nature the objective good is agent neutral, not agent relative. But this would necessarily favor morality, not rational egoism (for the latter only accepts agent relative values and reasons).[36] Indeed, both Rudd and Davenport are strong or robust moral realists (holding that moral judgments not only have truth value, but that some of these judgments are literally true since they correspond to stance-independent moral facts).

Davenport argues that moral standards provide a *firm point* outside of our first-order states that is much needed, since without such an objective basis, we have no stable ground for working upon ourselves; any attempt to better oneself will then be at the mercy of the contingencies of time. Moral

[35] Rudd goes as far as saying that "Rawlsian liberalism collapses into Schlegelian (or Rortian?) ironism – the valuing, not of *rational* choice, but of choice itself. But it is hard to see how such ironism can avoid collapsing into full-blown nihilism; for why should we treat the sheer power of choice as valuable, if there is nothing else that is genuinely valuable that it enables us to choose" (2012: 115).

[36] For the agent relative reasons and values of rational egoism, see, e.g., Hills 2010: 91.

norms and ideals thus provide a check (*Anstoß* in the Fichtean sense) by representing something radically different from subjective perspectives and first-order states (Davenport 2012: 98–9, 122–5; cf. Rudd 2012: 165).[37]

Here both Davenport and Rudd rely on Frankfurt's concept of care. For Frankfurt (2004: 17), caring is an activity that "connects and binds us to ourselves" by giving meaning and character to our lives. Caring brings volitional unity, coherence, and structure to our lives by identifying certain values that are particularly important to us. Davenport argues that

> caring and higher-order willing are naturally based on perceptions or beliefs about objective values; such a basis partially explains their nonderivative agent-authority. Within the "rational striving" conception caring (like identification) requires the agent's conviction that (i) the people or goals to which he is committed are inherently worth caring about, or that (ii) the process of caring about these ends and pursuing projects related to them is inherently valuable (or both), where (iii) such inherent value is independent of her prior desires and preferences, though not of her history. (2012: 105)

Based on Jeffrey Blustein, Davenport argues that we must suppose that the objects of our "deep-seated cares" are not merely subjective but that they must reflect values that are not derived from our individual cares for them (2012: 105). Our motivation and rationality would be undermined if our values and commitments were either pointless or "imposed by our accidental desires" or if "our interest in them derives solely from manipulation by others" (Davenport 2012: 106). However, we will see in the next chapter that the aesthete seems ruled by exactly such accidental desires. The ethicist, by contrast, evaluates desires and cares based on moral considerations instead.

[37] Discussing the rational stability of agency, Davenport writes: "[E]ven if we abstract from the social relationships involved in our cares, our loyalty to important values expressed in them cannot be stable without a deeper loyalty to ethical principles of consistency, honesty, and respect for persons as beings capable of caring. Agents who begin to form autonomous cares find that attentiveness to the values grounding these cares makes salient the deeper ethical considerations relevant to critically assessing nonmoral values and ordering cares together" (2012: 122).

Moral values with universal import seem to provide an adequate basis for the type of continuity of commitment that seems necessary if we are to recognize ourselves as the same agent-cause across different circumstances of action (cf. Irwin 2011: vol. 1, 299; Davenport 2012). This need for a firm basis seems to represent a practical analog to the need for assuming an identical I as a subject of consciousness over time through being conscious of an enduring world. I owe this suggestion to a reviewer.

CHAPTER 3

Moral Inescapability: Moral Agency and Metaethics

The Aesthete, Humeanism, and Wantonness

Both the aesthete and the ethicist are deeply concerned with love as an emotion (or a passion). The aesthete focuses on romantic (erotic) love, whereas the ethicist focuses on marriage as the paradigm case for the ethical stage. The aesthete believes in love as an experience that makes life beautiful and interesting, seeing marriage and its duties as incompatible with the freedom and spontaneity required by genuine love (cf. SKS 2, 145, 356 / EO1, 145, 367; SKS 3, 144 / EO2, 146). He sees love as a mere feeling, whereas the ethicist and Kierkegaard seem to approach it as a virtue with emotional (affective), dispositional, and cognitive aspects that ought to be cultivated.[1]

The aesthete experiences different emotions and desires, but he does not give his *assent* to them by endorsing them or by actively embracing their significance. He lacks higher-order motives that develop and cultivate lower-order motives and desires into coherent character traits and virtues. Indeed, he hardly views himself as the *owner* of his inclinations and desires, in the sense of taking responsibility for them – although they do make up the basis of his decisions, ends, and actions. He is free in the sense of being independent of his inclinations, but he does not recognize or affirm this freedom as the ethicist does (Irwin 2011: vol. III, 301, 304). He thus takes up the perspective of a *spectator* toward his own emotions and his own life. By doing this, he denies that he is already involved in life and therefore responsible for it (Furtak 2005: 58–9, 62–3, 66, 79).

A remarkably similar position is found in the Humean conception of acting for a reason (cf. Irwin 2011: vol. III, 293–6). As Sarah Buss explains, this conception says that

[1] Kierkegaard suggests, however, that there is some continuity between the different forms of love. *Stages on Life's Way*, for instance, describes different forms of love in a manner reminiscent of Plato's famous description of different forms of love in the *Symposium* (cf. Furtak 2005: 103–4).

> someone acts for a reason whenever both (a) her beliefs and desires "rationalize" her action (i.e., provide some justification for acting this way) and (b) her action is caused by the mental states that rationalize it. (1999: 400)

However, as Buss points out, this means that the agent must regard her ends

> as having been imposed upon her by the desires she happens to have. It is as if some third person (B) informed the deliberator (A) of *his goals*, and her job was simply to figure out the best way to achieve these goals . . . [But this] is like mistaking a traveler's action for the actions of his travel agent. (1999: 410)

Buss then concludes that

> *no matter what reasons are*, deliberators must make up their minds about what to do; and if they are to make up their minds, their reason must play the master role; it must determine the normative status of their desires. (1999: 411)

But neither the Humean agent nor the aesthete allows reason to play such a master role (Irwin 2011: vol. III, 293–304). Both are detached from their ends since the ends are imposed from without. The aesthete does not lack energy or dedication, but he sees his ends as *external* to himself, insofar as they are objects of inclination that are purely *accidental* to him. The aesthete would be less detached from his ends, however, if he could regard them as *appropriate* for him, as the sort of agent he is, because they represent the type of ends that he *ought* to choose irrespective of the strength of his inclinations (Irwin 2011: vol. III, 299). Terence Irwin explains:

> Since we regard ourselves as continuing selves; and think it right, irrespective of the strength of our desires, to plan for our continuing selves, we can also see – though we may not see – that a purely aesthetic attitude to ourselves cannot satisfy us. If we treat our ends as matters of mere inclination, we do not ask the questions that, as continuing agents, we recognize as legitimate, about whether we have reason to pursue this end rather than another. The aesthetic outlook does not fit the self that adopts it. (2011: vol. III, 299)

Irwin concludes that the aesthetic agent is liable to despair because aesthetic agency presupposes nonaesthetic agency (2011: vol. III: 299–300). The aesthete is double-minded, split between aesthetic and moral agency. Specifically, he thinks of himself as a particular continuing self that is free, but this self does not fit aesthetic agency, which is ruled by inclinations and desires that are accidental and external. Virtually the same point is made by Buss (in a different context):

> Practical deliberators cannot set *their own* goals without holding evaluative beliefs about the goals *their desires* incline them to pursue; and such evaluations necessarily involve the application of practical norms which are independent of the desires themselves. (Buss 1999: 403; cf. Taylor 1985: 26)

Love and Higher-Order Motives: Eros and Marriage

In *Either/Or*, the paradigmatic case illustrating this point concerning practical norms is romantic love. The ethicist argues that moral obligation is not opposed to love, something that is reminiscent of Schiller and Hegel (cf. Stern 2012: 190–9). Specifically, he stresses that moral duty should not be interpreted as something external that is opposed to my inner being, but rather seen as something that expresses my true being (SKS 3, 242–3 / EO2, 254–5). Freedom is realized *in* moral and social commitment – it is not opposed to it. In the words of Hegel (1991a: 133): "In doing my duty [for its own sake], I am at home with myself [*bei mir selbst*] and free."

The ethicist argues that romantic love needs to be both endorsed and restricted in marriage. The idea is that romantic love is transfigured in marriage so that love's needs are completed and fulfilled. On this view, marriage is not an alien imposition on romantic love, but something that allows romantic love to develop and endure (Evans 2009: 93). The ethicist proceeds by arguing that love itself wants to be strengthened, since it wants to ensure that it will last. Even in the absence of a marriage ceremony, lovers therefore swear faithfulness to each other in the name of something perceived to be higher (e.g., moon, stars, father's ashes) so as to bind themselves (SKS 3, 61–2 / EO2, 56.). This indicates that love itself seeks commitment and responsibility (SKS 3, 61, 66, 144–7 / EO2, 56, 60–1, 146–9).[2]

The ethicist argues that our lower-order motives, desires, and states can only have (lasting) significance by being actively endorsed and guided by practical rationality involving intersubjective standards of assessment.

[2] However, *Works of Love* argues that love's need for obligation shows that love is dimly aware that it is insufficient by itself; love is insecure, anxious about the possibility of change, anxious that love may vanish or change. As a result, love needs moral obligation (SKS 9, 40, 73 / WL, 32–3, 66). However, Kierkegaard's claim that difficulties remain with William's notion of marriage (SKS 7, 167 / CUP1, 181) need not undermine the justification of morality.

Specifically, lower-order motives only acquire real importance if we are ethically committed by relating to what happens to us, either by identifying with or distancing ourselves from lower-order motives. This can be done either by viewing lower-order motives as appropriate or as inappropriate, as something we ought or ought not to act on, based on the *merits* of different options that reflect normative *reasons* that hold irrespective of strength of inclinations (Irwin 2011: vol. III, 299–300). We thus need to introduce the idea of a *rational choice* based on the merits of different options, not just on inclinations and desires. This means that we enter the area of good and evil as features to be considered in a free choice (Irwin 2011: vol. III, 300). Specifically, we need strong evaluation, which is a higher-order evaluation of lower-order motives based on qualitative standards of merit or goodness (Taylor 1985: 17–28; Davenport 2012: 101–6).

The more general point, however, is that there is no free lunch. Things cannot have real importance or meaning if they do not imply some commitment or obligation. Specifically, emotions that are not actively endorsed and regulated are merely *episodic* sensations without meaning and significance. The aesthete therefore lives in a world of fleeting and abbreviated emotions, lacking emotional integrity (Furtak 2005: 59, 65). He may consider emotions and passion to be the deepest part of the human being; but these are wild and unruly as long as the aesthete does not have any definitive aim or end (Furtak 2005: 77). Without an active endorsement of emotions, these will disintegrate into mere fragments and the aesthete will be ironic and indifferent toward his own life. Furtak elaborates:

> He avoids taking anything seriously, and thereby guards himself against the emotional risk of being more than ironically involved. And the fragmentary nature of his temporal existence also keeps him from occupying any role that requires sustained care: he can be a dilettante but not a devoted artist, a temporary acquaintance but not a loyal friend ... Rather than letting his episodic emotions grow into longstanding attitudes, the aesthete lets them weightlessly pass away, so that both joy and torment end up meaning nothing. (2005: 68, 79)

Someone whose emotions lead him to form a consistent disposition will attain integrated selfhood in a manner unavailable to someone who lives merely momentary. Moreover, emotional responses involve an orientation toward value in two different senses. First, emotions themselves have either a positive or negative valence that involve evaluation or valuing as well as appraisals, assessments, or impressions of importance (Mulligan 2010).

Second, we can relate to these emotions again by valuing and evaluating them, forming higher-order motives that can vary from wanton indifference to full moral commitment.

Unlike the ethicist, aesthetes do not seem to sustain awareness of what moves them, something that makes them dishonest with themselves and untrue to relevant values and goods.[3] The immediate aesthete seems to be a *wanton* who does not evaluate his motives, since he lacks such higher-order motives. He therefore is simply moved by first-order desires. Reflective aesthetes, by contrast, may come in two different variants: One follows the strongest given desire, tacitly accepting it by using higher-order motives to reinforce it. Another forms higher-order motives that prevent evaluation of lower-order motives. At the higher level, the latter is a spectator who is indifferent to his lower-order motives (Rudd 2012: 80–5; cf. Davenport 2012: 123). This is paradoxical, since it is precisely the evaluative belief that all lower-ordered motives are indifferent that prevents choice and prioritization.

In any case, the aesthete is ruled by sensuousness, so that rationality and reflection serve sensuousness instead of morality (something that makes him heteronomous in a Kantian sense). But the reflective aesthete is not a mere natural being who could not have prioritized differently. He is not some animal that cannot be held responsible for his acts since he freely prioritizes sensuousness over morality. The latter means that morality is conditioned on nonmoral incentives or principles. This means that the aesthete acts morally in a very limited sense, that he, for instance, loves himself and his neighbor when he feels like it, but not all of the time.

However, this is deeply problematic since morality, by its very nature, seems to require unconditional and universal compliance. For if the will were to compromise on morality as the aesthete does, it would partially affirm its nature and partially affront it. It would partially express its essence and partially violate it, allowing itself to be determined sometimes by aesthetic standards and sometimes taking morality to be of absolute worth. But as Seriol Morgan points out, in trying to do so,

> the will would actually fail to achieve in any measure any of the things it half-heartedly attempted to commit to. You do not live up to the demands of morality at all by committing yourself to do so to a certain extent, and you cannot appreciate the dignity of humanity if you resolve to respect it only now and then. Rather, this would just show that you had failed to grasp the importance of any of these things in the first place. (2005: 96–7)

[3] I owe much of this point to a reviewer.

This is the doctrine of moral rigorism (concerning character) associated with Kant and Kierkegaard (Fremstedal 2014a: 25–8). However, this rigorism seems preferable to latitudinarianism (Allison 1995: 146–52; Firestone and Jacobs 2008: 127–33). At least, this may hold for a practical use of it, which strives for moral perfection involving a unity of the virtues (although an explanatory use of it seems problematic).

Following Gottfried Wilhelm Leibniz (1646–1716), Kierkegaard criticizes the idea of a fully indifferent will (*liberum arbitrium*) that could just as well choose one thing as another (Løkke and Waaler 2009: 74–5). Like Kant and Schelling, he is not so much concerned with alternative courses of action as choosing between good and evil, particularly at the level of one's character (cf. SKS 4, 414 / CA, 112). He agrees with Leibniz about how we should not conceive of freedom. Freedom should not be modeled after Buridan's ass, which could not decide between two equally attractive stacks of hay and hence starved to death. Here Leibniz invokes Plato and Augustine, saying that the will is never prompted to action except by the representation of the good.

Although he is not explicit, Kierkegaard relies on the same Platonico-Christian tradition, maintaining that good and evil are not on the same footing (Walker 1972: 6–9, 17–18, 118–26, 143–4). First, we will see that he takes moral goodness to be inescapable. Second, his notion of facticity implies that there is no neutral starting point from which we can choose rationally, since we are finite historical beings who are always situated in specific situations. Finally, we cannot avoid choosing. Even the choice not to choose is a choice. Indeed, even higher-order indifference relates to lower-order motives. The self cannot but form higher-order motives since it entails hierarchical agency (as seen in Chapter 1).

Insofar as this agency is also autonomous, it must also evaluate different motives based on whether they are appropriate and involve normative reasons for action. It is here that practical normativity enters the picture. However, specifically moral normativity seems necessary since our self-relation is intertwined with our relation to others (more on this later). And even if the relevant normativity is not exclusively moral, it still seems that morality must be involved and it cannot be second to other norms. Rather, it must have supreme authority (more on this later).

Against Subjectivism: The Critique of Autonomy in Metaethics

Kierkegaard seems concerned with autonomous agency. However, many readers also associate him with Kantian autonomy in metaethics in which agents create moral norms and obligations. Robert Stern writes:

> It has become commonplace to read Kierkegaard as ... inheriting the Kantian idea of the self-legislating subject, but as following it through to its logical conclusion, so that the apparent emptiness and arbitrariness in this subject's position becomes fully clear. This then leads to Alastair MacIntyre's famous account of Kierkegaard in *A Short History of Ethics* and *After Virtue*, as facing a situation of radical (because groundless) choice. (2012: 16–17)

This widespread reading associates Kierkegaard with post-Kantian autonomy and existentialism. But it has little support in his texts, apart from various aesthetes who appear to support subjectivism or antirealism. Indeed, Kierkegaard offers an explicit critique of Kantian autonomy (and an implicit critique of Sartre's radical choice) that attacks moral subjectivism and relativism:

> Kant held that the hum[an] being was his own law (autonomy), i.e., bound himself under the law he gave himself. In the deeper sense, what this really postulates is lawlessness or experimentation ... If I am to bind myself and there is no binding force higher than myself, then where, as the A, who binds, can I find the rigor I do not possess as B, the one who is to be bound, when, after all, A and B are the same self[?] (SKS 23, 45, NB 15:66 / KJN 7, 42)

If I can bind myself, I can also unbind myself at will:

> [T]he adult is simultaneously master and servant; the one who is to command and the one who is to obey are one and the same ... It can so easily happen that the servant meddles in the deliberation about the task, and conversely, that the master pays too much attention to the servant's complaints about the difficulties in carrying out the tasks. Then, alas, confusion develops; instead of becoming his own master a person becomes unstable, irresolute, vacillating ... Finally ... all his energy is expended in thinking up ever new changes in the task. (SKS 8, 389–90 / UD, 294–5; cf. SKS 11, 182–3 / SUD, 68–9)

The attempt to create one's own values and norms, without caring about anything for its own sake, leads not only to values and norms that are revocable and unstable but also to motiveless and arbitrary choice. Like the German Romantics and idealists, Kierkegaard here identifies a dilemma inherent to antirealist and subjectivist accounts of autonomy (self-determination) in metaethics (cf. Pinkard 2010; Stern 2012; Fremstedal 2020c: 300–4): Is autonomy based on reasons that are antecedently valid or not?

The first horn of the dilemma takes self-determination to be based on normative practical reasons that are antecedently valid and therefore have rational authority prior to self-legislation. Autonomy is then constrained by normative standards that are not self-imposed, something that appears to involve not only realism but also heteronomy. To avoid such heteronomy, the second horn rejects all normative standards and constraints that are not self-imposed.[4] Normative standards are therefore only considered authoritative if self-imposed. Any normative content is then valid, as long as it is self-imposed by contingent fiat.[5] But the content could change any time since nothing prevents an arbitrary change of will. Self-determination here collapses into a motiveless and arbitrary choice that is fundamentally groundless. Indeed, normativity is here constituted by a bootstrapping operation that is groundless, motiveless, and arbitrary.

Worse still, the lawgiver is but a finite, fallible, and imperfect subject who – in his motiveless choices – suffers from whims and moods, as well as laxness, procrastination, and corruption. Since lawgiver and subject are identical, the decisions of the lawgiver can be unduly influenced by the special interests of the subject. Specifically, the subject can influence the lawgiver to change and lessen his obligations instead of fulfilling them. Instead of realizing given tasks, he can therefore constantly change his mind about what to do, by lazily concocting new tasks (SKS 8, 389–90 / UD, 294–5). Instead of acting morally, he may deliberate about what his obligations are or what they could and should be. Self-determination therefore facilitates an unrestrained reflection that is self-consuming, something Kierkegaard associates with late modern European society.

Clearly, this form of autonomy is closer to Jena Romanticism and Sartre's radical choice than Kant or Hegel.[6] Indeed, it is closely associated with the subjectivism and relativism of the aesthetic stage. Kierkegaard here agrees with moral realists and theological voluntarists who worry that human autonomy collapses into an arbitrary self-launching that neither gives a convincing account of normativity nor of moral agency (Kosch 2006a: chs. 5–6; Stern 2012: ch. 7). Part 1 of *The Sickness unto Death*, for

[4] Kierkegaard refers to a "constraining factor"; see SKS 23, 45, NB 15:66 / KJN 7, 42.

[5] For a contemporary defense of a similar decisionism, which claims that it is possible to reject rational agency and thereby to become insane or to die, see Cohen 2008.

[6] Although Kant specialists discuss whether Kant is a metaethical realist or constructivist, many have taken autonomy to involve constructivism that creates valid norms by following valid procedure. Not just Rawls and Habermas but also Kierkegaard and some German Romantics and idealists associated Kantian autonomy with constructivism and subjectivism. See Pinkard 2010: 59–60, 115, 162–3, 187–9, 207, 277; Stern 2012; Fremstedal 2014a: ch. 10.

instance, argues that the phenomenon of defiance, or desperately wanting to be oneself, indicates that the self does not create or constitute itself normatively (SKS 11, 130 / SUD, 14). Defiance seems to presuppose norms that are given by someone else that I will not live up to, since I will not give up my own ends or projects.[7]

Here Kierkegaard's critique of autonomy anticipates debates about the source of moral obligations from Elizabeth Anscombe to contemporary moral realism and divine command theories of moral obligations (Stern 2012: ch. 7; Fremstedal 2014a: ch. 10). Like Anscombe, Kierkegaard objects to giving absolute overriding authority to something that is merely a human construct or creation, since human autonomy cannot bestow value on things that do not already have it.[8] Kierkegaard thus criticizes the view that morality is but a contingent creation of particular individuals. But many moral constructivists (e.g., Kantians) maintain that we construct valid obligations by being rational and by following valid procedure. Constructivism need not be based on what individuals actually or arbitrary do, since it could be based on what rational beings would do, or what they could agree to, under ideal circumstances.

Kierkegaard's argument has less force against the latter position than against subjectivists who see morality as a contingent construct of particular individuals. His argument is more convincing as an argument against subjectivist, relativist, and antirealist autonomy (including radical choice in existentialism), than against moderate forms of constructivism that see some moral claims as being literally true (i.e., moral success theory). Still, Kierkegaard may object that it is far from clear how idealized human choice or autonomy can bestow value on things that do not already have it, especially when actual human autonomy fails to bestow value (Rudd 2012: 149). He thus targets all forms of subjectivism, in which human valuing – idealized or not – somehow generates values and normativity.

[7] Kosch argues that defiance indicates that the self is neither normative self-sufficient nor its own ontological basis (the latter seems to entail the former): There does need to be *something* independent of the self and its activity from which norms can come, and this something must also be a plausible source of value, but something can fill those conditions without being the causal source of the agent's existence . . . the theological voluntarist model is not the only one to fit the constraints, even though it is clearly the one that Kierkegaard has in mind. This account of the structure of the self, by making the self dependent and oriented towards an outside source of norms, makes structurally possible a genuine alternative: turning away from that source and turning towards it. (2006a: 209)

[8] Anscombe (1958: 2–5) argues that the concept of legislation requires superior power in the legislator and that it is not possible to have such a conception of ethics unless you believe in God as a lawgiver.

Moral Realism and Divine Commands: Metaethics

Some take Kierkegaard to be a theological voluntarist in the traditions of nominalism and Lutheranism, while others read him as a strong moral realist in the Platonico-Christian tradition.[9] As it is mainly strong forms of these doctrines that are fundamentally incompatible, Kierkegaard can combine some form of theological voluntarism (or divine command ethics) with either strong (robust) realism or moral success theory.

Strong theological voluntarism sees the content of morality – what is right or wrong, good and bad – as contingent on God's will. Strong moral realism, by contrast, sees moral truths as facts (e.g., Platonic ideas) existing independently of both God's will and any other stance God or humans may take toward it. But minimal divine command theories allow for moral content (or moral facts) that hold independently of God's will (i.e., strong realism), while maintaining that morality only has a strictly morally obligatory *form* due to God's command (Evans 2014a: 142). Finally, there are hybrid views in which the content of morality partially depends on God's will and partially not (e.g., Duns Scotus). Although Kierkegaard's position is not perfectly clear, it nevertheless seems clear that he accepts at the very least moral success theory and some version of divine commands (although it is not clear if the latter amounts to a proper divine command theory of moral obligations).

Kierkegaard is sometimes thought to have contributed to the development of divine command theories of moral obligations by presenting the demands of neighbor-love in a particularly uncompromising manner.[10] Those who defend a divine command reading of him argue that divine command makes intelligible a morality that expects more of us than we are capable on our own, an ethics that transcends the ethical stage (and its appeal to human willpower) by accepting the *moral gap* between our moral obligations and our natural capabilities (as finite and sinful beings). On this reading, Kierkegaard makes sense of the moral gap by holding that (at least some) moral obligations are imposed by God, whose capacity to judge, assist, and forgive us differs from that of other kinds of obligating source (Stern 2012: 204–16).

9 For voluntarism, see Bohlin 1944: 63, 75–6; Wisdo 1987; Kosch 2006a: chs. 5–6; Irwin 2011: vol. III, ch. 77. For strong realism, see Davenport 2008a: 232–3 and 2012: 121–5; Rudd 2012: chs. 4–6; cf. Stern 2012: 221–2.

10 Quinn (1996 and 2006: 65–8), Evans (2006a), and Stern (2012: ch. 7) claim that Kierkegaard has a divine command theory of moral obligation, something Ferreira (2001: 40–2, 243–4), Roberts (2008: 79–90), and Manis (2009a) deny.

Proponents of the divine command reading argue that divine commands are sufficient for moral obligations on Kierkegaard's account, since seemingly immoral acts would be obligatory to us if commanded by God.[11] Indeed, *Fear and Trembling* seems to suggest that Abraham must sacrifice Isaac, since God commands it.[12] And *Works of Love* suggests that we should obey God in love, even if he requires something that seems harmful or overly demanding to us (SKS 9, 28 / WL, 20).[13] Even the duty of neighbor-love seems to rely on divine commands in *Works of Love* (Quinn 1996; Evans 2006a).

However, even if divine commands may impose some moral obligations, this need not rule out that some obligations have a different basis. *Works of Love* can be read as saying that the ultimate basis of moral obligations lies not in divine commands as such, but in the structure of the created world and God's relation to it (Ferreira 2001: 41; Manis 2009b). This reading accepts (strong, nonnaturalist) moral realism, but adds that moral obligations are based on the fact that we are created from nothing by God and that our neighbor is a fellow person, created in the image of God (Manis 2006: 137–41, 218; cf. SKS 9, 66–7, 94, 118, 219–26 / WL, 60, 88–9, 216–24). It suggests that Kierkegaard relies on a theology of creation in which – at least some – moral obligations depend on the fact that we belong to God as his creation. The central idea here is that we are worthy of love as a result of bearing God's image.[14] Our very dignity seems based on divine creation.

Similarly, "Purity of Heart" takes divine creation to be very good, although the fall partially corrupts it (SKS 8, 123 / UD, 7; cf. SKS 9, 66–7, 94, 118, 219–25 / WL, 60, 88, 115, 216–22). There is an element of goodness even in human evil that allows guilt-consciousness, faith, and sin-consciousness (although the two latter require divine revelation; cf. Fremstedal 2014a: ch. 2). Human beings are alienated from divine creation and goodness by sinfulness, something that makes divine grace, revelation, and divine commands decisive. Divine commands can then be necessary if we are to know and uphold our duty after the fall, although the duty to love the neighbor precedes God's command.[15]

[11] Or, if God counterfactually commands something, then it would be obligatory. See Manis 2009a: 290, 300.

[12] Quinn (2006: 60–72) takes Abraham's sacrifice of Isaac to mean that morality depends on God's will. For a discussion, see Davenport 2008a: 206–22.

[13] However, this passage is compatible with God promulgating obligations that hold independently of his command. See Manis 2006: 127.

[14] Manis 2006: chs. 3–4 and 2009. By contrast, Evans (2006a) maintains that we have only premoral obligations without divine commands.

[15] Manis 2006, 2009a, and 2009b. Manis (2006: 148–58) points to overlap between Kierkegaard and divine command theory when it comes to the possibility of individual obligations and callings and

Kierkegaard maintains that only neighbor-love makes us free and independent. By loving all humans without exception, we avoid being overly dependent on specific human beings:

> [I]n the world of spirit, precisely this, to become one's own master, is the highest – and in love to help someone toward that, to become himself, free, independent, his own master, to help him stand alone – that is the greatest beneficence. (SKS 9, 272 / WL, 274)

Charity makes us free, for "without law, freedom does not exist at all, and it is law that gives freedom" (SKS 9, 46 / WL, 38–9) – the reference to the law here probably includes the two great commandments of Christian ethics. In any case, autonomy here concerns independent-minded agency, not the creation of normative content.[16]

This allows for divine commands to play an important role within Kierkegaard's ethics, but it does not amount to a full-fledged divine command theory of moral obligation in which divine commands are necessary and sufficient for imposing moral obligations. Although there is some uncertainty and disagreement about Kierkegaard's exact position, it nevertheless seems clear that he develops an *intermediate* position between divine command ethics and moral realism, in which some parts of morality depend on God's will, while others do not (cf. Stern 2012: 222). Specifically, there are Platonico-Christian elements in Kierkegaard that support strong moral realism rather than theological voluntarism. Still, more research is needed – both historically and systematically – on moral realism and divine commands in Kierkegaard.

Inescapable Morality: Constitutivism Concerning Moral Normativity

Kierkegaard follows Socrates and Plato in arguing that the ethical is internal to human agency and selfhood. Rob Compaijen explains:

> Socrates' important idea that human beings in some sense already possess all knowledge is the background for Kierkegaard's claim that human beings are already in possession of the ethical (which is, of course, the reason why he emphasizes the Socratic notion of "recollection") . . . in the "Dialectic of Ethical and Ethical-Religious Communication" as well as in

the view that divine commands and grace are necessary to know and uphold obligations and to provide moral motivation.

16 Davenport (2012) focuses on autonomous agency, whereas Adams (2016) sees autonomy as a moral virtue of independent mindedness instead.

> *Concluding Unscientific Postscript*, Kierkegaard and Climacus stress that, in order to realize the ethical, there is nothing that needs to be put *into* the individual, but, instead the ethical needs to be brought *out* of the individual. Consequently, it is a central idea in Kierkegaard's authorship that the ethical is not external to, but already "inside" the individual. (2018: 184–5)

Specifically, Kierkegaard's relies on the guise of the good thesis introduced by Plato. A *subjective* version of it says that in ϕ-ing intentionally, we take ϕ-ing to be good (Tenenbaum 2021). An alternative version says that to desire or pursue something involves taking it to be good. In both cases, the good is merely a *perceived* (subjective) good. An *objective* (constitutivist) version of the thesis, by contrast, takes human agency to presuppose the objective good, even if the agent fails to realize it. In Kierkegaard, the idea seems to be that human selfhood and agency presuppose the objective moral good (cf. Walker 1972: 118–26, 138, 143–4). Any attempt to escape it is futile since nonmoral goods (and moral evil) are parasitic on it. Moral goodness, represented by the unconditional ethical task and moral normativity, is therefore constitutive of our selfhood and agency (cf. SKS 18, 279–80, JJ:420 / KJN 2, 258).

For Kant, the capacities that constitute responsible agency involve implicit commitment to their own inherent value as an end. Kant thus takes the normative bindingness of the categorical imperative to be grounded in the will's inescapable commitment to the shared value of freedom and reason (as potentials shared by all humans). Kierkegaard, by contrast, locates human dignity in our shared capacity for love (seeing the latter as a result of us being created in the image of God). However, for both thinkers the moral imperative arises from something *internal* to the volitional capacity that constitutes created personhood. This helps explain the fact that moral obligations do not feel like contingent inclinations. By expressing our shared nature, moral obligations differ from wanton and alien desires as well as from incentives resulting from coercion.[17]

However, Kantians see categorical and hypothetical imperatives as constitutive of intentional action and practical identity,[18] whereas Kierkegaard sees morality (and its obligations) as constitutive of wholehearted selfhood and autonomous agency. It does not represent

[17] I owe this point to a reviewer.

[18] See Korsgaard 2013. *Constitutivism* concerning practical normativity derives practical normativity from practical agency. Such constitutivism is found both in Kantianism and German idealism. Cf. Kosch 2018: esp. 36. For Kierkegaard, see Wietzke 2011.

a defeatable constitutive aim but rather an inescapable constitutive principle that cannot be overridden. This strong, objectivist and constitutivist view is developed particularly in "Purity of Heart."

"Purity of Heart," develops constitutivism by maintaining that we are only free to choose between being unconditionally good and being good to some extent, or in some respect (cf. SKS 8, 139–40 / UD, 24–5). Since it is inescapable, it is only the good that may be willed unconditionally and consistently without any contradiction or incoherence: "[T]he person who in truth wills only one thing *can will only the good* . . . the good is unconditionally the one and only thing that a person may will and shall will" (SKS 8, 138–9 / UD, 24–5). But full moral commitment does not rule out other concerns or norms (cf. Blattberg 2020). The point is only that the latter are a matter of secondary importance if moral duty is at stake.

Still, the agent is double-minded without full moral commitment:

> The person who wills one thing that is not the good is actually not willing one thing; it is an illusion, a semblance, a deception, a self-deception that he wills only one thing – because in his innermost being he is, he must be, double-minded. This is why the apostle says, "Purify your hearts, you double-minded." (SKS 8, 139–40 / UD, 25)

Elsewhere he writes: "You, too, are indeed subject to necessity. God's will is still done anyhow; so strive to make a virtue of necessity by unconditionally doing God's will" (SKS 11, 34 / WA, 30). (As we will see in Chapters 6–7, Kierkegaard consistently *identifies* the divine and the good, taking divine goodness and unity to be present in everything.) Indeed, it seems that we cannot step back from the good if it is absolute or infinite, as Kierkegaard (and Platonists) holds (Rudd 2012: 153). We are then "subject to necessity" in the sense that morality is inescapable. Thus, Kierkegaard writes: "Everyone in despair has two wills, one that he futilely wants to follow entirely, and one that he futilely wants to get rid of entirely" (SKS 8, 144 / UD, 30). However, getting rid of the good is futile and self-defeating, since it is inescapable (SKS 8, 123 / UD, 7). Immorality and amoralism therefore involve double-mindedness, a split between the (moral) good the person (futilely) wants to avoid and the nonmoral good that he prefers instead. Wholeheartedness or purity of heart, by contrast, requires full moral dedication. But human agents need *not* be aware of this. As a result, there is not only a tendency to depreciate ethical goodness and overappreciate nonmoral value but also a tendency to overlook the inescapability of the good.

Moral inescapability implies that the relation between good and evil is fundamentally *asymmetric*, since evil depends on good but not vice versa. Kierkegaard therefore concludes:

> [D]espite all his defiance, [a person in despair] does not have the power to tear himself away completely from the good, because it is the stronger, he also does not even have the power to will it completely [insofar as he is in despair]. (SKS 8, 146 / UD, 33)

Although sin deviates from the good or the eternal, it is still the case that the latter "is the dominant, which does not want to have its time but wants to make time [itself] *its own* and then permits the temporal also to have its time" (SKS 8, 127 / UD, 11). The good is eternal since it is both unchangeable and the root of time itself, including the future (particularly the eschatological future). The temporal, by contrast, represents an ever-changing manifold that does not allow true unity, unless dominated by the eternal in the form of the morally good (SKS 8, 140–51 / UD, 26–39). True unity therefore requires eternity, Kierkegaard argues in a Platonic manner (Walker 1972: 17–18).

To despair is "to lose the eternal" (Pap. VIII–2, B154:3 / JP 1, 747), since "the eternal" represents the present in which the self should take responsibility for its whole life. The self has something of the eternal in it, insofar as it cannot escape itself. Specifically, our self-relation, in which we relate to ourselves morally, seems inescapable since hierarchical agency must form higher-order motives (cf. Stokes 2015: 159–60).

Wholeheartedness requires not only a unified identity, which appears to take a narrative form, but also a minimal self that takes unconditional responsibility for its whole life in the present.[19] Unless the self takes full responsibility for itself, it cannot fully endorse itself reflectively or accept itself completely. Without full acceptance, or unconditional willingness to be itself, it is in despair, because it is split between actuality (that it does not fully accept) and ideals (that it identifies with).

Kierkegaard describes sin metaphorically as a divorce from goodness (SKS 8, 123 / UD, 7). This appears to involve a relational understanding of evil, as something that can only be understood as a polemic *reaction* against good. However, it also seems to imply that evil itself has a relational nature, since evil only exists by reacting against good. Kierkegaard therefore seems not only to make an epistemological claim about how we understand evil

[19] The narrative self then presupposes a minimal self, just as higher levels of unity in consciousness presuppose basic levels of unity. The two latter ones seem constitutive of selfhood, whereas the two former both seem normative (Rudd 2012: 196, 226; Stokes 2015: 104–6, 178–86).

but also an ontological claim about its very nature. This view of evil is difficult to reconcile with readings of Kierkegaard as a theological voluntarist who dismisses both the guise of the good thesis and (strong) moral realism.[20] Instead, it supports Platonico-Christian and Kantian interpretations of Kierkegaard (cf. Walker 1972: 17–18; Knappe 2004: chs. 3–4).

Discussion: Constitutivism, Reasoning, Dialogue, and Morality

Before we return to amoralism, we may ask how the theological views above relate to constitutivism, which derives moral normativity from agency? It seems that insofar as human agency is created by God, constitutivism could converge with creation theology, which sees morality as rooted in creation. Constitutivism derives practical normativity from practical agency, but the latter is part of divine creation. But it is neither clear that all practical normativity could be derived from agency (as strong variants of constitutivism would claim) nor that all moral obligations depend on divine creation. Rather, for Kierkegaard it is only some obligations – specifically the commandment to love thy neighbor – that depend on creation, while the quest for moral wholeheartedness depends on coherent selfhood and autonomous agency.

Kierkegaard's constitutivism regarding moral normativity is relatively unexplored and deserves more discussion before final judgment is passed. But it could easily prove more controversial than other forms of constitutivism, since it relies on Platonico-Christian metaphysics that many find unacceptable. But even other types of constitutivism indicate that the good is inescapable, by being constitutive of agency.[21] Korsgaard (2013), notably, takes the categorical imperative to be constitutive of intentional action and practical identity.

More recently, Robert Louden uses Habermas to argue that rational communication requires honesty about facts and evidence, as well as "respect for the equal right of others to participate in the discussion, and absence of coercion (refraining from violence) in attempting to justify one's position to others" (2015: 52). Similarly, Davenport argues that we must respect that other persons are "reasoners with practical experience

[20] Kosch (2006a) even seems to think that voluntarism gives a more satisfactory account of evil (as imputable and intelligible) than ethical intellectualism and Kantian rationalism – something that is quite controversial. See Irwin 2011: vol. III, 107, 308.

[21] For Humean constitutivism, see Leffler 2016: 559–62; Katsafanas 2018: 373. For Kantian constitutivism, see Korsgaard 2013. For Fichtean constitutivism, see Kosch 2018. For Nietzschean constitutivism, see Katsafanas 2015.

that may differ from ours" in order to cooperate with them "in articulating practical truth or warrant for beliefs" (2012: 110). John Skorupski (2012: 388) on the other hand says that "[p]ersonal normative knowledge is possible only through dialogical response to a collective state of judgment – which one can agree with or criticize but which provides an essential framework."

This focus on communication and intersubjectivity may seem unKierkegaardian however, although I think that this is far from the case. First, Judge William argues that it is only against a social and historical background that one can chose oneself and become moral. As we have seen, the self belongs to – and depends on – a social and historical context (cf. SKS 3, 243–4, 249–50, 261 / EO2, 255–6, 262–3, 274–5). Indeed, it has a social identity where others understand its place, roles, and rights, although it must break with this identity and return to it, by taking it over and reforming it in light of its commitments.

Second, even *Fear and Trembling* argues that one depends on the understanding of others for a right understanding of what to do. Specifically, one is likely to overlook relevant arguments unless one communicates openly with others:

> If [the tragic hero] remains silent, he takes a responsibility upon himself as the single individual, inasmuch as he disregards any argument that may come from the outside . . . His heroic deed requires courage, but part of this courage is that he does not avoid [*unddrager sig*] any argument. (SKS 4, 177 / FT, 87)

One has "responsibility for remaining silent" (SKS 4, 180 / FT, 91). But instead of withdrawing from public arguments, the hero "has the consolation that every counterargument has had its due" (SKS 4, 201 / FT, 113). More generally, Kierkegaard takes reason (or the understanding, *Forstanden*) to be a *social* enterprise (Westphal 1991: 22, 97; Emmanuel 1996: 49; Betz 2007: 306). Specifically, we cannot correct ourselves by relying on others feedback and critique if we shut ourselves away and are no longer interested in an exchange of ideas (SKS 15, 139–40n; Welz 2019: 285). Practical *reasoning therefore requires dialogue* rather than monologue. Here Kierkegaard anticipates the central idea of Habermas' discourse ethics (Hösle 1992: 7; Fremstedal 2006: 86; McCombs 2013: 56; Welz 2019: 285). But this idea has a much longer history. Fichte's *System of Ethics* particularly emphasized it, being the forerunner for Kierkegaard, Apel, *and* Habermas (Wood 2016: 212).

In any case, the aesthete faces a problem with normative knowledge. For he cannot know what is right for him to do (or even believe) unless he is willing to learn from others by relying on dialogue and open communication. In order to deliberate and reason to the best of his ability, he – like anyone else – must be open to the views and advice of others. He must therefore be open to alternative views that can correct his own views. Without this, his deliberation seems to involve self-centered stubbornness or methodological solipsism, which thinks that reasoning is monological (cf. Compaijen 2018: 67).

The aesthete then faces a *dilemma*. He can *either* embrace solipsism and self-centeredness *or* he can be truly open to the views and advice of others by following the best reasons and arguments. But the former would be at the mercy of mistakes, since it cannot test the correctness of its own judgements without using the understanding of others as an *external criterion* for truth – as Kant emphasizes (A 7:128). It cannot correct itself, unless willing to truly learn from others (cf. SKS 15, 139–40n; Welz 2019: 285).

Learning from others, however, would weaken the aesthete's commitment to amoralism for two different reasons. First, rational communication itself involves practical normativity that seems at least partially moral. It specifically requires honesty about facts and evidence as well as respect for the rights and expertise of others, as Louden (2015a) and Davenport (2012: 110, 122) argue. To be able to learn from others, the deliberator must therefore respect them, communicate openly, and treat them noninstrumentally and nonmanipulatively – something that involves clear moral constrains.[22] He cannot treat others instrumentally if he is to be truly open to others and really learn from them without having a hidden agenda, which is beyond critique and at the mercy of mistakes. To be open to a new self-understanding and to truly learn from others, he cannot only learn from others when it benefits himself; for even his understanding of his self-interest depends on being able to learn from others.

Second, and relatedly, anyone who enters a rational discourse must be open to the possibility of being mistaken in his or her beliefs. Any belief one might hold must therefore be revisable in light of potential arguments, reasons, and evidence. Even the aesthetic outlook must then be revisable and suspendible in a rational discourse, although it is difficult to see that it will allow rational deliberation as well as the ethical outlook does and that it will be supported by the best arguments. For rational communication

[22] Fichte (2005: 303–4 [IV, 319–20]) went as far as indicating that it would be a performative contradiction to argue for the truth of rational egoism. If egoism were true it would be best to keep it to oneself. At least, it makes little sense to convince others of its truth, since others have only instrumental value, according to egoism.

and deliberation not only favors morality but even seems to presuppose it (Louden 2015a).

Conclusion

Kierkegaard's work is so rich and multifaceted that it has the potential for adding something valuable to contemporary discussions on ethics and personal identity, as is exemplified by the work of Rudd, Davenport, Furtak, and others. What makes Kierkegaard's work interesting is not only its arguments and dialectics but also its vivid literary descriptions and examples as well as its rich use of phenomenology and psychology. Kierkegaard does provide strong motivation and reasons for transitioning from the aesthetic to the ethical stage by arguing that despair can only be overcome if we choose the ethical. The aesthete has strong practical reasons for becoming moral, since it overcomes despair and allows a cultivation of desires, love, and character traits. MacIntyre is therefore mistaken in claiming that Kierkegaard's existential choice between the aesthetic and the ethical is criterionless like the radical choice of Sartre (cf. Rudd 2012). Still, morality is not justified by nonmoral standards. But the aesthetic stage does collapse internally, making the choice of ethics defensible. Without this, a leap from one normative domain to another would not be rational.

The most characteristic feature of Kierkegaard's work, as compared to his predecessors, is the central role despair plays in it. He went beyond his predecessors by analyzing the importance of despair and hope for moral agency, offering a systematic analysis of despair that makes extensive use of phenomenology and (moral) psychology (cf. Grøn 1997: 137–42; Stokes 2010: 7–8). Still, it might seem that Kierkegaard's general methodology and his argumentative strategies are perhaps stronger than the specific arguments. In principle, the argumentative strategies seem sufficient to overcome the dilemma associated with the "why be moral?" question. However, the actual arguments offered are still somewhat incomplete and sketchy, standing in need of interpretation and reconstruction.[23]

[23] Theunissen (2005: 1, 143–4n) points out that there are relatively few attempts to defend or reconstruct Kierkegaard's theory in a rational or argumentative manner (although things have improved since he wrote this in the early 1990s).

PART II

Morality, Prudence, and Religion

CHAPTER 4

The Critique of Eudaimonism: Virtue Ethics, Kantianism, and Beyond

Terminology

In 1791 and 1793, the early Kantians G. C. Rapp and J. P. L. Snell introduced the terms "eudaimonist" (*Eudämonist*) and "eudaimonism" (*Eudämonismus*), respectively.[1] In the late 1790s, Kant popularized these terms, describing a eudaimonist as a *moral egoist* who is motivated by utility and personal happiness rather than moral duty (A 7:130). The eudaimonist "is moved to do his duty only *by means of* the happiness he anticipates" (MM 6:377, cf. Ak 8:395–6). Kant therefore concludes that eudaimonism involves "the *euthanasia* (easy death) of all morals," since morality is contingent on pathological grounds (MM 6:378).

He is clearly worried that moral virtue becomes a purely instrumental means to personal happiness, by becoming subordinated to premoral notions of prudence, sensuousness, and inclination.[2] As a result, the categorical imperative of morality would be replaced by a hypothetical imperative of prudence (which presupposes that happiness or self-interest is set as an end). Fichte, Schelling, Hegel, Schleiermacher, and Schopenhauer all follow Kant in criticizing eudaimonism, although the content of the criticism changes somewhat, partially because it is associated with Kant's controversial dualism of (Newtonian) nature and (libertarian moral) freedom (cf. Irwin 2011: vol. III, §§974, 1009–10, 1024, 1053).

In the late twentieth century, the reemergence of virtue ethics and eudaimonism renewed the discussion of egoism and instrumentalism concerning moral virtue (Toner 2017). Both today and in the past, many are worried that eudaimonism involves an objectionable egoism

[1] Rapp 1791: 3; Snell 1793. See also Ad. [pseudonymous reviewer] 1793: 552–7 and 559–60.

[2] Irwin (2011: vol. I, §161) argues that Plato and Aristotle clearly criticize instrumentalism concerning moral virtue, whereas Socrates and the Cynics do not clearly reject it.

and instrumentalism. The problems that are discussed today are therefore largely the same as those discussed by Kant and Kierkegaard, although the answers have become more sophisticated.

Kant seems to accept *psychological eudaimonism*, the view that we always act with happiness in mind (Hare 2002b: 74; cf. Timmermann 2013: 672–5). However, psychological eudaimonism need not imply *ethical eudaimonism*, the view that we should always act – at least mainly – for the sake of our individual happiness; for the former – unlike the latter – allows morality to dethrone the pursuit of (premoral) happiness. Instead of dismissing happiness, Kant requires that it be conditioned and limited by the moral law (Marina 2000: 344–5). Moral *virtue should represent the motive* (determining ground) of moral action and *happiness the object, aim or end* of morality (Wood 1970: ch. 3; Beiser 2006: 615–16). In the doctrine of the highest good, Kant thus reintroduces the striving for happiness as a rational – but secondary – element of ethics and religion. This doctrine is controversial, partially because virtue seems rewarded with happiness, in a way reminiscent of eudaimonism. In the late eighteenth and early nineteenth century, this led to extensive discussions of both eudaimonism and "the highest good," in Kant and other thinkers, in both Germany and Denmark (Thuborg 1951: chs. 8–12, 14; Koch 2003 and 2004: 146–58, 192; Beiser 2006: 591–9, 627–8; Irwin 2011: vol. III, chs. 71, 73–4, 76).

However, we need to distinguish between two different notions of happiness, which are both found in both Kierkegaard and Kant. First, we have happiness not constituted by moral virtue. This is the *premoral* happiness that Kierkegaard and Kant take "eudaimonia" to be.[3] This happiness could involve a *hedonistic* account of happiness, a *desire-satisfaction* account or an *objective list* account, in which happiness is constituted by nonmoral goods (e.g., honor, money and health).[4] All these views are eudaimonistic (van Zyl 2017: 186), and can involve both psychological and ethical eudaimonism.

Second, we have happiness constituted – at least in part – by virtue as a necessary component. Examples of such moral happiness includes not only Aristotelian and Stoic accounts of *eudaimonia* (Hursthouse 2013), but

[3] For Kant, see Irwin 1996. Kosch (2015a: 124) points out that "happiness, for Kant, is an end that is essentially agent-relative and that sets individual interests against one another" in a competitive manner.

[4] Kierkegaard classifies these as poorer or finite goods: SKS 10, 159–60, 163, 230–5 / CD, 151–2, 155, 222–8; SKS 4, 459 / CA, 160. *Either/Or* suggests both hedonism and desire-satisfactionism concerning happiness: SKS 2, 40 / EO1, 31; SKS 3, 32, 175 / EO2, 24, 179–80.

arguably also Kierkegaard's concept of eternal happiness (the "highest good") and Kant's doctrine of the highest good – a doctrine that conditions happiness on morality (without reducing it to morality). All these accounts entail *moralized* happiness, referring not merely to true or real happiness, the sort of happiness worth seeking or having, but also happiness entailing virtue (more on this later).

The Historical Context

Kierkegaard knew Kant's critique of ethical eudaimonism from his studies at the University of Copenhagen (B&A I, 10 / LD, 13–14; Green 1992: 7–8). In both Denmark and Germany, eudaimonism was the dominating position until Kant published *The Groundwork of the Metaphysics of Morals* (1785).[5] In both countries, Kantian criticism of ethical eudaimonism was highly influential, but not universally accepted. Therefore, it became ordinary to distinguish between the eudaimonistic tradition (from Socrates to Wolff) and Kantian ethics.[6]

Kierkegaard does not develop an ethical theory that is hierarchical, complete, and modelled after theories in modern science. Rather, he is concerned with ethics in much the same way that classical virtue ethics is concerned with ethics. He gives a conceptual exploration of moral character, virtue, and happiness that expresses and seeks practical wisdom (Roberts 2008; Vos 2016). Partially for that reason, most commentators associate Kierkegaard's ethical views either with virtue ethics or with Kantian ethics (including Fichtean and Hegelian ethics).[7] His focus on the cultivation of emotions, passion, and moral character is reminiscent of virtue ethics, whereas his emphasis

[5] See Thuborg 1951: chs. 8–11 and 14; Koch 2003; Kosch 2015a: 118–19. Duns Scotus, the third Earl of Shaftesbury, and the French quietists developed noneudaimonistic and antieudaimonistic positions (Irwin 2011: vol. I, chs. 25–6 and vol. II, 364–5, 549–50, 814). But neither Scotus nor Shaftesbury exercised any identifiable influence on Kierkegaard's critique of eudaimonism, except for Scotus' indirect influence on Lutheranism (e.g., Crusius) and Kantianism. Finally, Kierkegaard "touched only superficially upon" Fénelon's quietist doctrine of pure love (Šajda 2009: 142–3).

[6] Thinkers as different as Hegel and Schopenhauer ascribe eudaimonism to most of Kant's predecessors. Schopenhauer applauds Kant for dismissing eudaimonism, an apparently widely held view (Irwin 2011: vol. III, §§1009–10, 1044).

[7] Evans 2006a: 86–109. For virtue ethics, see Furtak 2005: chs. 7, 9; Rudd 2005: 78–80, 99–105; Evans and Roberts 2013. For Kantianism and idealism, see Lübcke 1991: 99–100; Hannay 1993: 225–7; Westphal 1998: 106–10; Søltoft 2000: 263–4; Knappe 2004: chs. 3–5; Kosch 2006b; Irwin 2011: vol. III, 304–9.

on purity of heart, moral duty, infinite guilt, universalism, and egalitarianism is reminiscent of Kantianism. Like Kant, he focuses on the formal aspects of ethics, but he does not show much interest in moral rules or procedures. Rather, he seems concerned with virtuous judgment and character formation – as virtue ethicists are. Therefore, his ethics seems agent-centered (Vos 2016: 329).

Many commentators have touched on Kierkegaard's view of eudaimonism, but we still lack a thorough analysis of what he meant by eudaimonism and why he found it lacking, something that also prevents a proper evaluation of his critique.[8] Commentators see Kierkegaard as an antieudaimonist or a noneudaimonist (Green 1992: 100–7), as a reformer of eudaimonism or as a highly unconventional eudaimonist (Evans 2006a: 142–6; Mendham 2007; cf. Irwin 2011: vol. 1, §162). These conflicting interpretations reflect interpretative difficulties and differing ethical views among the commentators.

Historical research indicates that Kierkegaard had relatively poor knowledge of Aristotle's *Nicomachean Ethics* (using the Kantian W. G. Tennemann as his main commentator on Aristotle; see Løkke 2010). This is surprising, given the historical and contemporary importance of Aristotelian ethics (cf. Irwin 2011) and the fact that Kierkegaard's own views often resemble virtue ethics. But it can be partially explained from the fact that Kierkegaard lived prior to the Aristotle (and Thomas Aquinas) renaissance of the 1870s, in a Danish context influenced heavily by German philosophy and theology (something that is reflected in his frequent use of German translations and commentaries).

Here I rely on a *broadly Kantian reading* of Kierkegaard's critique of eudaimonism for five reasons. First, it is worth considering a broadly Kantian approach to Kierkegaard, given the importance of Kantianism and idealism for Kierkegaard's historical context and their continued relevance for philosophy and theology (including Kierkegaard studies). Second, a Kantian reading has the advantage of reconciling Kierkegaard's critique of eudaimonism with his seemingly eudaimonist claim that "eternal happiness," the "highest good," represents our final end. Third, it helps explain his unusually broad use of self-love and sensuousness. Fourth, there is clear textual evidence indicating conceptual overlap

[8] See, however, Webb (2017). I emphasize egoism and Kantianism, whereas Webb emphasizes lack of alterity and communication. These two interpretations are largely compatible, although my discussion and evaluation of Kierkegaard differs from that of Webb.

between the views of Kant and Kierkegaard on eudaimonism.[9] At the very least, Kierkegaard's ethical views belong to the noneudaimonist tradition from Duns Scotus to Kant rather than to Aristotelianism or Augustinianism. As we saw, *noneudaimonism* holds that morality can be justified without appeal to happiness, so that "we have sufficient reason to pursue virtue above all other goods or advantages even if it conflicts with happiness or it does not affect it either way"; still, happiness is important for morality in other respects, since it can provide reasons for action and a further defense of morality (Irwin 2011: vol. 1, 289).

Finally, Kierkegaard is concerned with a *sacrifice* of self-interest that gives meaning only if one sacrifices something intrinsically valuable and recognizes it as such (see Lippitt 2013: 131). Moral sacrifice of self-interest therefore presupposes that *prudence has independent value* that conflicts with morality. But this is far more difficult to explain for *quietism* than for noneudaimonism. Quietism requires total self-forgetfulness and renunciation of all self-interested motivation. It holds that "any thought of the benefits one gains from" morality or religiousness "is entirely out of place, and incompatible with" proper virtuousness (Irwin 2011: vol. II, 549). Quietists are *antieudaimonists* who sees proper regard for moral virtue as demanding that virtue is not seen as a part of, or means towards, personal happiness. But such a view neither seems Kierkegaardian (cf. Olivares-Bøgeskov 2014: 138–41) nor very promising on its own terms (see Haybron 2010; Irwin 2011; Parfit 2013: vol. 1, ch. 6; Fremstedal 2018).

Like Kant, Kierkegaard seems to accept psychological eudaimonism, but not ethical eudaimonism. In both signed and pseudonymous writings, Kierkegaard repeatedly describes our final end, the "absolute telos," as "eternal happiness," and he identifies it with the "highest good" (SKS 7, 353–9, 388, 524 / CUP1, 387–94, 426–7, 502; SKS 9, 240–1 / WL, 239–40) – a key concept in the eudaimonistic tradition of classical and medieval philosophy and theology. Kierkegaard (Climacus) claims that we have an unconditional interest in eternal happiness, although this interest can be lost (SKS 7, 25 / CUP1, 16). Indeed, not everyone is concerned with eternal happiness, especially not in the Augustinian-Kantian sense of the term found in

[9] Criticisms of eudaimonism were widespread in post-Kantian philosophy and theology. It is therefore difficult to ascertain exactly which sources Kierkegaard relied on, although commentaries indicate that his knowledge of eudaimonism is mediated by the Kantian W. G. Tennemann 1798–1819; cf. Green 1992: 115–6; Løkke 2010: 47.

Kierkegaard's religious writings, which comprises virtue, happiness, and the "kingdom of God" (Glenn 1997: 260–1; Fremstedal 2014a: ch. 5) Still, it is perfectly possible to be concerned with other forms of happiness. Indeed, Kierkegaard's aesthetes and Judge William are all concerned with happiness, although they interpret it differently (cf. SKS 3, 119, 205, 207 / EO2, 118–19, 213, 216; cf. Olivares-Bøgeskov 2014).

Kierkegaard, Kant, and eudaimonism converge on the following claims (although they interpret them somewhat differently):

1. The general focus lies on how one should live one's life as a whole rather than on singular actions or special situations; moral character is therefore primary, while moral actions are secondary.
2. The pursuit of the "highest good" brings unity and meaning to life,[10] since it is our final end.
3. As such, the highest good should be pursued for its own sake (not because it is a means to something external to it).
4. It entails both moral and nonmoral elements, synthesizing morality and prudence (the Stoics, however, think that only virtue matters).
5. Moral virtue is not only a means to happiness but something that should be pursued for its own sake (although instrumentalism concerning virtue denies the latter).

Eudaimonism, Egoism, and Hypothetical Imperatives

Kierkegaard implicitly discusses eudaimonism in a great number of works. The most important texts are probably "Purity of Heart is to Will One Thing" and "Gospel of Sufferings," Parts I and III of *Upbuilding Discourses in Various Spirits* (1847), respectively. As seen (in Chapters 2–3), "Purity of Heart" takes morality to be inescapable, so that wholeheartedness requires valuing morality for its own sake and to prioritize it over all competing goods. Anything else entails a double-minded split between nonmoral and moral goods (SKS 8, 138–9, 149 / UD, 24–5, 37).

Unlike most commentators, I will here focus on Kierkegaard's *explicit* references to eudaimonism in order to understand and evaluate his critique of eudaimonism. There are a total of twelve occurrences

[10] For eudaimonism, see Annas 1993: 27–46; Irwin 1996: 72. For Kant, see Wimmer 1990: 2–5, 21–2, 56–7. For Kierkegaard, see Fremstedal 2014a: chs. 2–7.

of eudaimonism in the new, critical edition of Kierkegaard's works, including five in published writings and seven in journals and notebooks.[11]

The first group of passages in which Kierkegaard explicitly discusses ethical eudaimonism contrasts self-regard with other-regard, prudence with morality, and hedonism with duty. In 1839, Kierkegaard writes:

> Our time is more and more losing the teleological moment that belongs to a life-view [*Livs-Anskuelse*] – and among the educated classes one will certainly find many who regard a marriage without children as the highest – in this respect one thinks by way of contrast of the Jews; they almost entirely gave up their own existence and sought it only in that of another. (SKS 18, 15, EE:29 / KJN 2, 11)

He then adds the following comment:

> [I]n this domain it is often simply an altogether egoistic eudaemonism, which will not endure the resignation that goes with having one's life's goal in another; for marriage does indeed seem to demand a similar resignation, but for one thing, the fruit nevertheless arrives more quickly and almost simultaneously with the sowing, and for another, the reciprocal resignation involved in such a person's attitude is not as it should be, based in any third element, but is of the kind that seeks to calculate its *profit*. (SKS 18, 15, EE:29 / KJN 2, 11)

Kierkegaard is clearly concerned with the moral content of life here, especially whether eudaimonism involves self-regarding or other-regarding concern. The passage contrasts genuine concern for children (a "third') with eudaimonism that seeks profit by relying on egoistic calculations. Clearly, this eudaimonism involves egoism that is only concerned with others instrumentally. Kierkegaard clearly suggests that marriage without children may be based on egoistic calculations and payoff, whereas finding our purpose in children requires noninstrumental other-regard. He thus stresses that we should be willing to renounce personal interests for the sake of others. Otherwise, we do not have a proper life-view (*Livs-Anskuelse* – SKS 18, 15, EE:29 / KJN 2, 11).

11 For an overview, see "Search results for: eudaimoni," *Søren Kierkegaard's Skrifter*, electronic version 1.8, 2013, accessed on January 12, 2018, http://sks.dk/zoom/search.aspx?zoom_sort=1&zoom_query=eudaimoni*.

The commentary of SKS describes eudaimonism as the view that moral virtue and moral duty are motivated by (the prospect of) personal happiness and pleasure (SKS K7, 284). This definition may fit Kierkegaard perhaps, but it is certainly problematic if eudaimonism is interpreted in hedonistic terms or if psychological and ethical eudaimonism are confused.

In 1843, he similarly contrasts eudaimonism with the famous existential choice of oneself (which is identical to the choice of the ethical):

> "To choose oneself" is no eudaimonism, as one will readily perceive. It is quite remarkable that even Chrysippus sought to elevate [*hæve*] eudaimonia as the highest aim by showing that the basic drive in everything is to preserve and maintain itself in the original condition, and pleasure and happiness appear insofar as it succeeds. (Pap. IV, A246 / JP 5, 5636)[12]

Kierkegaard denies that the choice of oneself involves eudaimonism or egoism, implying that morality is not justified by prudence. However, the ethicist, Judge William, describes the aesthete A as an egoist (SKS 3, 258 / EO2, 271–2).[13] Like Kant, Kierkegaard here relies on a *broad* notion of egoism (or selfishness) as the prioritization of *sensuousness* over morality (cf. SKS 4, 382 / CA, 79; SKS 9, 59 / WL, 52–3; Pap. VIII–2, B71; JP 4, 4447), something that appears implicit in his account of the aesthetic way of life (as we saw in Chapter 2). He therefore speaks of "the aesthetic-sensuous pers[on]" (SKS 18, 272, JJ:395 / KJN 2, 251). The aesthetic is here taken in the original Greek sense of *aisthesis*, as perception from the senses, although Kierkegaard associates it with sensation, sensibility, and sensuousness more generally (cf. SKS 3, 29–30 / EO2, 21–2). The defining feature of the aesthete seems to be that he is ruled by sensuousness, so that rationality and reflection serve sensuousness.[14] The aesthete does what is in his sensuous interest, since the ground of action lies in sensuousness and inclinations rather than moral duty. Even if he is good-hearted, and wants the good of others, he still acts from sensuousness or self-love (Fremstedal 2014a: 29). Kant makes a similar point by saying: "All material practical principles are, as such, of one and the same kind and belong under the general principle of self-love or one's own happiness" (CPR 5:22). Paul Formosa explains:

> All principles are of two types: those that are categorical, and based on purely universal interests, and those that are hypothetical, and based on non-universal or particular interest. Kant labels the latter *en masse* under the rubric of self-love, as they encapsulate "selfish" (in the sense of

[12] *Fornøielse*, enjoyment or pleasure, is aligned with *eudaimonia* and happiness (*Lyksalighed*) here, although the passage discusses the Stoic Chrysippus. Kierkegaard's source is Tennemann 1798–1819: vol. IV, 318–19; cf. SKS K6, 167–8.

[13] Judge William also connects true, nonhedonistic happiness with the existential choice of oneself (SKS 3, 119, 205, 207 / EO2, 118–19, 213, 216).

[14] Judge William therefore says that the life of the aesthete is never qualified as spirit (SKS 3, 176 / EO2, 181).

> particular or non-universal interests), even if those interests are not [necessarily] prudential. Hence, Kant does not claim that whenever we act against morality, self-love is the *end* that we seek ... envy, malice, ideology and the like can be ends for which we act against morality and sometimes even in spite of our self-interest. But even so, all such cases involve the *principle* of self-love, for such ends can only be chosen in the light of hypothetical (or "selfish") and never categorical imperatives.[15]

Like Kant, Kierkegaard stresses that "virtue must be desired for its own sake" (SKS 19:403, Not13:39 / KJN 3, 401), not because of any reward (SKS 8, 149 / UD, 37). Moral obligations are therefore categorical imperatives, while prudential obligations are hypothetical, by being conditioned on sensuousness or happiness (cf. SKS 9, 123, 133–4, 194–5 / WL, 119–20, 130–1, 195–6; SKS 22, 78, NB11:131 / KJN 6, 74; Knappe 2004: chs. 3–5). This appears to be why he aligns eudaimonism with sensuousness and finitude in this 1843–44 passage:

> The transition from eudaimonism to the concept of duty is a leap or, assisted by a more and more developed understanding of what is most prudent, is one finally supposed to go over directly to virtue[?] No, there is a pain of decision that the sensuous (the eudaimonistic), the finite (the eudaimonistic) cannot endure. Man is not led to do his duty by merely reflecting that it is the most prudent thing to do; in the moment of decision reason [*Forstanden*] lets go, and he either turns back to eudaimonism or he chooses the good by means of a leap. (SKS 27, 277, Papir 283:1 / KJN 11.1, 276)[16]

Kierkegaard aligns eudaimonism not only with prudence but also with the sensuous and the finite. Prudence serves not only personal happiness and self-interest, but also sensuousness and inclination (cf. Irwin 1996). A radically evil agent, for instance, could be prudent by following sensuousness and nonmoral incentives, even if this differs from a rational pursuit of self-interest in any ordinary sense of the term. Like Kant, Kierkegaard then distinguishes sharply between morality and selfishness and between freedom (or spirit) and nature, respectively. Like Kant, he classifies nonmoral motives as selfish. Consider the following passage from 1847:

[15] Formosa 2009: 204–5. Kant is often accused of overlooking the possibility of other incentives than the those of morality and self-love. Specifically, he neither seems to leave room for demonic evil nor unselfish good-heartedness. Kant's approach here (and to a lesser extent that of Kierkegaard) may seem problematic, unless supported by further considerations about moral psychology and action theory. For a discussion, see Caswell 2007; Fremstedal 2014a: 30–1 and 2019b.

[16] For the claim that happiness (*Lykke*) is not a category of spirit but something that belongs to the sensate, see SKS 11, 141, 158 / SUD, 25, 43.

> The basis for erotic love is a drive [*Drift*], the basis of friendship is inclination, but drive and inclination are natural qualifications [*Naturbestemmelse*], and natural qualifications are always selfish; only the eternal qualification of spirit expels the selfish; therefore there is still a hidden self-love in erotic love and friendship ... To relate to one single human being in unconditional impetuous [*fremstormende*] preference is to relate to oneself in self-love; implicit in such a preference is conscious or unconscious obstinacy which arbitrarily wants to have its own will. (Pap. VIII–2, B71:6 / JP 4, 4447; cf. SKS 9, 238 / WL, 237; SKS 10, 126–7 / CD, 115–16)

We are now in a position to understand why "[t]he transition from eudaimonism to the concept of duty is a leap" (SKS 27, 277, Papir 283:1 / KJN 11.1, 276). There is no gradual transition from self-concern to proper other-concern, or from eudaimonism to morality. Kierkegaard therefore describes the transition from eudaimonism to moral virtue, duty, and the good as a *leap*, as a transition from one normative domain to another. Eudaimonists justify virtue in prudential terms. But virtue requires other-regarding moral concern that involves *self-effacement* that undermines the very self-concern that supposedly justifies virtue for the eudaimonist (cf. Davenport 2007: ch. 7; Clark 2016).

Kierkegaard (Climacus) elaborates upon this idea in *Concluding Unscientific Postscript* (1846), where he speaks of someone who makes a

> simulated movement, a simulated pass [*fingeret Udfald*] at the absolute [the highest good, eternal happiness], although he remains completely within the relative, a simulated transition [*fingeret Overgang*] such as that from eudaemonism to the ethical within eudaemonism. (SKS 7, 385 / CUP1, 423)

Immediately prior to the quote, he warns against making the pursuit of the highest good, an eternal happiness, into a "profitable stock-exchange speculation [*fordeelagtig Børs-Speculation*]" (SKS 7, 385 / CUP1, 423). The quote itself involves an analogy between transitioning from the relative to the absolute and transitioning from eudaimonism to the ethical. The quote describes both transitions as being false (as being *fingeret*), not only as being simulated (the Danish original is clearer than the translation here). The analogy indicates that morality involves unconditional obligations, whereas eudaimonism (or prudence) conditions obligations on self-interest.

Normative Conflict: Against Ethical Eudaimonism

Concluding Unscientific Postscript describes prudence and morality as follows:

> [T]here actually are not two [different] paths, or there are two [similar] paths of pleasure [*Lystens Veie*], one of which is a little more sagacious [*klogere* – prudent] than the other, just as when climbing a mountain to enjoy [*nyde*] the view it is more sagacious not to turn around too soon – in order to enjoy it all the more. Then what? Then the sensualist [*Vellystningen* – the libertine] (the eudaemonist) is not only lunatic because he chooses the path of pleasure [*Lystens Vei*] instead of the path of virtue, but he is a lunatic sensualist [*gal Vellystning*] for not choosing the pleasurable [*lystige*] path of virtue. (SKS 7, 367 / CUP1, 403)

Pleasure and enjoyment seem identical here (although both "*Lyst*" and "*at nyde*" are used).

Like other passages, this passage associates eudaimonism with hedonism, libertinism, and sensualism. The passage makes fun of the eudaimonist idea that it is *imprudent* to choose vice over virtue, since refusing vice on the grounds that it is imprudent involves being moral for the wrong reasons – something that amounts to legality and egoism, not morality or altruism. The eudaimonist allegedly misconceives the choice between virtue and vice by seeing it as a choice between prudent and imprudent self-interest, respectively.

The passage above even suggests that prudence supports vice and libertinism. This suggestion is important, not so much because it is provocative and may give the impression of immoralism and libertinism, but for two other reasons. First, it implies that prudence and morality are not coextensive, but rather divergent and *conflicting*. Second, it is exactly such divergence and conflict that allows unselfish morality. Indeed, we could *not* choose morality for its own sake only, unless it differed from prudence (cf. Timmermann 2013: 674–5; Fremstedal 2014a: ch. 4). *Postscript* then contrasts morality with prudence:

> It has been said often enough that the good has its reward in itself, and thus it is not only the most proper but also the most sagacious thing [*det Klogeste* – the most prudent thing] to will the good. A sagacious [*klog*] eudaemonist is able to perceive this very well; thinking in the form of possibility, he can come as close to the good as is possible, because in possibility as in abstraction the transition is only an appearance. But

> when the transition is supposed to become actual, all sagacity expires in scruples. Actual time separates the good and the reward for him so much, so eternally, that sagacity cannot join them again, and the eudaemonist declines . . . To will the good is indeed the most sagacious thing – yet not as understood by sagacity but as understood by the good. The transition is clear enough as a break, indeed, as suffering. (SKS 7, 313 / CUP1, 342–3)

Human history separates goodness from rewards in a manner that undermines eudaimonism (Green 1992: 107). Virtue does not guarantee happiness, nor vice unhappiness since the relation between the two is contingent and unpredictable in this life. Therefore, prudence and morality often diverge and conflict. *Fear and Trembling* says that

> imperfection is the fundamental law of the external world, and . . . he who does not work does get bread, and he who sleeps gets it even more abundantly than he who works . . . It is different in the world of the spirit. Here an eternal divine order prevails . . . only the one who works gets bread. (SKS 4, 123 / FT, 27)

The 1843–46 writings assume that it is incidental whether virtue brings happiness or unhappiness (SKS 4, 156 / FT, 63; SKS 7, 126 / CUP1, 134; SKS 15, 132–5). By contrast, the late Kierkegaard (1847–55) assumes that virtue brings unhappiness in this life. At least, imitation of Christ – as the paradigm of Christian ethics – results in suffering and hardship (SKS 20, 249, NB3:11 / KJN 4, 249; SKS 20, 293, NB4:13 / KJN 4, 293–4; SKS 27, 486, Papir 407 / KJN 11.2, 187–8; SKS 21, 152, NB8:17 / KJN 5, 159; SKS 8, 220, 319–431 / UD, 119, 217–341; SKS 12, 170 / PC, 167; SKS 25, 370, NB29:107 / KJN 9, 375; SKS 13, 307 / M, 251). But Christ is crucified by human sinners, not by an amoral nature. Kierkegaard's view of the latter does not change here. Rather, his view of the former does. It is human evil that impairs and subverts virtue, not an amoral nature. Still, even Kierkegaard (Climacus) points to overlap between prudence and morality in 1846:

> All worldly wisdom is indeed abstraction, and only the most mediocre eudaemonism has no abstraction whatever but is the enjoyment of the moment. To the same degree that eudaemonism is sagacious [*klog*], it has abstraction; the more sagacity, the more abstraction. Eudaemonism thereby acquires a fleeting resemblance to the ethical and the ethical-religious, and momentarily it can seem as if they could walk together. And yet this is not so, because the first step of the ethical is infinite abstraction, and what happens? The step becomes too great for eudaemonism, and although some abstraction is sagacity, infinite

> abstraction, understood eudaemonistically, is lunacy. (SKS 7, 387–8n / CUP1, 426n)

Here "infinite abstraction" characterizes moral impartiality and selflessness, whereas "some abstraction" describes *enlightened* self-interest, a broadened or idealized form of prudence. There seem to be at least three senses in which self-interest and eudaimonism can become abstract or idealized. First, through a focus on long-term interests rather than short-term interests. Second, by valuing other goods instead of hedonism. Finally, by avoiding extreme partiality (i.e., rational egoism) and by considering the interests of some other human beings (i.e., a weak form of partiality).

The most mediocre (*maadeligste*) eudaimonism is said to lack such abstraction, since it is concerned with the pleasure of the moment, whereas improved types involve enlarged self-interest. Indeed, Kierkegaard (Climacus) concedes that an abstract form of prudence may appear congruous with the ethical (and religious), at least for a moment. This clearly indicates that there does *not* appear to be a total conflict between morality and prudence. Still, he denies that there is a gradual transition from prudence to morality, describing the transition from self-interest to moral impartiality as an infinite abstraction or a leap to a different category (SKS 27, 277, Papir 283:1 / KJN 11.1, 276; SKS 7, 313 / CUP1, 342–3). Morality and prudence thereby represent different normative domains.

A Problematic View of Prudence?

Kierkegaard's Kantian interpretation of prudence seems problematic. Irwin argues compellingly that prudential imperatives, or prudential principles, need not be derived from inclination or sensuousness:

> [T]he very fact that something would promote my welfare makes it reasonable for me to do it, whether or not I happen to care about my welfare, and whether or not I happen to regard this as an element of my welfare. At any rate, it seems quite natural to criticize people for acting unreasonably if they act in ways that violate their welfare, whether or not they happen to care about this. (1996: 75)

Following Bishop Joseph Butler, Irwin (1996: 76) argues that "my reason for pursuing my own happiness justifies my inclination to do it, not the other way round," as assumed by Kant. Prudential imperatives do involve nonmoral principles, but we can have good, external, and categorical reasons to follow such imperatives or principles apart from our desire, or inclination, for it (Irwin 1996: 76–82, 95). Prudential reasons for action need not be subjective reasons that are contingent on the desires of the agent. Instead, prudential reasons (e.g., to be healthy) can hold *categorically*, independently of the agent's desires. We can therefore criticize those who violate their own well-being. Personal happiness and self-interest can therefore represent objective goods that benefits us, whether we recognize it or not (cf. Haybron 2010: 187). Prudential reasons can then be objective in this sense (cf. Parfit 2013: vol. 1, chs. 2–4).

However, if prudential imperatives are not hypothetical imperatives dependent on inclination, then neither must eudaimonism subordinate practical rationality to inclination.[17] Kierkegaard suggests that eudaimonism involves subjectivism and anthropocentrism concerning ethical normativity, whereas Christocentrism involves objectivism concerning ethics (more on this later). But Augustinians can object that virtue and happiness are not only good for us, but also good for God. Virtue and happiness are therefore good in an objective (agent-neutral) sense (theological voluntarists might deny this, but Augustinians favor moral realism over voluntarism typically). Thus, *eudaimonia* can benefit us, even if we fail to acknowledge it. A life of excellence and flourishing can be objectively better than vice and unhappiness, even if we fail to realize it. Eudaimonism need therefore not involve subjectivism or anthropocentrism concerning practical reasons and values.

Self-interest also has moral implications, given duties of beneficence and a requirement to promote the happiness of others. Subjectivist and preferentialist views of happiness and prudence then have problematic, counterintuitive consequences. Based on Fichte's *System of Ethics*, Michelle Kosch (2018: 84) points out that it would be very strange if "we owe less assistance to people who have lower expectations" or less demanding subjective interpretations of happiness. On such views,

> beneficence might in principle require helping another to do something the beneficiary finds overwhelmingly important but the benefactor sees as utterly pointless. It also absolves the benefactor of any duty to elevate the level of the beneficiary's health, education, nutrition, or what have you,

[17] Still, eudaimonism does subordinate morality to the "highest good," "eudaimonia," a good that can involve nonmoral goods if it also involves a clear moral component (Irwin 1996: 81).

> above the beneficiary's own subjective norm, which will be indexed to local conditions that may be quite abject. (Kosch 2018: 84)

We can avoid these problems by considering prudential reasons to be objective (agent neutral) and categorical. Still, this solution comes at a cost. If morality and prudence both issue categorical reasons for acting, this allows normative conflict in the form of a *dualism of practical reason*. This dualism threatens not only the rational authority of morality but also practical rationality more generally since it undermines all-things-considered rationality.

It is exactly this stark dualism Kant and Kierkegaard avoid by interpreting prudence as hypothetical imperatives and morality as categorical imperatives. This allows prudence to be conditioned on and limited by morality (cf. Fremstedal 2014a: ch. 5; Bader 2015). Indeed, prudence need not involve categorical imperatives if it is conditioned on a general inclination for happiness that is contingently found in human agents.[18] For it seems that we cannot but desire happiness if some form of psychological eudaimonism is true (as both Kant and Kierkegaard seem to think).

Still, there are different interpretations of Kant here. Some deny normative conflict between morality and prudence, holding that morality *silences* prudence in cases of motivational conflict (however, the power of choice must still chose between competing incentives – see Bader 2015: 198n9). Others allow normative conflict (as normative pluralism normally does; see Chang 1997a), but deny that prudential reasons are generally *overriding*. That is, morality overrides prudential reasons, by having lexical *priority* (cf. Timmermann 2013: 674–7). At least, this seems to hold for strict moral duties if not for all moral reasons. Kierkegaard seems committed to such lexical priority since he assumes normative conflict in which morality overrides prudence (McDaniel 2020: 431). However, such priority could even allow morality to defeat categorical *pro tanto* reasons issued by prudence.

Concluding Discussion and Assessment

Kierkegaard's view of eudaimonism is essentially consistent in the 1839–54 period. It does not appear to have changed much over time, and the different pseudonyms and Kierkegaard himself all seem to be

[18] Again, I am indebted to a reviewer.

in essential agreement (except for the aesthetes). It is then difficult to understand why it would be wrong to attribute claims about eudaimonism made by Climacus to Kierkegaard, given that Kierkegaard's views correspond to, or overlap with, views expressed by Climacus (cf. Kosch 2006a: 12).

However, Kierkegaard's critique of ethical eudaimonism remains controversial. Eudaimonists can argue that overriding normative reasons for action may coincide perfectly with the demands of one's happiness; they need not claim that all overriding reasons for action arise from the demands of one's own happiness (Wedgewood 2008: 189). And the content of morality need not be self-regarding or egoistic if the virtues merely involve formal egoism. Virtue has both an instrumental value (by bringing happiness) and an intrinsic value, since it is valued for its own sake. Formally, the virtuous agent is concerned with his own happiness, but he can only strive for happiness by developing other-regarding virtues (such as justice) that are valued noninstrumentally (Annas 1993: 127, 224–90, 322–3).

This distinction between formal and substantive egoism is familiar today, but it is not clear that it was used in Kierkegaard's Danish context or that Kierkegaard recognized it (cf. Thuborg 1951; Koch 2003 and 2004). At this point, Kierkegaard simply seems more Kantian than Aristotelian. The translation of the Greek *fronesis* to the Latin *prudentia* may indeed suggest that Greek eudaimonism concerns prudence rather than morality. However, this involves an oversimplification of eudaimonism in its nonhedonistic and noninstrumentalist forms (Irwin 1996). Kierkegaard's Kantian critique of eudaimonism is therefore more successful against hedonist versions of eudaimonism (Epicureanism) than against Stoicism or Aristotelianism; the two latter can easier ascribe a noninstrumental role to virtue than the former can since they moralize happiness (Annas 1993). Hedonism, by contrast, does not moralize happiness by seeing it as constituted by moral virtue. Hence, it cannot rule out the possibility of happiness without virtue.

Kierkegaard's tendency to associate eudaimonism with hedonism and libertinism indicates that he – like Kant – focuses on weaker or extreme forms of eudaimonism (cf. Mendham 2007: 609). But instrumentalism concerning virtue should not be confused with egoism. *Consequentialists* and utilitarians value virtue instrumentally insofar as virtue produces good consequences (utility). Virtue is here a means towards general utility or universal welfare, not personal happiness. Instrumentalism regarding virtue is therefore combined with altruism, not egoism

(Driver 2017: 322–6). The widespread Kantian critique of eudaimonism tends to overlook this, although it is equally relevant to consequentialism.

Recently, Davenport defends a broadly Kantian critique of eudaimonism at length. By discussing different cases, Davenport argues convincingly that it is possible to lose self-interested motives for action, while retaining other-regarding motives for action. Although self-interested and other-regarding motives often coexist, they nevertheless represent two independent motives that can come into conflict. For virtue has an intrinsic value that cannot be only a means to happiness, since happiness is at best an unintended by-product of virtue, Davenport argues.[19] However, eudaimonism rules out moral purity or self-forgetfulness that does good *only* because it is good. Eudaimonists cannot rationally sacrifice anything significant for the sake of the other unless it somehow contributes to *eudaimonia*. Genuine other-regard therefore seems incompatible with eudaimonism's focus on personal happiness (*eudaimonia*) as the highest good.[20] Thus, Kierkegaard's central claim seems supported.

Kant and Kierkegaard both dismiss the eudaimonistic idea that morality can be justified prudentially. Both assume conflict between morality and prudence, which ethical eudaimonism denies. Indeed, Kierkegaard's critique of eudaimonism is difficult to reconcile with most forms of virtue ethics since the latter normally presupposes ethical eudaimonism. Kierkegaard's (first and second) ethics therefore come closest to Kantian-idealistic ethics that breaks with eudaimonism, hedonism, and consequentialism.[21] Here Ronald Green (2011: 140) claims that Kant's general influence on Kierkegaard finds its expression in Kierkegaard's repeated affirmation of a strict, demanding ethics and moral awareness of our own guilt and sin. Even if there is not much hard evidence for this claim, it still seems largely plausible. In Denmark, Kant was known for his strict and rigorous ethics, an ethics that Kierkegaard seems largely sympathetic to. Indeed, Kierkegaard's understanding of ethics seems Kantian insofar as it is

[19] Davenport 2007: chs. 5–7. However, the argument is developed independently of Kierkegaard.

[20] Still, eudaimonism can overcome this problem by denying individuality (Davenport 2007: chs. 6–8). Clark (2016) represents a more promising approach, however. He defends a weak eudaimonism where morality is prioritized *above* prudence at the level of particular actions, local deliberations, and motives, although prudential considerations still justify morality (at least mainly) at the global level of life as a whole.

[21] A widespread view of the early nineteenth century, which is forgotten today, took Kantianism to be the only viable alternative in philosophical ethics (Kosch 2015a: 116–29).

noneudaimonistic, deontological, anticonsequentialist, rigoristic, egalitarian, and highly demanding in a way that Aristotelian and Hegelian ethics are not (cf. Stern 2012: 204, 244–52; Fremstedal 2014a: 230–1).

Still, Kierkegaard does not only belong to the tradition of Kantian ethics. Many scholars have identified elements reminiscent of virtue ethics in his theory, such as the cultivation of emotions (cf. Furtak 2005; Evans and Roberts 2013). It therefore seems best to consider Kierkegaard's ethics to lie somewhere between Christian virtue ethics and Kantianism. I think that this holds for both the first and second ethics, although Kierkegaard's last writings emphasize Christian suffering and martyrdom in a manner that goes beyond non-Christian ("first") ethics.

CHAPTER 5

Noneudaimonistic Ethics and Religion: Happiness and Salvation

Ethics and Theology: Paganism and Christianity

Kierkegaard (Climacus) writes:

> Just as some have deceitfully wanted to form a transition from eudaemonism to the ethical through sagacity [*Klogskab*], so it is also a deceitful device to want to identify becoming a Christian as closely as possible with becoming a human being and to want to make someone believe that one becomes that decisively in childhood. (SKS 7, 546 / CUP1, 602)

This passage compares the transition from eudaimonism to the ethical (by means of prudence) with the identification of being a human being and being a Christian. The implication is that just as little as eudaimonism (or prudence) suffice for the ethical, just as little does being a human being (or a child) suffice for being a Christian. Since Kierkegaard interprets Christianity in ethical terms (in the second ethics), he also suggests that pagan eudaimonism differs from Christian ethics (SKS 15, 237–8). Like Kant, he then contrasts *eudaimonistic, pagan ethics with Christian ethics*, suggesting that the former involves egoism and instrumentalism concerning virtue, while the latter pursues good for its own sake. Kant claims that Christianity has a purer notion of morality than the Greeks and Romans had (LPDR 28:1123; LE 29:604; CPR 5:129; Stern 2012: 244). Like Kierkegaard, Kant relies on Gospel passages that seem to contrast righteousness with prudence in a noneudaimonist manner. Particularly the following passage seems important:

> Be not . . . anxious, saying, What shall we eat? or, What shall we drink? or, Wherewithal shall we be clothed? For after all these things do the Gentiles seek; for your heavenly Father knoweth that ye have need of all these things. But seek ye first his kingdom, and his righteousness; and all these things shall be added unto you.[1]

[1] Matthew 6:31–3 (American Standard Version).

The pagan concern for food, drink, and clothing is here contrasted with moral justice and the kingdom of God. It is claimed that moral justice has priority over other concerns – although pagans seek nonmoral goods instead. Perhaps this is why *Works of Love* follows the Church Fathers in describing pagan virtues as "glittering vices" (SKS 9, 60 / WL, 53; SKS K9, 136). Similarly, *The Concept of Anxiety* indicates that Greek ethics is not ethics proper, since it contains an aesthetic element that is incompatible with the ideality or demandingness of ethics. Discussing Aristotle, Kierkegaard (Vigilius Haufniensis) says that for the Greeks virtue is not sufficient, since earthly goods are also needed (SKS 4, 324 / CA, 16–17; cf. SKS 19, 389, Not13:20 / KJN 3, 387). The Greeks and Aristotle were concerned not only with moral virtue but also with nonmoral goods (something that is not wrong insofar as the "highest good" includes nonmoral elements, such as external goods).

However, for Kierkegaard this point about pagan virtue is more radical than anything found in Augustine or even Kant. Augustine (1998: Books 19–20) accepts (ethical and psychological) eudaimonism but identifies the "highest good" with the "kingdom of God." Although Kant dismisses eudaimonism, he nevertheless identifies (1) the "highest good" with the "kingdom of God" and (2) proper Christian ethics with philosophical ethics.[2] Kierkegaard accepts (1) but not (2), since he distinguishes systematically between philosophical ("first") and Christian ("second") ethics (Glenn 1997: 260–1; Fremstedal 2014a: ch. 5). Kierkegaard follows Augustine and Kant in seeing the highest good as essentially shared, although it singles out each individual in their individuality as if they were facing judgment day.

Like Augustine and Kant, the *Postscript* assumes that pagans and Christians are both rightly interested in the highest good (SKS 7, 522, 529, 560 / CUP1, 574, 581, 617–18). The point here is not that everyone in fact shares this interest but rather that they have moral and prudential reasons to do so. Indeed, Kierkegaard (Climacus) suggests that Christianity requires unreserved ("infinite") interest in the highest good (SKS 7, 25, 57 / CUP1, 16, 52). Like Augustine and Kant, he then assumes that only Christianity makes the realization of the highest good possible (SKS 7, 25, 560 / CUP1, 15–16, 617).

However, Kierkegaard interprets both Christian and pagan ethics in noneudaimonistic terms. In the 1847–54 period, he repeatedly attacks Christian eudaimonism. In 1847, he writes:

> It is really peculiar that thanking God for good things (i.e. worldly and temporal advantages and good fortune, etc.) should be enough to constitute

[2] Like Augustine, Kant thinks that Christianity has a truer notion of the highest good than the philosophical schools of antiquity (Forschner 1992; Beiser 2006: 625–6).

> Christianity. In this way Christianity easily becomes the intensified enjoyment of life (eudaemonism). The pagan became anxious when he was very fortunate; he had a certain mistrust of the gods. But there was also something else in this, because rightly understood, his anxiety expressed the consequences of clinging tightly to worldliness. But in Christianity! A person strives for and seeks earthly goods, and then, in order to be free of anxiety, a person thanks God. Aha! In this way this sort of Christendom becomes even more worldly than paganism itself. To thank God for good days ought first and foremost mean to investigate, to test oneself with respect to how one clings to such things; presumably this ought to mean that one has learned to think less of all such things. But on the contrary, one clings to them all the more, and then one thanks God – in order to have permission to remain in possession quite calmly and securely. Oh, how people in fact defraud Christianity. (SKS 20, 223, NB2:211 / KJN 4, 222)

It is all too easy to be a Christian when it pays off, since one can then be moved by rewards instead of God's call or goodness for its own sake. This appears to be why Kierkegaard thinks that Christendom risks becoming preoccupied with an intensified life-enjoyment or eudaimonism. Presumably, it is intensified because providence is perceived to contribute to the enjoyment by rewarding the believer. Kierkegaard here aligns eudaimonism with intensified life-enjoyment or hedonism, thereby focusing on extreme and weaker forms of eudaimonism. These have difficulty in explaining why genuine other-regard is necessary for *eudaimonia* when the latter consists in pleasure that need not entail other-regard.

In 1848, Kierkegaard also connects eudaimonism with Christian sectarianism in Denmark:

> [T]he Grundtvigians tell themselves that they are the only true [Christians] . . . [T]hey must be reproached for . . . [that] they do nothing to bring other [people] to [Christianity]. It is a kind of eudaemonism, a kind of opulence to live such a way with Christianity. It is kind of disloyalty to Christianity to keep it to oneself. (SKS 20, 336, NB4:106 / KJN 4, 337)

The Grundtvigians are concerned with their own salvation, instead of the salvation of others. Kierkegaard connects this "kind of eudaemonism" not only to sectarianism but also to group egoism and partiality that undermines the impartial, universal, and egalitarian character of Christianity.[3] He objects to the self-regarding nature of sectarianism, which lacks proper regard for humanity as a whole. Again, he criticizes ethical eudaimonism for

[3] Humanity entails equality for Kierkegaard (SKS 16, 87 / PV, 111). He believes that salvation is universally available, although not everyone accepts it. Cf. Jackson 1998: 238.

egoism and special interests.[4] The idea seems to be that egoism treats others merely instrumentally, preventing openness to the alterity (otherness), fragility, and risk that comes with participation in social practices (cf. Webb 2017: 439–56). Still, eudaimonists can object that the egoism here is formal, not substantial, since the agent strives for happiness by being virtuous in a noninstrumental manner (cf. Annas 1993: 224–6).

In 1854, Kierkegaard attacks the theological establishment (especially Bishop Jacob Mynster) in Denmark for its eudaimonism and hedonism (SKS 26, 248–9, NB33:5 / KJN 10, 253). He then prescribes the following treatment for the Danish church:

> [J]ust as natural eudaemonism must regard [Christianity] as poison, and wanting to be [a Christian] as the same as taking poison, so must [Christianity] regard this eudaemonistic, Protestant – especially the Danish – Epicureanism as poison, and therefore it is appropriate to take a counter-poison in order, if possible, to be able to resist the infection. (SKS 25, 376, NB29:114 / KJN 9, 380)

Again, the idea is that eudaimonism, especially Danish Epicureanism or hedonism, is poison to Christianity (cf. SKS 26, 248–9, NB33:5 / KJN 10, 253). Kierkegaard then prescribes Schopenhauer as an antidote against eudaimonism, targeting the Grundtvigians rather than Augustine. Presumably, the reason is that Schopenhauer, in Book IV of *The World as Will and Representation*, recommends asceticism and denying the will to life.[5] The suggestion is that such a cure would undermine eudaimonism. If the eudaimonist pursues happiness, then try asceticism and life-denying values instead; if the Epicurean pursues pleasure, try suffering instead.

But a conflicting passage (also from 1854) argues that even Schopenhauer is an eudaimonist. Kierkegaard writes: "If existence itself is suffering, then asceticism easily becomes a form of eudaimonism, a point [Schopenhauer] himself makes against the Stoics" (SKS 25, 390, NB30:12 / KJN 9, 394). Kierkegaard adds the following explanation:

> In his own view, through the mortification of the will to life the ascetic aims to reach a state that, despite the fact that one exists as though one does not – to this extent the ascetic is dead in relation to everything. But if to exist is to suffer, then it is clear that existing as though one does not exist, so that one scarcely knows whether one exists or not – is eudaemonism, though naturally of

[4] SKS 19, 389, Not13:20 / KJN 3, 387 contrasts Aristotle's *eudaimonia* with religious communication (*Meddelelse*), suggesting that eudaimonists are self-centered rather than sharing with others.

[5] Schopenhauer 1969: vol. 1, §§ 34, 36, 38, 54, 67–71. Kierkegaard's reading of Schopenhauer in 1854–55 may not have caused Kierkegaard's pessimism in this period, but it may have strengthened it somewhat.

> a modest sort; that is, it is the highest eudaemonism provided one assumes, as does [Schopenhauer], that to exist is to suffer. If to exist is to suffer, eudaemonism of course cannot be sought in the direction of existing; it must be sought in the direction of nonexistence, and the highest possible eudaemonism becomes the closest approximation to nonexistence. (SKS 25, 390, NB30:12, margin / KJN 9, 394, margin)

Even Schopenhauer's pessimism and antinatalism represent a form of eudaimonism in which happiness is found in nonbeing that escapes suffering. Schopenhauer (1969: vol. 1, §§ 34, 36, 38, 54, 67–71) wants to escape suffering, not only momentarily in aesthetic experience but permanently in asceticism and voluntary death by starvation. This appears to be a negative form of eudaimonism and hedonism that minimizes unhappiness, pain, and suffering. It flees misery instead of seeking bliss, Kierkegaard suggests.

Alterity and Christocentric Ethics

Kierkegaard's critique of eudaimonism goes far beyond the Kantian criticism of egoism considered so far. Instead of beginning with the human desire for happiness, Kierkegaard starts with divine goodness, contrasting God's descent to us with human striving toward perfection:

> We human beings want to look upward in order to look for the object of perfection (although the direction is continually toward the unseen), but in Christ perfection looked down to earth and loved the person it saw ... Christianly to descend from heaven is boundlessly to love the person you see just as you see him. Therefore if you want to be perfect in love, strive to fulfill this duty, in loving to love the person one sees, to love him just as you see him, with all his imperfections and weaknesses, to love him as you see him when he has changed completely, when he no longer loves you but perhaps turns away indifferent or turns away to love another, to love him as you see him when he betrays and denies you. (SKS 9, 174 / WL, 174)

Kierkegaard contends that eudaimonism is concerned with personal well-being rather than other-regard, alterity, or Christocentrism for their own sake (SKS 9, 161 / WL, 160). Its starting point is fundamentally self-referential and anthropocentric, since eudaimonism concerns what contributes to personal happiness or flourishing. Indeed, even moral virtue and friendship are pursued for the sake of self-fulfillment (although the egoism here seems formal rather than substantial, see Annas 1993). Christianity, by contrast, starts not from our desire to possess the "highest good," but from imitation of Christ and loving the neighbor for his own sake. Its starting point is therefore Christocentric and *other-regarding*, not anthropocentric or self-regarding (cf. Jackson 2017: 288).

Christian neighbor-love in particular renounces self-interest for the sake of concrete help to others who are in need. This is the imitation of Christ that results in suffering. Indeed, Christian suffering is to suffer precisely because one does good (SKS 16, 218 / JFY, 169). By freely accepting suffering and temporal loss, Christian charity is noneudaimonistic. This view is found not only in Kierkegaard's pessimistic 1854–55 writings but also in 1847 and 1850 (SKS 8, 138–84, 220, 319–431 / UD, 24–79, 119, 217–341; SKS 9, 174 / WL, 174; SKS 12, 170 / PC, 167).

Thus, Kierkegaard adds a specifically Christian, Christocentric dimension to Kant's criticism of eudaimonism. However, this Christocentrism is closely related to the concept of *alterity* (otherness). Unlike Kant, Kierkegaard interprets genuine other-regard in terms of otherness or alterity (cf. Webb 2017: 440–1). Whereas Kant thinks that we deserve respect as humans, Kierkegaard adds that we should be loved both as humans *and* as individuals. The other should therefore be valued as an irreplaceable individual, not just as a member of the human species. Kierkegaard thus emphasizes irreducible individuality in a manner that is reminiscent of German Romanticism and theories of intersubjective recognition in Fichte and Hegel as well as twentieth-century accounts of alterity (e.g., Levinas).[6]

"Eternal Happiness": A Noneudaimonistic "Highest Good"

Although Kierkegaard criticizes eudaimonism, he nevertheless assumes that the highest good represents our final end. Morality is necessary for the "highest good," in a manner reminiscent of noninstrumentalist eudaimonism. Like Kant, Kierkegaard therefore comes closer to eudaimonism than he admits (or realizes).[7] Indeed, even Kierkegaard occasionally uses the concept of prudence (*Klogskab*) in the wide, classical sense of *prudentia* that covers both morality and prudence (SKS 8, 197–201 / UD, 93–7). Here, prudence does not represent one normative domain among others. Rather, it represents practical normativity more generally. As such, it concerns what we ought to do all-things-considered.

Like eudaimonists, Kant occasionally uses the concept of morality in a broad, holistic, classical sense that includes prudential concerns and social norms that concern life as a whole. The concept of the highest good, notably, concerns virtue, happiness, and the kingdom of God. However,

6 For Kierkegaard, see Assiter 2009: 73–8; Stan 2017: esp. ch. 6. For Romanticism, Fichte, and Hegel, see Pinkard 2010: chs. 5–9.

7 This is partially why Kant's "highest good" is criticized for its alleged eudaimonism. Cf. Beiser 2006: 614–16, 627–8

it is only rational to promote this good, and to prioritize morality above prudence, if we compare morality to prudence (Timmermann 2013: 674–5). Morality is then not one normative domain isolated from prudence and religion. Rather, it represents pure practical rationality.

In both Kant and Kierkegaard, the "highest good" thus reintroduces some of the problems raised by eudaimonism. For both, it entails a synthesis of morality and prudence in which morality causes personal happiness, if only indirectly in the afterlife.[8] Even if morality is not motivated by happiness (but happiness is its *foreseeable* result), this still resembles eudaimonism by *ascribing both an instrumental and an intrinsic role to morality.* Morality is valued for its own sake *and* assumed to bring happiness indirectly.

Indeed, Kierkegaard (and Climacus) speaks of *expecting* the highest good or eternal happiness (SKS 5, 19–25 / EUD, 9–15; SKS 7, 387 / CUP1, 426). Kant, on the other hand, argues that we should promote (*befördern*) the highest good with all our powers, although we cannot realize it without divine assistance (R 6: 120, 138–9). This clearly indicates that the highest good is not merely an unintended by-product of moral action. Rather, it must be possible to *aim* at the highest good and hope for it insofar as its happiness is somehow a foreseeable result of morality and prudence (given, for example, Christian belief). Clearly, Kant views the highest good as the aim or *end* of morality (Wood 1970: ch. 3; Beiser 2006: 615–16). And John Silber argues that we should promote it by furthering distributive justice, in which there is proportionality between moral desert and happiness.[9]

However, a full, immediate realization of the highest good would seem to reward morality in an eudaimonist manner. But Kant and Kierkegaard both seem to avoid this problem by assuming *conflict* between morality and prudence. In this life, this conflict allows an unselfish morality that prioritizes virtue over happiness. Yet the realization of the highest good in the afterlife nevertheless brings happiness to the virtuous (who need not be perfect if divine grace is introduced).

However, for both Kant and Kierkegaard, the highest good is an object of hope that is *not* based on sufficient epistemic evidence. The *Postscript* states that "the specific sign that one relates oneself to the absolute [telos, eternal happiness] is that not only is there no reward to expect but suffering to endure" (SKS 7, 366 / CUP1, 402; cf. SKS 5, 326–8 / EUD, 337–9). First,

[8] Fremstedal 2014a: chs. 5–6. For Kant, see Wood 1970; Beiser 2006. For Kierkegaard, see Evans 1999: 140–7.

[9] Silber (1963: 183) argues that we work towards the idea of the highest good by promoting proportionality between desert and happiness, in many different activities such as grading of papers, serving on juries, and rearing children.

one suffers by relinquishing the tendency to relate unconditionally or absolutely to finite, lesser goods. Indeed, one must sacrifice all goods that conflict with eternal happiness. Unlike "finite" or "poorer goods" (such as money, fame, or power),[10] "the highest good" is categorically and supremely good (SKS 7, 358–65 / CUP1, 394–401), overriding all other goods (Westphal 1996: 158–65; Evans 1999: 168–73).

Second, one suffers by being separated from one's final end, eternal happiness, since this end cannot be properly realized in human history (SKS 7, 353–9, 388, 524 / CUP1, 387–94, 426–7, 502; cf. Westphal 1996: 161–5). One the one hand, one suffers by experiencing hardship or injustice, insofar as morality neither brings happiness nor realizes the kingdom of God. On the other hand, one suffers by being passive or even sinful since one cannot save oneself by one's own unaided power (cf. Westphal 1996: 161). This holds both for Christian salvation and for the realization of the highest good.

Like Kant, Kierkegaard (Climacus) suggests that the "highest good" requires morality (SKS 7, 354–9, 388 / CUP1, 389–94, 426–7). Indeed, "eternal happiness, as the absolute good," has "the remarkable quality that *it can defined only by the mode in which it is acquired*" (SKS 7, 388 / CUP1, 426–7). Clearly, Kierkegaard's view is that it is not acquired by human power but by the free acceptance of divine *grace* (more on this later). Elsewhere, he therefore aligns it with Christian religiousness (SKS 5, 19–21, 24–5 / EUD, 9–11, 14–15), saying that the highest good is to love God (SKS 10, 209 / CD, 200). Strictly speaking, however, eternal happiness, or the highest good refers to final salvation and bliss in the hereafter (SKS 7, 354–91, 560 / CUP1, 389–430, 617; SKS 10, 219, 230–5 / CD, 211, 222–28).[11] Unlike temporal happiness, such happiness is stable, designating a state where one lacks nothing, since one is independent of pressures and needs (Fremstedal and Jackson 2015: 4).

The *Postscript* dismisses accounts of "eternal happiness" that do not involve moral commitment. Instead of giving a detached, theoretical account of it, the *Postscript* therefore connects it to ethico-religious existence which is infinitely interested in "eternal happiness" (SKS 7, 25, 57 / CUP1, 16, 52).[12] Natural

[10] For poorer goods, see SKS 10, 230–5 / CD, 222–8. For finite goals, see SKS 4, 459 / CA, 160. Kierkegaard writes that Christianity "is not of the opinion that wealth cannot, in a certain sense, be termed a good. It is precisely for this reason that it says, [']Give everything to the poor.[']" (SKS 25, 390, NB30:12 / KJN 9, 394).

[11] "*Evig Salighed*" is normally translated "eternal happiness," although "eternal salvation" also occurs (SKS 5, 250–68 / EUD, 253–73). Still, Kierkegaard's use of the term seems consistent with the use of it by Climacus and de silentio. See Fremstedal 2014a: ch. 5.

[12] In a narrow sense, the term "ethico-religious" seems associated with immanent (natural) religiousness in the *Postscript*. But in a general sense it fits *all* views which combine ethics and religion, including Christianity and the ethical stage of Judge William. See Chapter 7 for a discussion.

religion seems seriously concerned with such soteriological happiness, and Christian religiousness even seems to anticipate it (cf. SKS 5, 19–21, 24–5, 250–68 / EUD, 9–11, 14–15, 253–73; SKS 10, 201, 209 / CD, 191, 200). Specifically, eternal happiness seems anticipated existentially by *hope, faith, and charity* as Christian virtues. Hope, notably, expects the good for both oneself and others, by being based on charity that loves all without distinction (SKS 9, 259 / WL, 260). Hope is nothing without charity, although charity itself is nourished by hope (SKS 9, 248, 258 / WL, 248, 259). However, hope in God requires faith and trust in God and vice versa (Gouwens 1996: 157). Even though Kierkegaard does not speak of the theological virtues here (cf. Vos 2016), he nevertheless assumes that faith, hope, and charity are *interconnected*, since all three are necessary for avoiding despair (SKS 8, 204–5 / UD, 100–1; SKS 9, 227–62 / WL, 225–62; SKS 10, 127–32 / CD, 116–22; SKS 11, 195–6 / SUD, 81; SKS 13, 99, 103–4 / FSE, 77, 82–3).[13]

Still, this leaves room for a *regulative* reconstruction of the highest good that does not require religious faith. This nonreligious reconstruction aims to minimize (inescapable) *normative conflict* between morality and prudence in this life. Even if a perfect synthesis of morality and prudence would – in Kantian terms – transcend all experience, the "highest good" can nevertheless be interpreted as a *regulative* idea that we should promote and approximate, although we can never reach it completely (cf. Fremstedal 2018: 5). The basic argument here can be reconstructed roughly as follows: First, we have prudential reason to avoid normative conflict in which morality weakens prudence. Second, we have a decisive moral reason to avoid demoralization that results from conflict between morality and prudence, which makes morality highly demanding (more on this in Chapters 9–10 and 13). Finally, and partially as a result of this, we have moral reason to promote *distributive justice*, in which there is proportionality between moral desert and happiness (Silber 1963; Beiser 2006: 596–7). We should therefore minimize conflict between morality and prudence by removing disincentives to distributive justice (if not by

[13] Cf. Fremstedal 2020b: 84–6. The emotions and virtues dealt with by Kierkegaard (especially hope, faith, and charity) are often Christian, belonging to an Augustinian-Lutheran tradition. See Roberts 2008; Evans and Roberts 2013; Vos 2016. Commenting on the theological virtues (but not Kierkegaard), John Bishop suggests that "faith is taking it to be true that there are grounds for the hope that love is supreme – not simply in the sense that love constitutes the ideal of the supreme good, but in the sense that living in accordance with this ideal constitutes an ultimate salvation, fulfilment or consummation that is, in reality, victorious over all that may undermine it (in a word, over evil). The supremacy of love is linked to the supremacy of the divine itself since love is the essential nature of the divine. What is hoped for, and what faith assures us is properly hoped for, is a sharing in the divine itself, loving as God loves . . . people of faith take reality to be such that their hope (for salvation, the triumph of the good) is well founded, and not merely an attractive fantasy or inspiring ideal" (2016: Part x).

creating incentives for such justice, since the latter would effectively encourage instrumentalism concerning justice).

Thus, both prudence and morality generate reasons to promote the highest good. The highest good avoids prudential normativity that is morally objectionable and moral normativity that is prudentially objectionable. As a result, we avoid a dualism of practical reason (cf. Bader 2015). Instead of competing, morality and prudence would then support each other reciprocally. Our lives then become less conflicted and more integrated, since we avoid conflicts that undermine ought-all-things-considered practical normativity. We would therefore be much more disposed to act correctly morally and prudentially since one type of normativity would not undermine the other or threaten practical rationality more generally.

This brief sketch therefore indicates that the regulative use of the highest good is supported independently of religious faith.[14] But this regulative use of it does not amount to a Christian hope of universal salvation for all sinners. Rather than being a kingdom of God based on divine grace, it involves an ethical commonwealth based on distributive justice as a regulative idea. However, immorality would seem to exclude one from this commonwealth. And the commonwealth is not realized in the hereafter; it is only something we approximate asymptotically through historical progress.

Still, both secular and religious versions of the highest good represent an efficacious *moral order* that prevents moral action from being in vain. For it seems that moral agents must not only assume the reality of freedom but also that moral actions can be efficacious and successful. Otherwise, it would simply not make sense to act morally (cf. Beiser 2006: 597, 616–23; Ak 5:446, 458). However, the realization of morality cannot be simply postponed to the afterlife since morality must be able to make some difference in this life. Still, conflict between morality and prudence prevents the moral order from being fully efficacious in human history. In addition, the realization of the highest good is hindered both by immorality and problems with uniting agents in a universal kingdom or commonwealth. Therefore, a full realization of the highest good, as opposed to a mere approximation to it, is only possible eschatologically (Beiser 2006; Fremstedal 2014a: chs. 4–9).

[14] Similarly, even nonbelievers can interpret eternity and judgment day as a regulative ideal (Rudd 2012: 166). Nonbelievers can understand perfectly well the idea of caring about "a final status that gathers together our lives as an implicit finished totality" (Stokes 2015: 229).

Conclusion: Neither Predestination Nor Pelagianism

For Kierkegaard, "eternal happiness," which is identical to "eternal salvation," concerns the state of the person who is saved and transformed by receiving God's grace. Pieter Vos writes:

> Transformation implies more than just the perfection or completion of nature, but less than the complete replacement of nature by grace . . . Rather than by (natural) progress or a Thomistic completion of natural capacities, in this view virtue is marked by transformation that requires "inversion" and "conversion." In the end, this has to do with the radical nature of human fallibility and sin . . . [H]uman character is formed via a relation to God in Christ, who not only atones for human sin but also constitutes the qualitative criterion and ethical goal for human selfhood. (2016: 325)

Christ has "decisive significance" by making "a new person [*Menneske*]" of the disciple, Kierkegaard (Climacus) maintains (SKS 4, 226–8 / PF, 17–19; cf. SKS 12, 145–6 / PC, 142–3). But it is *not* the case that divine grace is irresistible or that we are predestined to either salvation or damnation, irrespective of how we live. Kierkegaard therefore claims that "[i]n eternity everyone as a single individual must make an accounting to God," but, with respect to "the highest," "every human being, God be praised, is capable of it if he wills" (SKS 8, 228, 224 / UD, 128, 123). However, Kierkegaard accuses the doctrine of predestination of overlooking this capability and for fostering moral passivity (SKS 18, 23, EE:50 / KJN 2, 18–19; SKS 24, 289–90, NB23:175 / KJN 8, 289; SKS 27, 93, Papir 49 / KJN 11.1, 48; SKS 27, 93–4, Papir 51:1–3 / KJN 11.1, 95).

On the other hand, Kierkegaard accuses Pelagianism of frivolity and thoughtlessness (SKS 11, 195 / SUD, 81). He maintains that we are neither morally perfect nor powerful enough to save ourselves without divine assistance. Happiness is therefore not something we can expect or deserve, as something owed to us as morally perfect beings without any character flaws. Indeed, we can neither save ourselves nor be morally perfect; we can only choose whether or not to accept divine grace (SKS 5, 267–8 / EUD, 272–3; SKS 7, 390–91, 421 / CUP1, 429–30, 463; SKS 10, 228 / CD, 220–1; SKS 24, 190–1, NB22:159 / KJN 8, 188–90). Indeed, Kierkegaard thinks that we ignore the decisive importance of the atonement if we assume that human agency contributes positively toward salvation (cf. SKS 22, 123–4, NB11:201 / KJN 6, 120–1; SKS 22, 373–4, NB14:46 / KJN 6, 377–8). Thus, he rejects both Pelagianism and predestination, preferring an intermediary view where faith is both a divine gift and a human task (Jackson 1998):

> In order to constrain subjectivity it is rightly taught that no one is saved by good works, but by grace – and, consequently, by faith. Fine. But am

> I myself therefore unable to do anything with respect to becoming a believer? Here one must either immediately answer with an absolute No, and then we have a fatalistic understanding of election by grace, or one must make a little concession ... subjectivity cannot be excluded unless we want to have fatalism. (SKS 22, 415, NB14:123 / KJN 6, 420–1)

For Kierkegaard, an "anguished conscience," which is conscious of moral failure, is a requirement for serious interest in personal salvation (SKS 20, 69, NB:79 / KJN 4, 68; SKS 21, 285, NB10:55 / KJN 5, 296). Specifically, the conversion to Christianity is both preceded and motivated by the problem of human guilt and sin. The problem of guilt and sin leads to the collapse of non-Christian ethics, due to human inability to live up to its own standards; despair is inevitable due to the moral gap between ideals and the actual extent to which they are realized (cf. SKS 4, 323–31 / CA, 16–24). Christian ethics, by contrast, involves not only sin-consciousness but also divine and human forgiveness of sins. It relies on divine grace, whereas pagan ethics relies on human willpower (Fremstedal 2014a: chs. 2–10).

Although the nature of divine assistance remains mysterious, Kierkegaard still sketches a three-step account of how it works together with human effort. In 1852, he suggests the following development of the dialectics between human effort and divine grace:

1. [I]mitation, tending toward decisive action, through which the situation for becoming [a Christian] comes into existence
2. [Christ] as gift – faith
3. [I]mitation as the fruit of faith (SKS 24, 460, NB25:35 / KJN 8, 466)

The process of becoming a Christian who imitates Christ here starts (1) with the agent's unaided attempt to do good by imitating Christ (something that can contribute to anguish, although the interest in Christianity must itself presuppose anguish). To be consistent, Kierkegaard must deny that this attempt to do good represents good works that contribute positively to our salvation. Rather, he must assume that it removes hindrances by preparing for (2), the reception of divine grace that results in faith as gift. Finally (3), true imitation of Christ is then seen as the fruit of faith, implying that human efforts are *transformed* by divine assistance. This is not far removed from Kant's view that we can only hope and believe to receive divine assistance if we first start by doing good to the uttermost of our capability (see R 6:117–18). Both Kant and Kierkegaard thus approach divine assistance from the practical, forward-looking perspective, by emphasizing that we must take the initiative toward good by acting morally, although practical agency depends on divine agency for its creation and development.

CHAPTER 6

The "Teleological Suspension of the Ethical" and Abraham's Sacrifice of Isaac

Introduction: The Traditional Reading and Its Problems

The "teleological suspension of the ethical" and Abraham's sacrifice of Isaac in *Fear and Trembling* represent perhaps Kierkegaard's most controversial contributions to philosophy and theology. Traditionally, the teleological suspension is seen as a reaction against Kant and German idealism (especially Fichte and Hegel).[1] Paolo Diego Bubbio explains:

> There is no doubt that there is, for Hegel, a strong connection between ethics and religion. The extent to which this connection turns into a dependence of religion on the ethical (mutual recognition), however, has been, and still is, an object of dispute. From this angle, a reaction against the risk of turning faith into a mere statement of social fact rather than a personal and existential commitment was inevitable. Kierkegaard well represents this reaction ... *Fear and Trembling* is clearly critical of the Kantian reduction of (natural) religion to moral philosophy ... The risk of reducing religion to moral philosophy is what leads Johannes [de silentio] to draw a strong distinction between (and often to contrast) *ethical* behavior and *religious* behavior. (2014: 85, 89)

Bubbio mentions (without acceptance) the dominant view that Kant reduces genuine religion to ethics.[2] Kierkegaard, by contrast, is taken to dismiss this view by claiming that *religion transcends ethics*. This traditional reading (as I call it) involves three distinct claims:

1. That religion and ethics are distinct and *nonidentical*, at least in part
2. That ethics and religion diverge and *conflict*, at least in part
3. That religion *overrides* ethics normatively[3]

[1] See Fahrenbach 1968: 124; FT, 348–9 (Hongs' note); Knappe 2004: 80–1; Green 2011: 8.

[2] Terry Pinkard (2001: 37) writes, "Kant's Christianity was exclusively a religion of morality, and for the radical Kantians, Jesus was only the foremost teacher of morality, not some supernatural God-man walking the earth." Cf. Wood 2016: 7, 19.

[3] The ethical is overridden, not silenced. See McDaniel 2020: 430. See also Davenport 2008a: 219–20.

Conceptually, the last claim presupposes the two former claims. It also seems less plausible and more dangerous than the former claims (see Mulder 2000: 321; Stewart 2003: 319), since it contradicts the unconditional and overriding nature of morality – two ideas even Kierkegaard endorses. The two former claims, by contrast, only say that religion somehow diverges and conflicts with morality – a view that is widespread. Still, it is difficult to see how there could be serious conflict between religion and ethics, unless God somehow undermines morality. As we will see, Kierkegaard takes the latter to be a pagan idea that contradicts the Christian idea that God is love.

A closely related reading sees Kierkegaard as representing *moral exceptionalism*, in which someone (e.g., Abraham) is beyond or above morality, by virtue of possessing some higher justification that is typically religious.[4] Since it is typically religion (and no other domain) that is assumed to be above morality, moral exceptionalism typically overlaps with the traditional reading, in which religion overrides ethics. Both readings thus grant religion autonomy from ethics, something the present reading denies. Both appear supported by the "teleological suspension of the ethical" and the closely related binding of Isaac (the *Akedah*) in *Fear and Trembling*. Famously, the *Akedah* is described in ethical terms as murder and in religious terms as a paradigmatic case of sacrifice and belief. The ethical stage of existence is also transcended by the religious stage in both *Stages on Life's Way* and *Concluding Unscientific Postscript*. Since 1877 the traditional reading has been used to criticize Kierkegaard.[5] More recently, Irwin concludes that Kierkegaard's "position is stronger if he does not emancipate himself from the ethical as far as he thinks he should" (2011: vol. III, 324). However, in what follows, I argue that the traditional and exceptionalist readings are false as readings of Kierkegaard. The problem with both readings is not just that they fail to make sense of Kierkegaard's views on ethics and religion (and how he relates to Kant and Fichte) but

[4] Fox-Muraton (2018: 8) speaks of individual "moral exceptionalism" instead of Charles Taylor's cultural "moral exceptionalism."

[5] The traditional reading of Kierkegaard originates in the 1870s when Georg Brandes and others classified Kierkegaard's work and its positions as belonging to the aesthetic, ethical, and religious stages. In a highly influential work, Brandes (1877) uses Abraham in *Fear and Trembling*, and the "teleological suspension of the ethical," as *the* paradigm case for the religious stage. Brandes and later commentators highlight the conflict between the ethical and the religious stages, taking the religious stage to entail moral exceptionalism. Brandes emphasized how the religious stage looks suspiciously like the aesthetic stage insofar as both contradict universalistic ethics. This approach to Kierkegaard influenced not just the cultural radicals in Scandinavia but also German interpretations of Kierkegaard and existentialism (Tullberg 2006; Stewart 2009). See also Malantschuk 1978: 60–75; Irwin 2011: vol. III, 309–24.

also that they make it very difficult to understand his relation to contemporary metaethics and theories of personal identity (cf. Evans 2006a; Rudd 2012). Instead of softening Kierkegaard, I suggest that commentators since Brandes have radicalized him unnecessarily by reading "the teleological suspension" and the *Akedah* out of context (pace Mulder 2002: 304).

Briefly on the Kantian Background

In a much-referred passage, Carl Schmitt refers to Kant's concept of God as a "parasite of ethics."[6] Indeed, Kant bases religion on morality by viewing the good as more basic than the divine *and* by arguing that we have moral reasons to postulate a God who reconciles morality and happiness.[7] Although *Opus Postumum* identifies God with pure practical reason, the critical philosophy does not identify these two.[8] Still, the majority view is that the critical philosophy reduces religion to ethics, something the minority view rejects.[9]

Kant defines religion as the recognition (*Erkenntnis*) of all our moral duties as divine commands (CPR 5:129; R 6:153). Here divine commands concern the subjective *form* (i.e., the obligatoriness) – not the content – of ethics (i.e., what is right or wrong; cf. Evans 2014: 142). Religion adds a subjective dimension to ethics by seeing moral duties as divine commands. For the religious believer, the awareness of moral duty is therefore subjectively enlivened by the idea of God and his commands (Wood 2000: 501).

In addition, religion involves statutes or positive laws, which introduces normative content that transcends morality, just as positive law transcends natural law. Kant therefore distinguishes *moral faith* from *statutory faith*,

6 Schmitt 2007: 83–4. Schmitt's use of quotes indicates that he did not coin this expression but that it was already established at the time (1929).

7 For Kant's moral argument for God, see CPR 5:111–47; Ak 5:446–84. For the priority of the good over the divine, see R 6:154, 185; Ak 9:450–1.

8 For a controversial (and unconvincing) attempt to refute this standard view, see Schwarz 2004; cf. Fremstedal 2014a: 267. Louden (2015b: 124–5) points out that some parts of the *Opus Postumum* describes God as an independent being, whereas other parts describe him as a projection of reason.

9 Palmquist 1992: 129–48; cf. Bubbio 2014: 89. Palmquist defends the minority view (as does Hare 2002b: 45), whereas Wood (2016) and Pinkard (2001) represent the majority view. The majority view makes Kant's philosophy of religion problematic both for secular and religious readers. For secular readers, the reduction of religion to ethics makes religion appear superfluous or unnecessary (although it is *not* supposed to be an eliminative reduction). For at least some religious readers, the reduction is problematic because there does not appear to be anything unique about religion since religion is reduced to ethics that seems largely secular. However, the minority view makes Kant less controversial since it is closer to the widespread view that religion and ethics both overlap and diverge somewhat.

a form of faith based on statutes or positive laws that concern religious rituals and practices. Since these statutes or laws are revealed and mediated historically by tradition, scriptures, and churches, Kant aligns statutory faith with revealed faith, historical faith, ecclesiastical faith, and church faith (R 6:102–32; CF 7:36–7).

Still, statutory and moral faith need not exclude each other. Religious statutes do good work if they strengthen moral faith and are unproblematic if compatible with morality. But religion that hinders morality is pagan and superstitious (R 6:111–12; CF 7:47, 50, 65). Statutory faith without moral faith is motivated by fear of punishment and hope of reward since morality is then but a means for reaching something external to morality (e.g., a community with God). Moral faith, by contrast, conditions faith on morality.

Kant is clear that statutory faith should be the *vehicle* and *shell* of moral faith (R 6:85, 101, 104, 121, 135), and that the former should therefore be interpreted and justified by the latter (cf. R 6:109–14, 130; CF 7:48). There is a partial overlap or identity between moral and statutory faith, whereby different statutory faiths share the same rational core (Ak 23:95; Wimmer 1990: 94). Thus, there are many different statutory faiths but only one moral faith (Ak 8:367).[10]

Still, it is only when "all earthly life comes to an end" that the visible churches of statutory faith will be dissolved (R 6:135). "[Statutory] faith is not to be '*abolished* by progress. Rather, it is to come to an understanding of itself as a vehicle for pure religious faith, so better to serve the pure faith which is its essence'" (Louden 2002: 129–30 quoting Wood 1970: 196). Instead of dismissing historical religions, Kant therefore calls for rational *reform* of existing religions (Collins 1967: 164–5; Despland 1973: 244).

It is very difficult to see that Kant reduces either the content or form of religion to morality (or moral faith). And it is far from clear that such a reduction is necessary or convincing. Kantians need not reduce religion to ethics but must prioritize morality above religious rituals and practices. Religion should be compatible with morality, but neither its content nor its form needs to be exclusively moral.[11]

[10] Kant views Christianity as the most developed religion, saying that it "treads in the closest proximity to reason" (R 6:167; cf. 193–4). Christianity's "best and most lasting eulogy is its harmony [*Zusammenstummung*] ... with the purest moral belief [*moralischen Vernunfts*glauben]," a harmony Kant believes to have demonstrated in *Conflict of the Faculties* (CF 7:9, 44; cf. Ak 10:180; Ak 11:429).

[11] The material aspect of religion can therefore contain duties known through experience. Cf. MM 6:487; Wimmer 1990: 168–71; Palmquist 1992: 133; Hare 2002b: 45.

Still, it is possible that statutory (positive) religion represents *nonideal* practical normativity that includes punishments and rewards (Firestone and Jacobs 2008: 196). The important distinction would then be between nonideal and ideal moral normativity, not between morality and religion.[12] On this reading. the content of statutory religion would be moral in a nonideal sense.

In any case, Kant does moralize religion greatly, even if he does not reduce it to morality. However, Fichte and Kierkegaard go further than Kant does here. First, at least prior to 1800, Fichte identifies God with our moral order (and the supersensible world), whereas Kant and Kierkegaard distinguish more clearly between Creator and creation (cf. Stolzenberg 2010: 6). Second, Fichte seems to anticipate Feuerbach by viewing God as a human projection and construction, something neither Kant nor Kierkegaard does.[13] Still, I argue that Kierkegaard *moralizes* religion completely (although both ethics and religion have theoretical implications).

The Ethical in *Fear and Trembling* and *Either/Or, Part II*

The single most influential text for understanding the relation between the ethical and religious in Kierkegaard is probably *Fear and Trembling*. This text interprets the ethical not as secular but as divine. After asking whether there "is an Absolute Duty to God," Kierkegaard's nonreligious pseudonym de silentio writes:

> The Ethical is the universal, and as such it is also the divine. Thus it is proper to say that every duty is essentially duty towards God, but if no more can be said than this, then it is also said that I actually have no duty towards God. The duty becomes duty by being traced back [*henføres*] to God, but in the duty itself I do not enter into relation to God. For example, it is a duty to love one's neighbor. It is a duty by being traced back to God, but in the duty I enter into a relation not to God but to the neighbor I love. If in this connection I then say that it is my duty to love God, I am actually pronouncing only a tautology, insomuch as "God" in a totally abstract sense is here understood as the Divine – that is, the universal, that is, the duty. (SKS 4, 160 / FT, 68)

Here God is identical to the divine, the ethical, duty, and the universal (*Almene*). This implies a *universalistic* account of ethics *and* religion, which

[12] Horn (2014) finds nonideal normativity in Kant's writings on history, politics, and law, whereas Korsgaard (1996b: 147–53) finds it in his ethics. Neither of them discusses the philosophy of religion.

[13] For Kierkegaard, see Chapters 1 and 3. For Fichte, see Wood 2016: 18. For Kant, see Düsing 1973.

differs from the particularistic account of Abraham as an exception. Furthermore, the passage above concludes that on this universalistic picture "God comes to be an invisible vanishing point, an impotent thought; his power is only in the ethical" (SKS 4, 160 / FT, 68). In his drafts for *Fear and Trembling*, however, Kierkegaard himself nevertheless explicitly describes the ethical as representing "God's commandment" (Pap. IV, B67 / JP 1, 908). As such, the ethical is neither false nor invalid – quite the opposite.

The identification of (universalistic) ethics and the divine in *Fear and Trembling* suggests the moral order itself is divine (similar to what we find in Fichte) or that God is a personification of social morality (a more Hegelian view).[14] Existing scholarship has rightly interpreted this passage, and the ethical in *Fear and Trembling*, as a denial of an absolute duty towards God at the ethical stage (or first ethics) and as following Kant and his early successors (notably Fichte and Hegel) in Germany and Denmark. To understand this, we need to consider two different taxonomies of ethical duties that were widespread in the eighteenth and nineteenth centuries. The old taxonomy, from A. G. Baumgarten in Germany and Bishop N. E. Balle (1791) in Denmark, distinguishes categorically between (1) duties of religion (or duties to God) and duties to (2) others and (3) duties to ourselves. By contrast, the taxonomy of Kant and Fichte denies that are any special duties towards God (in addition to duties to human beings), because this would require that God as such is a possible object of experience (R 6:241; cf. LE 27:709; CPR 5:83; Wood 2016: 236–7). The ethical in *Fear and Trembling* follows the latter taxonomy by assuming that we only relate to God indirectly through our neighbor (although Abraham in *Fear and Trembling* appears to follow the old taxonomy instead, by involving an exception from universalistic ethics).[15]

The interpretation of the ethical as universal in *Fear and Trembling* is clearly reminiscent of, if not identical to, the ethical position of Judge William in *Either/Or, Part II* (Evans 2009: 101; Rudd 2012: 145; Westphal 2014: 47–50). However, the ethics of Judge William, often described as the ethical stage, is *not* secular but religious, since he stresses the continuity and interdependence between ethical and religious virtues (SKS 3, 249 / EO2, 262). Here ethical life is religious as Westphal (1998: 109) points out:

> God is very much a part of [William's] world, he is so complacent (wretched contentment!) in his piety and civic virtue, which are but two sides of the

[14] For the latter, see Evans 2009: 105; cf. Bubbio 2014: 85. For Fichte, see Stolzenberg 2010.

[15] Similarly, Karl Barth claims that religious prayer and worship is relatively distinct from morally good work. See Jackson 2010: 13n.

> same coin, that he cannot really imagine himself in the wrong against God. The established order, into which he has been thoroughly and successfully socialized, is pretty much identical with the Kingdom of God. If the ethical universal is the highest, "then the ethical is of the same nature as a person's eternal salvation" (*FT*, 54). In other words, socialization is salvation because "the ethical is the divine" (*FT*, 60). Judge William is the embodiment of Christendom. (Westphal 2014: 48–9)

On this Hegelian reading, the ethical "universal," which is identical to the divine, is not an abstract, Kantian universal but the concrete universal, or society's (Christendom's) institutions, laws, and customs. For Judge William, and de silentio, the ethical and divine is therefore immanent to society and its practices rather than something transcendent like Platonic or Kantian ideas (Westphal 2014: 43; cf. Stern 2012: 198–9). Still, the *Akedah* contradicts both Hegelian ethics (*Sittlichkeit*) and Kantian morality (*Moralität*). *Sittlichkeit* is partially based on *Moralität*, and the concept of the universal may refer to deontological norms and natural law, not just to Hegel's concrete universal (Knappe 2004: 77–85; Rudd 2005: 145; Davenport 2008a: 211).

De silentio explicitly identifies the divine with the ethical (as universal), whereas Judge William seems to identify the two implicitly (see Westphal 2014: 48–9; cf. Evans 2009: 101). Specifically, William holds the world order to be rational (SKS 3, 277, 305 / EO2, 292, 323; SKS 6, 145 / SLW, 155), and tends to identify the rational, good, and divine with the practices and institutions of society (see Westphal 1991: 76–7; Furtak 2005: 92–6; Bubbio 2014: 91). William and de silentio both tend to see the universal and divine as *immanent* or internal to human society (whereas Climacus in the *Postscript* sees the divine as *transcending* society, since Creator differs from creation).[16] Also, William stresses the human ability to be moral and happy and appears to be a Pelagian who dismisses the (closely related) doctrines of original sin and radical evil (SKS 3, 170–1, 173 / EO2, 174–5, 178).

"The Teleological Suspension of the Ethical" in *Fear and Trembling*

It is often assumed that "the teleological suspension of the ethical" in *Fear and Trembling* cancels the ethical (as universal). But the text is clear that "that which is suspended is not relinquished [*forskjærtset*] but is preserved

[16] Evans (2006a: 329) takes Kierkegaard to argue that what is truly divine and transcendent cannot be identified with a worldly order without thereby becoming corrupted.

[*bevaret*] in the higher, which is its τέλος" (SKS 4, 148 / FT, 54). The ethical (as universal) is therefore *aufgehoben* or recontextualized, not negated completely. It goes from being absolute to being relativized by finding a new *telos* or grounding (Westphal 2014: 49–50). In this passage, the (human) *telos*, which suspends the ethical, is identified with "eternal happiness," (SKS 4, 148 / FT, 54) a concept that appears in Kierkegaard's pseudonymous and signed writings alike, and described as "the highest good" (see Chapter 5). The ethical (as universal) therefore seems recontextualized (*aufgehoben*) with reference to the "highest good" – a concept that involves virtue, happiness, and the kingdom of God.

Moreover, the "teleological suspension" cannot suspend all ethics but only some variant (or aspect) of it, since the ethical *remains in force* as we will see. Judeo-Christian ethics is not suspended; only pagan ("first") ethics or some variant of it is suspended (e.g., Hegelian *Sittlichkeit* or Kantian *Moralität*, which both represent the ethical as universal).[17] Indeed, we will see (in the next chapter) that the second (Christian) ethics suspends the first ethics in *Concluding Unscientific Postscript*. The "teleological suspension" cannot then negate ethics in general if it represents Judeo-Christian ethics.

Finally, this is not just a suspension of a certain type of ethics but also a suspension of a correlated type of religiousness. Kierkegaard therefore describes the *Akedah* "not [as] a collision between God's command and man's command but between God's commandment and God's commandment" (Pap. IV, B67 / JP 1, 908). The normative conflict here is between God's general prohibition against killing and his specific command to sacrifice Isaac (*both* of which are ethico-religious). It is not conflict between ethics and religion as such but rather between a universalistic, natural interpretation of both and a particularist, Judeo-Christian interpretation of both. Unlike the former, the latter is based on supernatural revelation, which "refers to putative divine action that is not included in God's ordinary activity of creating and sustaining the world" (Wahlberg 2020: Part 1.1).

Westphal characterizes the relation between God and ethics in *Fear and Trembling* as follows:

> [T]he text supports the claim "what makes it right to sacrifice Isaac is that, and only that, God commands it." No other ground seems remotely plausible. But it goes beyond the evidence available to us to assume that

[17] For suspension of Hegelian *Sittlichkeit*, see Evans 2009: 106; Westphal 2014: 43. For the suspension of Kantian *Moralität*, see Knappe 2004: 77–85. I have not found any commentator claiming that the second ethics is suspended, but some suggest that it is *either* the ethical stage *or* ethics in general (the latter is clearly implausible, given the textual evidence presented in this chapter and the next). For an overview, see Boldt 2006: 101–11.

> this is a general, meta-ethical principle for Silentio. This is especially true in light of the relative validity of the ethical sphere. We have duties derived from the laws and customs of our people (society, nation, state, church, sect, *Volk*) so long as these are not trumped by a special command from God. But nothing Silentio says about *Sittlichkeit* suggests that it presupposes a divine command meta-ethic. (2014: 68)

Westphal concludes:

> First, there is no strong divine command ... meta-ethic in *Fear and Trembling*, namely the general claim that divine command is the necessary and sufficient condition for (categorical, moral, or/and religious) obligation. Second, a weaker principle is implied, if not stated theoretically, by Silentio (who insists he is not a philosopher), namely that a divine command is a sufficient condition for obligation. Within the horizon of biblical faith, and most particularly within the story of Abraham, if God commands it, it becomes my duty. No other ground seems remotely available to acquit Abraham of the charge of murder. We may not like this fact about the Bible or about Silentio's telling of the Abraham story, but that is no reason to deny its presence in both. (2014: 71–2)

Even those who defend a (strong) divine command reading of Kierkegaard, notably C. Stephen Evans and Philip Quinn, typically deny that the whole content of morality is contingent on God's will (Evans 2006a; Quinn 1996 and 2006: 65–72). Instead, they argue that the content of morality is literally true and valid, at least in part independent of divine commands. Divine commands are supposed to explain the form rather than the content of morality. Specifically, divine commands give morality a strictly obligatory character that goes beyond what is merely good for us (Evans 2014a: chs. 1–3). Divine commands therefore presuppose standards of moral goodness that are at least partially independent of divine volition. Hence, divine commands cannot negate or contradict moral goodness (at least not in general).

Indeed, since the *ethical remains in force* during the *Akedah*, not even the command to sacrifice Isaac negates ethics in general (or silences it either wholly or in part). Davenport explains:

> Abraham *remains* under the requirement to love Isaac wholeheartedly, as a parent should. He is not excused from this obligation ... Rather, it is only because he must continue to love Isaac that he is faced with sacrifice and loss, and is unable on his own to pursue what he wills: namely, that Isaac live to father a holy nation. (2008a: 219–20; cf. McDaniel 2020: 447)[18]

[18] Davenport (2008a: 201) denies that Abraham tries to murder Isaac: "Abraham believes he can sacrifice Isaac without murdering him." The explanation for this lies in the fact that Abraham

Davenport argues that Abraham's love for Isaac is suspended only in the sense that its realization is dependent on divine agency. Instead of rejecting ethics, Abraham reaffirms it by relying on divine assistance. Similarly, Kierkegaard takes eschatology to reaffirm ethics. Davenport explains:

> Eschatological promises and their eucatastrophic fulfillment can issue from the free creative will of God only if the [morally] Good itself is not a free creation of this will, but remains ontologically prior to it, as a metaphysically necessary truth. The eschatological, properly understood, depends on the ethical for its sense or meaning, rather than the other way around. (2008a: 232)

Morality depends on divine agency not for its grounding but for its successful realization in the highest good. But *Fear and Trembling* is often thought to break with such a Kantian view. In order to understand that this need not be the case, we must examine Abraham in *Fear and Trembling.*

The *Akedah* Cannot Be Imitated: Abraham as Special Case

Fear and Trembling has provoked much controversy by describing Abraham's sacrifice of Isaac both as murder and as paradigmatic religiousness, which is based on a private revelation beyond public reasoning. Indeed, many different readers and commentators associate it – and Kierkegaard – with *religious fanaticism, extremism, intolerance, or even terrorism.*[19] Recently, Stewart (2003: 319) writes that "de silentio's argument is potentially the same as that of any given fanatical religious terrorist. In short, it justifies any action." Particularly after the 9/11 terrorist attacks, *Fear and Trembling* seems more problematic than ever since religious terrorists actually try to justify terror as an Abrahamitic sacrifice (Mjaaland 2007: 133–5).

Worse still, these problems may not only concern Abraham but also religiousness *in general,* since Abraham seems to be a paradigmatic believer, as the traditional reading emphasizes (in an unnuanced manner – see Brandes 1877: esp. 186). Although this reading generates many problems, there are still Kierkegaardians who accept it and its associated religious

believes that God will return Isaac after the sacrifice. Still, "Abraham expects to lose Isaac forever [by sacrificing him] *if* his faith is wrong" (2008a: 224).

[19] Fremstedal 2006 and 2008. For *fanaticism*, see Evans and Walsh 2006: xxv–xxvi. For *terrorism*, see Mjaaland 2007: 133–5. For *extremism*, see Marshall 2013: 301; Tudvad 2013: 141. For *intolerance*, see Stan 2011: 309–10.

sacrifices of the highest good (cf. Malantschuk 1968: 227–34 and 1978: 58–67, 198–9, 252). Like Stewart, I cannot see what could possibly justify Abraham's sacrifice or attempts to imitate it. Still, I do not think that Kierkegaard's position is therefore indefensible, although many think so (see Hösle 1992; Mjaaland 2007). Thus, I contend that we must distinguish between the *special case* of Abraham and general features of religiousness. The former, not the latter, contradicts the prohibition against killing.

Like Paul, *Fear and Trembling* describes Abraham as the father of faith (SKS 4, 105 / FT, 9). Indeed, *Fear and Trembling* uses Abraham to exemplify both the "the teleological suspension of the ethical" and the "double movement of faith" (SKS 4, 149–59, 130–45 / FT, 55–67, 34–52). The double movement of faith explicates general features of Judeo-Christian faith, as we will see later (in Chapter 11). "The teleological suspension," by contrast, involves a recontextualization (*Aufhebung*) of the ethical, which may not only concern the *Akedah* but also Christian ethics, according to *Postscript* (more on this in Chapter 7).

As we saw, Kierkegaard describes the *Akedah* as "a collision between ... God's commandment and God's commandment" (Pap. IV, B67 / JP 1, 908). Abraham experiences normative conflict between God's *general* prohibition against killing and his *specific* command to sacrifice Isaac (Pap. IV, B67 / JP 1, 908). Here the unconditional duty of neighbor-love conflicts with the unconditional duty to love and obey God, at least from the nonreligious perspective of de silentio (Jackson 2010: ch. 6).

Clearly, the command to sacrifice Isaac generates problems, although these problems only concern Abraham. It is therefore crucial that his situation is unique and unrepeatable in several respects (Rocca 2002; Fox-Muraton 2012): *Historically*, it belongs to an *archaic* context where child sacrifice was practiced and considered pious (Hösle 1992: 18–19; Jackson 2010: 183–99; Evans 2015: 69). Originally, the *Akedah* was not considered murder but rather as Abraham's sacrifice of his most prized possession (Green 1988: 90–1), something *Fear and Trembling* downplays. *Theologically*, God intervenes directly in Abraham's world by calling and electing him especially, giving him a revelation that *Fear and Trembling* considers private, unwavering, unrevisable, and infallible (more on this later). *Morally and epistemically*, *Fear and Trembling* assumes that Abraham is without sin and guilt and that he is *infallible* in connection with the commanded sacrifice of Isaac (Rocca 2002; Boldt 2006: 109; Evans 2006a: 80; Fremstedal 2006). "Problema III" explains that

> [u]p until now I have assiduously avoided any reference to the question of sin and its reality. The whole work is centered on Abraham . . . for Abraham did not become the single individual by way of sin – on the contrary, he was a righteous [*retfærdige*] man, God's chosen one. (SKS 4, 188, w. note / FT, 98–9, w. note; cf. SKS 7, 243–4 / CUP1, 268–9)

Unlike other human beings, Abraham is not a sinner in *Fear and Trembling* (Rocca 2002; Evans 2006a: 80). Unlike us, he neither suffers from the moral nor epistemic (noetic) problems of sin. Nor is he self-deceived. Quite the opposite: He is "a devout and God-fearing man . . . worthy of being called God's chosen one" (SKS 4, 127 / FT, 31).[20] His motives are *pure*, since his own interests coincide perfectly with God's interests (SKS 4, 116–17, 127, 153 / FT, 20–1, 31, 59).

But ordinary believers are closer to *Fear and Trembling*'s Merman than to Abraham, since they are not without guilt or sin (SKS 4, 183–9 / FT, 94–9). Except for Abraham, Kierkegaardian religiousness is deeply concerned with guilt and sin. As a result, the first ethics is suspended by the second ethics; the former's unforgiving demand for moral perfection gives way to a Christian ethics based on divine grace and forgiveness.[21] The failure to fulfill the law – which is written in our hearts (cf. SKS 5, 91 / EUD, 84) – leads to the collapse of the first ethics (more on this in the next chapter).

Still, the unique case of Abraham represents a structural analogue to sinful believers in that both he and believers depend on divine intervention. Whereas the latter needs God's grace to overcome sin, Abraham confronts an analogous obstacle: For him, the commandment to sacrifice Isaac represents a contingent barrier to fulfilling his moral obligation to love Isaac and the duty not to murder (Davenport 2008a: 228–31). Like others, he must therefore perform a double movement of faith. First, he resigns completely since he is incapable of realizing the highest good by his own, unaided power. Second, he nevertheless believes that this good can be realized by divine power and intervention (SKS 4, 129–45 / FT, 34–52).

Unlike others, Abraham is not only especially elected by God; he is also assumed to receive a *private* revelation and calling beyond question or doubt. As such, it cannot be discussed or argued about, since it is inaccessible to all others (SKS 4, 153, 172–83, 201–7 / FT, 59, 82–93, 113–20). This leads Vittorio Hösle (1992: 14) to criticize Kierkegaard for attempting to

[20] By contrast, Climacus writes that "the conception of being the [divinely] elect [*Udvalgte*] that esthetically wishes to be, for an example, in an apostle's place is so repulsive [*væmmelig*]" (SKS 7, 530 / CUP1, 582).

[21] Lübcke (2006: 411–12) shows that both de silentio and Climacus present the transition from the first to the second ethics by emphasizing guilt-consciousness.

immunize faith from all critique. Still, Hösle (1992: 7) and others nevertheless argue that Kierkegaard anticipates the central idea of Habermas' discourse ethics (McCombs 2013: 56; Westphal 2014: 56–7). As we saw, Kierkegaard (de silentio) writes:

> If [the tragic hero] remains silent, he takes a responsibility upon himself as the single individual, inasmuch as he disregards any argument that may come from the outside . . . His heroic deed requires courage, but part of this courage is that he does not avoid any argument. (SKS 4, 177, cf. 180 / FT, 87, cf. 91)

Instead of withdrawing from public arguments, the hero "has the consolation that every counterargument has had its due" (SKS 4, 201 / FT, 113). Although these passages concern the sacrifice of the tragic hero, they nevertheless have a broader scope, as indicated in Chapter 3. The general idea is that practical *reasoning requires dialogue* since we are likely to overlook relevant reasons unless we communicate openly. We cannot know if we act for a "valid reason" or not, unless we are willing to learn from others by relying on their feedback and critique (SKS 15, 182, 207 / BA, 59, my transl.; cf. SKS 15, 139–40n; Welz 2019: 285). It seems to be for this reason that Kierkegaard (Climacus) says that inwardness without outwardness represents "the most difficult interiority, in which self-deception is easiest" (SKS 7, 369 / CUP1, 406). Indeed, to close oneself off from communication involves demonic self-enclosure (*Indesluttethed*; see SKS 4, 430 / CA, 130; SKS 11, 186 / SUD, 73), which should not be confused with inwardness (discussed on Chapter 8) .

Moreover, *Fear and Trembling* hardly claims that Abraham is given a private revelation. Rather, it only sees what follows *if* we grant such a revelation (Johansen 1988: 100–1). Thus, it makes conditional claims about the consequences of a private revelation that is assumed to be unwavering, unrevisable, and infallible. But Kierkegaard elsewhere views our beliefs as revisable and fallible (cf. SKS 15, 130; Westphal 1996: 119 and 2014: 192–5). He (Climacus) writes that "[e]ven the most certain of all, a revelation, *eo ipso* becomes dialectical when I am to appropriate it . . . As soon as I take away the dialectical, I am superstitious" (SKS 7, 41n / CUP1, 34–5n). Indeed, faith without uncertainty and dialectics involves superstition, deceit, falsity, and narrow-mindedness (SKS 7, 41n, 59, 412 / CUP1, 35n, 55, 454). *Postscript* then goes on to explicitly contrast the finished and completed faith of Abraham with existential faith that is always in a state of becoming, since it remains a normative task that is never finished (SKS 7, 453–4n / CUP1, 500n).

Fear and Trembling assumes – at least hypothetically – that God intervenes directly in Abraham's world, requiring him to sacrifice Isaac (SKS 4, 105, 113–8 / FT, 9, 16–22). But this differs strongly from the hidden God found elsewhere in Kierkegaard's authorship. Mélissa Fox-Muraton (2012: 381) therefore points out that the hidden God "does not manifest himself on Earth; our only means of attaining him is through our [ethical] relations with others."

Finally, *Fear and Trembling* warns explicitly against *imitating* Abraham by killing someone. In an often-overlooked part of the work, Kierkegaard (de silentio) criticizes a sleepless person who is obsessed with Abraham and who wants to imitate him by sacrificing someone (SKS 4, 124–5 / FT, 28–9). The sleepless person is influenced by a priest who praises Abraham. However, the selfsame priest responds by condemning the sleepless imitator: "You despicable man, you scum of society, what devil so possessed you that you want to murder your son" (SKS 4, 124 / FT, 28). Kierkegaard (de silentio) then concludes that the sleepless imitator "probably will be executed or sent to the madhouse" (SKS 4, 125 / FT, 29). However, this is not just a prediction of what will happen; it is also an implicit recognition that the state is justified in punishing the imitator or sending him for psychological treatment.

Thus, no one is justified in imitating the sacrifice of Isaac. Fox-Muraton comments:

> [D]e Silentio confesses that he is incapable of giving an example of a real case to which [the teleological] suspension could be applied, aside from Abraham. He is, moreover, very clear about the fact that it would be not only a serious error but also a sin and an abomination, to try to take Abraham as an example . . . the Biblical texts set out Abraham as the figure of faith . . . whom we are meant merely to *contemplate*, and not as the hero whom we are meant to admire or emulate, or as a representational character with whom we might identify . . . The teleological suspension of the ethical is thus applicable only because Abraham is elected by God – an exceptional circumstance, and by no means an ordinary, quotidian or imitable event. (2012: 372–5)

But even Abraham can be criticized for sacrificing Isaac. In 1851, Kierkegaard is explicit that it would have been "an error on [Abraham's] part," if he were to kill Isaac, since "it was not God's will" that he acted earnestly (*gjorde Alvor*) on "God's requirement . . . to sacrifice Isaac" (SKS 24, 375, NB24:89 / KJN 8, 379). In this passage, Kierkegaard suggests that God never intended the sacrifice, since God's requirement represents *irony*. The very same interpretation of Abraham's sacrifice is developed independently of this passage by Jackson (2010: ch. 6), who argues that God's command to sacrifice Isaac is ironical, and that it breaks with the tradition of child sacrifice. This tradition assumes that God demands child sacrifice, but Abraham realizes that that is not the case and therefore he breaks with tradition (Hösle 1992: 18–19).

But what was Kierkegaard's view of this in 1843 when he wrote *Fear and Trembling*? In 1846, he explicitly distanced himself from both Abraham and de silentio:

> In *Fear and Trembling*, I am just as little, precisely just as little, Johannes de Silentio as the knight of faith he depicts, and in turn just as little the author of the preface to the book. (SKS 7, 570 / CUP1, 626)

Clearly, the pseudonym de silentio is a nonbeliever who largely refrains from concluding, since he mainly presents a dilemma, according to which Abraham is either a murderer or a genuine believer (SKS 4, 126, 150, 183 / FT, 30, 57, 93). Still, Kierkegaard himself concludes in 1843 by saying: "The greatness of Abraham was not that he sacrificed Isaac, but that he believed, that he was glad and prepared" (Pap. IV, B73, my transl.). Even de silentio is explicit that "[i]t is only by faith that one achieves any resemblance to Abraham, not by murder" (SKS 4, 126 / FT, 31). It is only by resigning completely *and* believing (i.e., the double movement of faith) that we may resemble Abraham and be believers in a Judeo-Christian sense.

In *Fear and Trembling*, the story of Abraham entails individual *moral exceptionalism* in which Abraham seems above the general, categorical, moral prohibition on killing (cf. SKS 4, 159 / FT, 66).[22] This radical suspension of the ethical differs from all other cases. Apart from Abraham, *Fear and Trembling* therefore says that religious believers look like a public servant and merchant (*Rodemester* and *Kræmmersjæl*), not like fly-by-nights or itinerant geniuses (*løse Fugle og landstygende Genier*; SKS 4, 133–4, 167 / FT, 39, 75). In addition, the text contrasts the genuine believer, who is "a witness, never the teacher," with sectarianism that make noise; the former is concerned with inwardness, the latter with externalities (SKS 4, 170–1 / FT, 79–80).

Concluding Unscientific Postscript is even clearer, claiming that religiousness is not compatible with murder, since legality is necessary (SKS 7, 453n / CUP1, 500n; more on this in Chapters 7–8). Indeed, we will see that the *Postscript* sketches a moderate suspension of the first ethics that does

22 Fox-Muraton's Kierkegaardian critique of exceptionalism targets a radical suspension of ethics, not a suspension of the first ethics by the second ethics (2018: 8).

not involve any moral exceptionalism. But even Abraham's suspension only entails exceptionalism from the perspective of nonbelievers such as de silentio: for Abraham believes that there is *only apparent* conflict between the prohibition against killing and the command to sacrifice Isaac. He is confident that God will be true to his promise (that "in his seed all the generations of the earth would be blessed") so that Isaac can live to father a holy nation (SKS 4, 114 / FT, 18).

Conclusion: Religion Entails Ethics

The traditional reading and moral exceptionalism are mainly supported by *Fear and Trembling,* and both appear contradicted by Kierkegaard's later works (more on this in the next chapter). Both rely greatly on the *Akedah*, although Abraham is an exceptional individual without sin, guilt, or fallibility who is elected specially by God. Abraham's sacrifice of Isaac is important insofar as it exemplifies religious resignation and faith (i.e., the double movement of faith). But the exceptional command to sacrifice Isaac is problematic as a paradigm case for ethics and religion since no one can be in the situation of Abraham. Neither is it clear that the double movement of faith, as presented in *Fear and Trembling* and later works, needs to break with ethics. Rather, it presupposes the second ethics (see Davenport 2008a; Fremstedal 2014a: ch. 7). For infinite resignation presupposes the highest good that *Fear and Trembling* identifies with eternal happiness and our *telos* (SKS 4, 148 / FT, 54; cf. SKS 7, 372 / CUP1, 409). And this is something that can only be realized with divine assistance. Although there are difficulties with the case of Abraham, Kierkegaard does not endorse moral exceptionalism or anything immoral. Rather, he interprets religion in moral terms by identifying the good with the divine (as we will see in Chapter 7).

CHAPTER 7

Moralized Religion: The Identity of the Good and the Divine

The Book on Adler

Like *Fear and Trembling*, *The Book on Adler* discusses whether a private revelation can break with morality.[1] Specifically, it discusses the private revelation that the Danish Pastor Adolph P. Adler allegedly received from God. For Kierkegaard, however, Adler is not just a special case but also an epigram for the confusion of contemporary Christendom. Specifically, there is a tendency in both Adler and others to confuse the concepts of divine revelation and authority (cf. SKS 15, 106 / BA, 3–4, 21), something that calls for clarity and consistency.[2]

The question is not if it is possible to receive a revelation but rather what a revelation would require of the receiver intellectually and morally. Kierkegaard writes:

> The whole book is basically an ethical inquiry into the concept of a revelation, into what it means to be called by a revelation, into how the one who has had a revelation relates himself to the human race, to the universal. (Pap. VIII–2, B27, 76 / BA, 3)

However, *The Book on Adler* hardly investigates

1. the first-order question of whether Adler received a revelation or not (something that would transcend the limits of human cognition).

Rather, it investigates

[1] *The Book on Adler* was written 1846–47 and edited until 1855 but only published posthumously in 1872, since Kierkegaard was worried about how it could affect Adler personally (cf. BA, vii, xiii–xv). Note that the text in BA *deviates substantially* from SKS. In some – but not all – versions of the manuscript, *The Book on Adler* is attributed to the pseudonym Petrus Minor. Unlike BA, SKS does *not* include this pseudonym, although earlier editions did so (SKS 15, 89–295 / Pap. VII–2, B235). The name "Petrus Minor" suggests that the pseudonym is concerned with authority, apostolicity, and the continued possibility of revelation – although he lacks authority. See Millay 2015: 219.

[2] My discussion here is indebted to Emmanuel 1996; Evans 2006b: 246–52; Fox-Muraton 2018: 11–18.

2. the second-order question of whether he is justified in claiming and believing to have received a revelation or not (cf. SKS 15, 171, 173 / BA, 49, 51; Emmanuel 1996: 37); and
3. if he can be justified in drawing practical conclusions about how he ought to act therefrom (Fox-Muraton 2018: 14).

We cannot know if Adler received a private revelation or not. But we can nevertheless understand and asses its alleged doctrinal (propositional) content, based on Adler's account of it (SKS 15, 216–26 / BA, 176–87). However, this account is so confused and contradictory that not even Adler has reason to believe in it (SKS 15, 171–204, 216–26, 245, 276 / BA, 49–80, 176–87). Specifically, Adler confuses revelation with enthusiasm and being saved. He appears to change and revoke the revelation several times, without acknowledging that he introduces any changes (cf. SKS 15, 195 / BA, 71).

In this context, Kierkegaard argues that not even divine revelation can justify exceptions from morality (Fox-Muraton 2018: 14–17). Instead of supporting moral exceptionalism or a religious suspension of ethics, divine revelation entails a "terrible [moral] responsibility" (SKS 15, 137 / BA, 163). For Kierkegaard, a revelation "would essentially be related to the ethical because . . . this is the divine's medium of communication" (SKS 25, 187, NB27:72 / KJN 9, 188). He therefore concludes:

> The ultimate standard [*sidste Maalestok*], which humans are rated according to, is the ethical, in comparison to which all differences (even that of being God's chosen one in an exceptional sense) are but an infinitesimal amount. (SKS 15, 127, my transl.)

Even if one were to receive a private revelation, this could not justify immoral speech or action. Kierkegaard is therefore clear: "The religious sphere includes or ought to include the ethical" (SKS 15, 106 / BA, 21). Thus, he makes the *normative* claim that justified religion requires ethics.

Kierkegaard (both the pseudonyms Petrus Minor and H. H.) argues that a divine revelation must be completely heterogeneous with, and indifferent to, the domain of politics and power.[3] Therefore, an apostle "would have forfeited his cause" by using "power in the worldly sense" (SKS 11, 109 / WA, 105; Pap. VII–2, B235, 106–7 / BA, 186). The exact same holds for an extraordinaire individual (e.g., Adler) who receives a revelation from God. Kierkegaard therefore argues that the latter must "jest lightly about being victorious in the world, because he knows very well that if only everything is in order with his relation to God, his idea will surely succeed even if he fails" (SKS 15, 132 /

[3] For these pseudonyms, see notes 1 and 4 in the present chapter.

BA, 157). Whether he is Adler or an apostle, the extraordinaire individual must therefore be willing to suffer everything for his cause (SKS 15, 130, 132, 225 / BA, 154, 157, 186). He must then be humble and patient, leaving the matter in God's hands (Pap. VIII–2, B12, 56–7 / BA, 166–7; Evans 2006b: 249).

Based on this, Evans concludes that for Kierkegaard

> a person who has genuinely received a revelation will not use worldly means to ensure the triumph of revelation, but will rest content in God's providence. This person will not manipulate or coerce others into accepting the revelation, and he or she will not fear rejection, confident that the ultimate outcome is in God's hands. (2006b: 248)

Presumably, we should not believe that worldly persons who make use of power and politics are recipients of a revelation, since a revelation (as such) differs essentially from the worldly (as such). This, however, "fits the traditional claim that genuine sanctity or holiness is one criterion of a true prophet" (Evans 2006b: 249). Indeed, the above represents a *negative criterion* that indicates the falsity of claims concerning a putative revelation. Still, it is not perfectly clear if it indicates that (1) one is not justified in claiming or believing to have received a revelation in the first place; *or* if (2) one is drawing wrong practical conclusions from the revelation. Kierkegaard suggests that Adler is mistaken in *both* regards, since his confused words and deeds undermine and contradict his claim to be an extraordinaire individual who receives a private revelation.

Two Ethical-Religious Essays

Two Ethical-Religious Essays (written 1847, published 1849) is based on a part of *The Book on Adler*. The first part of these essays, "Does a Human Being Have the Right to Let Himself be Put to Death for the Truth," asks if violence can be justified religiously (Fox-Muraton 2018: 19–20). Specifically, the text (attributed to the pseudonym H. H.[4]) asks:

1. Can one ever be justified in knowing that one possesses the truth and has privileged access to it?
2. Can one be justified in making others guilty of the crime of murder by letting oneself be put to death for the truth?

[4] The character, personality, and identity of the pseudonym H. H. seems irrelevant to the content of the argument. See Martens 2015: 93–4.

The discussion assumes that we have *categorical duties* both toward truth and toward others (SKS 11, 73–6 / WA, 68–72). Thus, it assumes that we have unconditional reasons and obligations both to seek truth and to care for others. It is then argued that it is only justifiable to let oneself be put to death for the truth if both of the two following conditions are met:

A. One can be justified in knowing that one has a privileged access to truth that is clearly not accessible to others, since one knows something others cannot know (e.g., by receiving a private revelation).
B. On the basis of this knowledge (#A), one is morally justified in becoming a martyr for truth who is put to death at the hands of others, thereby making them guilty of murder.

The idea here is that becoming a martyr for truth represents a moral sacrifice and achievement, in which the martyr suffers precisely because he is doing good. However, the text categorically denies that any of these conditions can possibly be met by any human being (although it can be met by Christ). For no one can be justified in thinking that he has a privileged accessed to truth that places him on a fundamentally different level than his neighbors (SKS 11, 77–9, 87 / WA, 73–5, 83). And no one is justified in contributing to the moral corruption of others (unless he can forgive them as Christ does). Therefore, the categorical conclusion follows that "a human being does not have the right to let himself be put to death for the truth" (SKS 11, 88 / WA, 84).

More generally, the implication is that one cannot justify violence or anything categorically immoral because one thinks that one possesses some truth. Indeed, the whole argument presupposes that our categorical moral obligations cannot be overridden by any claims to possess truth (SKS 11, 73–89 / WA, 68–85). Fox-Muraton therefore concludes:

> [I]t is never justifiable to use religious grounding or the appeal to religious authority to exempt oneself from the sphere of moral responsibility toward others . . . one never has the right to intentionally provoke his own being put to death in virtue of some higher authority . . . While Kierkegaard's writings do not give us any precise specification as to what can and ought to be considered a just cause, they do, however, offer a set of meta-principles which can be used to evaluate our moral responsibilities. (2019b: 366–7)

Fox-Muraton argues that this conclusion holds both for individuals and groups who claim to have a privileged access to truth (2018: 24–5).

Pseudonymous Writings (1843–1846)

However, it is not just these lesser-known writings that criticize moral exceptionalism or attempts to let religion override ethics. The better-known pseudonymous writings also criticize moral exceptionalism and religious attempts to override morality. By targeting mysticism, *Either/Or, Part II* criticizes attempts to relate to God isolated from other human beings. It is claimed that such attempts are not only morally objectionable but also that they reduce God to an idol (SKS 3, 230–3 / EO2, 241–4). The clear implication is that a genuine relationship to God requires a moral relation to one's fellow human beings, something that anticipates later works.

Concluding Unscientific Postscript offers an important discussion of *Fear and Trembling*. As we will see (in Chapter 8), the *Postscript* is explicit that religiousness is not compatible with being a murderer, since moral legality – doing the right thing – is necessary yet insufficient for religiousness (SKS 7, 453n / CUP1, 500n). Immediately after saying this, the *Postscript* criticizes the account of Abraham in *Fear and Trembling* for being a "rash anticipation" of religious existence that falsely depicts it as something finished and completed, rather than something that is always in a state of becoming (SKS 7, 453–4n / CUP1, 500n). Abraham thus seems too idealized and perfect to be realistic or even human (see Rocca 2002). *Postscript* then offers the following interpretation of the "teleological suspension":

> The teleological suspension of the ethical must have an even more definite religious expression [than being a mere passing thought]. The ethical is then present at every moment with its infinite requirement, but the individual is not capable of fulfilling it ... The suspension consists in the individual's finding himself in a state exactly opposite to what the ethical requires. (SKS 7, 242 / CUP1, 266–7)

The next paragraph then interprets our failure to fulfill the ethical in terms of sinfulness:

> Duty is the absolute, its requirement the absolute, and yet the individual is prevented from fulfilling it ... The dreadful exemption from doing the ethical, the individual's heterogeneity with the ethical, this suspension from the ethical, is sin as a state in a human being. (SKS 7, 243 / CUP1, 267)

The "teleological suspension" cannot possibly negate ethics, since it *represents* the second ethics.[5] Ethics is therefore supported – not contradicted – by

[5] This supports the Pauline-Lutheran interpretation of *Fear and Trembling* as a work that concerns soteriology and eschatology (see SKS 24, 154, 163–4, NB22:92, NB22:112, NB22:115 / KJN 8, 92, 112, 117; Green 2011: 167–94; Westphal 2014: Part 1).

religion. Elsewhere, the *Postscript* states that "there is nothing between [the individual] and God but the ethical" (SKS 7, 128, cf. 131, 144 / CUP1, 137, cf. 140, 155), claiming that "[t]he ethical is and remains the highest task assigned to every human being" (SKS 7, 141 / CUP1, 151). Both here and elsewhere, Kierkegaard (Climacus) views the ethical as necessary for the religious, describing the religious stage as "the ethico-religious sphere" (SKS 7, 510n / CUP1, 561n). Someone who lacks an awareness of ethics thereby lacks an awareness of God (SKS 7, 222–3 / CUP1, 244; Evans 2006a: 88).[6]

Signed Writings (1847–53)

Like *Postscript*, *Works of Love* claims that conscience involves taking part in God's moral knowledge (SKS 7, 144 / CUP1, 155; SKS 9, 145, 370 / WL, 143, 377). Indeed, "to relate to God is precisely to have conscience" and that "[i]n the conscience it is God who looks at a person; so now in everything the person must look at him" (SKS 9, 145, 370 / WL, 143, 377; cf. SKS 10, 202–3 / CD, 192–3). Kierkegaard writes:

> A person should begin with loving the unseen, God, because then he will himself learn what it is to love. But that he actually loves the unseen will be known by his loving the brother he sees; the more he loves the unseen, the more he will love the people he sees. It is not the reverse, that the more he rejects those he sees, the more he loves the unseen, since in that case God is changed into an unreal something, a delusion . . . God demands nothing for himself, although he demands everything from you. (SKS 9, 161 / WL, 160–1)

Neighbor-love depends on God, but we only love God by loving our neighbor. We serve God by serving our neighbor, and sacrifice to God by reconciling with our brother (SKS 10, 43–4, 292 / CD, 32–3, 273–4). Therefore,

> With love of God and love of one's neighbor it is the same as with double doors that open up at the same time, so that it is impossible to open the one without also opening the other, and impossible to close the one without also closing the other. (SKS 24, 165, NB22:117 / KJN 8, 163)

Thus, "Kierkegaard repudiates the idea that duties towards God could replace or compete with duties towards one's fellow humans" (Evans

[6] However, *Postscript* associates the term "ethico-religious" with natural religion, although it seems fitting for all views which combine ethics and religion.

2006b: 212). However, love of God seems prior to neighbor-love conceptually although not temporally. As the good, God is a middle term that mediates between different individuals, making us all into human beings who are created in his image (SKS 9, 94, 111, 124, 219–26, 299 / WL, 88–9, 106–7, 121, 216–24, 301; cf. SKS 10, 43–4 / CD, 32–3). And we can only resemble God by loving our neighbor (SKS 9, 69–70 / WL, 62–3).

Substantial conflict between morality and religion seems possible if God is not good and almighty but rather a mighty tyrant that we must accept for prudential reasons. Despite appearances, *Fear and Trembling* tries to rule out this scenario by stressing that Abraham believes in divine love (Pap. IV, B66; cf. SKS 4, 129–30 / FT, 34–5). But the pseudonymous author of *Fear and Trembling*, de silentio, is a nonbeliever who does not share this belief in divine love. Therefore, he characterizes Abraham's faith as absurd. However, it is only from this nonreligious perspective that there is apparent conflict between loving God and loving one's neighbor (Jackson 2010: ch. 6). Kierkegaard later elaborates on this topic of believing in divine love in *Upbuilding Discourses in Various Spirits*:

> [I]f you have experienced a human life's heaviest moment, when all became dark for your soul, as if there were no love in heaven or as if he who is in heaven were nevertheless not really love, when it seemed to you as if there were a choice you had to make, the dreadful choice between being in the wrong and gaining God or being in the right and losing God – is it then not true that you have found the blessedness of heaven in choosing the former, or rather in this, that it really was not a choice, that on the contrary it was heaven's eternal claim on you, its claim on your soul, that there must be no doubt, that God was love! (SKS 8, 364 / UD, 267–8)

Kierkegaard continues by contrasting the Christian idea that God is love with paganism:

> Alas, although many call themselves Christians and yet may seem to be living in uncertainty as to whether God actually is love, it would truly be better if they made the love blaze just by the thought of paganism's horror: that he who holds the fate of everything and also your fate in his hand is ambivalent, that his love is not a fatherly embrace but a constraining trap, that his secret nature is not eternal clarity but concealment, that the deepest ground of his nature is not love but a cunning impossible to understand. We are not, after all, required to be able to understand the rule of God's love, but we certainly are required to be able to believe, and believing [*troende forstaae*], that he is love. It is not dreadful that you are unable to understand God's decrees if he nevertheless is eternal love, but it is dreadful if you could not understand them because he is cunning. (SKS 8, 365 / UD, 268)

This quote suggests that, since God's very nature is love, he cannot require anything morally bad of us; even though we may not understand all he does or requires.

The interrelationship of the moral and the divine is also apparent in Kierkegaard's understanding of individual accountability to God:

> Each human being, as a single individual, must account for himself to God; and while no third person dares to intrude into this settling of accounts between God and the single individual [*den Enkelte*], the speaker dares to and ought to remind us with his question that this is not forgotten ... in eternity everyone as a single individual must make an accounting to God ... And eternity will bring out before his consciousness everything he has done as an individual ... What else, indeed, is the accounting of eternity than that the voice of conscience is installed eternally in its eternal right to be the only voice! What else is it than that in eternity there is an infinite silence in which the conscience speakers only with the single individual about whether he as an individual has done good or evil. (SKS 8, 227–8 / UD, 127–8; cf. SKS 11, 235 / SUD, 124)

Kierkegaard continues by saying that conscience is often suppressed in temporality. Yet, he insists that the individual "does not get rid of it; it is still his, or, rather he belongs to it ... in eternity the conscience is the only voice heard ... there is no place to escape it" (SKS 8, 228 / UD, 129). The conclusion is that conscience and God are only concerned with "what he as a single individual has said and done and thought – good or evil" (SKS 8, 229 / UD, 129).

The same point is made again in *Christian Discourses*: "What is the only distinction God makes? The one between right and wrong. And what distinction does he make? That he is wrath and malediction upon the one who does wrong" (SKS 10, 232 / CD, 224).[7] In 1849 again, he stresses, "the only thing [God] looks at is the ethical" (SKS 22, 351, NB14:13 / KJN 6, 356). *The Sickness unto Death* makes a related point:

> From the Christian point of view, everything ... ought to serve for upbuilding ... It is precisely Christianity's relation to life (in contrast to a scholarly distance from life) or the ethical aspect [*Side*] of Christianity that is upbuilding. (SKS 11, 117 / SUD, 5)

The ethical is not just one aspect of Christianity since it is identified with the upbuilding that "everything ... ought to serve." The text later describes

[7] Immortality *is* the separation of the just from the unjust (SKS 10, 212–16 / CD, 202–8).

the ethico-religious "'thou shalt' . . . as the sole regulative aspect of man's relationship to God. This 'thou shalt' must be present in any determination of the religious" (SKS 11, 226 / SUD, 115). In 1852, Kierkegaard insists that the meaning of Christianity "arranges everything ethically; all [humans are] alike, the ethical alone decides the difference" (SKS 25, 10, NB26:4 / KJN 9, 7). In 1853, he concludes,

> The medium, the sole medium, through which God communicates with "humanity," the only thing he will talk about with humanity, is: the ethical. But in order to speak ethically of the ethical . . . it is necessary that everything else be absolutely relegated to the level of infinite unimportance. Stick to the point . . . – that is, stick to the ethical. (SKS 25, 186, NB27:72 / KJN 9, 187)

Here Kierkegaard claims that God only speaks of ethics and that anything else is totally unimportant or indifferent. Clearly, his God is still the *moral God.* However, Christianity is concerned with personal salvation and immortality, not just with moral action and character formation. But salvation and immortality involve a moral judgment based on divine justice *and* grace (cf. SKS 20, 289, NB4:5 / CD, 378; SKS 8, 227–8 / UD, 127–8; SKS 18, 309–10, JJ:508 / KJN 2, 284–5). And faith in it is morally advantageous, since it avoids demoralization and despair (see Chapter 10).

Kierkegaard's emphasis on the interconnection of religion and the ethical is also expressed in his response to critique of religion based on modern science. The 1853 passage quoted above responds to such critique by arguing that it is ethically indifferent whether science supports geocentrism or heliocentrism (SKS 25, 187, NB27:72 / KJN 9, 188). For Kierkegaard the scientific critique of the supernatural elements of revelation masks a desire to remove the core of Christianity, namely the ethical:

> [T]here is a profound cunning in . . . objections from the natural sciences [concerning inaccurate explanations of natural phenomena]. For, indeed – even after one concedes, on the greatest possible scale, that the natural sciences are right with respect to revelation – what remains entirely unchanged, is the Christian ethic, its requirement to die away, etc., etc. – natural science, after all, has made no corrective discoveries in this connection. But that is not what people want: they want to enjoy life in pagan style, and to that end they want to get rid of [Christianity]: but half-afraid of [Christianity] as they still are, people hypocritically want to do it – on the basis of science. (SKS 25, 187, NB27:72 / KJN 9, 188)

Discussion

For Kierkegaard, religion is essentially different from science (in the wide sense of *Wissenschaft,* which includes the humanities).[8] Science concerns explanatory and descriptive questions, whereas religion concerns normative ethics.[9] Clearly, Kierkegaard is concerned with ethics not just in the narrow sense, which concerns moral duties, but also in the wide sense, which concerns living well, authentic selfhood, the proper use of freedom, and living in a meaningful and valuable manner (cf. Wood 2016: 125). For him, this wide notion of ethics seems to coincide with religiousness and ought-all-things considered practical normativity. It is very difficult to see how the 1846–53 passages above can be reconciled with the traditional reading (introduced by Brandes), since Kierkegaard rules out both that ethics and religion diverge *and* that religion overrides ethics. Indeed, he often criticizes religious views on ethical grounds. As we have seen (in Chapter 5), he criticizes Christian eudaimonism for its (alleged) egoism and instrumentalism concerning moral virtue. In addition, he attacks believers who think they are justified in letting themselves be put to death for the truth. This all implies that some religious views are false simply because they are morally inadequate. This criticism thus presupposes that religion must be compatible with ethics. For him, justified religion therefore requires ethics (SKS 15, 106 / BA, 21).

For Kierkegaard, religiousness is a way of living rather than a theoretical belief about the world. It concerns virtues such as faith, hope, and charity rather than mythology or cosmology. He therefore agrees fully with Kant that religious texts should be read morally or existentially as something that concerns how I live my life instead of being read literally or in a historical-critical manner.[10] In 1854, he therefore describes Christian faith as an ethical determination (*Bestemmelse*) of the relationship between God and man:

> In the New Testament, faith is not an intellectual category but an ethical category [*Bestemmelse*] designating the relation of personality betw[een] God and a hum[an] being. Therefore faith is required (as an expression of devotion) – to believe against reason, to believe even though one cannot see

[8] This idea is particularly associated with liberal theology after Kant. See Dorrien 2012.

[9] However, *Wissenschaft* includes different forms of normative theory (e.g., legal theory, political philosophy, and economy), something that Kierkegaard may overlook. Yet he could be right that *Wissenschaft* does not include ethical normativity (or even ought all-things-considered normativity), unless ethics is seen as a *Wissenschaft* (as claimed in SKS 4, 323–6 / CA, 16–20).

[10] Bubbio 2014: 100; Dalferth 2015: 70–5. Kant and Kierkegaard here anticipate Bultmann's existential interpretation of scripture. See Bayer 2007: 161–8.

> (entirely a category of personality and the ethical). (SKS 27, 616, Papir 486 / KJN 11.2, 318, 320)

This passage speaks of believing against reason, although it may not amount to more than belief that is based on practical considerations instead of epistemic evidence and intellectual considerations (see Chapter 13). In any case, Kierkegaard relies on an ethical interpretation of Christianity that is modern and post-Kantian (see Dorrien 2012: ch. 5). Wood writes,

> Kant, like Kierkegaard, regards all religion as entirely a matter of "subjectivity". It has to do with one's way of regarding one's duties, and with one's moral disposition or attitude in fulfilling duties. Religiousness, then, is solely a matter of a person's subjective attitude towards the moral life. A moral agent is religious if she associates her moral duties with the thought that they are commanded by God, and observes her duties in that spirit. (2000: 498)

For both Kant and Kierkegaard, religion concerns our subjective attitude towards the moral life; it concerns dispositions, intentions, and characters that are scrutinized by God (R 6:47–8; MM 6:438–9; SKS 7, 144 / CUP1, 155; SKS 9, 145, 370 / WL, 143, 377). Like Kant, Kierkegaard holds that religion is based on moral knowledge of what to do. Specifically, we become aware of God by reflecting on our moral tasks.[11] Particularly the *moral gap* between our moral obligations and our natural capabilities is decisive for Christian ethics (Quinn 1998; Hare 2002b; Evans 2006a: 49; Stern 2012: 204–16). We have seen that Kierkegaard stresses that having an "anguished conscience," that is, being conscious of one's failure to meet the requirement of the law, is a prior condition for serious interest in the Christian offer of salvation (SKS 20, 69, NB:79 / KJN 4, 68). The conversion to Christianity and the reception of divine grace is preceded and motivated by the failure of the first ethics.

Still, the second ethics cannot eradicate the first ethics. The latter is necessary for motivating conversions to Christianity and it is also needed in the public realm and outside of Christian communities. Although the first ethics on its own collapses, it is still necessary for becoming a Christian. This may even be the reason why *Stages on Life's Way* describes the ethical as "only a transition sphere" (SKS 6, 439 / SLW, 476). This is sometimes taken to mean that ethics is left behind by religion (see Brandes 1877: 185–6), although nothing could be further from the truth if Kierkegaard is right.

11 Cf. Evans 2009: 113–4. Evans (2010) defends this view of religious knowledge as based on moral knowledge.

The Euthyphro Dilemma

In his notes on Leibniz's *Theodicy*, Kierkegaard asks: "Is the Good good because God wills it to be, or is it good in and of itself?" (SKS 19, 408, Not13:43 / KJN 3, 406). Theological voluntarism holds the former, whereas moral realism and Platonism hold the latter. Many assume that Kierkegaard is a theological voluntarist, but the main proponent of this reading, David Wisdo, admits that Kierkegaard is neither clear nor explicit on this point. Wisdo (1987: 222–3) merely says that Kierkegaard *probably* grounds goodness in divinity or that he *suggests* it.

Recently, Stern argues that Kierkegaard's position is more moderate since it is an intermediary view between voluntarism and realism. On this reading, Kierkegaard allows that what is right or good is independent of God's command, although it only becomes obligatory as a result of the command. Moral obligations depend on divine commands, but God commands actions because they are right in themselves and because he is good. Stern explains:

> God puts us under obligations but without operating outside any prior order of value or norms, even thought that order may not be wholly within our grasp as finite beings. As a result ... the Euthyphro objection to Kierkegaard's position drops away.[12]

Religion cannot conflict with ethics, if God is morally good and commands something that is antecedently moral. Nor can religion override – or contradict – ethics, if ethics is derived from God's will, as theological voluntarism maintains. Not even voluntarism can therefore allow conflict between ethics and religion since morality is here derived from God's will. At least, a good and omnipotent God cannot allow serious conflict between morality and religion. Timothy Jackson is therefore right that "what is forbidden by Christian ethics must also be forbidden by Christian faith, because God is the author of both" (2010: 193). Both interpretations – both theological voluntarism and Stern's intermediary view – thus undermine the traditional reading of Kierkegaard, in which religion overrides ethics normatively. On both readings, a conflict between ethics and religion would imply that our relation to God is *conflicted*, either because we misunderstand God or because God himself is somehow conflicted.[13]

[12] Stern 2012: 221–2. Stern argues that the Euthyphro dilemma has limited effectiveness, as it only really bites against radical theological voluntarism. It is mainly the latter that has problems with arbitrary, abhorrent, and heteronomous commands. See also Davenport 2008a: 232–3; Bubbio 2014: 97 (referencing Hannay).

[13] The latter possibility seems absurd; see Pap. x–6, B72, 82; Jackson 2010: 194.

However, there is a *third* reading. Jackson describes this as the identification of the divine and moral goodness:

> [F]or the Augustinian the dilemma is malformed. God *is* Goodness and, as such, the source and destiny of all that is. God does not discover goodness outside Himself and belatedly enjoin it; nor does He artificially order that evil be good. Goodness and God are the same, so there is no need and no way to prioritize them relative to each other. Asking about facts or values without God is like asking about space or time without the Big Bang that brought them simultaneously into being . . . once we see that, in God's necessary existence, scientific fact and moral value are one, we realize that the ancient Euthyphro dilemma is a nonstarter. (2014: 539)

This Augustinian position seems essentially identical to Kierkegaard's position (although he sees God as necessary morally, not metaphysically). Goodness is neither prior to God's will, as Stern and Davenport think, nor does it result from His will, as Wisdo assumes. Instead, the good and divine are *identical.* This is exactly the view that Kierkegaard puts forward in many different passages that consistently *identify* the good and the divine. In 1843, he (de silento) writes:

> The Ethical is the universal, and as such it is also the divine. Thus it is proper to say that every duty is essentially duty towards God . . . "God" in a totally abstract sense is here understood as the Divine – that is, the universal, that is, the duty. (SKS 4, 160 / FT, 68)

In 1844, Kierkegaard speaks of the "sacred word[s]" of virtue, love and fear of God (SKS 5, 355 / EUD, 370). This suggests that "virtue" and "love" are sacred, because divine. In 1845, he (Frater Taciturnus) claims that "the ethical . . . requirement is so infinite that the individual always goes bankrupt" (SKS 6, 439 / SLW, 476). In 1846, he (Climacus) similarly says that "[t]he ethical is . . . present at every moment with its infinite requirement" (SKS 7, 242 / CUP1, 266–7; cf. SKS 9, 252 / WL, 252). The ethical is not only infinite but also "absolute" and therefore "infinitely valid in itself" (SKS 7, 133 / CUP1, 142).

Specifically, the moral task seems *infinite* by virtue of being

1. *divine*, since the good and the divine are identical;
2. *inexhaustible*, since we can never finish the ethical task (SKS 7, 143 / CUP1, 153–4);
3. categorically *overriding*, since strict moral duties trump all other considerations; and

4. highly *demanding*, since it requires everything of us and involves a moral gap between our moral obligations and our natural capabilities as finite beings with moral character flaws (cf. Quinn 1998; Hare 2002b; Evans 2006a: 49; Stern 2012: 204–17).

In 1847, Kierkegaard himself states, "That the good is its own reward . . . is eternally certain. There is nothing so certain; it is not more certain that there is a God, because this is one and the same" (SKS 8, 151 / UD, 39). Indeed, it is impossible to choose between God and moral rightness, since God himself *is* love (SKS 8, 364 / UD, 268).

Here and elsewhere (SKS 9, 252 / WL, 252), Kierkegaard *identifies* God with moral goodness in general and charity in particular. His view seems to be that morality and charity *orient* us towards the good, which is identical to God. Specifically, we relate to God, and take part in his moral knowledge, with our conscience (see SKS 7, 144 / CUP1, 155; SKS 9, 145, 370 / WL, 143, 377). Although God differs from creation, we are nevertheless created in his image, with his law written in our hearts (cf. SKS 5, 91 / EUD, 84). Indeed, we even resemble God insofar as we are charitable (SKS 9, 69–70 / WL, 62–3). Still, it is God, rather than the divine source of love within us, that is identical to the good. Rudd comments:

> Kierkegaard . . . follows Plato in seeing the Good as "Eternal" and distinct from particular goods. Furthermore – now following a long tradition of Christian (and for that matter, Jewish and Islamic) Platonism – he goes on to identity the Good with God. (2012: 45–6)[14]

Evans writes:

> Climacus actually seems to identify God with the ethical at various points . . . [In *Purity of Heart*,] Douglas Steere was correct to translate "*det Gode*" as "the Good", indicating the very specific character of what Kierkegaard is discussing. It seems clear enough in many cases that the Good is identical with "the Eternal" or with God. One might compare Kierkegaard here with Robert Adams in *Finite and Infinite Goods*, who consciously evokes Plato by capitalizing "the Good" . . . In fact, I believe that implicit in *Works of Love* is an identification of God with the Good, an identification that . . . is made explicit in *Purity of Heart*. (2006a: 88, 105n, 183)

Heiko Schulz (2015: 120, 123), on the other hand, contends that "moral goodness (viz. love)" is "the sole *substantial* attribute of God, so that

[14] For Kierkegaard's Christian Platonism, see also Walker 1972; Evans 1999: 58–64; Wyller 1999: 190–206 (who was a Plato scholar); Rudd 2012: 49–50, 141–61.

[divine] omnipotence is but one of its properties"; goodness therefore entails and functions as a sufficient condition for God's almightiness.[15]

Thus, Kierkegaard seems to follow Christian Platonism not only by accepting moral realism but also by identifying God with the good. But in any case, none of these interpretations are compatible with the traditional reading of Kierkegaard (originating with Brandes 1877). None of them give *conceptual room* for conflict between ethics and religion. First, theological voluntarism does not allow such conflict since it derives ethics from God's will (cf. Jackson 2010: 193). Second, Stern's intermediary reading cannot allow such conflict either, since God is morally good and therefore only commands actions that are right in themselves. Finally, any such conflict is precluded by the identity of the good and the divine.

We should thus not attribute to Kierkegaard conflict between ethics (as such) and religion (as such) or the overriding of ethics by religion. Instead, there is conflict *internal* to the ethico-religious since it is different interpretations of the ethico-religious that conflict with each other. In any case, Kierkegaard is explicit that God is only concerned with ethics (SKS 8, 228–9 / UD, 129; SKS 10, 232 / CD, 224). For him, there are no higher standards than the divine moral standards (see SKS 7, 133–41 / CUP1, 142–51; SKS 15, 127). The question of what we ought to do all-things-considered is then a specifically ethico-religious question.[16] Indeed, a God who reconciles morality and prudence would support the overridingness of morality, without giving up prudential rationality and ought-all-things-considered rationality (cf. Hare 2002b; Fremstedal 2014a: ch. 6).

Still, it is not perfectly clear how the content of the first and second ethics relate to each other. Some think that the content is *identical*, whereas others think that Christian ethics has a *more specific and demanding* character that involves suffering and sacrifice based on the imitation of Christ.[17] The first ethics includes a natural understanding of goodness and divinity that is limited by human finitude or even sinfulness. The second

15 Dalferth (2015: 89) argues that Kierkegaard "understands God not as a perfect being but as the fundamental dynamic reality of love, without which nothing else could and would exist . . . God is . . . the infinite or eternal actuality of creative and transforming love: a love that is self-communicating and the source of all life and love in heaven and on earth."

16 Existential questions are therefore ethico-religious questions for Kierkegaard (cf. Dalferth 2015: 75). Existential authenticity is nothing beyond or above ethico-religious normativity.

17 Following Davenport (2008a: 218–19), Krishek (2009: 106) suggests that the content remains the same. Also, Piety (2010: 128) thinks the content is "essentially the same," whereas Evans (2006a: 110–11, 146–55, 161) thinks that the second ethics *clarifies, specifies, and corrects* the first ethics. Quinn (1998: 374), however, takes the second ethics to appear harsh, offensive, and demanding to non-Christian ethics that does not allow recourse to divine grace. See also Irwin 2011: vol. III, 313–19; Stern 2012: 223.

ethics, by contrast, is based on divine revelation and seems to add content that is more specific and demanding than the content of the first ethics. *The Sickness unto Death*, for instance, indicates that suicide is permissible within the first ethics and impermissible within Christian ethics (SKS 11, 161, 163–4 / SUD, 46, 48–9). Thus, the first and second ethics give two different interpretations of moral goodness, which overlap at least partially; the second ethics seems to retain and transform the first ethics, at least in part.

However, several commentators associate the first ethics with moral impartiality and *universalism*, and the second ethics with *particularism*. *Either/Or, Part II* and *Fear and Trembling* both identify the ethical with the universal, something that is reminiscent of Kantian-Hegelian ethics (Knappe 2004: 77–86; Irwin 2011: vol. III, 304–9). Judge William, notably, emphasizes that the individual should become the universal man by doing his duty; particularity should be taken over and reformed so that it becomes compatible with universality (SKS 3, 248–51, 276–7, 285 / EO2, 261–4, 292–3, 302).

The second ethics, by contrast, is often interpreted as a form of moral particularism in which moral obligations and callings can be unique to the individual (Evans 2006a: 15, 170–9; cf. Davenport 2013: 245–6). Indeed, Kierkegaard writes: "[A]t every person's birth there comes into existence an eternal purpose for that person, for that person in particular. Faithfulness to oneself with respect to this is the highest a person can do" (SKS 8, 198 / UD, 93). Particularist readings are often based on the concept of exception (*Undtagelse*), seeing the religious stage as an exception from the universal and the ethical (see Brandes 1877: 186). However, it is difficult to find good examples of such exceptions apart from Abraham's sacrifice of Isaac and Søren's alleged sacrifice of Regine (see Buber 2002: 60–9). These examples do not justify moral exceptionalism; not even moral particularism (e.g., Aristotelianism) allows such exceptionalism. Still, particularism could constrain how we fulfill our imperfect duties. And in some cases, unique vocations could probably rule out certain social roles as inappropriate for specific individuals. In any case, Kierkegaard scholars should clarify the relations between moral universalism, particularism, exceptionalism, partiality, and impartiality.

Presumably, the second ethics modifies and reinterprets the notion of goodness from the first ethics, rather than contradicting it. It seems clear that there must be both some continuity and discontinuity for this approach to work. Evans argues that the second ethics answers to problems implicit in the first ethics, while going beyond it by completing, clarifying, specifying, and correcting it (2006a: 103, 110–11, 146–55, 161; cf. Irwin 2011: vol. III, 313–24; Stern 2012: 223). However, Kierkegaard's non-Christian pseudonyms tend to stress the discontinuity and incongruity between the first and second ethics by depicting revelation and the *Akedah* as something absurd that offends natural man. However, we will see that the pseudonyms stand in danger of pushing this approach into the extreme, unless read as a corrective against those who represent the opposite approach by viewing Christian revelation as being merely continuous with pagan categories. Even though faith appears absurd to nonbelievers, it is not absurd to believers, as we will see in Chapters 11–13.

Conclusion: A Myth in the Kierkegaard Literature

Despite all the attention given to the second ethics, Kierkegaard's identification of the good and divine, ethics and religion, has received relatively little attention. One explanation lies in the tendency to interpret the first ethics as secular ethics (Quinn 1998: 349; cf. Lübcke 2006); another lies in the traditional reading of Kierkegaard with its emphasis on the "teleological suspension" in *Fear and Trembling*.

If we interpret *Fear and Trembling* in terms of the other works, as Davenport and others do, this has the advantage of ascribing to Kierkegaard a much more consistent view that is less problematic ethically and rationally than the traditional reading. If we take *Fear and Trembling* to contradict my reading (and Davenport's reading), we end with a picture of Kierkegaard that appears less consistent and more provocative. In any case, the traditional reading has less support in Kierkegaard's texts than the moralist reading that I am suggesting. Philosophically, the traditional reading appears more problematic than my reading, since it implies that ethics can be (partially) overridden by religion – something that is practically dangerous, rationally problematic, and very difficult to defend. We therefore have both philosophical and textual reasons for replacing the traditional reading. It is not clear that there are theological reasons for protesting against this, unless we dismiss religious ethics in general or the overridingness of morality and the identification of the good and the divine in particular. At least, that seems to be Kierkegaard's view.

PART III

"Subjectivity, Inwardness, Is Truth"

CHAPTER 8

"Hidden Inwardness" and Humor: Kantian Ethics and Religion

Background: The Concept of Inwardness

In *Concluding Unscientific Postscript*, Kierkegaard (Climacus) complains that we have "forgotten what it is to exist and what inwardness means" (SKS 7, 455–8 / CUP1, 502–5). Hidden inwardness is described as the true religiousness, which uses all its tricks (*Kunst*) to prevent it from being noticed (SKS 7, 430 / CUP1, 475). Still, the meaning of "inwardness" is hardly clear, perhaps precisely because it is hidden and forgotten.

Recently, Alastair Hannay described Kierkegaard's concept of inwardness as follows:

> "Inwardness" is by no means a perfect translation of "Inderlighed". As with Hegel's *Innerlichkeit*, the sense is not that of inward-directedness . . . [but of] an inner warmth, sincerity, seriousness and wholeheartedness in one's own concern for what matters, a "heartfeltness" not applied to something but which comes *from* within. However, since "inwardness" has become a standard translation for Kierkegaard's "Inderlighed" and in this sense even finds a place in the *Oxford English Dictionary*, it has been retained here. (Hannay 2009: xxxviii–xxxix)

In the late eighteenth century, the Danish Wolffians and Kantians coined many Danish philosophical terms (cf. Høffding 1909: 16, 21, 26–7; Thuborg 1951: 17–18, 121–49, 181; Holm 1967: 13, 33–43; Koch 2003). *Inderlighed* in particular is a Danish equivalent of the German *Innerlichkeit* and *Innigkeit*, terms Kantians and idealists associated with a moral-religious character or disposition (*Gesinnung*) that is hidden. Although Kant repeatedly uses the term "inward [*innerlich*]," (MM 6:222, 306, 354, 357, 377, 418, 441, 463, 470) he prefers the term *Innigkeit* instead of *Innerlichkeit*. Still, he uses *Innigkeit*, not in the sense of intimacy but in the sense of inwardness. Therefore, he speaks of "the inwardness of a benevolent disposition [*der Innigkeit der wohlwollenden Gesinnung*]" (MM 6:456). Like Kierkegaard, he claims that "the outer . . . does not disclose the inwardness of the [moral] disposition [*der innern sittlichen Gesinnung*]" (R 6:63, cf. 95, 99).[1] Indeed, "when moral worth is at issue, what counts is not actions, which one sees, but those inner principles of actions that one does not see" (G 4:407). We do not know hearts and reins – neither in our own case nor in the case of others (R 6:47–8).[2]

Hegel claims that Kant "revived the consciousness" of "absolute inwardness," associating inwardness with Kant's principle of freedom and the independence of reason:

> The main effect of Kant's philosophy has been that it has revived the consciousness of this absolute inwardness [*Innerlichkeit*]. Although, because of its abstraction, this inwardness cannot develop itself into anything and cannot produce by its own means any determinations, either cognitions or moral laws, still it altogether refuses to allow something that has the character of outwardness to have full play in it, and be valid for it. From now on the principle of the independence of reason, of its absolute inward autonomy [*absoluten Selbständigkeit*], must be regarded as the universal principle of philosophy, and as one of the assumptions of our times.[3]

However, rather than using an idiosyncratic terminology, Kierkegaard uses the terms Kantians and idealists developed in order to describe the distinction between the free, moral disposition and intersubjective phenomena, as well as the related distinction between internal freedom (*homo noumenon*) and external freedom (independence from being constrained by another's choice).[4] The distinction between the inner (*det Indvortes*) and the external (*det Udvortes*) in Kierkegaard (and Climacus in particular) seems to correspond to Kant's distinction between the supersensible (*übersinnliche*)

[1] Henrich argues that in the *Inquiry Concerning the Distinctness of the Principles of Natural Theology and Morality*, Kant admired Francis Hutcheson's recognition of the "original inwardness of the ethical [*ursprünglichen Innerlichkeit des Sittlichen*]." See Henrich 1957–58: 64, my transl.

[2] Kant presents his account of the disposition or character as a philosophical reconstruction of the biblical idea that only God knows hearts and reins (MM 6:438–9). I prefer "hearts and reins" (King James Bible) to "hearts and minds." The former is closer to Kant and Kierkegaard, since "reins" means not only the seat of feelings and passions but "kidneys," like Kant's "*Nieren*" and Kierkegaard's "*Nyrer.*"

[3] Hegel 1991b: §60, 107; cf. Hegel 1991c: §60, 85. Note that Hegel and Kierkegaard both view Socrates as the founder of inwardness and subjectivity. See Stewart 2015b: 138, 164, 172.

[4] For examples of how external and internal freedom were rendered inward (*indvortes*) and external (*udvortes*) freedom by the Danish Kantians and Fichteans, see Thuborg 1951: 125. My Kantian approach to "inwardness" in this chapter is partially anticipated by Wimmer (1990: 207) and Palmquist (2016). Wimmer takes Kierkegaard's concepts of inwardness and subjectivity to correspond to Kant's noumenal *Gesinnung*, something that is also suggested by Palmquist. Harbsmeier (1999), by contrast, focuses on the importance of Romanticism and pietism for Kierkegaard's "inwardness."

disposition (*Gesinnung*) and phenomena that are intersubjectively available, including the consequences of our acts (cf. MM 6:237, 418, 340; CPR 5:161).[5] For both Kant and Kierkegaard, "inwardness" refers not so much to lower-level maxims that underlie various actions, as to the moral character (the supreme maxim) that in turn underlies all these maxims. However, we will start by examining Kierkegaard's critique of consequentialism in ethics before we turn to the concepts of legality, morality, and character.

Kierkegaard's Ignored Critique of Consequentialism

In normative ethics, Kierkegaard (Climacus) insists that the moral worth of actions lies in the will or intention behind an action, not in its consequences (SKS 7, 270n / CUP1, 296n). This view is often associated with Kantian deontology (see Evans 1982: 97–8), although it is better described in German as *Gesinnungsethik* and in Danish as *sindelagsetik* (i.e., an ethics of disposition – see Søltoft 2000: 263–4). *Fear and Trembling*, *Concluding Unscientific Postscript*, and *The Book on Adler* all sketch such an ethical view. These writings rely on an argument that can be reconstructed as follows:

1. Moral action is necessarily intentional action.
2. Morality is practically oriented or action guiding.
3. Morality is therefore forward-looking.
4. Actual or objective consequences of moral acts can only be known in retrospect.
5. Actual or objective consequences are of theoretical, not practical, importance, since they concern our assessment and knowledge of the past, not how we should act.
6. Objective versions of (act) consequentialism are therefore concerned with the theoretical question of what makes an action right, something that is irrelevant practically (cf. Das 2017: 332).

Kierkegaard (Climacus) claims that moral actions only belong to the agent if the actions are intentional. He therefore says that "[e]thically, what makes the deed the individual's own is the intention" (SKS 7, 144 /

[5] See also note 11 below. Palmquist (2016: 748) argues that *Gesinnung* should be translated as "conviction" rather than "disposition" or "attitude." However, I focus on our fundamental *Gesinnung* in the sense of our supreme maxim, which is identical to our moral character (or moral personality).

CUP1, 155). The intention also decides the moral value of actions. Kierkegaard (de silentio) writes:

> [I]f one is truly going to learn something from greatness [*af det Store*] one must be particularly aware of the beginning. If the one who is to act wants to judge himself by the results, he will never begin. Although the result may give joy to the entire world, it cannot help the hero, for he would not know the result until the whole thing was over, and he would not become a hero by that but by making a beginning. (SKS 4, 156 / FT, 63)

The intention is here described as "the beginning" and the actual consequences as "the result [*Udfaldet*]," although the *Postscript* describes them as "the intention [*Hensigten*]" and "the effect [*Virkningen*]," respectively (SKS 7, 144 / CUP1, 155). In the passage above, Kierkegaard (de silentio) argues that one cannot even start to act if one were to judge oneself based on the actual consequences of one's acts, since these consequences are only known retrospectively. At the time of acting, one only knows one's intentions, *including* the intended consequences of acts. It is these intentions (and these consequences) that matter morally, not the actual consequences.

Indeed, the *Postscript* goes to the extreme of claiming that "it is plainly immoral to care about the outcome" of one's acts (SKS 7, 270n / CUP1, 297n). But it is only immoral to care about the consequences if morality becomes a mere means towards self-interest, as we saw in Chapters 4–5. Kierkegaard (Climacus) writes:

> True ethical enthusiasm [*Begeistring*] consists in willing to the utmost of one's capability, but also, uplifted in divine jest, in never thinking whether or not one thereby achieves something. As soon as he [*Villien* – the will] begins to cast a covetous eye on the outcome, the individual begins to become immoral – the energy of the will becomes torpid, or it develops abnormally into an unhealthy, unethical, mercenary hankering [*lønsyg Higen*] that, even if it achieves something great, does not achieve it ethically – the individual demands something other than the ethical itself. A truly great ethical individuality would consummate his life as follows: he would develop himself to the utmost of his capability; in the process he perhaps would produce a great effect in the external world, but this would not occupy him at all, because he would know that the external is not in his power and therefore means nothing either *pro* or *contra*. He would remain in ignorance about it, lest he be delayed by the external and fall into its temptation. (SKS 7, 126–7 / CUP1, 135–6; cf. SKS 7, 270–1, 125–6, 129–44 / CUP1, 296–7, 134–5, 138–55)

It is morally desirable to remain ignorant about whether actions in fact produce happiness or not. This presupposes that we have prudential reasons to pursue personal happiness that tend to conflict with morality. To avoid instrumentalism concerning moral virtue, the *Postscript* insists in a Kantian manner that "[t]he ethical as the absolute is infinitely valid in itself and does not need embellishment in order to look better" (SKS 7, 133 / CUP1, 142).

Still, there is a tendency to judge based on embellishments or actual consequences:

> When in our age we hear these words: It will be judged by the results – then we know at once with whom we have the honor of speaking. Those who talk this way are a numerous type whom I shall designate under the common name of assistant professors [*Docenterne*]. With security in life, they live in their thoughts: they have a *permanent* position and a *secure* future in a well-organized state. They have hundreds, yes even thousands of years between them and the earthquakes of existence; they are not afraid that such things can be repeated, for then what would the police and the newspapers say? Their life task is to judge the great men, judge them according to the result. Such behavior towards greatness betrays a strange mixture of arrogance and wretchedness – arrogance because they feel called to pass judgement, wretchedness because they feel that their lives are in no way allied with the lives of the great. (SKS 4, 155–6 / FT, 62–3; cf. SKS 15, 132–5)

Objective versions of consequentialism are miserable insofar as they fail to achieve the great results aimed at; and they are arrogant, presumptuous, or overconfident by judging others morally. But we may object that Kierkegaard overlooks subjective versions of consequentialism that focus on intended, expected, and foreseeable consequences instead of actual consequences. He does not discuss subjective consequentialism in any detail.[6] Still, it is possible to sketch a Kierkegaardian critique of subjective consequentialism, by considering the implications of some of Kierkegaard's more general points about consequences, some of which are the following:

7. Actual or objective consequences tend to diverge from intended or subjective consequences (a broadly Kantian view).
8. Specifically, it is absolutely not the case that morally good intentions guarantee objectively morally good results.
9. Nor is it the case that objectively great results (welfare or utility) imply good moral motivation.

[6] Primary and secondary sources suggest that Kierkegaard had little knowledge of, and interest in, consequentialism and utilitarianism, associating such views with reflected aesthetes rather than morality proper. Cf. Evans 2009: 91–3.

10. The 1843–46 writings assume that it is entirely incidental whether moral virtue produces happiness or unhappiness (SKS 7, 126 / CUP1, 134); accordingly, consequences represent prices of a *lottery* that is fundamentally indifferent to moral desert and justice (SKS 4, 123, 156 / FT, 27, 63).
11. The late writings (1847–55), by contrast, assume that moral virtue brings unhappiness in this life. Specifically, imitation of Christ, as the paradigm of Christian ethics, results in suffering and hardship (SKS 8, 220, 319–431 / UD, 119, 217–341; SKS 12, 170 / PC, 167; SKS 13, 307 / M, 251).

The 1843–46 view undermines subjective consequentialism since there is no reliable connection between our intentions (and the intended consequences) and actual consequences. Whether our acts produce happiness or welfare is then entirely incidental, unforeseeable, and uncontrollable.[7] But it is hardly plausible that we cannot foresee such welfare in any reliable or significant manner. Even if welfare and consequences generally involve significant side effects that are often unintended or nontargetable, it still seems that Kierkegaard is exaggerating here (cf. Evans 2006b: 318).

In any case, his extreme 1847–55 view allows a perverse form of consequentialism, because it assumes that good intentions will be punished, suggesting that bad intentions escape this punishment. Since it is still assumed that we have an interest in happiness, this view could have demoralizing consequences because we would then have prudential reasons to be immoral.

Yet intended consequences matter morally to Kierkegaard as well as subjective consequentialism (indeed, it even matters for Kant, as part of the agent's maxim). But Kierkegaard and Kant both insist that a good will, which seeks good only *because* it is good, is morally necessary, something consequentialism denies. Even if a good motive aims at good ends, they nevertheless insist that the moral rightness of motives is not a function of (probability-discounted) expected results. Some motives for action are inherently right and should therefore be cultivated for their own sake, even if they do not produce benefits. And sufficiently good ends cannot justify immoral means of producing them.[8]

In any case, consequentialism in ethics concerns the evaluation of moral actions (or rather the legality of actions). Therefore, it is difficult to apply

[7] This view is still found in *The Book on Adler* (written 1846–47); see SKS 15, 134–5n, 172n, 238–40 / BA, 49n.

[8] I am heavily indebted to an anonymous reviewer here.

consequentialism to the evaluation of moral characters. As we have seen, consequentialists like Mill and Moore concede that we can only evaluate characters if we consider motives (Mill 1969: 219–20; Zimmerman 2015: 18). Motives are important for "understanding character, which concerns desires and commitments just as much as conduct" does (Martin 2012: 108). And it is not at all clear that morality only concerns the different actions we perform; for it also concerns character traits, as emphasized by eudaimonists, Kant, and Kierkegaard.

Legality Versus Morality

Like Kant, Kierkegaard distinguishes between doing the right thing and doing it for the right reason. He writes: "even if people did *what* duty commands, they would still not [necessarily] be doing their duty" (SKS 10, 215 / CD, 206). *Works of Love* stresses that "[n]o one can decide" "whether it is actually out of love" that one acts or not; "it is possible that it is vanity, pride – in short something bad, but it is also possible that it is love" (SKS 9, 367 / WL, 374).

Clearly, Kierkegaard distinguishes between *legality and morality*, between acting in accordance with the law and acting out of respect of the law. We can know the legality of actions based on experience, but we do not know their morality in any straightforward manner. Because of this, legality is compatible with egoism *and* altruism, with immorality *and* morality.

Still, we can know that acts without legality are *not* moral. Since legality is necessary, Kierkegaard (Climacus) concludes that "the religious person's incognito . . . does not mean that his . . . is the actuality of a robber, a thief, a murderer" (SKS 7, 453n / CUP1, 500n).[9] Thus, one cannot possibly have the right reasons or motivation (e.g., faith) if one does the wrong thing (e.g., kill). In this sense, legality is necessary, although it functions as an *incognito*. The legality in question is moral, rather than juridical, since the discussion centers on ethics, religion, and character traits.

Like Kant, Kierkegaard holds some acts to be incompatible with morality (and genuine religion). Particularly *Works of Love* describes several types of behavior that are incompatible with neighbor-love. In the case of bitter mockery, poisonous distrust, and cold callousness, he says that "it will be

[9] Kierkegaard also relies on the distinction between legality and morality in his journals (SKS 23, 384, NB19:86 / KJN 7, 392). Like Kant, he even contrasts Jewish legality with Christian morality (SKS 18, 381, KK:11 / KJN 2, 348; SKS K18, 558, cf. SKS 11, 196 / SUD, 82; SKS K11, 216).

recognizable from the fruits that there is no love within" (SKS 9, 15 / WL, 7). And someone who accuses and condemns others morally is thereby said to indirectly reveal and condemn himself (SKS 9, 373–4 / WL, 380–1).[10] After this, Kierkegaard emphasizes that one must forgive one's neighbor if one is to be forgiven by God, since "the forgiveness you give is the forgiveness you receive" (SKS 9, 373 / WL, 380).

Perhaps because he focuses on character rather than actions (and the formal aspects of morality rather than its material aspects), Kierkegaard tends to be vague (if somewhat traditional) about the content of morality. It is therefore difficult to ascertain what accepting legality would amount to on Kierkegaardian terms. Surely, it should not mean that we always ought to accept whatever practice is established by society. Kierkegaard is clearly opposed to an ethics that justifies and deifies the established order, associating such a view with the pseudonym Judge William (see Westphal 2014: 48–9).

Moral Character

Characters underlie and constraint actions, although we know characters from actions. For this reason, characters are more hidden, or less explicit, than actions. For Kant, an action presupposes a lower-level maxim, which in turn presupposes a character (supreme maxim). Indeed, Kant describes the character as a disposition (*Gesinnung*), which is supersensible and therefore not directly accessible to us (R 6:63, 67).[11]

Kierkegaard also denies that we have direct access to our own disposition or character. Although he seems less explicit about whether the disposition is supersensible or not, it is nevertheless clear that it cannot be experienced directly in space and time. Instead of being an empirical object, the fundamental disposition or character therefore seems intelligible or even supersensible. Indeed, Kierkegaard describes it in Kantian terms as an "*an sich*" that differs from intersubjectively available phenomena (SKS 1, 317 / CI, 281). He therefore suggests that the inner sphere hides behind historical phenomena (SKS 7, 58 / CUP1, 54), while the religious author hides behind worldly phenomena (for the latter, he even uses Kant's German term "*Erscheinung*"; see SKS 16, 50 / PV, 69–70).

10 *Practice in Christianity* makes a similar point by claiming that condemning a Christian for confessing his faith is to condemn yourself (SKS 12, 215–6 / PC, 220).

11 Louden 2002: 136, 152. See also note 5 in this chapter. In his 1833–34 lecture notes, Kierkegaard refers to Kant's view of the moral rebirth that establishes moral character (SKS 19, 57, Not1:7 / KJN 3, 52).

In a passage that discusses Kant and Hegel, Kierkegaard (Climacus) goes as far as saying, "The only *an sich* that cannot be thought is existing [*det at existere*], with which thinking has nothing at all to do" (SKS 7, 300 / CUP1, 328). Just like inwardness, existence is here understood as the disposition or character that underlies action. The existential perspective is therefore understood as a practical perspective that concerns character formation. The cryptic claim that existence is "*an sich* that cannot be thought" belongs to a passage that contrasts Hegel's theoretical philosophy with Kant's practical philosophy. The former is retrospective and theoretic, whereas the latter is forward-looking and moral. It is claimed the former cannot deal adequately with practical or existential issues that are essential to practical agency (see Evans 2006b: 38). Specifically, theoretical thought cannot capture moral inwardness fully. Theoretical questions are important, but insufficient for practical questions concerning how to live.

Clearly, Kierkegaard insists that we have an unconditional obligation to be moral, irrespectively of how others act. Still, it is very difficult, if not impossible, to avoid acting free of assumptions about our moral characters (and personalities). In many situations, for instance, we need to choose who to trust and who not to trust. It seems impossible to do this, unless there is a way to distinguish a life of virtue from one of evil that stays within the bounds of legality. It thus seems that inwardness cannot be entirely hidden, even if it has legality as its incognito. Jack Mulder writes:

> [T]he problem with hidden inwardness is not that it is inward, the problem with hidden inwardness is that it is *hidden*. To hide something one necessarily contains it. And this is the problem. An inwardness that confines itself (in order not to be seen for what it is) is not in fact inwardness, but negative outwardness. (2002: 317)

An entirely hidden inwardness seems to be a false inwardness, a "negative outwardness." Kant, however, argues that we need many observations to confirm that someone has a moral character, but only one observation to know that there is no (moral) character.[12] One act without legality (e.g., murder) indicates an evil character, whereas acts that appear good need not involve a good character (R 6:71, 63). This presupposes that characters are either good or evil, something Kant dubs moral *rigorism* (R 6:22–5).

[12] "Reflexionen zur Anthropologie," in Ak 15:55–654, esp. 15:541, *Reflexion* 1230; cf. 15:526, *Reflexion* 1191; R 6:20, 68.

Even though Kierkegaard holds some acts to be incompatible with morality, he nevertheless claims:

> [T]here is nothing, no "thus and so," that can unconditionally be said to demonstrate unconditionally the presence of love or to demonstrate unconditionally its absence. (SKS 9, 22 / WL, 14)

Kantians could concede that there is nothing that unconditionally demonstrates the presence of charity (practical love). Although some acts *are* incompatible with morality (e.g., murder) and would seem to demonstrate the absence of love (given sanity and accountability), Kierkegaard is probably right that the absence or presence of love cannot be demonstrated unconditionally with a single proof or consideration. To know this, we would not only need to know the nature of an individual act but also the relevant context, intentions, reasons, causes, and whether the person was sane or not. We need not only an act but also an autonomous action and relevant character traits. We must then rely on inferences from the outer to the inner that involve judgments that are uncertain, as Kant points out (R 6:63–7; Louden 2002: 136–52). These judgments are conditioned on many different fallible considerations about the agent and the context, as Kierkegaard in turn suggests (SKS 9, 15 / WL, 8–9; SKS 15, 256–7 / BA, 100–1).

In the case of neighbor-love, Kierkegaard contrasts the hiddenness of love with its visible fruits (SKS 9, 15–24 / WL, 8–16). Words and deeds indicate something about the underlying character, even if the latter remains hidden. Instead of being absolutely hidden, inwardness then represents a disposition to act that takes the form of a *character* that grounds ethico-religious actions.[13] Indeed, we will see that the *Postscript* takes inwardness to involve not only subjective truth but also moral wholeheartedness. Such inwardness is only possible if the agent's character is fully committed towards morality (as we have seen in Chapters 2–3) and if it thereby expresses itself in words and deeds.

Still, "inwardness" is better described negatively than positively, because it is easier to make the case that "inwardness" is lacking than to make the case that it exists. The concept of hidden inwardness need, then, not be as problematic as it seems, since it mainly involves the broadly Christian and Kantian idea that we do not know the hearts and reins of others – or even ourselves (SKS 11, 79 / WA, 75; cf. SKS 20, 325, NB4:78 / KJN 4, 326).[14] It is

[13] Cf. Evans (2006b: 179) on the dispositional character of inwardness. Vos (2016: 317–18) notes that inwardness functions more or less as the equivalent of character for Kierkegaard.

[14] See note 2 in the present chapter.

only God, as a scrutinizer of hearts, who knows our innermost being (SKS 10, 244 / CD, 237), including whether there is inwardness or not (Harbsmeier 1999). Gordon Michalson therefore comments:

> Indeed, Kierkegaard's position is thoroughly Kantian ... just as there is a noumenal shield protecting the Kierkegaardian object of faith, there is a corresponding noumenal shield protecting the inner recesses of this all-important subject of faith, the true disciple. This becomes clear in Kierkegaard's claim that we can never truly "know" or recognize an authentically religious person, the presumptions of Christendom notwithstanding. The Kantian attitude toward the profound concealment of the true moral worth of another person is recapitulated almost exactly in Kierkegaard's idea of the "knight of faith," whose identity remains forever hidden from the scrutiny of others. (1985: 90)

As Marilyn Piety indicates, this "hidden inwardness" is closely related to the idea of moral freedom:

> Kierkegaard clearly holds something like a Kantian view of the relation between the phenomenal and noumenal view of a person. This view can be found, for example, in the section of *Either-Or Part II* entitled "The Aesthetic Validity of Marriage". It may be challenging to make sense of how the phenomenal and noumenal aspects of a person can be brought together in such a way as to preserve human freedom, but Kant asserts they can be, and Kierkegaard appears to follow Kant in this respect. In fact, Kierkegaard distinguishes between "rationalism" and "naturalism" in a journal entry that examines this aspect of Kant's thought (*SKS* 19, 159 [Not 4:11 / KJN 3, 139–40]). (2017)

Yet, Kierkegaard does not seem to accept Kant's transcendental idealism (Knappe 2004: chs. 1–2; Fremstedal 2014a: 229). Nor does Kierkegaard see moral freedom as being merely atemporal (although even Kant speaks of a temporal conversion to good; see R 6:48).[15] But he does accept closely related Kantian ideas about the finitude and limits of human cognition (cf. Green 1992: 121–46; Evans 2006b: 39), denying knowledge of the *Gesinnung* (Lippitt 2013: 139), the supersensual, and God (as assumed by Platonists and rationalists concerning knowledge). He also accepts Kant's related critique of theoretical proofs for the existence of God, seeing "the difference between divine and human knowledge as fundamental for philosophy" (Westphal 2014: 168). Thus, even if he is not a transcendental idealist, Kierkegaard nevertheless accepts broadly Kantian points about the limits and finitude of human cognition, as sketched by Kant in *Dreams of a Spirit-Seer* prior to the

[15] For discussion, see Wimmer 1990: 151–60, 207; Fremstedal 2014a: 67–70.

transcendental idealism of the *Critique of Pure Reason.*[16] However, we will see (in Chapter 10) that he associates these ideas not only with Kant but also with Lessing and Socrates.

Did Kierkegaard's View of Inwardness Change?

Many scholars point out that Kierkegaard's earlier works tend to defend hidden inwardness, whereas his later works tend to attack it instead (see Boldt 2006: 108–10; Schreiber 2018: ch. 9). In 1846, he (in the guise of Climacus) calls for inwardness, whereas he takes up the persona of Anti-Climacus when he calls for outwardness in 1850.[17] Kierkegaard sketches the following historical narrative. First, medieval Christianity overemphasizes outwardness by privileging the monasteries. As a corrective, Protestantism and the *Postscript* emphasize worldliness *and* inwardness. Finally, Kierkegaard's later writings react against the latter by stressing outwardness in the form of Christian suffering, martyrdom, and imitation of Christ (see SKS 22, 241, NB12:162 / KJN 6, 243; SKS 23, 435, NB20:74 / KJN 7, 443; SKS 24, 368, NB24:78 / KJN 8, 373; SKS K26, 243).

The late Kierkegaard is worried that Christendom uses "hidden inwardness" as an excuse for moral laxness and mere legality. If inwardness is essentially hidden, nobody can know whether I am moral or not. Keeping up appearances, or negative outwardness, would then suffice. To counteract such laxness, the late Kierkegaard therefore stresses the moral need for action and for renouncing self-interest, holding that neighbor-love must either express itself outwardly or die (Ferreira 2001: 253; cf. Palmquist 2016). Although love as such is hidden, its presence is still indicated by its visible fruits (SKS 9, 15–24 / WL, 8–16). Christian discipleship – *imitatio Christi* – in particular involves confession, suffering, and martyrdom that is polemical against worldliness. The late Kierkegaard therefore stresses the scandalous nature of Christianity as a corrective against "hidden inwardness" and Christendom (more on this in Chapters 11–12).

However, it is not so much the view of inwardness that changes here as two other things. First, the view of virtue and happiness changes. As we have seen, the early Kierkegaard thinks that the relation between virtue and happiness is contingent, whereas the late Kierkegaard assumes that virtue brings unhappiness, at least in the case of Christ. Second, he assumes that

16 Kierkegaard quotes *Dreams of a Spirit-Seer*; see SKS 18, 198, JJ:179 / KJN 2, 182–3; SKS K18, 312.

17 Ferreira 2001: 254. Even Anti-Climacus is originally described as an extraordinaire Christian in hidden inwardness (Pap. x–6, B48 / JP 6, 6349). And Kierkegaard himself calls for inwardness in 1846–47 (SKS 15, 256–60 / BA, 100–4).

the historical situation changes by overemphasizing inwardness instead of outwardness (as was earlier the case). Therefore, his response must also change if it is to be adequate.

But the view of inwardness does not change radically; it is best considered a change of emphasis, which counteracts the misuse of "hidden inwardness" in Christendom. In 1844, Kierkegaard (now using the persona of Haufniensis) stresses that inwardness is *in* action, and that it can only be achieved *through* action (SKS 4, 439 / CA, 138). In 1846, he (now as Climacus) admits that inwardness without outwardness can easily involve self-deception. Indeed, it represents "the most difficult interiority, in which self-deception is easiest" (SKS 7, 369 / CUP1, 406). Indeed, this self-deception resembles demonic uncommunicativeness or self-enclosure (*Indesluttethed*), which is inwardness in deadlock (see SKS 11, 186 / SUD, 73; SKS 4, 430 / CA, 130). Implicitly, Kierkegaard thus contrasts inwardness with self-enclosure. The former seeks outward manifestation, whereas the latter tries to avoid outwardness (Grøn 1997: 82–5).

Nevertheless, inwardness as such cannot be seen or contemplated, since it can only be expressed or realized (SKS 7, 292 / CUP1, 320). For this reason, the point is that inwardness can only be achieved through ethico-religious words and deeds. It involves not only global character traits but also a disposition to act morally. As Stephen Palmquist (2016: 738) notes, this sounds paradoxical, since "principles or ideals that are by their nature essentially inward end up requiring outward manifestation in order to be confirmed or fully justified as real." This "paradox of inwardness . . . is already present (though so easily overlooked) in Kant and (more overtly) in Kierkegaard" (Palmquist 2016: 750).

Inwardness, Self, and Second-Order Volitions

The ethicist Judge William describes "the inner [*det Indvortes*]" as a "will [that] is directed towards itself" (SKS 3, 96 / EO2, 94). Instead of being an "inner world" (the Hongs' translation of "*det Indvortes*"), it represents second-order volitions, wills to will something. It does not concern first-order volitions (i.e., the different things I will). Rather, it concerns my will to act on first-order volitions or not. "[T]he inner" therefore concerns *volitional identification* with, or alienation from, first-order volitions and desires. As seen in Chapter 1, this second-order volition separates selfhood from human nature, since the self is a reflexive self-relation that relates actively to the human synthesis (of facticity and freedom) by identifying with some first-order states, while alienating itself from other such states (SKS 11, 129 / SUD, 13).

In this respect, "inwardness" is like "the inner" and selfhood, since all these concepts concern second-order volitions (as well as higher-order motives and hierarchical agency more generally). Neither of these presupposes anything essentially private that cannot be expressed publicly (see Mooney 2012: 79–80). Still, not just any second-order volition or desire would qualify as genuine inwardness or authentic selfhood. Demonic self-enclosure, notably, would not qualify. For proper inwardness and selfhood require unconditional ethico-religious commitments that are *long term*, by being grounded on one's very character (see Vos 2016: 317–18). Therefore, Judge William describes the categorical choice of the ethical in terms of inwardness (SKS 3,164 / EO2, 167), whereas Climacus reserves inwardness for natural religion and Christian faith. However, William's use of the term seems somewhat loose, sporadic, and nontechnical, whereas the use of it in the *Postscript* is more consistent, technical, and systematic. Still, both see it as being based in one's fundamental attitude towards one's life as a whole. Indeed, we will see that inwardness seems to require *moral* wholeheartedness in the *Postscript*. Specifically, inwardness is described in terms of subjective truth that requires moral wholeheartedness.

Inwardness can then be interpreted either as a perfect moral character or as a character that is fundamentally committed towards morality by wholeheartedly engaging in self-evaluation and self-improvement. Kierkegaard clearly opts for the latter view, by claiming that one must be unconditionally striving for the good if one is to achieve wholeheartedness (SKS 8, 139–40 / UD, 24). Welz comments:

> Remarkably, Kierkegaard does not identify purity of heart with the goodness of one's heart. Instead of speaking of kindheartedness, he only speaks of the heart's longing, yearning, and craving for the good. (2019: 288)

However, the process of moral improvement can be interpreted both as a never-ending temporal process of reform (i.e., a process of sanctification that gradually improves moral behavior) and as a sudden rebirth or conversion at the level of character. Unlike many pietists, Kierkegaard finds it unimportant to specify a point in time for conversion (SKS 10, 225 / CD, 217; Stokes 2015: 213). He emphasizes that being good is a never-ending task, and that it is always possible to lapse back into evil. Whereas Judge William describes the process of moral improvement in terms of human effort, Kierkegaard focuses on the dialectics between human effort and divine grace. As we will see, even Climacus, who is a mere humorist, sees moral improvement and eternal happiness, as lying beyond our human ability. He thereby anticipates a religious perspective on ethics that is Augustinian and anti-Pelagian.

Irony and Humor as Incognitos in *Concluding Unscientific Postscript*

Kierkegaard (Climacus) does not only connect religion to "hidden inwardness" but also to humor. For him, religious inwardness is not entirely hidden but expressed as humor, whereas the ethical is expressed as irony (SKS 7, 457–77 / CUP1, 504–25). Irony here refers to a specific way of existing that requires

1. legality (a point that is implicit);
2. personal awareness of unconditional moral responsibility; and
3. that one ironically comprehends all the relativities of life by seeing the conflict between the infinite moral demand and everything finite or relative (SKS 7, 455–8 / CUP1, 502–5).

Irony contrasts the moral demand with everything finite or relative, since the latter represents an imperfect reality that falls short of moral ideals. Not only does irony require first-order representation of the ethical task and reality but it also requires a second-order representation of how these first-order representations conflict. Nevertheless, *the ethicist* goes beyond mere irony by being wholeheartedly committed towards morality. Since we cannot verify if someone is fully committed towards morality, we cannot know whether he is an ethicist or a mere ironist. The latter sees the contrast between morality and reality but is not seriously committed to morality as the ethicist is. However, both must presuppose legality – otherwise, we could distinguish between them. An ironist without legality would differ externally from an ethicist with legality.

Humor, on the other hand, transcends irony (although it may presuppose it) by requiring that one "joins the conception of God together with everything [else] and [then] sees the contradiction" (SKS 7, 458 / CUP1, 505). Instead of focusing on the conflict between ethical ideals and reality, the humorist focuses on the conflict between a transcendent (or hidden) God and reality. Humor requires not only first-order representations of God and everything else but also a second-order representation of how these first-order representations conflict. This clearly involves an *incongruity* account of humor. Humor is not based on a formal contradiction but on incongruity (the Danish term "*Modsigelse*" covers both, although it is generally translated "contradiction" in English).

Still, humor does not require inwardness (SKS 7, 458–63 / CUP1, 505–11). Nor does it require theistic belief, since humor need not involve natural religion or Christian faith (SKS 7, 483n / CUP1, 531–2n). The mere humorist is said to have an abstract relation to God (SKS 7, 408n / CUP1, 448n). Presumably, he relies on a regulative idea of God as a transcendent idea,[18] or sees God as possible rather than actual. It therefore seems that the mere humorist does not have to be a theist who ascribes a constitutive role to God. Instead, he could be an agnostic or he could ascribe a regulative role to the God-idea, either practically or theoretically; humor contrasts reality with a God that is transcendent, hidden, or merely possible. (In any case, Kierkegaard does not distinguish between faith and belief, since the Danish "*Tro*" covers both terms, just as the German "*Glaube*" does.)

However, the *Postscript* claims that humor requires the concept of infinite guilt (SKS 7, 477–503, 519 / CUP1, 525–54, 571–2). "Infinite guilt" is the rigorist idea that any immoral action or character flaw involves total guilt (Fremstedal 2014a: ch. 2). Any moral failure involves a radical and essential failure, rather than a partial one (something which seems to presuppose the traditional view known as the unity of the virtues). To the humorist, any finite human attempt to improve the human condition then appears to be a jest, given the infinite ethical task (or God's will) and our infinite guilt (Lippitt 2000: 94). The mere humorist is aware of "infinite guilt," but he revokes it with jest, despite being committed towards morality. He has some awareness of his guilt but does not take it seriously, something that separates him from the religious believer who sees himself as infinitely guilty and therefore totally in need of divine forgiveness. But since we cannot verify if someone is a believer or serious about his personal guilt, religiousness expresses itself as humor that contrasts God and world.[19]

[18] Kierkegaard's notes from Martensen's lectures refer explicitly to the regulative status of God as a transcendent ideal that we should strive to approximate (SKS 19, 140, Not4:11 / KJN 3, 139). Even if these notes do not represent Kierkegaard's own view, he nevertheless went on to sketch a regulative approach to God later on. See Pattison 1997; Verstrynge 2004; Bubbio 2014: ch. 4; Fremstedal 2014a: 100; Dalferth 2015: 75.

[19] Unlike *Either/Or*, the *Postscript* is clear that inwardness requires religious suffering. Both immanent (natural) and Christian religion require suffering, in which one suffers by being separated from the highest good, one's final end (as we saw in Chapter 5). However, neither the religious believer nor the ethicist wants to appear better outwardly than other humans do. See Evans 1999: 193, 205.

Conclusion: Neither "Negative Outwardness" Nor a Hidden Domain

"Hidden inwardness" represents one of Kierkegaard's more controversial contributions to European philosophy and theology, since it seems to involve either a private, inner domain or a "negative outwardness" (Mulder 2002: 317). Still, this chapter indicates that it is not as problematic as it may seem if we employ a charitable, Kantian reading of Kierkegaard. Specifically, "hidden inwardness" describes an ethico-religious character that is only indirectly available through its expressions in words and deeds. As such, it is opposed to legalistic and consequentialist ethics and closer to religious variants of Kantianism and virtue ethics.

Notoriously, Kierkegaard is concerned with the *inner* transformation of the person, not the outer reformation of society. Therefore he writes: "Christianity does not want to make changes in externals; neither does it want to abolish drives or inclination – it wants only to make infinity's change in the inner being" (SKS 9, 141 / WL, 139). However, this is often taken to mean that he is concerned with a religious *conversion*, not with political or moral action. But a conversion is both a religious and a moral matter, for it is a conversion to good that establishes moral character with divine assistance (cf. Fremstedal 2014a: chs. 2–9).

Still, the difference between *external* reform and *inner* conversion remains. For Kierkegaard, morality is not so much a matter of performing good actions, as a matter of establishing good character and forming good intentions. Indeed, we have seen that he describes it in terms of hidden inwardness and hidden love. Still, inwardness and love require "outward manifestation in order to be confirmed or fully justified as real" (Palmquist 2016: 750). If not, inwardness and love must die (cf. Ferreira 2001: 253). Thus, moral actions and deeds are still decisive. Indeed, they express inwardness or character, although it is this very fact that makes them *secondary* on Kierkegaard's view.

CHAPTER 9

Subjective Truth: "Kierkegaard's Most Notorious … Claim"

"Subjectivity Is Truth" – and Untruth

Kierkegaard, and particularly *Concluding Unscientific Postscript*, is notorious for offering a subjective justification of religious belief and a closely related account of *subjective truth*.[1] However, we will see that the concept of hidden inwardness sheds light on the controversial theses "subjectivity is truth" and "[s]ubjectivity is untruth" in the *Postscript*. Indeed, "subjectivity is truth" is expanded on as "subjectivity, inwardness, is truth," with the further addition "that existing, the inward deepening in and through existing, is truth [*det at existere, Inderliggjørelsen i og ved at existere, er Sandheden*]" (SKS 7, 186–8 / CUP1, 204, 206). "Subjectivity is untruth," on the other hand, is described as a more inward expression of "subjectivity is truth" (SKS 7, 189 / CUP1, 207). Note however that the *Postscript* is only concerned here with the cognition of truth *essential* to ethical and religious agency (SKS 7, 181 / CUP1, 197–8).

"[S]ubjective truth" is described as "the truth of appropriation [*Tilegnelsens Sandhed*]" (SKS 7, 29 / CUP1, 21). On a straightforward reading, it refers to the subjective appropriation of objective truth, in the realist sense of holding and existing independently of the subject's response (stance) towards it.[2] Indeed, the *Postscript* seems to presuppose objective truth and some form of metaphysical and metaethical realism.[3] Its discussion and appropriation of Gotthold Lessing, for instance, presupposes an objective or realistic notion of truth. Kierkegaard (Climacus) attributes the following theses to Lessing: The subjective existing thinker relates to truth

[1] Helms (2013: 439) describes "truth is subjectivity" as perhaps "Kierkegaard's most notorious – though pseudonymous – claim."

[2] For similar interpretations sketched by Thomas Heywood and Walter Schulz, see Law 1993: 96–7.

[3] For metaphysical realism and realism concerning truth, see Evans 2006b: 40, 307. For theological realism, see Carr 1996: 238–9. For metaethical realism, see Davenport 2012: 8–10, 39–42, 55–9, 70–2, 86–9, 151–6; Rudd 2012: 91–5, 112–16; Stern 2012: 221–2; Fremstedal 2014a: ch. 10. For realism concerning language, see Fox-Muraton 2019a: 403.

as a process of becoming; he has the preference of never-ending striving for truth over the possession of it (SKS 7, 80, 103 / CUP1, 80, 106). These theses, which seem endorsed by Kierkegaard (Climacus), do not deny an eternal truth but deny the possession of certain and final knowledge of it. The point seems to be that we strive for objective truth without ever reaching it completely (cf. Howland 2012: 115–29).

On the straightforward reading, truth becomes subjective insofar as an agent appropriates (objective or realistic) truth (cf. SKS 7, 176, 186, 220–1 / CUP1, 192, 203, 242), presumably by *wholeheartedly* identifying with it and by acting upon it by letting higher-order motives affirm truth. This requires full moral commitment if the identification is to be wholehearted. Hermann Deuser writes:

> *Appropriation* thus means that one "essentially appropriates the essential only by doing it" [SKS 5, 416 / TD, 38]. The significance of *knowledge* and intellectual decisions is thereby neutralized, and the significance of *ethics* is taken up into the self-relation as the defining perspective for action. (1998: 385)

Conversely, "[s]ubjectivity is untruth" insofar as one alienates oneself volitionally from truth, thereby failing to act on it (since higher-order motives differ from truth). Both these responses involve higher-order motives, just like inwardness and selfhood do.

But the *Postscript* is clear that even the acknowledgment that "[s]ubjectivity is untruth" involves inwardness insofar as one acknowledges personal failure by being conscious of one's state of sin. Indeed, "[s]ubjectivity is untruth" is more inward than "subjectivity is truth," since true inwardness lies not in human perfection without God, but in human *sin-consciousness* before God (SKS 7, 189–92 / CUP1, 207–10). Still, it is not sufficient to stop with sin-consciousness, since one must also strive towards good. The terminology here is like Kant's use of subjective and objective principles in ethics. Whereas the moral law is an objective principle, our maxims are subjective principles that we act on. We only exist in truth then if our subjective principles, which define *how* we exist, are based on objective principles. Ulrich Knappe (2004: 84n) therefore writes: "The 'how' to which Kierkegaard refers characterizes the subjective or motivational aspect of a moral action and … the how is in truth if it denotes an act from duty." On this Kantian interpretation, the subjective aspect of moral action can only be said to be true if we act from duty, if the motivational reasons are also normative reasons. The much-discussed subjective "how" then refers to the inwardness and seriousness of the moral disposition.

One difficulty with this reading is that subjective truth – and belief – concerns "*objective uncertainty*" held fast in the "*most passionate inwardness*" of faith (SKS 7, 186 / CUP1, 203). But how can "objective uncertainty" involve objective truth? As we will see, objective uncertainty entails a lack of epistemic evidence, which allows belief based on practical reasons – something that in turn is compatible with an objective truth.

A subjectivist reading, by contrast, may give a literal account of "subjectivity is truth," according to which truth is created by subjective responses such as valuing or volition. But it is hard to see how it can account for "[s]ubjectivity is untruth," and why the latter is described in terms of *sin* in the Christian sense (cf. SKS 7, 189–92 / CUP1, 207–10). It also overlooks the assumed correspondence between the subjective "how" and the objective "what" (SKS 22, 414, NB14:121 / KJN 6, 420). Both here and elsewhere, Kierkegaard (Climacus) presupposes a notion of truth that *is neither relativistic nor subjectivistic.*[4] Clearly, he presupposes that there is a *true* God, an eternal happiness, and an ethical task. Take for example this notorious passage:

> *If someone who lives in the midst* of Christianity enters, with knowledge of the true idea of God ... the house of the true God, and prays, but prays in untruth, and if someone lives in an idolatrous land but prays with all the passion of infinity, although his eyes are resting upon the image of an idol – where, *then*, is there more truth? The one prays in truth to God *although* he is worshipping an *idol*; the other prays in untruth to the true God and is therefore in truth worshipping an *idol.* (SKS 7, 184 / CUP1, 201)

This passage suggests that the best is a Christian who prays truly or sincerely to the true God. The second best is a sincere pagan who prays truly to an idol. The third best is an insincere Christian who prays to the right God untruly. The worst is an insincere pagan who prays to an idol untruly. The passage thus distinguishes between subjective and objective aspects of faith. Westphal (2014: 163) argues that the subjective "how" here refers to the faith whereby we believe, a faith that can be either sincere or insincere. By contrast, the objective "what" refers to doctrine that is believed. On this interpretation, "subjectivity is truth" therefore implies that dogmas are less important than the faith whereby we believe.[5] Simpleminded although sincere believers who are confused about religious

[4] Still, different subjectivist readings exist. For a brief overview, see Law 1993: 91–7.

[5] Law points out that "Kierkegaard does not reject doctrine, but aims to shake people out of complacently accepting Christianity as *only* a doctrine and not as a way of life that demands self-sacrifice and renunciation (*SKS* 22, 95, NB11:160 / KJN 6, 91), and for which the genuine believer should be prepared to *suffer*" (Law 2015: 258; cf. Evans 1999: 209–10).

doctrine are then preferable to insincere believers who have got the dogmas right. Having the right inward disposition is more important than holding exactly the right beliefs. The latter would privilege elite theologians, whereas the former is available to all humans. However, we will examine alternative interpretations of this passage after we have discussed subjective justifications of religious belief and Kierkegaard's theory of truth.

Subjective Justifications of Religious Belief

The *Postscript* seems to connect subjective truth to subjective and practical concerns that motivate and justify religious belief. In the middle of the discussion of subjective truth, the *Postscript* introduces God as a postulate:

> God is indeed a postulate, but not in the loose [*ørkesløse* – pointless] sense in which it is ordinarily taken. Instead, it becomes clear that this is the only way an existing person enters into a relationship with God: when the dialectical contradiction brings passion to despair and assists him in grasping [*omfatte*] God with "the category of despair" (faith), so that the postulate, far from being the arbitrary, is in fact *necessary* defense, self-defense [Nød*verge*]; in this way God is not a postulate, but the existing person's postulation of God is – a necessity [*Nødvendighed*]. (SKS 7, 183n / CUP1, 200n)

The necessity here is not objective but subjective and practical since God must be postulated to avoid despair (more on this in Chapter 13). Both here and elsewhere, the subjective perspective is represented by practical concerns that are typically moral, religious, and prudential. The objective perspective, by contrast, is taken in a narrow sense by being represented by theoretical concerns that seem epistemic. Like Kant, Kierkegaard therefore *aligns the subjective with the practical and the objective with the theoretical* in this context (Evans 1982: 77–83; Emmanuel 1996: 35; cf. Wood 1970: 16; Beiser 2006: 609–10). Presumably, the objective here concerns external epistemic evidence, which holds independently of our subjective responses to it. The subjective, by contrast, concerns the subjective ends of agents insofar as these ends are rational or justified. More particularly, it concerns the highest good as the final end of ethico-religious agency (cf. LL 9:69).

In any case, Kant is clear that faith (or belief) is *not* objective in the sense that it has an objective ground in epistemic evidence as knowledge has. But it must nevertheless be objective in the broad sense of being *intersubjectively valid*, communicable, and sharable (*mitteilbar*; see Chignell 2007: 326–7, 355). And the same seems to hold for Kierkegaard (including Climacus and the *Postscript*). Thus, Kierkegaard is *not* denying objectivity in general, but only a specific form of it that is inadequate for dealing with faith. Whereas Kant argues that it is morally necessary to postulate God (in order to think consistently), Kierkegaard argues that it is necessary for wholeheartedness. However, both forms of necessity are supposed to hold universally for all practical, autonomous agents who adopt the highest good as their final end.

Kant says that "to *orient* oneself in thinking in general means: when objective principles [*Principien*] of reason are insufficient for holding something true, to determine the matter according to a subjective principle [*Princip*]" (O 8:136). Here Kant speaks of orientation based on practical reasons, since epistemic reasons for and against it are lacking. Similarly, the *Postscript* describes both subjective truth – and belief – as "*objective uncertainty*" held fast in the "*most passionate inwardness*" (SKS 7, 186 / CUP1, 203). Objective uncertainty entails insufficient evidence from the epistemic perspective. It is exactly this uncertainty that allows belief (or faith) as opposed to knowledge (SKS 7, 187 / CUP1, 203), something that is also Kant's view (A822–30/B850–8; cf. Furtak 2012: 101–2). Here Kierkegaard (Climacus) warns explicitly against "conflating knowledge with belief [*forvexle Viden med Tro*]" (SKS 7, 36 / CUP1, 29; cf. SKS 4, 281 / PF, 83; Pap. X–6, B79 / JP 1, 10; SKS 27, 487, Papir 408 / KJN 11.2, 188–9). He writes:

> Whereas up to now faith has had a beneficial taskmaster in uncertainty, it would have its worst enemy in ... certainty. That is, if passion is taken away, faith no longer exists, and certainty and passion do not hitch up as a team [*Vished og Lidenskab spændes ikke*]. Let an analogy illustrate this. Whoever believes that there is a God and also a providence has an easier time (in preserving the faith), an easier time in definitely gaining the faith (and not an illusion) in an imperfect world, where passion is kept vigilant, than in an absolutely perfect world. In such a world, faith is indeed inconceivable. Therefore it is also taught that faith is abolished in eternity. (SKS 7, 36 / CUP1, 29–30)

Belief involves a subjective response to objective uncertainty not based on evidence. As such, it necessarily involves a risky *venture* that is neither warranted by evidence nor probability (Emmanuel 1996: 39–40, 157–8). But it is exactly this subjective response that allows passionate and inward belief that dares to venture beyond existing knowledge (SKS 7, 36–49, 187 / CUP1, 29–44, 204). Today, this view is known as a "doxastic venture" model of faith (Bishop 2016: Part VII) .

We cannot possibly have sufficient objective knowledge of the existence of God and immortality (eternal happiness), since such knowledge lies beyond the limits of human cognition (see Michalson 1985: 90–1; Green

1992: 121–46; Evans 2006b: 39; Piety 2017). But this still leaves room for belief based on practical reasons. The view known as pragmatism (or practical nonevidentialism) concerning belief, developed by Kant and William James, holds that practical reasons can justify belief if epistemic evidence is lacking (Beiser 2006: 610; Gava and Stern 2017; Chignell 2018). Kant writes:

> [N]ow enters *the right* of reason's *need*, as a subjective ground for presupposing and assuming something which reason may not presume to know through objective grounds, and consequently for *orienting* itself in thinking, solely through reason's own need, in that immensurable space of the supersensible, which for us is filled with dark [*dicker*] night. (O 8:137)

Practical reasons justify belief that is unwarranted epistemically. Specifically, moral faith is necessary to escape the antinomy of practical reason, which undermines the realization of the highest good (CPR 5:107–19). Kant therefore thinks that the subjective response of the religious believer is fitting and valid since (only) it resolves the antinomy.

Similarly, the *Postscript* claims that "Christianity is a perfect fit" if "subjectivity is truth," since the Christian "paradox and [human] passion [thereby] fit each other perfectly" (SKS 7, 210 / CUP1, 230). Putting it differently, there is a subjective "how" that *only fits one object* (SKS 7, 182, 557n / CUP1, 199, 613–14n; SKS 22, 414, NB14:121 / KJN 6, 420; SKS K22, 528). This fit between the subjective "how" and the objective "what" rules out subjectivism and relativism.

Here the subjective "how" is represented by passion and the maximum of religious inwardness (SKS 7, 210, 554–9 / CUP1, 230, 610–6; SKS 22, 414, NB14:121 / KJN 6, 420). It concerns the formal aspects of inwardness, whereas the objective "what" concerns the material aspects. The latter is represented both by the paradox, in the Christological sense of being both human and divine (SKS 7, 210 / CUP1, 230), and by "eternal happiness" (SKS 7, 354–9, 388 / CUP1, 389–94, 426–7), a synthesis of virtue and happiness associated with the kingdom of God (Glenn 1997: 260–1; Fremstedal 2014a: chs. 5–9). The object of faith, the "what," therefore, represents Christian doctrine, whereas the "how" concerns the faith whereby we believe. Faith is therefore assumed to fit the doctrines of the incarnation and the kingdom of God as the highest good.[6] Again, the assumption is that Christianity allows the realization of the highest good.

[6] McCombs (2013: 211) interprets subjectivity as rationality, claiming that "Christianity and rationality are a perfect fit, that Christianity is the perfection of reason, and that the rationality of Christianity can be discovered by subjective striving."

For Kierkegaard, these doctrines cannot be objectified or described by detached observers (cf. Barrett 2021). Instead, they call for a passionate and committal response from human agents. Indeed, the doctrinal content cannot be adequately disclosed unless the agent takes interest in it as something that concerns him personally. Put in phenomenological terms, this suggests that the subjective "how" involves a practical noetic attitude that *correlates* with a specific noematic content (doctrine). And this seems to fit neatly with the straightforward reading of subjective truth.[7]

Kierkegaard's Theory of Truth (Watts)

Subjective truth not only concerns religious belief but also truth. However, it is often assumed that Kierkegaard does not have a theory of truth (Westphal 1996: 116; Fremstedal 2019c). Daniel Watts (2018) rejects this assumption. He argues compellingly that Kierkegaard sketches an original theory of truth as self-coincidence. In the *Postscript*, the discussion of truth starts by introducing two traditional accounts of truth described as the realist (or empirical) and idealist accounts or formulas (SKS 7, 173–5 / CUP1, 189–92). Watts explains:

> On the realist's formula, it is *being* that is supposed to have the priority [over thought]. The pursuit of truth, accordingly, is the aim to bring our representations [or thinking] into conformity with the ways things are. On the idealist's definition, by contrast, the priority is given to *thought*. Here, the pursuit of truth is the aim to render being intelligible in the form of a coherent system of thought. (2018: 200–1)

However, this leads to a problem. On both accounts, truth requires *coincidence* between thought and being. But such coincidence can only be perfect if being is taken in a sufficiently abstract sense so that it can coincide perfectly with thought (e.g., as being that is thought to be). The problem is then that "thinking and being signify one and the same" or that thought and being mean one and the same (SKS 7, 174 / CUP1, 190). There cannot be any relation between thought and being if they mean the same and are identical. Truth is then nothing but the *identity* of thought and being, and the difference between the realist and idealist accounts therefore collapses. Watts offers the following summary and reconstruction:

> [N]either the idealist nor the realist definitions of truth say more than that truth is the identity of thought and being. Uninformative though it seems to

[7] Again, I am indebted to a reviewer here.

> be, there is nevertheless a way to interpret this formula as a substantive definition of truth. On this interpretation, the formula applies, in the first instance and paradigmatically, to God; that is, to God *qua* perfectly self-coinciding agent. (2018: 203–4)

This interpretation is based on the remark that "for God" thought and being actually represent a self-identity or agreement (SKS 7, 175 / CUP1, 190). The *Postscript* speaks of "redoubling [*Fordoblelse*]" and "reduplication [*Reduplication*]" here (SKS 7, 175–6 / CUP1, 190–1), suggesting that God paradigmatically exemplifies truth as the self-identity of thought and being. Although God's being agrees perfectly with his thought or self-awareness, there is nevertheless a duality within God (Watts 2018: 202–3). Watts writes:

> [I]f it is to be substantive, the concept of truth must apply, paradigmatically, to . . . a form of agency that . . . [i] must exhibit the duality of self-relation; and (ii) it must remain in agreement with itself, being in no wise self-estranged . . . It is no doubt a further question whether this ontologically committed interpretation of truth can be defended, for example against deflationary or eliminativist accounts. Climacus offers no such defence. His conclusion is best viewed as a conditional: *if* it can be given a substantive interpretation, *then* truth must be interpreted by reference to God *qua* perfect-self-coinciding agent. (2018: 203–4)

The idea seems to be that divine agency involves not just thinking but also a self-relation that avoids double-mindedness and self-estrangement completely. Human agency, by contrast, is often conflicted or double-minded. To the extent that that is the case, such agency cannot be said to live truly or to be true to itself.

It is mainly agents that are truth bearers on this account, not propositions.[8] The truth predicate therefore plays a fundamentally *adverbial* role for Kierkegaard (Watts 2018: 205–6). He therefore writes: "truth in the sense in which Christ is the truth is not a sum of statements, not a definition [*Begrebsbestemmelse*] etc., but a life" (SKS 12, 202 / PC, 205). Truth here describes wholehearted existence, not true propositions (or beliefs). An agent can be self-estranged, double-minded, and mad, while still uttering true propositions and possessing true beliefs (see SKS 7, 178–80 / CUP1, 194–6). Stating true propositions or having true beliefs is therefore compatible with living untruthfully or being untrue to oneself.

[8] Watt's view here is anticipated by Furtak 2005: 43–4 and 2012: 88.

Truth therefore has different meanings in different contexts. Indeed, the *Postscript* is infamous for distinguishing between objective and subjective truth:

> To objective reflection, truth becomes something objective, an object, and the point is to disregard the subject. To subjective reflection, truth becomes appropriation, inwardness, subjectivity, and the point is to immerse oneself, existing, in subjectivity [*det gjelder netop om existerende at fordybe sig i Subjektiviteten*]. (SKS 7, 176 / CUP1, 192)

Objective truth seems to involve an idealized third-person perspective that is objective by virtue of being fully informed yet disinterested, detached, and impartial. As such it belongs to an idealized spectator, or epistemic agent, who describes an object from all perspectives simultaneously. As such, it resembles both a divine spectator and an ideal spectator, understood as a self-coinciding agent without any special interests, self-dividedness, double-mindedness, or duplicity.[9] Objective truth here becomes a *regulative* idea that human spectators should approximate asymptotically. As such, it represents a heuristic principle which guides theoretical, *descriptive* inquiry and epistemic agency, possibly by bringing objects under systematic unity as Kant argues (cf. A509/B537, A647/B674, A663/B691).

Subjective truth, by contrast, is not a different truth but rather the same truth approached in a different context or from a different perspective. Both concern wholehearted agency. But only subjective truth concerns the normative first-person perspective of *practical* agency. Specifically, it concerns wholehearted or coherent practical agency that avoids despair, something that requires self-awareness, inwardness, and moral commitment (as we have seen in Chapters 2–3 and 8). In addition, it may require faith, hope, and charity (cf. Chapter 5). Only such agency exists truly, or is true to itself, by properly occupying the first-person perspective of practical agency (cf. Watts 2018: 215).[10] Like objective truth, subjective truth seems to be a regulative idea that human agents may approximate only asymptotically. At least, it requires wholeheartedness that longs for the good indefinitely (cf. Welz 2019: 288).

9 Watts (2018: 211–12) argues that objective truth is not mainly propositional. However, he (2018: 198–211) speaks of empirical inquiry here, something that seems too restrictive.

10 Evans (1982: 77–80) claims that subjectivity is concerned with practical possibilities that have objective content. Helms (2020: 9), on the other hand, suggests that subjectivity "offers a synthesis of possibility and actuality that does not follow directly from what precedes it" since subjectivity must actively synthetize possibility with actuality.

By contrast, practical agency that is double-minded or conflicted is not true to itself. Watts argues that the discussion here turns on the Kantian thesis that "[r]elating to oneself merely as an object among objects is itself a form of self-estrangement," because "human subjectivity cannot be exhausted by empirical self-consciousness since the standpoint of practical agency cannot be objectified" (2018: 213). Living truthfully in the first-person perspective therefore differs from being an objective spectator. In practical contexts, it is wholeheartedness and self-awareness that seems to confer truth to practical agents, whereas it is a view from everywhere (and nowhere in particular) that confers truth to epistemic agents in theoretical inquiry (cf. Watts 2018: 220).

This view is anticipated as early as the famous 1835 Gilleleje passage that asks: "What is truth other than living for an idea?" (SKS 17, 26n5, AA:12.5 / KJN 1, 21n5). Here Kierkegaard writes:

> *[T]he* thing is to find a truth which is truth *for me*, to find *the idea for which I am willing to live and die*. And what use would it be in this respect if I were to discover a so-called objective truth, or if I worked my way through the philosophers' systems ... And what use would it be in that respect to ... construct a world which, again, I myself did not inhabit but merely held up for others to see? What use would it be to be able to propound the meaning [*Betydning*] of Christianity, to explain many separate facts, if it had no deeper meaning *for myself and my life?* ... That's what I lacked for leading a completely human life and not just a life of knowledge [*Erkjendelsens*], to avoid basing my mind's development on – yes, on something that people call objective – something which at any rate isn't my own, and to base it instead on something which is bound up with the deepest roots of my existence, through which I have, as it were, grown into the divine, clinging fast to it even if the whole world were to fall apart. *This, you see, is what I need* [mangler], *and this is what I strive for.* (SKS 17, 24–6, AA:12 / KJN 1, 19–21)

This passage anticipates the distinction between subjective and objective truth in the *Postscript*. Both in 1835 and 1846, the focus lies on the practice perspective, not on the epistemic perspective. Only practical concerns necessitate religion; and religion itself concerns practical issues.

Kierkegaard's approach here mirrors a *duality* in the very concept of truth. Truth concerns that which not only (objectively) agrees with facts or reality but is also (subjectively) expressed in truthfulness, faithfulness, fidelity, loyalty, and veracity. Truthfulness in particular involves not only accuracy but also sincerity and authenticity, which is true to itself (Williams 2004). For Kierkegaard, the latter requires wholeheartedness and moral commitment that avoids self-deception and conformism alike.

Concluding Discussion: Neither Subjectivism Nor Relativism

The unusual theory of truth that Watts finds in the *Postscript* is relatively unexplored and deserves more discussion before judgment is passed on it. It seems clear, however, that there are objective, formal constraints on selfhood that prevent relativism and subjectivism (cf. Welz 2019: 288). Specifically, wholeheartedness, or being true to oneself, requires unconditional moral commitment that unifies facticity and freedom. Indeed, it even seems to require faith, hope, and charity. Moreover, note the adverbial use of the truth predicate in the controversial passage quoted earlier :

> *If someone who lives in the midst* of Christianity enters, with knowledge of the true idea of God ... the house of the true God, and prays, but prays [*untruly*], and if someone lives in an idolatrous land but prays with all the passion of infinity, although his eyes are resting upon the image of an idol – where, *then*, is there more truth? The one prays [*truly*] to God *although* he is worshipping an *idol*; the other prays in [*untruly*] to the true God and is therefore [*truly*] worshipping an *idol*. (SKS 7, 184 / CUP1, 201, modified transl. based on Watts' suggestions)

Here the pagan embraces practical agency by being seriously interested in his own existence. He thinks that religion is a matter of practical concern since it concerns how he should live his own life in earnest. The false Christian, by contrast, seems to objectify Christianity by trying to be a disinterested spectator who contemplates Christianity and its dogmas without seeing their relevance for his own life. He privileges the third-person perspective of epistemic agency, whereas the pagan privileges the first- and second-person perspective of practical agency (cf. Watts 2018: 217). But practical agency cannot be escaped, so that any attempt to avoid it by privileging epistemic agency involves self-deception, self-estrangement and despair.

This notorious passage then suggests the following hierarchy of religious existence:

1. Wholehearted practical agency believing in the true God
2. Virtually wholehearted practical agency believing in a false god
3. Incoherent practical agency, which tries to escape practical agency by objectifying, describing, and theorizing the true God in a detached manner
4. Incoherent practical agency, which tries to escape practical agency by objectifying, describing, and theorizing a false god in a detached manner

The important thing is not so much if the agent is *sincere* as if he is *wholehearted* and if he is thereby true to himself. A pagan can then be more wholehearted than a self-estranged (incoherent) Christian. Still, complete wholeheartedness seems to involve objective content that is only available to a coherent Christian. For Kierkegaard, it is only possible to overcome despair and sin if one receives divine assistance, something he connects to the Christian virtues of faith, hope, and charity. *The Sickness unto Death* therefore contrasts despair with Christian faith, while *For Self-Examination* contrasts it with hope against hope and *Works of Love* contrasts it with hope and charity (SKS 9, 248–59 / WL, 248–60; SKS 11, 195–6 / SUD, 81; SKS 13, 99, 103–4 / FSE, 77, 82–3). The implication is that only faith, hope, and charity avoid double-mindedness or despair (cf. SKS 8, 204–5 / UD, 100–1; SKS 9, 227–62 / WL, 225–63; SKS 10, 127–32 / CD, 116–22). Subjective truth therefore requires these Christian virtues, since only the latter allow full wholeheartedness (cf. Fremstedal 2020b: 84–6).

The straightforward reading, by contrast, takes subjective truth to concern subjective appropriation of truth that holds and exists independently of the subject's response to it. Here truth becomes subjective insofar as an individual appropriates objective truth by identifying with it and by acting upon it by letting higher-order motives reinforce or affirm truth. This approach presupposes truth that is independent of the agent's response to it, at least to a significant extent. As such, it seems clearly compatible with Watt's interpretation of objective truth as truth described from the third-person perspective of epistemic agency. It also seems compatible with subjective truth described from the first-person perspective of practical agency if the agent acts on (objective or realistic) truth instead of contemplating it.

Finally, even the pragmatic reading of subjective truth, which justifies belief on practical and subjective grounds, is compatible with different truth theories. Unlike pragmatic theories of truth, pragmatism concerning belief is compatible with different truth theories, such as the correspondence theory. For pragmatism concerning belief assumes both practical and epistemic reasons for belief, but it does *not* say what truth itself is.

We may then conclude that instead of involving objectionable subjectivism, the notorious idea that "subjectivity is truth" involves an original theory of truth as self-coincidence or wholeheartedness that is relatively unexplored. In addition, it is closely associated with subjective, practical justifications of religious belief found in pragmatism concerning religious belief. Still, subjective justifications of belief need not involve subjectivism or fideism, since faith could be supported by practical reasons that are objective by holding even if they are not subjectively recognized.

PART IV

Faith and Reason

CHAPTER 10

A Leap of Faith? The Use of Lessing, Jacobi, and Kant

The Leap and the Pantheism Controversy: Jacobi (and Leibniz)

In the context of religious belief, *Concluding Unscientific Postscript* develops the category of the leap (*Springet*[1]) by discussing Friedrich Heinrich Jacobi (1743–1819) and the Pantheism Controversy.[2] The Pantheism Controversy was the biggest public controversy of the late German Enlightenment. It was started by Jacobi's *Concerning the Doctrine of Spinoza in Letters to Herr Moses Mendelssohn* (published in 1785 and 1789), which claimed that Gotthold Ephraim Lessing (1729–81) was a Spinozist. By doing this, Jacobi (2005: 243–56) effectively accused the most prominent German philosopher between Leibniz and Kant of pantheism and atheism. Because of his central role in this controversy, Jacobi exercised an important influence on the late Enlightenment and German idealism. Specifically, Jacobi argued influentially that the Enlightenment project, and its rational philosophy, involves not just pantheism but also atheism and nihilism. Against this background, he and his allies presented a choice between rational nihilism and seemingly irrational faith (or *fideism*).

Whereas the former was associated with the rational and explanatory philosophy (*Alleinphilosophie*) of the Enlightenment, the latter was associated with a philosophy of freedom and becoming (*Unphilosophie*) based on faith. Jacobi (2005: 246) argued that a "mortal leap [*salto mortale*]" from the former to the latter is necessary, because of the nihilism, inconsistencies, and contradictions implied in any rational and systematic philosophy that is mainly explanatory. However, Jacobi does not advocate a blind leap of faith but only a leap that brings the Enlightenment philosophy of Lessing

[1] In *The Concept of Anxiety*, by contrast, the leap refers to the fall from good to evil (SKS 4, 413–15 / CA, 111–13).

[2] Jacobi is associated with German anti-Enlightenment and religious irrationalism, although the latter is contested. See Beiser 1987: ch. 2; Di Giovanni and Livieri 2018.

back on its feet. Specifically, he maintains that truth cannot be reached by rational thinking that is merely explanatory (Beiser 1987: ch. 2; Rasmussen 2009; Di Giovanni and Livieri 2018). He therefore writes "that even the greatest thinker must end up in absurdities if he insists absolutely on explaining everything, on making sense of it by means of clear concepts and refusing to accept anything else" (Jacobi 2005: 250). Even rationalists must resort to faith in order to choose reason, something that anticipates the Popperian view that even rationalism presupposes a basic choice of faith (Hannay 2006: 55).

Despite his reputation for irrationalism, Jacobi did not see himself as an irrationalist. Although his early works contrast faith and reason, his later works instead contrast a narrow, explanatory form of rationality – dubbed the understanding – with a higher reason based on faith (Di Giovanni and Livieri 2018: Part II.v). Although this distinction between the understanding and reason, *Verstand* and *Vernunft*, influences Kierkegaard's contemporaries (e.g., Magnús Eiríksson), Kierkegaard does not accept it (cf. Westphal 2018). Instead, he typically contrasts faith with the understanding (Danish, *Forstanden*, cf. German, *der Verstand*). However, we will see (in Chapter 12) that the understanding still represents a narrow form of rationality for Kierkegaard (although it is not clear that it is merely explanatory for him). Furthermore, I will argue that Kierkegaard's concept of dialectics represents a form of rationality that transcends the understanding. But it is *not* a higher reason based on faith. Rather, it represents a form of practical rationality that can allow faith. In any case, both Jacobi and Kierkegaard are here concerned with the issue known as "faith and reason," namely how religious faith relates to human rationality (including reason as a natural faculty).[3]

Anders Moe Rasmussen (2009: 41) argues that the *Postscript* reformulates Jacobi's either/or between rational nihilism and fideism as a choice between systematic and scientific philosophy on the one hand and religious faith on the other. Kierkegaard (Climacus) associates the former with Hegelianism and pantheism (rather than Spinozism), and the latter with Christian faith. Still, both Jacobi and Kierkegaard seem to advocate a leap from human understanding to religious faith associated with fideism. Specifically, both deny that faith is justified theoretically by epistemic reasons, although it is hardly clear whether it could be supported by normative practical reasons instead (more on this in Chapter 13) .

[3] For Kierkegaard, see Westphal 2018. For Jacobi, see Beiser 1987: ch. 2; Jacobi 2005; Rasmussen 2009; Di Giovanni and Livieri 2018.

In addition, Jacobi's distinction between disinterested and interested thinking, between being a spectator and a participator, respectively, clearly anticipates Kierkegaard's project (Rasmussen 2009: 43–4). As we saw in the previous chapter, Kierkegaard contrasts the third-person perspective of objective, epistemic thinking with the first-person perspective of subjective, practical thinking. However, we will see that Kierkegaard seems to combine, or align, this distinction with a Leibnizian distinction between necessity and historical belief, where the latter represents the contingent beliefs and interests of historical agents who participate in society.[4]

Based on Leibniz's *Theodicy: Essays on the Goodness of God, the Freedom of Man and the Origin of Evil* (1710), the "Interlude" of *Philosophical Fragments* argues that necessary truths (e.g., 2 + 2 = 4) differ from contingent truths, in historical and empirical disciplines. The former, but not the latter, holds necessarily so that its negation would involve a formal logical contradiction.[5] Kierkegaard (Climacus) uses this distinction to distinguish between the sphere of *essences* (or thought), where things exist *necessarily* and can be known as such by mere reason, and the sphere of *existence*, where things exist only *contingently* and the cognition of which is (historical) belief (Løkke and Waaler 2009: 60; Nason 2012).

But things that exist contingently are not arbitrary for Leibniz since they are dependent on the principle of sufficient reason where everything happens for a reason. Although Kierkegaard (Climacus) is inspired by Leibniz here, it seems clear that he deviates from Leibniz's rationalism and idealism, including the principle of sufficient reason and theoretical proofs for God's existence (Løkke and Waaler 2009: 60–1). Here Kierkegaard (Climacus) mainly uses Leibniz to develop a new understanding of historical belief and contingency where contingent existence is not arbitrary.[6]

4 Kierkegaard (Climacus) combines ideas from Leibniz with ideas from Jacobi, Hume, and Schelling. Following Jacobi, he claims that inferences from effect to cause cannot be drawn by way of proof or explanation but only by means of belief (SKS 4, 283 / PF, 84). In addition, Jacobi introduces an "exception" from the universalistic ethics of Kant and Fichte that prefigures the concept of the exception in Kierkegaard's *Fear and Trembling* and *Repetition* (Di Giovanni and Livieri 2018).

5 Kierkegaard's relation to Leibniz seems based mainly on a reading of the *Theodicy* in 1842–43 (cf. SKS 19, 390–4, Not13:23 / KJN 3, 388–91). Specifically, Kierkegaard mentions Leibniz when dealing with faith and reason in the journals and when analyzing *modal* categories in *Philosophical Fragments*. Although Kierkegaard was influenced to some extent by Leibniz's conceptual apparatus (particularly on the modalities), it nevertheless seems clear that most of the conceptual distinctions and nuances in Leibniz are neglected by Kierkegaard. Thus, it is not clear that Kierkegaard's references to Leibniz are very substantial. See Løkke and Waaler 2009.

6 In the *Theodicy*, Leibniz argues that we can cognize things that exist only contingently by forming beliefs that are more or less certain (unlike *a priori* knowledge of necessary truths in mathematics and

The "Interlude" argues that it is not only the future that is contingent but also the past (SKS 4, 269–70 / PF, 79–80). The facticity of the past does not mean that it exists by necessity. History, both future and past, involves transitions from possibility to actuality that cannot be predicted or fully comprehended (Løkke and Waaler 2009: 69), since it is based on free agency that contingently intervenes in the world by actualizing some possibilities, while annihilating others. These transitions involve a leap from possibility to actuality (SKS 7, 313 / CUP1, 342; SKS 19, 395, Not13:27 / KJN 3, 393). In the Napoleonic Wars, for instance, the king decides that Denmark is allied with France, not England.

§1 of the "Interlude" introduces the Aristotelian notion of *kinesis* (movement, change) as the transition from potentiality to actuality in reality (not in logic). §2 then uses this notion to interpret history as process where something (historical) comes into existence by "a relatively freely acting cause" (SKS 4, 276 / PF, 76), something that probably refers to *kinesis* being brought about by human agents (or possibly God) who start new causal chains by intervening in the world. Free agency thus intervenes contingently in the world by actualizing some possibilities, and not others.[7]

It is not only history itself that is fundamentally contingent, however, but also our interpretation of it. *Philosophical Fragments* suggests that we should relate to the past just as we relate to the future, namely by forming historical beliefs (SKS 4, 276 / PF, 76–7). Such beliefs are contingent and normally involve considering different interpretative possibilities. Of the different possibilities, some are actualized, while others remain unrealized.

Here Kierkegaard (Climacus) goes beyond Leibniz and Jacobi by stressing the normative nature of belief, combining the epistemic aspect of historical belief with an ethical aspect. He claims that "belief is not a knowledge but an act of freedom, an expression of will" (SKS 4, 281 / PF, 83). Despite appearances, the point is *not* that we change beliefs at will, as doxastic voluntarism maintains (SKS 4, 264 / PF, 62; cf. Evans 2006b: 299–304). Rather, beliefs are contingent and revisable, involving

metaphysics). Leibniz uses the term "belief" to describe knowledge that is concluded by judging from effects (Løkke and Waaler 2009: 62). To arrive at a belief, we must infer the cause from its effect (e.g., inferring Homer from the *Iliad*). At this point, the "Interlude" of *Philosophical Fragments* (especially §4) develops this idea further by distinguishing between the uncertainty of (historical) belief and the certitude of immediate sense perception and cognition (SKS 4, 281 / PF, 82).

[7] For Kierkegaard, such agency cannot be constituted by Leibnizian individual monadic essences that determine actions, since freedom operates in the history of individuals. Indeed, Kierkegaard is not only a libertarian concerning freedom but also a noncompatibilist (Kosch 2006a: ch. 5). Again, I am indebted to a reviewer here.

interpretation. We are not only morally responsible for the actions we perform but also for the (contingent) beliefs we form and the interpretations we develop (cf. Rasmussen 2009: 43). As early as 1838, Kierkegaard therefore claims that we are morally responsible for our intellectual views, not just our actions (SKS 17:271–2, DD:180 / KJN 1, 262). Indeed, belief choices are actions for Kierkegaard (Emmanuel 1996: 57). Both here and elsewhere, he is therefore concerned with the *ethics of belief*, the epistemic and practical normativity that governs the formation, maintenance, and relinquishment of beliefs (see Chapter 13).

When developing the category of the "leap," the *Postscript* references Jacobi's notion of the leap as a "*salto mortale*" (a mortal leap, heels over head). However, Kierkegaard (Climacus) immediately distances himself from Jacobi's *salto mortale* and its associated religious fideism or irrationalism by presenting two objections to Jacobi (SKS 7, 98–9 / CUP1, 100–1). First, he objects that Jacobi's leap is nothing but a transition from the objectivism of Spinoza's philosophy to subjectivism. This was a well-known objection found in Hegelianism (Rasmussen 2009: 38–9). Second, he sketches an objection to the effect that Jacobi's attempt to persuade Lessing to make the leap was mistaken, since a true leap cannot be communicated straightforwardly, since it is an "isolating act" that cannot be conveyed directly (Hannay 2006: 60). Thus, Kierkegaard seems generally critical of Jacobi's position (cf. SKS 7, 227 / CUP1, 250).

Still, Jacobi is often seen as a forerunner of Kierkegaard.[8] George di Giovanni and Paolo Livieri indicate some of the reasons why Jacobi is seen in this way:

> Because of Jacobi's insistence on the primacy of immediate existence over reflective conceptualization, and of the rights of the "exception" [against Kantian universalization in ethics], the possibility is there to interpret his position as a case of proto-existentialism, and to treat him, just as Kierkegaard, as an essentially religious thinker (Beiser, 1987). Indeed, some of the language Jacobi uses, and the themes he explores, are to be found in Kierkegaard again. (Whether the latter was himself an existentialist is, of course, itself an open question.) One must however keep in mind that the language of the "leap of faith" does not belong to Jacobi. The *salto mortale* he had proposed to Lessing was no leap into the unknown but, according to his explicit testimony, a jump that would have brought Lessing, who had been walking on his head in the manner of philosophers, back to his feet . . .

[8] Much the same holds for Johann Georg Hamann (1730–88), who was Jacobi's colleague and ally. See Betz 2007.

> In sum, Jacobi's figure, including its place within the Enlightenment, is much more complex than usually assumed, and still in need of discussion ... It might well be that the secret of this complexity is that Jacobi, just like Kierkegaard after him, was motivated by deeply conservative beliefs which he saw threatened by the culture of the day; but, again like Kierkegaard, in trying to reassert them, developed a language that was later to be used, contrary to anything he would have ever imagined, to undermine them instead. (2018: Part v)

Scholars point out that Kierkegaard never speaks of a "*leap of faith*." But it is not well-known that this notion (or its German equivalent) was first attributed to Kierkegaard in 1896 by Christoph Schrempf (a controversial German translator of Kierkegaard, who is not known for reliability).[9] Still, by a "leap of faith," Schrempf means a leap *into* a state of faith, not a leap which is itself an act of faith (Schreiber 2018: 257–9). This usage is in line with the *Postscript*, which describes a leap into Christian faith (although faith itself is an act rather than a state). Specifically, the *Postscript* speaks of "the qualitative transition of the leap from [nonbeliever] to believer [*Springets qvalitative Overgang fra Ikke-Troende til Troende*]" (SKS 7, 21 / CUP1, 12). But Christian faith hardly results from leaping alone. Rather, it seems to involve Christian doctrine combined with the double movement of faith (see Chapters 6, 7, 9, and 11).

In any case, it has been objected that a leap into faith cannot be based on faith, since faith is the *result* of the leap, not its *presupposition*.[10] Still, we must distinguish between two different beliefs or faiths here (the Danish *Tro* and the German *Glaube* both cover both). The Christian belief after the leap differs from the pre-Christian belief that the leap is based on. But *both are nevertheless beliefs*. Specifically, the leap into Christianity seems based on a pre-Christian belief in which one's situation is deemed desperate or hopeless. It is not a blind leap in the dark since one abandons hopelessness and despair by converting to Christianity (Grøn 1997: ch. 7). Therefore, one knows what one is leaping from and what one is leaping to (cf. Evans 2006b: 129). Indeed, the leap seems based on a comparative judgment of old and new standards.

Such a comparison need not be blind or irrational. But since the leap of faith has exactly such irrational and fideist connotations it is misleading to attribute it to Kierkegaard (although it would be fitting in other respects

[9] Schreiber 2018: 257 references Christoph Schrempf (1896) "Vorwort," in Harald Höffding, *Sören Kierkegaard als Philosoph*, Stuttgart: Frommann, iii–x, vi.

[10] Schreiber (2018: 257) referencing Alastair McKinnon (who traces the "leap of faith" to Walter Lowrie's 1945 translation of the *Postscript*).

since it is a leap from and to faith). Still, there is a deeper problem here concerning *normative pluralism* since the leap involves a transition from one normative domain to another. Any comparison of standards therefore seems based *either* on old standards *or* on new ones. Kierkegaard recognizes this, frequently using the Aristotelian expression "*metabasis eis allo genos*" to describe a transition from one genus to another (cf. SKS 7, 96–7 / CUP1, 98). However, we will return to this problem later since it motivates irrationalist and fideist readings of Kierkegaard (to be discussed in Chapters 11–13).

In addition, there is a further problem which has to do with *reasons internalism*. Since Christian faith relies on divine revelation, not mere reason alone, it seems clear that it *cannot* be internal to the actual motivational set of pagans or potential believers. To allow revelation, the actual motivational set of potential believers must therefore be *enlarged* so that new normative reasons can be articulated and discovered. The motivational set must then be changed by acquiring new beliefs (particularly sin-consciousness seems important here).

Leaping Across "the Broad and Ugly Ditch": Lessing

In this context, *Concluding Unscientific Postscript* introduces Lessing's notion of the leap. In the famous dialogue with Jacobi, the leap is described as follows:

> *Lessing* . . . I rather like your *salto mortale*; and I can see how a thinking head might perform this kind of headstand just to get out of the bit [to get going]. Take me with you, if you can!
> [*Jacobi*]. If you will just step on the springboard which lifts me off, the rest will take care of itself.
> *Lessing*. But even that would mean taking a leap which I can no longer impose on my old legs and heavy head. (Jacobi 2005: 251–2)

In Lessing's own words, the leap is described as follows:

> If no historical truth can be demonstrated, then nothing can be demonstrated *by means of* historical truths. That is: *contingent truths of history can never become the proof of necessary truths of reason* . . . But to make the leap from this historical truth into a quite different class of truths . . . – if this is not a "transition to another category [*metabasis eis allo genos*]", I do not know what Aristotle meant by that phrase . . . this is the broad and ugly ditch [*der garstige, breite Graben*] which I cannot get across, no matter how often and earnestly I have tried to make the leap. (Lessing 1777: 9, 12, 13; 2005: 85, 87)

Lessing portrays the leap as a transition from historical truths to necessary truths, relying on a broadly Leibnizian distinction between contingent and necessary truths (see Thompson 2009). Unlike Kierkegaard, however, Lessing equates necessary truths of reason with the central truths of Christianity (Howland 2012: 112). When Kierkegaard (Climacus), in response to Lessing and Jacobi, develops his own notion of the leap, the leap still concerns the conversion to Christianity. But it is no longer a transition from contingent truths of history to necessary truths of reason. Instead, it is a transition from *natural ethico-religious truths to historical Christianity* (Michalson 1985: 73–4; Thompson 2009: 103–4). The *Postscript* describes it as a transition from immanent to transcendent religiousness, that is a transition from presuppositions we possess naturally by our own powers to presuppositions that are *supernaturally* revealed by God (SKS 7, 234–8 / CUP1, 258–62).[11] Thus, Kierkegaard (Climacus) changes the meaning of the term "leap," something he seems aware of, speaking of possible theses (rather than actual theses) by Lessing in this context (Michalson 1985: ch. 4). This indicates that Kierkegaard (Climacus) is not only interested in what Lessing actually said but also what he could have said. Still, Lessing and Kierkegaard agree that religious faith is not based on information or knowledge that is empirical or historical. For Kierkegaard, Christian revelation is supernatural, whereas Lessing takes religious truths to be *a priori* and necessary.

Lessing was a leading Enlightenment philosopher who advocated theological naturalism, whereas Kierkegaard is typically seen as reacting against the Enlightenment, and against naturalism and rationalism in matters of religion by insisting on the supernatural and paradoxical nature of divine revelation. However, it seems that Kierkegaard was not only influenced by Lessing's literary style but also appears to have found Lessing useful for acknowledging the limits of reason, for avowing the never-ending quest for truth, for valuing subjectivity, irony, humor, and polemics (Thompson 2009).

Indeed, the *Postscript* devotes a section comprising two chapters to Lessing (SKS 7, 65–120 / CUP1, 61–125). These two chapters are called "An Expression of Gratitude to Lessing" and "Possible and Actual Theses by Lessing." The *Postscript* attributes the following four theses to Lessing:

1. The subjective existing thinker is aware of the dialectic of communication.

[11] Mats Wahlberg (2020: Part 1.1) explains: "the counterpart to natural revelation . . . is supernatural revelation . . . 'Supernatural', in a theological context, refers to putative divine action that is not included in God's ordinary activity of creating and sustaining the world."

2. The subjective existing thinker relates to truth as a process of becoming.
3. The transition from historical to eternal truth takes the form of a leap.
4. The never-ending striving for truth is preferable to the possession of truth (SKS 7, 73, 80, 92, 103 / CUP1, 72, 80, 93, 106).

Of these four theses, the latter two are more definitely traceable to Lessing than the first two, although the second resembles the fourth (Thompson 2009: 97; cf. Westphal 1996: 59–99). The first thesis indicates that Kierkegaard (Climacus) took Lessing (like Kant) to be a Socratic and maieutic philosopher, associating Lessing with irony and jest. Lessing is taken to say that we only relate to the Deity one at a time, without the mediation of others (SKS 7, 67–70 / CUP1, 65–7). The second thesis does not deny that there is an eternal truth but denies that we possess certain and final knowledge of it. The third point makes creative use of Lessing by developing Lessing's notion of the leap (and Jacobi's *salto mortale*) further in order to fit Kierkegaard's (Climacus') own purposes.

Finally, the *Postscript* quotes approvingly a famous remark by Lessing:

> *If God held all truth enclosed in his right hand, and in his left hand the one and ever-striving drive for truth, even with the corollary of erring forever and ever, and if he were to say to me: Choose! – I would humbly fall down to him at his left hand and say: Father, give! Pure truth is indeed only for you alone!* (SKS 7, 103 / CUP1, 106; original emphasis)

This quotation suggests, in a Socratic manner, that we should strive for truth rather than possess it. This is in line with the approach to Lessing elsewhere in the *Postscript* where Lessing is seen as a Socrates whose jest betrays a sense of the objective uncertainty of all that is important (Hannay 2006: 61; cf. Howland 2012; SKS 7, 192 / CUP1, 210). Elsewhere, Kierkegaard tries to improve on Lessing by saying:

> [N]o, if God held salvation in his right hand and also held in his left hand the concern that had become the content of your life, would you not yourself choose the left although you nevertheless became like someone who chose the right? (SKS 5, 267 / EUD, 272).

We are not saved by choosing salvation or happiness as such, but by choosing the concern or striving for good and truth for its own sake. Instead of being motivated by personal happiness and salvation, we should be motivated by moral goodness and seek truth for its own sake. In this context, Kierkegaard (Climacus) explicitly breaks with eudaimonism (SKS 7, 367, 385–7, 546 / CUP1, 403, 423–6, 602), favoring a Kantian approach to morality and prudence (as seen in Chapters 4–5).

"An Uncertain Leap" and Kant's "Honest Way"

Kierkegaard is clearly familiar with Kant's philosophy of religion and the heated discussions over the existence of God and immortality among Kant's successors in Germany and Denmark. Indeed, it is these very discussions that make up the context for Kierkegaard's ethical and religious thought.[12] Existing scholarship points to considerable overlap between the theories of Kant and Kierkegaard, although it is generally difficult to identify the Kantian influence on Kierkegaard in detail. Kierkegaard knew Kant from many secondary sources (e.g., Hans M. Martensen's lectures), but only quotes from three primary sources (*Dreams of a Spirit-Seer*, "An Answer to the Question: What Is Enlightenment?," and *Conflict of the Faculties*).[13] The Kantian elements in Kierkegaard can be summarized as follows.

As we saw in Chapter 8, Kierkegaard's notion of finitude comes close to Kant's critical philosophy. Both thinkers hold that human reason fails through its essential finitude to be an absolute (perspectiveless) perspective of the world.[14] Therefore, we cannot see the world from an absolute point of view nor have any knowledge of the supersensible or supernatural. Here Kierkegaard seems to follow Kant in dismissing theoretical proofs for the existence of God. Specifically, he takes Kant's critique of the ontological argument for God's existence to show that being is not a predicate, and that thought and being, ideality and reality, are therefore heterogeneous (SKS 4, 319 / CA, 11; SKS 19, 139–40, Not4:11 / KJN 3, 139; SKS 22, 215, NB12:121 / KJN 6, 217; SKS 22, 435, NB14:150 / KJN 6, 440). For Kierkegaard, this clearly indicates that being, existence, and actuality are fundamentally contingent and factual, something thought, essences, and possibilities are not. Pure reason can know the latter but not the former, since the former involves historical contingencies and free agency that initiate new causal chains that cannot be known a priori. Thus seen, Kant anticipates the crucial distinction between *being and thought*,

[12] For Kierkegaard's references to Kant's philosophy of religion, see SKS 18, 343, KK:4 / KJN 2, 320; SKS K18, 503; SKS 19, 141–3, Not4:12; KJN 3, 140–2. For related references to Kant, see also SKS 18, 44–5, EE:118 / KJN 2, 40; SKS 18, 204, JJ:202 / KJN 2, 188. For the Danish debate on immortality (particularly Poul Martin Møller), see SKS 7, 159 / CUP1, 172; SKS 17, 134, BB:41 / KJN 1, 127; cf. Koch 2004: 258–64.

[13] Green 1992: ch. 1. But the quote from *Conflict of the Faculties* is somewhat uncertain since the exact same quote occurs in *Toward Perpetual Peace*. See Fremstedal 2014a: 233–4.

[14] Westphal (1991: 89) argues that if the Kantian distinction between the noumenal and phenomenal worlds is that between the way in which one world appears to God and us, then the Kantian dualism is fundamental to Kierkegaard's epistemology too. Cf. Green 1992: 121–46.

actuality and possibility, existence and essence, the concrete and abstraction that was developed more systematically by the late Schelling and Kierkegaard.[15]

In connection with the physico-theological proof for God's existence, Kant criticizes the "mighty leap" from "the territory of nature and experience" to "the realm of mere possibilities" (A630/B658). He thus speaks of a leap from actuality to mere possibility that clearly anticipates Kierkegaard. However, instead of leaping across Lessing's "ugly, broad ditch," Kant speaks of making "only an uncertain leap over the narrowest ditch [*über den schmalsten Graben einen nur unsicheren Sprung thun*]" (WE 8:36). For Kant, this leap represents a leap into enlightenment, which dares to think for itself. Still, even such enlightenment seems to require moral faith. It is presumably because of its rationality that Kant describes the leap as "an uncertain leap over the narrowest ditch." The point seems to be that the leap can be justified rationally, despite epistemic uncertainty. In any case, Kierkegaard would be familiar with Kant's use of the "leap" here since it occurs in a text he refers to explicitly, namely "An Answer to the Question: What Is Enlightenment" (see SKS 23, 129–30, NB16:48 and NB16:50 / KJN 7, 130–2; SKS K23, 212–14).

Due to the limits of reason, both Kant and Kierkegaard hold that we cannot decide theoretically whether or not God exists. Epistemic evidence neither proves nor disproves God's existence. Still, we can – and must – decide the matter on subjective and practical grounds. Indeed, Kierkegaard repeatedly associates these points with Kant's critical philosophy (SKS 1, 194 / CI, 144; SKS 4, 319 / CA, 11; SKS 7, 502 / CUP1, 552–3; SKS 19, 139–40, Not4:11 / KJN 3, 139; SKS 19, 331, Not11:20 / KJN 3, 329; SKS 22, 435, NB14:150 / KJN 6, 440). Again and again, he contrasts Kant's "honest way" with the dishonesty of post-Kantian philosophy, particularly with Hegelianism (SKS 6, 142 / SLW, 152; SKS 19, 170, Not4:46 / KJN 3, 167; SKS 20, 229, NB2:235 / KJN 4, 229; SKS 22, 215, NB12:121 / KJN 6, 216–17; SKS 27, 390, Papir 365:2 / KJN 11.2, 92; SKS 27, 415, Papir 369 / KJN 11.2, 117).

In *Critique of Pure Reason*, Kant reconciles faith and reason by "deny[ing] *knowledge* in order to make room for *faith*" (B xxx). However, knowledge

[15] SKS 19, 311–12, Not11:8 / KJN 3, 309–10; cf. Pinkard 2010: 320–9; Stewart 2010: 80–1, 93–4; Hühn and Schwab 2013: 69. Hühn and Schwab (2013: 70) argue that Kierkegaard reserves actuality in a preeminent sense for the individual human existence in its concretion, defining existence in terms of singularity and interest. As a result, the hiatus between actual and possible posited by Schelling is deepened so that existing entities are outside any logical system. For the importance of Hamann regarding the priority of existence to thinking, see Betz 2007: 307.

(*Wissen*) and faith (*Glaube*, sometimes translated belief) are both technical notions, explained in "The Canon of Pure Reason" (A822–30/B850–8). Knowledge requires sufficient epistemic evidence. Faith, by contrast, is not based on epistemic evidence, since it concerns issues that we cannot possibly have knowledge of (notably, God and immortality). That is to say, we can neither have sufficient epistemic reasons for nor against faith. Still, there can be perfectly good reasons to have faith. Instead of being justified epistemically (as knowledge is), faith is justified by practical (and moral) reasons. In contemporary terms, Kant therefore seems to be a pragmatist (practical nonevidentialist) concerning faith.[16] Faith requires a subjective, practical justification, whereas knowledge requires an objective, theoretical justification. But faith must nevertheless be objective in the broad sense of being intersubjectively valid and communicable (Chignell 2007: 355). However, its theoretical content does not provide any knowledge but only serves to guide action (Neiman 1997: 158).

In one variant of the moral argument for the existence of God and immortality, Kant argues that the alternative to religious faith and hope is *demoralization* that involves despair and a loss of moral resolve. This seems to be a point about the moral psychology of ordinary agents who do not know if they are making a difference for the better by being moral. Without faith and hope, agents tend to become demoralized when their moral efforts do not seem to be making a difference.

Specifically, Kant argues that moral agents who face normative conflict between morality and prudence, in which virtue leads to unhappiness and vice to happiness, tend to be demoralized, in the sense that their moral motivation is weakened or deteriorates (see Adams 1987: 151–6). First, there is a tendency towards general moral *despair* in the face of such normative conflict (or moral injustice).[17] Second (and partially because of this), demoralization involves a psychological loss of resolve to continue to be moral.[18] In the face of normative conflict, injustice, and personal unhappiness, moral agents tend to lose moral resolve. Kant therefore concludes

[16] Cf. Chignell 2007 and 2018; Gava and Stern 2017. However, Stern (2017) suggests that Kant relies on moral evidence instead of epistemic evidence. But this is hardly evidentialism in an ordinary sense. Even the moral evidentialism discussed in Chignell (2018: Part V.II) holds that evidence is epistemic, not moral, although it adds that we have moral reason to follow epistemic evidence. Finally, it should be mentioned that not all nonevidentialist belief needs to be practical. Chignell (2007: 345–54, 359) suggests that Kant allows doctrinal belief about theoretical issues (e.g., noumena).

[17] Both Kant and commentators describes the antinomy of practical reason in terms of (moral) despair (LPDR 28:1076; Wood 1970: 160; Wimmer 1990: 68, 156–9, 206; Marina 2000: 354; Kuehn 2001: 313; Beiser 2006: 616; Henrich 2008: 102).

[18] I am indebted to Andrew Chignell and Darrel Moellendorf here.

that, without faith in a God who makes possible a moral order (which provides justice), we are led to an unstable condition (*schwankender Zustand*), in which we continuously fall from hope into doubt, mistrust, and despair (LPDR 28:1076, 1151).

In the "Dialectic of Pure Practical Reason," in the second *Critique*, Kant analyzes conflict between morality and prudence: Instead of merely invoking empirical evidence that indicates normative conflict, Kant sketches a transcendental argument in which morality must deviate from our prudential striving for happiness (CPR 5:146–7). Jens Timmermann explains:

> [If we] cannot experience any tension between prudence and the demands of morality [we] cannot be moved by, or take a pure interest in, the moral law as such . . . We need the "subjective antagonism" . . . of moral law and inclination for the law to affect our subjectivity. When we perceive that selfishness and moral judgement conflict, we realize for the first time that we are *not* enthralled by inclination, and that there is something within us that is active and radically free. This inspires respect, which in turn enables us to act independently of self-regarding considerations. (2013: 674–5)

We cannot chose morality for its own sake only unless it deviates from and conflicts with prudence. For morality would serve self-interest if it coincided perfectly with prudence (cf. Chapter 5). Still, we should promote and approximate the highest good, a moral world in which (only) the virtuous are happy (CPR 5:113–33; R 6:97–102). We have moral reasons to minimize normative conflict and injustice, since these problems tends to produce demoralization and despair. But morality is then committed to an end, the highest good, the realization of which lies beyond human powers. Specifically, divine assistance is needed for morality to cause happiness *and* for uniting the forces of separate individuals so that they participate in the ethical commonwealth or church (R 6:139).

Kant therefore concludes that faith in God (and immortality) is morally necessary and not some arbitrary assumption we could do without if we are to think consistently (CPR 5:132, 142–6, 152; Ak 5:451n; O 8:137–9). Religious faith is justified on the grounds that it resolves the antinomy of practical reason, a form of moral despair in which the highest good appears both necessary and impossible simultaneously (cf. Fremstedal 2014a: ch. 6). Specifically, Kant resolves the antinomy by arguing that the impossibility of the highest good is only apparent if God and immortality exist.

In his reply to critics, Kant concedes that he postulates the existence of God and immortality based on a human need. However, he denies that this involves wishful thinking, since the postulate is based on a *need of reason* rather than inclinations (CPR 5:143–4). Despite lack of evidence, reason must make a judgment based on practical reason in order to orient itself (O 8:137). Kant concludes that "I *will* that there be a God . . . this is the only case in which my interest, because I *may* not give up anything of it, unavoidably determines my judgment" (CPR 5:143). The proof for the existence of God lies "merely in the moral need" (LE 27:718). Dieter Henrich comments:

> To believe that the world order does not allow moral life would be to precipitate absolute despair. For that reason I *do not* believe it. Even if I think that I believe it, I am wrong. I do not believe that this is the case, no matter what I say. To read Kant this way is to encounter a sort of existential philosophy: there are well-founded beliefs that precede and survive all arguments. (2008: 102)

The existential philosophy Henrich sketches here comes close not only to religious existentialism but also to fideism and pragmatism concerning religious belief. It particularly fits Kierkegaard's claim that "[t]he best proof that there is a just governance [*Styrelse*] is to say: 'I will believe it, come what may'" (SKS 18, 296, JJ:469 / KJN 2, 273).

Still, Kant insists that belief, faith, and hope can be justified by practical reason, which transcends epistemic evidence. He therefore speaks of "rational belief" and "moral belief" (as well as a rational hope). Instead of being a fideist or irrationalist, Kant relies on a practical *reductio ad absurdum* argument. This argument clearly anticipates Kierkegaard by arguing that the alternative to religious faith (and hope) is despair and demoralization. Kant particularly anticipates this passage from the *Postscript*:[19]

> God is indeed a postulate, but not in the [pointless] sense in which it is ordinarily taken. Instead, it becomes clear that this is the only way an existing person enters into a relationship with God: when the dialectical contradiction brings passion to despair and assists him in grasping God with "the category of despair" (faith), so that the postulate, far from being the arbitrary, is in fact *necessary* defense, self-defense; in this way God is not a postulate, but the existing person's postulation of God is – a necessity. (SKS 7, 183n / CUP1, 200n, slightly modified transl.)

The necessity here is not epistemic but practical and subjective, since God must be postulated to avoid despair (cf. SKS 11, 195–6 / SUD, 81). This

[19] Rapic (2007: 43) interprets this passage as a comment on Kant, whereas Green (1992: 139) claims that Kierkegaard *follows* Kant in postulating God's existence. Also, Ferreira (1998: 232–3n4) and McCombs (2013: 213) see it as a reference to Kant's God-postulate. See also Fremstedal 2014a: ch. 6.

suggests a *reductio ad absurdum* of nonbelief, in which the absurdity involves practical absurdity in the form of hopelessness and despair. Like Kant, Kierkegaard here sketches a practical *reductio ad absurdum* argument, in which nonbelief is rejected as absurd practically.[20]

Kierkegaard therefore seems influenced not only by Kant's critique of theoretical proofs for God's existence but also by his moral argument for the existence of God and immortality. Specifically, the postulation of God in the *Postscript*, the related critique of purposelessness in *Fear and Trembling*, and the "new argument" for immortality in *Christian Discourses* overlap significantly with Kant's moral argument (SKS 7, 183 / CUP1, 200; SKS 4, 112 / FT, 15; SKS 10, 214–21 / CD, 205–13; SKS 20, 289, NB4:5 / KJN 4, 288–9).[21] Both Kant and Kierkegaard justify religious faith on subjective and practical rather than objective and theoretical grounds. Both rely on a *reductio* argument in which nonbelief involves despair and an absurdity or antinomy, in which the highest good is simultaneously necessary and impossible. For both, God makes the highest good possible, despite its apparent impossibility. And both take religion to be first and foremost a practical matter that concerns how we live our lives (see Chapters 5–9).

In this context, Kierkegaard appears influenced by Kant's account of the dialectics of reason.[22] Kant argues that reason has a natural and inevitable tendency to exceed the limits of the understanding, since it seeks the unconditioned for everything conditioned in order to make the chain of conditions complete (A307/B364). However, the unconditioned as such cannot be reached since it lies outside the boundaries of our finite reason. Nor can God as such be reached, although the natural dialectic of reason in

[20] For Kant, see Wood 1970: 29–34. In Denmark, Møller developed a similar practical *reductio* in his article on immortality. Specifically, he argued that the alternative to belief in immortality is suicide or nihilism. Belief in immortality avoids these problems, while allowing unity and meaning in life. See Møller 1842: 162, 164, 176, 210, 226, 230; cf. Koch 2004: 258–64.

[21] Green 1992: 139; Fremstedal 2014a: ch. 6. Although Kierkegaard does not explicitly criticize Leibniz's theoretical approach to theodicy, his general approach nevertheless comes closer to Kant than Leibniz. Instead of accepting theoretical theodicy, both Kierkegaard and Kant think that the limitations of human rationality give us reasons for not having reasons to defend, to justify, or accuse God. The critical project of using reason to determine, and acknowledge, the limits of reason lead Kant and Kierkegaard to reject theoretical efforts to defend God in light of moral and natural evil in the world, since we cannot know God's relation to good and evil by inferring from the physical world. Both therefore interpret theodicy as a practical rather than a theoretical problem, opposing not only Leibniz's theodicy but also Hegel's theodicy through history. Cf. Welz 2008: 14–17, 83–7, 176–8.

[22] There is strong consensus here. See Thomas 1980: 203; Westphal 1991: 113; Green 1992: 77–8; Evans 1999: 222–4; Verheyden 2000: 157; Tjønneland 2004: 88–95; Pinkard 2010: 348; Fremstedal 2014a: chs. 5 and 11.

its theoretical use leads to the idea of God as a regulative principle (A670–82/B698–710). Here Kierkegaard (Climacus) seems influenced by Kant's view that the dialectic use of reason leads to the question of God. For Kierkegaard (Climacus), the highest passion of the understanding lies in it dialectically transcending its limit by becoming faith (SKS 7, 444–5 / CUP1, 490–1; SKS 4, 242–53 / PF, 37–47).

Kierkegaard also makes sporadic use of Kant's related distinction between regulative and constitutive principles (SKS 17, 270, DD:176 / KJN 1, 261; SKS 1, 311 / CI, 275; SKS 4, 86 / R, 219; SKS 11, 226 / SUD, 115). In his notes from Martensen's lectures, Kierkegaard refers not only to the regulative (heuristic) use of ideas (and Kant's moral argument) but specifically to the regulative status of God as an ideal we should strive for although it is outside of our reach (SKS 19, 139–43, Not4:11–12 / KJN 3, 139–42, 539, esp. SKS 19, 140, Not4:11 / KJN 3, 139). Even elsewhere, Kierkegaard interprets human selfhood in terms of an endless striving tending towards an endpoint of completion that seems to involve a regulative God-idea that is Kantian (cf. Pattison 1997; Verstrynge 2004; Bubbio 2014: ch. 4; Dalferth 2015: 75). Such regulative ideas are *transcendental*, surpassing all boundaries of experience; experience cannot therefore provide objects adequate for the ideas (A327/B384). Any progress towards transcendent ideas will therefore at best involve an asymptotic approximation that never reaches the transcendent as such.

Like Kant, Kierkegaard interprets symbols of religion and art as visible representations of transcendent ideas (that lie beyond the limits of our understanding).[23] Both see symbols and images as transitional forms that mediate between transcendent ideas and experience. For both, the invisible must be represented and symbolized by something visible if we are to grasp it practically. Religious language is therefore symbolic, allegoric, metaphorical (Winkel Holm 1998: 135–7, 319–20; Pattison 2002: 122–33). Kant writes:

> God's way can perhaps be so mysterious that, at best, he could reveal it to us in a symbolic representation in which the practical import alone is comprehensible to us, whereas theoretically, we could not in the least grasp what this relation of God to the human being is in itself, or attach concepts to it, even if God wanted to reveal such a mystery to us. (R 6:171)

Bubbio comments:

> [T]he answers provided by the two philosophers are very similar. For Kant, moral laws need to be symbolized: religious symbols, therefore, must be used

[23] Kant develops this in the third *Critique* and in *Religion within the Boundaries of Mere Reason*. Cf. Tjønneland 2004: 84–96; Bubbio 2014; Fremstedal 2014a: ch. 8.

> to apply the principles of practical reason to experience, so that they can serve as models for our behavior and play a regulative role in the application of moral ideas to the world [R 6:65]. The religious symbol *par excellence* is represented by Kant in the figure of Christ, "the Master of the Gospels." Christ represents the *prototype* of a pure moral disposition, one willing to undergo the greatest sacrifices (sacrifice unto death) to be morally perfect. (2014: 105)

Bubbio here takes Kant to develop a *kenotic* approach to sacrifice that anticipates Kierkegaard (2014: chs. 1, 4). Indeed, Kierkegaard's view is very similar to that of Kant (Bubbio 2014: 105–6). For Kierkegaard, the transcendent is symbolized by something visible, while Christ in particular represents – and symbolizes – moral perfection. Christ thus represents a prototype and paradigm that we should imitate. Christ and his suffering then take on a regulative role for Christian existence. Specifically, it requires a kenotic attitude of sacrifice that is unselfish and without reward, while still being something that constitutes the Christian as a Christian (Bubbio 2014: 106–9; cf. SKS 9, 123–4, 133, 274 / WL, 119–20, 131, 276).

In *The Jäsche Logic* (1800), Kant also anticipates Kierkegaard by stressing the personal nature of faith:

> I see myself necessitated through my end, in accordance with the laws of freedom, to accept as possible a highest good in the world, but I cannot necessitate anyone else through grounds (the belief is free) . . . on account of its merely subjective grounds, believing yields no conviction that can be communicated and that commands universal agreement, like the conviction that comes from knowledge. (LL 9:69–70)

Faith cannot be commanded since it is only authentic if each individual freely accepts it personally (CPR 5:144). Even if faith cannot be communicated just like knowledge is communicated, it nevertheless seems that faith must be intersubjectively *valid* and possible to share or communicate (Chignell 2007: 326–7, 355). Still, Kant suggests that every individual must reach faith on his own by realizing that he must believe in order to avoid despair and demoralization.

In this context, Kant warns not only against demoralization but also against passivity and undecidedness:

> [N]o more miserable condition for man can be thought . . . than the condition that leaves us undecided [*unentschloßen*] . . . particularly . . . when it affects our interests. Everything that holds us up and makes us inactive, leaves us in a certain kind of inaction, is quite opposed to the essential determinations of the soul. (LL 24:203)

Kant then uses Socrates as an example: "Even in the context of utter uncertainty in speculation there can be complete decisiveness in action. Socrates was uncertain [about immortality], but he acted as if he were certain."[24] This interpretation of Socrates clearly anticipates Kierkegaard's interpretation of him in the *Postscript* (cf. Westphal 2012: 142; Stewart 2015b: 153–4, 163–4). Like Christians, Socrates does not know if he has an immortal soul, but he nevertheless stakes his life on his faith (SKS 7, 187–92 / CUP1, 205–10), although it is based on practical reasons, not epistemic evidence. To Socrates, philosophy is then not so much a theoretical doctrine as a way of life based on moral faith. To Kant and Kierkegaard, Socrates is a protoexistential philosopher who unifies thought and life to the extent that he risks his life for his faith.

Like other enlightenment thinkers (*Aufklärer*), Kant appeals to Socrates as a forerunner of the Enlightenment and as a champion of its project.[25] Kierkegaard continues this trend by appropriating Socrates for his own purposes, interpreting him as a protoexistentialist (cf. Stewart 2015b). However, Kierkegaard's interpretation of Socrates is not only influenced by Lessing (Howland 2012) but also by Kantianism and Kant's friend Hamann. *The Concept of Anxiety* quotes Hamann by saying, "For Socrates was great in 'that he distinguished between what he understood and what he did not understand'" (SKS 4, 310 / CA, 3). Kierkegaard writes:

> [T]his theoretical ignorance [of Socrates], for which the eternal nature of the divine remained a mystery [*Hemmelighet*], must have had its counterpart in a similar religious ignorance of the divine dispensations [*Styrelser*] and direction in human life, a religious ignorance that seeks its edification and discloses its piety in a total ignorance. (SKS 1, 223 / CI, 176)

Particularly the following elements in Kierkegaard's Socrates seems Kantian:[26]

1. The idea of staking life on religious faith that is theoretically unfounded yet supported by morality (cf. Westphal 2012: 142).
2. The interpretation of Socrates as a midwife or occasion (Danish, *Anledning*; *Foranledning*), who reveals truth by throwing the learner back on his own natural resources, appears based on Kant's use of the notion of occasion (German, *Veranlassung*) in *Conflict of Faculties* (Green 1994: 173–5; 2011: 129–30; Fremstedal 2014a: 165–7).

24 Ak 24:433, translated in Zammito 2002: 277.
25 For this Enlightenment use of Socrates, see Betz 2012: 63.
26 For Kierkegaard's Kantian interpretation of Socrates, see Wyller 1999: 161, 171; Habermas 2019: vol. II, 672.

3. Socrates in the *Postscript* represents natural religion (immanent religiousness) that includes infinite guilt-consciousness and awareness of the human inability to realize the highest good (SKS 7, 390–1, 503, 519 / CUP1, 429–30, 554, 571–2). But this presupposes Augustinian and Kantian ideas such as moral rigorism, infinite guilt, and the highest good.
4. Both here and elsewhere, Kierkegaard's knowledge of the history of philosophy is colored by Kantianism, particularly that of Tennemann (1798–1819) (cf. Green 1992: 114–19; Løkke 2010: 47).

Still, Kierkegaard goes beyond Kantianism by relying on Hamann, viewing Socrates as a proto-Christian (something there is a long Christian tradition for – Betz 2012: 63–82).[27]

Kierkegaard generally views Kant as a prominent or exemplary Socratic philosopher who stresses human finitude and ignorance. But this also indicates Kant's limitation for Kierkegaard. Kant identifies the antinomy of practical reason and moral despair, but he hardly makes room for anything uniquely Christian in his rational theology. Here and elsewhere, Kierkegaard uses Kantian ideas to reinforce – and partially reinterpret – his own Christian convictions, combining the moral argument with Lutheran ideas about supernatural revelation and sin that go beyond Kant's critical philosophy. This is also related to the fact that Kant is associated with Enlightenment theology, theological rationalism, natural theology, and liberal theology, whereas Kierkegaard is seen as a critic of these movements (see Dorrien 2012: chs. 1, 2, and 5).

Still, Kierkegaard speaks approvingly of Kant's "radical evil" (SKS 20, 88–9, NB:125 / KJN 4, 88), a controversial doctrine that reinterprets original sin. Kierkegaard seems to agree with Kant on the following points: First, both evil and religion should be approached practically. The point is not to invent a theoretical doctrine of sin but to allow moral improvement (and salvation) by making us aware of our shortcomings (SKS 12, 80 / PC, 68). Second, we cannot be morally indifferent, or will the good to some extent only, since morality requires unconditional and complete compliance (i.e., the doctrine of moral rigorism). Third, evil or sin cannot be inherited biologically, but it is nevertheless contingently true that all humans (who have not yet converted to the good) are evil or sinful. Fourth, evil entails a corrupted character, or a character flaw, that cannot

[27] In addition, *The Concept of Irony* applies romantic irony to Socrates (something the later works do not do). See Tjønneland 2004: 67–9, 79–95.

be extirpated through human power. Fifth, we are responsible for the fall into evil, since it involves a misuse of freedom. Finally, both Kant and Kierkegaard argue that consciousness of freedom (in the sense of the power of choice, *Willkür*) leads to anxiety, which in turn precedes the fall into evil.[28]

Conclusion

Kierkegaard's use and appropriation of his German predecessors belongs for the most part to the period between 1841 and 1846, but the use of Kant and Fichte extends from 1833 to 1851.[29] Although Kierkegaard was fluent in German and familiar with classical German philosophy, his use of it is ambivalent, selective, eclectic, and assimilated to his own ends. Kierkegaard generally uses his German predecessors to develop a distinction between the spheres of existence and thought and to reinforce what he took to be genuine Christian faith. He particularly criticized naturalist, rationalist, and idealist interpretations of Christianity and attempts to synthetize Christianity with philosophy and culture.

Still, Kierkegaard's interpretation of religion in general and Christianity in particular is clearly influenced by his German predecessors. The "leap" is inspired by the Pantheism controversy, and the distinction between thought and being is influenced by Leibniz, Jacobi, Hamann, Kant, and Schelling. Finally, Kierkegaard's interpretation of arguments for religious belief seems influenced by Kant.

[28] The idea here seems to be that by giving in to anxiety, we tend to fall short of the moral requirement. For an analysis, see Fremstedal 2014a: 25–52, 165–7, 176.

[29] For Fichte, see Chapters 1–2 of the present monograph.

CHAPTER 11

Faith Neither Absurd Nor Irrational: The Neglected Reply to Eiríksson

Forgotten Sources: Eiríksson's Book and Kierkegaard's Reply

Kierkegaard responds not only to his German forerunners but also to his Danish contemporaries. Particularly his response to Magnús Eiríksson, a forgotten Icelandic theologian who lived in Copenhagen, is decisive for understanding his view of faith and reason. Ever since Eiríksson wrote his critique of Kierkegaard, *Is Faith a Paradox and "By Virtue of the Absurd"?* (1850), scholars have debated whether or not Kierkegaard is an irrationalist. Indeed, since the start of the Kierkegaard literature between 1850 and 1877, commentators have emphasized conflict between faith and reason, or between faith and knowledge (*Tro og Viden*) as it is known in Danish and German (cf. Koch 2004: chs. 10–12; Tullberg 2006: 12–15, 19–33, 46–54, 73–83).[1] Even today, many of the same issues are still discussed. The scholarly topics have thus been relatively constant over a 170-year period.[2]

Given this, it is astonishing that most of the literature ignores or downplays what is arguably *the* most important primary source for understanding Kierkegaard's views on absurdity, faith, and reason, namely his response to Eiríksson (esp. Pap. X–6, B68–B82 / JP 1, 9–12; JP 6, 6598–6601). As we will see, Kierkegaard rejects Eiríksson's claim that faith is irrational and absurd. In addition, his reply to Eiríksson is clearly relevant for understanding his much-discussed use of *pseudonyms* and the relation between *Fear and Trembling* and *Concluding Unscientific Postscript*. However, Kierkegaard did not publish the reply since he did not see the point of a public discussion with Eiríksson (Pap. X–6, B68–B82 / JP 1, 9–12; JP 6, 6598–6601).

[1] Eiríksson (1850) is the very first dedicated monograph on Kierkegaard to be written and published. But Nielsen (1849) published a book-length review of Kierkegaard and Martensen in 1849.

[2] For some examples, see Bohlin 1944: 29–109; McKinnon 1980: 126–7; Thomas 1980; Jackson 1987; Westphal 1991: vii, 21–7, 85–125; Knappe 2004: 59, 80–1, 118–20; Evans 2006b: 120–3; McCombs 2013.

Although the secondary literature often discusses absurdity and paradoxes, and faith and reason, Kierkegaard's response to Eiríksson's forgotten 1850 book was not published until 1934 when *Papirer* X–6 arrived. Still, it was only in 1962 that scholars discovered and partially analyzed Kierkegaard's response.[3] But even after this, most contributions overlook it,[4] probably because they overlook Eiríksson's book, upon which Kierkegaard is commenting, and so naturally find Kierkegaard's response difficult to understand. Indeed, Kierkegaard's drafted reply to Eiríksson is not even included in the new, critical edition of Kierkegaard's works in Danish (*Søren Kierkegaards Skrifter*; this edition is incomplete, largely leaving out the voluminous B sections of the *Papirer*). Nor is it included in the new translations in *Kierkegaard's Journals and Notebooks* since this work is based on *Søren Kierkegaards Skrifter*. Still, a few brief passages are included in Kierkegaard's *Journals and Papers* (JP 1, 9–12; JP 6, 6598–6601). Some of these passages make up some of the first passages of the first volume of *Journals and Papers* (JP 1, 9–12) – an indication of their importance. Although these passages are sometimes referenced by scholars,[5] they do not give any adequate overview of Kierkegaard's reply to Eiríksson's book. The present chapter will partially attempt to remedy these problems by showing the relevance of Kierkegaard's reply to Eiríksson, although it will also include some other relevant material.

In *Is Faith a Paradox and "By Virtue of the Absurd"?*, Eiríksson argues against the portrayal of religious faith as absurd in *Fear and Trembling* and *Concluding Unscientific Postscript* by claiming that faith is rational, although it transcends human understanding. Eiríksson makes the case that Kierkegaard's pseudonyms should have said something other than what they say, given fundamental ideas about Abrahamic religious faith that are shared by the pseudonyms and Eiríksson.

In 1850, Kierkegaard read *Is Faith a Paradox and "By Virtue of the Absurd"?* and drafted a long, interesting response that he did not publish (Pap. X–6, B68–B82 / JP 1, 9–12 and JP 6, 6598–6601).[6] In this draft, Kierkegaard (and his pseudonyms) praises the efforts of Eiríksson (or the pseudonym Nicolaus), as being sincere, honest, selfless, religious, and as

[3] Fabro 1962: 179–88. Bohlin (1944: 86) refers briefly to Pap. X–6, B68, and B79 without mentioning Eiríksson.

[4] See note 2 above for examples. [5] E.g., McCombs (2013: 22) refers briefly to JP 1, 10.

[6] Although the book was published pseudonymously, Kierkegaard seems to know that Eiríksson is behind the pseudonym Theophilus Nicolaus since he refers not just to Eiríksson's pseudonymous 1850 book but also to his signed 1846 book on rationality. See Pap. X–6, B68, 74 / JP 6, 6598, 301, which references Eiríksson 1846.

having moral worth (Pap. X–6, B68, 75–6 / JP 6, 6598). This is no small praise coming from Kierkegaard. Yet, he objects that Eiríksson's 1850 book is *not* sufficiently well-informed and that it lacks sharpness and dialectical rigor (Pap. X–6, B79, 85–6 / JP 1, 10). Thus, Kierkegaard concludes that Eiríksson's efforts are well-meant but that he lacks the necessary *theoretical* abilities. In addition, he distances himself from Eiríksson because Eiríksson's relentless public attacks on Martensen threatens to undermine Kierkegaard's indirect, pseudonymous critique of the establishment (Schreiber 2009: 86–9).[7] Kierkegaard therefore concludes that there is hardly any hope of real understanding between himself and Eiríksson. As a result, he (or his pseudonyms) will not publicly deal with Eiríksson. This appears to be why Kierkegaard never published his response to Eiríksson.

While Kierkegaard seems to think that he has little or nothing to gain from entering a public discussion with Eiríksson, his comments on Eiríksson's book show that Eiríksson's critique forces him to clarify important points. One could wish that Kierkegaard had engaged more with his contemporaries for the clarification of his points to which it would have led. Still, Kierkegaard indicates that *if* he were to answer Eiríksson, then the response should be attributed to himself and Anti-Climacus (Pap. X–6, B77, 84 / JP 6, 6600). But as it stands, Kierkegaard's seventeen-page response is attributed to the pseudonyms de silentio, Climacus, and Kierkegaard himself, although he mentions that one part may be attributed to Anti-Climacus.[8] De silentio and Climacus seem to be used because it is these authors that Eiríksson criticizes, while Anti-Climacus could be invoked to add some Christian seriousness and authority to the response.

Kierkegaard claims that pseudonyms make it possible to avoid a straightforward public attack on personal acquaintances (Pap. X–6, B128 / JP 6, 6596; Pap. VII–1, B88–B92). In addition, different

[7] Eiríksson is much more explicit and less polite than Kierkegaard when it comes to publicly singling out and attacking his enemies. Eiríksson identifies not just the Hegelians Heiberg and Martensen but also Hegel himself as enemies (1850: 118, 120, 122 and 1846: 10, 17–18, 30; cf. Pap. VII–1, B88–B92). He also tries to ally himself with Danish critics of Hegelianism, including not just Kierkegaard but also Rasmus Nielsen and Peter Michael Stilling (Eiríksson 1850: 160, 174). However, Eiríksson emphasizes that the Hegelians and Christendom represent the establishment, while he, Kierkegaard, and Nielsen are the underdogs. He contends that Kierkegaard and his allies have not received the attention they deserve, and that the establishment is using a *totschweigetaktik* (death by silence) against their critics (Schreiber 2009: 51–2).

[8] Pap. X–6, B68–B69, 72–8 and Pap. X–6, B72–B74, 80–3 are attributed to Climacus, while Pap. X–6, B70–B71, 78–80 is attributed to de silentio. Pap. X–6, B75–B76, 83–4 is not explicitly attributed to a pseudonym, although Pap. X–6, B75 mentions de silentio and appears to be a reworking of Pap. X–6, B68 that is attributed to Climacus. Pap. X–6, B77–B82, 84–8 is attributed to "me," apparently Kierkegaard. Finally, it is said that Pap. X–6, B79–B82, 85–8 (and possibly B78, 84–5) may best be attributed to Anti-Climacus. Cf. Schreiber 2009: 81n206.

pseudonyms represent different *perspectives* (SKS 23, 182–3, NB17:28 / KJN 7, 185). As mentioned, de silentio and Climacus speak as nonbelievers, whereas Anti-Climacus and Kierkegaard speak as Christian believers (see SKS 16, 17, 64–5n / PV, 31–2, 85–6n; Pap. X–6, B68 / JP 6, 6598; SKS 23, 182–3, NB17:28 / KJN 7, 185).

Kierkegaard faults Eiríksson for overlooking this perspectival approach when he bluntly identifies Kierkegaard with his pseudonyms (SKS 23, 182–3, NB17:28 / KJN 7, 185; Pap. X–6, B71, 80; Pap. X–6, B128 / JP 6, 6596). But even if Kierkegaard does not want to be simply identified with his pseudonyms (SKS 7, 571 / CUP1, 627), it does not follow that he disagrees with the pseudonyms or that the different voices are at odds with each other. Indeed, he writes:

> I would be glad to have another pseudonym, one who does not like Johannes de Silentio say he does not have faith, but plainly, positively says he has faith – Anti-Climacus – repeat what, as a matter of fact, is stated in the pseudonymous writings. (Pap. X–6, B82, 88 / JP 6, 6601)

We will see that Kierkegaard criticizes Eiríksson's contention that de silentio and Climacus are at odds with each other. Rather, the pseudonyms agree and repeat each other.

Like Kierkegaard, Eiríksson wants to promote genuine religious faith and to attack the inauthentic and complacent faith of bourgeois Christendom.[9] Both Kierkegaard and Eiríksson attack speculative theology for confusing authentic Christianity with bourgeois Christendom (Pap. X–6, B68, 72 / JP 6, 6598). Eiríksson's critique of *Fear and Trembling* and the *Postscript* thus belongs to a larger context where Eiríksson tries to ally himself with Kierkegaard against the Hegelians and the mainstream Danish intellectuals (something Kierkegaard does *not* appreciate; see Schreiber 2009: 51–2, 71–91).[10] Although he tries to ally himself with Kierkegaard and to supplement *Fear and Trembling*, Eiríksson's book focuses on his disagreement with de silentio and Climacus (1850: 2, 148). Indeed, Eiríksson indicates that he agrees with Martensen in the *principle* that Christian faith cannot possibly

[9] Eiríksson 1850: iv–v, 5–6, 9–12. Like Kierkegaard, Eiríksson criticizes those who believe that religious faith represents a defeated and outdated stage (1850: 13).

[10] For this reason, Eiríksson's critique of Kierkegaard's pseudonyms is much less harsh and satirical than his attack on Martensen. Eiríksson takes Kierkegaard much more seriously than most of his contemporaries did, and recommends *Fear and Trembling* highly to potential readers, partially because of its psychological insight. He describes de silentio as an ingenious and profound thinker and has deep respect for Climacus as well (Eiríksson 1850: 1, 18, 175). Eiríksson is interested in describing the character and state of mind of authentic religious believers (1850: 66). Although Eiríksson speaks highly of de silentio's psychological insight, he nevertheless objects that de silentio's descriptions are too idealized to be psychologically realistic (1850: 78).

be grounded in absurdity (although Martensen's application of this principle is said to be false; see Schreiber 2009: 65).

Eiríksson (1850: 20) accepts the Kierkegaardian view that authentic religious faith is about more than assenting to doctrine or dogma. Faith is not just about holding correct theoretical beliefs but also about how one leads one's life.[11] Like Kierkegaard, he therefore argues that Christendom puts too much emphasis on dogmas, confessions, ceremonies, and customs and too little emphasis on how we live our lives.[12] Both believe that authentic religiousness must be reintroduced in Christendom. Like de silentio, Eiríksson (1850: 71, 143, 147) appeals to Abraham, the father of faith, as a paradigmatic case of religious belief, contrasting Abraham with Danish Christendom.[13]

Faith Only Seemingly Absurd

As indicated by the title *Is Faith a Paradox and "By Virtue of the Absurd"?*, Eiríksson's central concern is whether religious faith is absurd, as claimed by de silentio and Climacus. Eiríksson (1850: 159) argues that de silentio and Climacus do not offer any real proof for the alleged absurdity of faith and concludes that faith is neither absurd for religious believers nor for God, although it may appear absurd to nonbelievers (e.g., de silentio and Climacus). To believers, however, faith is rational and reasonable, although it transcends human understanding and knowledge.

Like the late Jacobi, Eiríksson contrasts a higher reason (based on faith) with mere understanding.[14] Kierkegaard, by contrast, denies that there is

[11] Eiríksson (1850) describes the necessary doctrines in a minimalist manner as the belief that God is wise, good, and powerful (omnipotent). More emphasis is put on the believer's unconditional trust (*tillid*) in God as well as his obedience towards God. This trust and obedience should be expressed in the whole life of the believer, Eiríksson maintains. By being obedient and imitating God, the believer becomes not just morally good but also God's instrument. This is related to the fact that, for Eiríksson, authentic religiousness involves not just belief (faith) but also neighbor-love and hope.

[12] However, Eiríksson goes beyond Kierkegaard by criticizing the role baptism plays in Christendom, attacking the idea that infant baptism is somehow necessary and sufficient for being a Christian and that it therefore needs to be enforced by the state. Eiríksson goes as far as to suggest that Christendom is misled by a well paid and corrupt clergy and that it is motivated by laziness and impure motives (1850: 5–6, 9–12). For the Danish controversy over baptism in the 1840s, see Koch 2004: 499–500.

[13] However, Eiríksson departs from *Fear and Trembling* (and Kierkegaard) by emphasizing that Abraham is common not just to Judaism and Christianity but also to Islam (Mohammedanism). By focusing on these three Abrahamic religions, Eiríksson advocates syncretism and ecumenism (1850: 8, 103, 134, 137, 162–3).

[14] Eiríksson appears to follow Martensen, Mynster, and Jacobi by stressing the etymology of the Danish *Fornuft* from the German *vernehmen* (Schreiber 2019: 263–8). Indeed, Eiríksson's distinction

such a higher reason, contrasting faith and understanding instead (although this leads to problems discussed in the next chapter). Eiríksson (1850: 18) thus breaks with Kierkegaard by introducing a notion of reason (*Fornuft*) as a higher faculty – the sense (*Sands*) for the infinite and eternal. Indeed, Eiríksson (1846: 27, 40) describes reason as the faculty (or sense) for perceiving God and his revelations inside and outside of us. As such, reason is receptive (passive), involving an immediate, intuitive, and nondiscursive ability to make judgments about God, the supernatural, and supersensual.

The understanding (*Forstanden*), by contrast, is for Eiríksson an active, discursive, and mediating ability to make judgments that comprehend what is given from reason and sense perception (1846: 24–49; cf. Koch 2004: 295–6). While reason receives or perceives something (e.g., Christian revelation), understanding processes and analyzes it propositionally. Reason makes the judgment that something is given (or not), whereas the understanding analyzes it by asking what it is, how it is, and why it is (Eiríksson 1846: 36–43).

Eiríksson maintains that reason is certain, unless obscured by the understanding (1846: 37) – something that involves a cognitive failure. The idea seems to be that unbelief (*Vantro*) is caused by the understanding not accepting facts given to it by reason but rather relying on sense perception. The unbeliever uses the understanding alone, apart from reason, to judge and exclude faith as that which is an absurdity (Eiríksson 1850: 51–5). Presumably, this is a weak absurdity where one denies what transcends understanding and the humanly possible (typically supernatural revelation).

Superstition (*Overtro*), by contrast, is belief that is neither constrained by reason nor by the understanding (Eiríksson 1850: 54–5). It involves a total (strong) absurdity where one believes something untrue. A clear example of this would be to believe in something logically impossible, by embracing a formal contradiction. As we will see, Eiríksson (1850: 55) interprets faith by virtue of the absurd as a classical expression of (the principle of) superstition.

Eiríksson (1850: 51–2) stresses that the category of the absurd (or paradox) belongs to the understanding (something Kierkegaard accepts), but he adds that it does not belong to reason. He also distinguishes between *weak and strong absurdities*. A strong or true absurdity is something that is neither conceivable nor reasonable (Eiríksson 1850: 164). Although

between reason and understanding is reminiscent of the later Jacobi (for the latter, see Di Giovanni and Livieri 2018).

Eiríksson does not say so, this type of absurdity seems to involve a formal, logical contradiction, something it would be irrational to believe in. A weak absurdity, by contrast, represents something that is impossible for human understanding independent of reason to think or realize, although it is possible for God (1850: 68, 164). This type of absurdity represents something logically possible that we cannot grasp in a clear and determinate manner, something that *appears* to conflict with the everyday calculations of the understanding (Eiríksson 1850: 48). Eiríksson then argues that authentic Abrahamic faith and original Christianity only involve weak absurdity and that de silentio and Climacus are not sufficiently clear about this since they portray Abrahamic and Christian religion as being irrational by involving a strong absurdity (i.e., a logical contradiction presumably).[15]

Eiríksson starts by asking: "What is really faith? In what does it consist? What is its basis and motivating force? Is it based on reason or what is reasonable? Or is it based on the nonrational, the irrational, the absurd?" (1850: 14, my transl.). As can be seen from this passage, Eiríksson – unlike Kierkegaard – equates or aligns the absurd (in a strong sense) with the irrational. Eiríksson therefore takes de silentio and Climacus to portray faith in *irrationalist* terms, something that has also been assumed by many later readers.[16]

Both Kierkegaard and Eiríksson use the absurd and paradox interchangeably.[17] But Kierkegaard does *not* equate the absurd with something irrational or a formal contradiction, since he indicates that it is *above* reason, not against it (unlike Eiríksson and Hegel, Kierkegaard does *not* distinguish between reason and understanding, although he rarely speaks

[15] Here Eiríksson distinguishes between the believer's general confidence in God and his specific confidence in particular objects or events promised, or hinted at, by God (1850: 116). While the former involves believing in providence and having hope for the future, the latter involves expecting specific things. Eiríksson is clear that Abrahamic faith must be supported or accompanied by supernatural revelation, something that he aligns with miracles and wonders, hints, and signs from God. Eiríksson takes these hints and signs to involve communication from God, but this communication does not consist in theoretical doctrine as much as a divine promise and covenant that make up the basis for religious hope and trust (1850: 113–15, 140–7). Like Kierkegaard, Eiríksson follows Paul in describing religious hope as a hope against hope. And like Kierkegaard, he takes this Pauline term to mean that religious hope (and its associated faith) transcends human understanding, since it is not based on ordinary rational inferences (Eiríksson 1850: 33). Therefore, Christian and Abrahamic hope and faith *are* seemingly absurd.

[16] Thomas (1980: 215) therefore points out that "Kierkegaard's use of 'Paradox' has been the chief source of the charge of irrationalism because it was generally assumed that it was the assertion of a contradiction or an absurdity."

[17] I have therefore not distinguished systematically between the paradox and the absurd since this would only seem to complicate matters unnecessarily.

of reason). Here both Kierkegaard and Eiríksson use the term "*Modsigelse*," which covers everything from an incongruity to a logical self-contradiction. Still, Eiríksson (1850: 15, 54) claims that the Tertullian *credo quia absurdum* is pushed to the extreme by *Fear and Trembling* (and the *Postscript*). Eiríksson takes this principle to prescribe believing something (only) because it is absurd, and cannot be comprehended and proved by the understanding. He then claims that this would commit one to believing all manner of absurdities.

Eiríksson argues that the absurd is neither the motivating force nor the cause nor the basis of genuine religious faith (1850: 11). Authentic religious faith cannot be motivated by absurdity as such since any absurdity, logical contradiction, or untruth would then suffice for motivating religious faith. If that were the case, there is nothing religious about believing absurdities. And it does not make sense to believe something just because it is absurd, irrational, or untrue. Neither can absurdity nor irrationality be the cause or basis of genuine faith; if this were the case, faith would not be genuine or true. Indeed, faith based on absurdity would be nothing less than superstition, Eiríksson concludes.[18]

In his reply, Kierkegaard stresses that religious absurdity should not be confused with "the absurd in the ordinary [*vulgair*] sense" (Pap. X–6, B80 / JP 1, 11). Elsewhere, he (and Climacus) contrasts religious absurdity with nonsense, adding that "not every absurdity is the absurd or the paradox" in the religious sense (SKS 23, 23, NB15:25 / KJN 7, 20). Indeed, "the believing Christian ... uses the understanding – in order to see that he believes against the understanding. Therefore he cannot believe nonsense" (SKS 7, 516 / CUP1, 568). The understanding prevents or rules out nonsense. But it still leaves room for faith above reason unless it insists on being self-sufficient (see Chapter 12). Kierkegaard thus draws a distinction between nonsense and absurdity that Eiríksson appears to overlook although this distinction is already at work in the *Postscript*.

Kierkegaard suggests that Eiríksson's attempt to make religious belief reasonable results in him completely overlooking the teleological suspension of the ethical (Pap. X–6, B68, 76 / JP 6, 6598; Pap. X–6, B72, 82; Pap. X–6, B80, 86 / JP 1, 11). In this respect, Eiríksson's book differs from much of the later literature since Eiríksson shows no interest in the question of whether Abraham tries to commit murder by sacrificing Isaac.

[18] Absurdity is said to be the principle of superstition. See Eiríksson 1850: 16. Kierkegaard (Climacus), by contrast, associates superstition with attempts to exclude dialectics in order to find a firm footing for faith (SKS 7, 50 / CUP1, 44).

Still, Kierkegaard is clear that religious faith is *not* absurd to believers, although it appears absurd to nonbelievers such as de silentio and Climacus who are offended or scandalized by it. He (Anti-Climacus) writes: "When the believer has faith, the absurd is not the absurd – faith transforms it, but in every weak moment it is again more or less absurd to him" (Pap. X–6, B79, 85 / JP 1, 10). A longer passage (attributed to Climacus) makes essentially the same point:

> When I believe, then assuredly neither faith nor the content of faith is absurd. O, no, no – but . . . for the person who does not believe, faith and the content of faith are absurd, and . . . as soon as I myself am not in the faith, am weak, when doubt perhaps begins to stir, then faith and the content of faith gradually begins to become absurd for me. But this may have been the divine will: in order that faith – whether a man will have faith or not – could be the test, the examination, faith was bound up with the absurd, and the absurd formed and composed in such a way that only one force can prevail over it – the passion of faith – its humility sharpened by the pain of sin-consciousness. (Pap. X–6, B68, 75 / JP 6, 6598, page 301)

Like the paradox (and offense), the absurd is *relative to the perspective* of nonbelief since there is no absurdity for believers (Schreiber 2018: 79; cf. Wrathall 2019: 240–1). Unlike de silentio and Climacus, Kierkegaard does not portray faith as absurd or paradoxical or offensive in his signed writings, because these writings typically speak from the perspective of belief (SKS 23, 182–3, NB17:28 / KJN 7, 185; Pap. X–6, B68–B82 / JP 6, 6598–6601 and JP 1, 9–12; cf. McKinnon 1980; Carr 1996: 240).

Kierkegaard indicates that Eiríksson is somewhat misled by reading the pseudonymous writings and not the signed ones.[19] Like many later commentators, Eiríksson overlooks Kierkegaard's perspectival approach, in which the absurd is relative to a nonreligious perspective offended by faith (see Schreiber 2018: 85). However, Kierkegaard's reply to Eiríksson is important since it makes explicit this perspectival approach.

This point is also related to an important methodological issue where Eiríksson and Kierkegaard disagree. Throughout his book, Eiríksson (1850: vi, 11, 36–7, 101) argues that religious faith must be described from the inside and not from the outside perspective if we are to get a true description of it. Kierkegaard, by contrast, distinguishes systematically between the *perspectives of the believer and the nonbeliever*. While the former stays

[19] Kierkegaard also finds it necessary to remind Eiríksson of the motto from Hamann that suggests that *Fear and Trembling* should not be read literally (Pap. X–6, B70, 80). But he does not specify what Eiríksson misses by reading too literally.

within the perspective of faith (SKS 19, 126, 129–30, Not4:3 and Not4:5 / KJN 3, 125–9), the latter describes it from the outside (cf. Grøn 1995). This dual approach avoids reducing the divine to the humane, while still making it possible to motivate the transition to Christianity by identifying problems with paganism that Christianity avoids.[20] Religion is thus described from the perspectives of unaided reason *and* Christian faith.

Christian Faith Overcomes Both Absurdity and Offense

Practice in Christianity says that

> [t]he possibility of offense is the crossroad, or it is like standing at the crossroad. From the possibility of offense, one turns either to offense or to faith, but one never comes to faith except from the possibility of offense. (SKS 12, 91 / PC, 81)

Confronted with the incarnation, we can only choose to believe *or* to take offense, since indifference is impossible (SKS 4, 291 / PF, 93–4). The nonbeliever takes offense, since the incarnation represents something radically different and heterogeneous that provokes and therefore *seems* absurd by virtue of its *alterity* (SKS 4, 245, 249, 255 / PF, 39–40, 44–5, 51). Specifically, it makes us aware of our sinfulness and how it differs from the divine. It is sin-consciousness – granted by God – that makes possible the deepest self-reflection that understands and recognizes divine revelation as such (SKS 4, 251–2, 255, 290–1 / PF, 47–8, 51, 93). Karen Carr therefore claims that

> offense is not ultimately offense at a doctrine, not hostile denunciation of the claims of Christianity as self-contradictory and irrational (although this denunciation is a manifestation of the most intense forms of offense). It is rather offense at a particular way of living ... that requires acknowledgement of one's own sinfulness. (Carr 2019: 370)

The nonbeliever takes offense at the life of Christ and the ideal of *imitatio Christi*. *Either* he takes offense at a human being who is supposedly divine, performs miracles, and forgives human sinners. *Or* he takes offense at the suffering and passion that God must undergo unjustly (SKS 12, 87–8, 103–27 / PC, 75–6, 94–121).

Unlike the believer, the nonbeliever refuses to acknowledge personal sinfulness and the need for divine forgiveness. Nor will he accept the

[20] Grøn (1997: 296–9, 230–2, 364, 407) points to a similar duality in *The Sickness unto Death* in which Anti-Climacus argues that different positions fail *either* on their own terms *or* on Christian terms.

ethical ideal of *imitatio Christi*. But although offense primarily reacts against the Christian way of life, there is nevertheless an epistemic aspect to it, since offense involves a clash between human understanding and the alterity of the incarnation (SKS 4, 245, 249 / PF, 39–40, 44–5; SKS 12, 92 / PC, 81–2). It is precisely that which cannot be understood that seems *absurd* and untrue to the nonbeliever (Evans 2012: 215). Specifically, divine revelation appears absurd by differing from our understanding or reason (SKS 4, 249 / PF, 44–5; Betz 2007: 324). Insofar as the latter insists on its own supremacy, it must reject as absurd what it cannot understand (Emmanuel 1996: 59; cf. Helms 2017). Steven Emmanuel writes:

> Revelation . . . absolutely transcends human standards of knowledge (and morality). Revelation is marked by its complete heterogeneity with respect to the purely human order of things. It is the communication of a truth which is so superior that it reveals our judgments (both epistemic and moral) to be in error. (1996: 45)

On this reading, wanting revelation to conform to our understanding would be to reaffirm our sinfulness by putting reason above faith (Emmanuel 1996: 59). Revelation judges us and our standards, but we cannot judge it with our reason:

> When confronted by revelation, reason is left with only two choices: either to acknowledge the impossibility of assimilating revelation to the categories of human understanding, or to reject it. The former choice opens the way to faith, the latter ends in offense. (Emmanuel 1996: 50)

But Kierkegaard is more nuanced and philosophical than this. The cognitive, doctrinal *content* of a putative revelation can be a subject of thought and philosophical discussion, although we cannot understand how it enters the world by a divine revelation (SKS 15, 216–26 / BA, 176–87). Only the latter is *above* reason, by transcending the limits of human cognition (see Chapter 12).

Faith requires a limitation of the scope of the understanding or reason. Indeed, the understanding recognizes revelation (or the infinite) as something it cannot think or understand. It therefore plays a *negative* role, by limiting itself and identifying the absurd (as well by ruling out nonsense; see SKS 7, 516 / CUP1, 567–8; Michalson 1985: 83; Czakó 2015: 283). It makes room for faith by limiting itself, becoming aware of its own ignorance in religious matters. Kierkegaard writes: "The absurd is the negative criterion of that which is higher than human understanding and knowledge" (Pap. X–6, B80, 87 / JP 1, 11). The absurd is *above* understanding, not against it (SKS 19, 390–1, Not13:23 / KJN 3, 388). He writes:

> The absurd is the negative determinant [*Bestemmelse*] which assures ... that I have not overlooked one or other possibility which still lies within the human area. The absurd is the expression of despair: that humanly it is not possible – but despair is the negative sign of faith. (Pap. X–6, B78, 84 / JP 1, 9)

The absurd prevents the divine from being confused with something merely human (Pap. X–6, B68, 74 / JP 6, 6598). It should therefore differentiate faith from human knowledge and human possibilities (Jackson 1987: 82). Specifically, it concerns supernatural *revelation*, divine assistance, miracles and grace, which are all mysterious by transcending the limit of human rationality (SKS 27, 481, Papir 402 / KJN 11.2, 182; SKS 27, 487, Papir 408 / KJN 11.2, 188–9; SKS 27, 487–8, Papir 409:1 / KJN 11.2, 189–90; SKS 27, 489, Papir 410 / KJN 11.2, 191). It is the supernatural, supersensual, infinite, unconditioned, absolute, and divine (as such) that defy understanding, although the same seems to hold for original sin, atonement, and forgiveness.

Religious absurdity seems to consist in a veridical or truth-telling paradox in that it can be interpreted as indicating rightly (though surprisingly) that something is (divinely) possible (Jackson 1987: 79–81). Kierkegaard therefore suggests that it is incredible but true, following Hamann's use of Seneca (SKS 27, 150, Papir 185 / KJN 11.1, 154). He writes:

> All *Problemata* [in *Fear and Trembling*] should end as follows: This is the paradox of faith, a paradox which no reasoning is able to master – and yet it is so, or we must obliterate the story of Abraham. (Pap. IV, B75 / JP 3, 3079)

Against Eiríksson, Kierkegaard insists that Eiríksson's theological rationalism is at odds with his endorsement of supernatural revelation. Kierkegaard thinks that Eiríksson tries to evade this problem by presenting supernatural revelation as natural, while appealing to a higher rationality that resembles the speculative theology of right-Hegelians like Martensen (Pap. X–6, B68, 73–4 / JP 6, 6598). Kierkegaard explicitly objects to this peculiar notion of reason, although he does not object to discursive understanding (Pap. X–6, B68, 73–4 / JP 6, 6598; Pap. X–6, B72, 82; Pap. X–6, B75, 83). The implication is that Eiríksson must choose between rationalism and belief in supernatural revelation if he is to be consistent. As it is, Eiríksson risks that what he calls "reason" will represent not the divine but something all too human (such as confused thinking or intellectual hang-ups). Kierkegaard thus thinks that Eiríksson faces the same basic problem as Hegelians who try to mediate between rationalism and supernaturalism in matters of faith. Clearly, Kierkegaard views rationalism as incompatible with supernaturalism, denying that these terms could be mediated as Eiríksson and Hegelians think.[21]

But it is not obvious that rationalism in matters of faith needs to preclude the possibility of supernatural revelation as Kierkegaard suggests. To illustrate this, Kant's typology of religious belief seems sufficient. Consider the distinction between

1. *denying* supernatural revelation and affirming natural religion (i.e., naturalism),
2. *agnosticism* concerning supernatural revelation and affirmation of natural religion (i.e., rationalism),
3. to allow *affirmation* of supernatural revelation without taking it to be necessary as natural religion is (i.e., pure rationalism), and
4. holding supernatural revelation to be necessary (i.e., pure supernaturalism, see R 6:154–5).

This typology suggests that there are more conceptual options available to Eiríksson than Kierkegaard indicates. Kierkegaard contrasts naturalism (in the Kantian sense) with (pure) supernaturalism and tends to ignore the intermediary views (rationalism and pure rationalism).[22]

Still, Eiríksson's position hardly fits this Kantian typology, since Eiríksson wants to be a rationalist who not only affirms supernatural revelation but also takes it to be necessary. Thus, Eiríksson wants to combine, or mediate between, rationalism and supernaturalism in a manner that neither Kierkegaard nor Kantians see as possible. Although more work is needed on Eiríksson's notion of rationality, it nevertheless seems that he advocates a pre-Kantian notion of reason as intuitive cognition of the supernatural and supersensual – which Kierkegaard cannot accept.

Conclusion: *Fear and Trembling* Versus *Concluding Unscientific Postscript*

Eiríksson's short chapter on *Concluding Unscientific Postscript* (Chapter 3) starts by comparing the *Postscript* with *Fear and Trembling*. Eiríksson

[21] Bishop Mynster started the Danish debate on rationalism and supernaturalism by arguing that the law of excluded middle must hold true, and that the revelation of Christ is therefore either supernatural as the supernaturalists maintain or not supernatural as the rationalists maintain. See Stewart 2003: 78–9.

[22] The Kantian terminology here differs from pragmatism concerning belief. Pragmatism only assumes that belief is rational practically; it need not deny or affirm supernatural revelation.

argues that the *Postscript* represents a partially new form and content compared to *Fear and Trembling*, particularly by introducing the incarnation as a historical event and central dogma (1850: 150).[23]

Eiríksson starts by noting that the *Postscript* interprets absurdity in Christological terms, as the belief that Christ was finite and infinite, temporal and eternal. He then argues that this means that there is no absurdity before the birth of Christ, concluding that Abraham cannot be absurd as *Fear and Trembling* maintains (Eiríksson 1850: 152; Schreiber 2009: 79). Thus, Eiríksson uses the *Postscript* to support the central thesis that Abraham, and Abrahamic faith, is not absurd (1850: 154–5, 158). But Eiríksson only shows that Abraham is not absurd in the Christological sense of the term found in the *Postscript*; he does not show that Abraham is not absurd in another (non-Christological) sense.

Eiríksson proceeds by arguing that traditional Christianity, unlike the faith of Abraham, is truly strongly absurd, because of its problematic (absurd) dogmas. To support this point, he references the work of his contemporary Peter Michael Stilling (1812–69), briefly mentioning the dogmas of the trinity, the incarnation, the fall, heredity sin, vicarious atonement, and Christ's presence in the sacraments. Based on this, he concludes that traditional Christianity involves not just the Christological absurdity of Climacus but also several other strong absurdities (Eiríksson 1850: 162–3).[24] Indeed, Christianity is the only absurd religion known to us, he contends (1850: 165–6).[25]

[23] Eiríksson uses *Concluding Unscientific Postscript* to criticize *Fear and Trembling*. While Eiríksson's analysis of the *Postscript* (and *Philosophical Fragments*) is selective, eclectic, and relatively short (1850: 149–81), the analysis of *Fear and Trembling* is far more comprehensive. Indeed, his commentary on *Fear and Trembling* is longer than the book itself (see esp. 1850: 13–148).

[24] Kierkegaard does not accept this plurality of absurdities; see Pap. X–6, B79, 85 / JP 1, 10. For Stilling, see Stilling 1850; Koch 2004: ch. 14.

[25] Eiríksson (1850: 163) thinks Christianity is strongly absurd, by going against both our understanding and our reason. He continues by arguing that, even though these absurd dogmas are central to traditional Christianity, they are not to be found in original Christianity (Eiríksson 1850: 169–78). He suggests that the absurd dogmas belong to Christendom rather than scripture. The idea is that original Christianity is based on Abrahamic theism, whereas traditional Christianity has been corrupted by the church, creeds, and theology of Christendom. Somewhat rhetorically, Eiríksson concludes that the *Postscript* does not go far enough, since Climacus is blinded by the traditional dogmas of Christendom, especially the incarnation (1850: 175–78). Kierkegaardian polemics against Christendom is inconsistent because it accepts traditional dogmas and creeds in an uncritical manner instead of returning to authentic Abrahamic faith. The upshot is that the genuine religious believer, or even the genuine Christian, needs to follow the Kierkegaardian spirit rather than the letter by returning to Abrahamic faith. It is hardly surprising that Kierkegaard objects to this idea of being Christian without believing in the incarnation. Kierkegaard says that Eiríksson wants to abolish the dogmas of faith and to replace Christianity with the Old Testament. He thinks this shows how confused Eiríksson is (Pap. X–6, B68, 73, 76 / JP 6, 6598; Pap. X–6, B72, 81; Pap. X–6, B74, 83). Still, Eiríksson anticipates later readings of Kierkegaard that see Kierkegaard as a somewhat

Eiríksson's comparison of *Fear and Trembling* and *Concluding Unscientific Postscript* is one of the most interesting parts of his book. Here (Chapter 3) Eiríksson (1850: 154–8) argues persuasively that the Kierkegaardian faces a problem: Does Abraham's faith belongs to natural *or* supernatural religion, *or* to immanent or transcendent religiousness? The latter basically amounts to interpreting Abraham as a Christian who believes in the incarnation, something that is not just anachronistic but also nonsensical. The former, by contrast, appears to deny that there is any special revelation and promise available to Abraham, putting him on the same footing as the Greeks and pantheists.[26] But neither option represents Abraham's religious faith accurately. Eiríksson (1850: 152, 154–5, 158) therefore concludes that Abraham does not fit into the stages or spheres developed in the *Postscript* and that *Fear and Trembling* and the *Postscript* therefore are fundamentally at odds with each other. Even though Abraham is the father of faith, or a paradigmatic case of religious belief, he cannot be considered religious if we accept the *Postscript*'s interpretation of religion (Eiríksson 1850: 154–8).

Here Eiríksson identifies a problem that has occupied and troubled commentators until the present day. More recently, Davenport claims that

> "the holy grail" remains finding a single consistent understanding of "religiousness" that makes sense of what is said about resignation and faith in *Fear and Trembling* while also explaining what is said about religiousness A and B in the *Concluding Unscientific Postscript*.[27]

Kierkegaard replies that Eiríksson is quite right to distinguish between the absurd in *Fear and Trembling* and the paradox in the *Postscript* (Pap. X–6, B80, 86 / JP 1, 11). But this does not amount to a distinction between paradox and absurdity as such but rather to a distinction between *Fear and*

inconsistent thinker who was the last Christian or the last Protestant. While Eiríksson uses Kierkegaard to criticize Christendom and to defend Abraham, Brandes (1877) and other cultural radicals attack religious faith more generally. Similar tendencies are found in existentialism and in the Catholic reception of Kierkegaard in Germany and Austria, in which Kierkegaard was sometimes seen as the last Protestant. See Stewart 2009.

26 Eiríksson (1850: 150) interprets religiousness A as pantheism and B as Christianity. Although Kierkegaard attacks pantheism, he does *not* protest against Eiríksson's interpretation of religiousness A as natural religion.

27 Davenport 2008b: 880. Krishek points to similarities between *Fear and Trembling* and the *Postscript* but concludes that there is still need for more research on the relation between these works. Theunissen indicates that the double movement of faith belongs to Kierkegaard's Christian religiousness, whereas Davenport argues that Kierkegaard gives a single unified conception of religious belief that describes the subjective attitude of believers in *many different religions* (including religiousness A *and* B, as well as the belief of Zoroastrians and Socrates). See Theunissen 1991: 346; Davenport 2008a: 214, 222, 233; 2008b: 905–7; Krishek 2009: 143; cf. Fremstedal 2014a: ch. 7.

Trembling and the *Postscript*. He then goes on to say that Eiríksson does not grasp what the difference between these two works consists in. Eiríksson is wrong to suggest that these two works are fundamentally at odds with each other (Pap. X–6, B81, 87 / JP 1, 12), and he is also mistaken in identifying de silentio with Climacus (Pap. X–6, B71, 80) and with Kierkegaard himself (Pap. X–6, B128 / JP 6, 6596). Then comes the interesting part where Kierkegaard compares the notions of faith and absurdity in *Fear and Trembling* and the *Postscript*. This is perhaps the most important part of Kierkegaard's response to Eiríksson, a part that has yet to receive the attention it deserves.

Kierkegaard responds that the absurd in *Fear and Trembling* "is the mere personal definition [*Bestemmelse*] of the existential belief," whereas the paradox in the *Postscript* is belief related to a doctrine (Pap. X–6, B80, 86 / JP 1, 11). De silentio speaks of believing "by virtue of the absurd," whereas Climacus speaks of "to believe the absurd" (Pap. X–6, B80, 87 / JP 1, 11). *Postscript* uses absurdity (and paradox) in a Christian, Christological sense in which the absurd refers to the dogma of the incarnation (as something finite and infinite, temporal and eternal).[28] *Fear and Trembling*, by contrast, does not use the absurd in this Christological sense. So far, Eiríksson is right.

The incarnation does appear absurd to those who take offense at it. But Kierkegaard is nevertheless explicit that it "contains no self-contradiction [*Selvmodsigelse*]" (SKS 23, 137, NB16:60 / KJN 7, 139; cf. SKS 4, 298 / PF, 101). He contrasts Christianity and Abraham as follows:

> [A]ccording to the New Testament Abraham is called the father of faith, and yet it is [*vel* – arguably] clear that the content of his faith cannot be Christian – that Jesus Christ has been in existence. But Abraham's faith is the formal definition [*Bestemmelse*] of faith. (Pap. X–6, B81, 87 / JP 1, 12)

The faith of Abraham, as interpreted in the double movement of faith in *Fear and Trembling*, explicates the formal structure of faith rather than its content. The latter refers to the dogmas or objects of faith, whereas the former corresponds to the *act* whereby one believes (in the sense of trusting God or putting one's confidence in him). The content of Judaism differs

[28] Even Tertullian suggests that the incarnation involves paradoxicality. Eric Osborn writes: "If God, who is wholly other, is joined to mortal man in a way which is not inept, then either God is no longer God or man is no longer man, and there is no true incarnation. Truth on this issue can only be achieved by ineptitude. Tertullian does not universalize his claim; most ineptitude is false. This argument is put into paradox, to imitate Paul and to make it more striking and provocative. Paradoxes are useful because they are wonderful and against common opinion [*doxa*]" (1987: 58).

from that of Christianity, but Kierkegaard claims that they share a structure that formally defines or determines what faith is.

This structure is known as the double movement of faith. It consists of two movements:

1. The movement of infinite resignation, in which the ethico-religious agent renounces completely his ability to realize the highest good by his own unaided efforts.
2. The movement of faith, in which the same agent nevertheless believes that the highest good can be realized by divine power and intervention (SKS 4, 129–45, 167, 189–90, 197, 203 / FT, 34–52, 75–6, 99–101, 109, 115).

Both movements concern the act of believing,[29] although the first comes before the second in a logical rather than a temporal sense. Both represent higher-order motives or beliefs in which the agent relates to his highest good or value. On its own, the movement of resignation prevents the agent from acting in order to realize this value or good, since it is seen as impossible to realize by his own unaided efforts. Still, the movement of faith allows action, since the same good or value is seen as realizable by divine power and intervention (Johansen 2002: 267; Fremstedal 2014b: 190). It is decisive, however, that divine assistance and divine grace are something *supernatural and mysterious* that appear absurd by transcending mere reason (SKS 27, 481, Papir 402 / KJN 11.2, 182; SKS 27, 487–8, Papir 409:1 / KJN 11.2, 189–90; SKS 27, 489, Papir 410 / KJN 11.2, 191).

Thus, absurdity in *Fear and Trembling* refers to an (subjective) attitude or act, whereas absurdity in the *Postscript* refers (in addition) to the incarnation as an offensive object (dogma).[30] *Fear and Trembling* analyzes

[29] This is in line with the lexical meaning according to which the Danish word for movement, "*Bevægelse*," can mean an (subjective) "attitude" or "state of mind." See Fremstedal 2014b: 192.

[30] Eiríksson (1850: 56–7, 61, 68–9, 87, 89–90, 113) also presents another objection to Kierkegaard that the latter responds to. Eiríksson argues at length that the example of the princess in *Fear and Trembling* is not suited for the purpose of understanding religious faith. Eiríksson claims that the example portrays religiousness in subjectivist terms. This claim seems to be based on the fact that de silentio introduces the princess as an example of what is subjectively most valuable (SKS 4, 136 / FT, 41–2). De silentio states that only the single individual can give himself a more precise explanation of what is subjectively perceived as the highest (SKS 4, 163 / FT, 71). However, de silentio actually identifies what is objectively highest with eternal happiness and the human *telos* (SKS 4, 148 / FT, 54). Thus, he distinguishes what is objectively valuable (eternal happiness or salvation) from what is subjectively perceived as valuable (getting the princess). In his response, Kierkegaard (Climacus) says, that the story of the princess is only a minor illustration, an (subjective) approximation to faith, and not the chief substance as Eiríksson thinks (Pap. X–6, B68, 76–7 / JP 6, 6598; Pap. X–6, B74, 83). He concludes that Eiríksson developed a somewhat unhealthy obsession with the parable of the princess and that he misunderstood the point (Schreiber 2009: 83–4).

the subjective attitude of the religious believer, an attitude that is common to Judaism *and* Christianity (but probably not immanent religiousness). Yet, absurdity in the *Postscript* does not merely include the incarnation as an absurd or offensive object but also the subjective *attitude* of the believer (indeed, the incarnation itself not only reveals God as Christ but also involves divine forgiveness and atonement).

The attitude of the believer is absurd insofar as it goes beyond the understanding by transcending human possibilities and embracing divine grace and forgiveness (SKS 27, 481, Papir 402 / KJN 11.2, 182; SKS 27, 487–8, Papir 409:1 / KJN 11.2, 189–90). It is *not* absurd by virtue of believing something logically or objectively impossible, but only by believing something that is humanly impossible (SKS 4, 141 / FT, 46–7), such as the absolution of sins, getting Isaac back after sacrificing him, resurrecting the dead, or realizing the kingdom of God. The absurd is here a *modal* category, referring to what is metaphysically possible through supernatural, divine intervention but not practically possible for unaided human agency. However, Kierkegaard sometimes describes it in terms of (subjective or agent-relative) improbability (SKS 23, 24, NB15:25 / KJN 7, 20).

Elsewhere, Kierkegaard indicates that the pagan can exercise resignation only if he realizes that loss is inevitable. The piety of Judaism, by contrast, is capable of both resignation and faith (only) if the believer is put through an ordeal (as Abraham and Job were). Finally, the Christian differs from both by being capable of *voluntary* resignation and belief (SKS 10, 189 / CD, 178–9; SKS 25, 152–3, NB27:39 / KJN 9, 151–2; SKS 15, 268 / BA, 112–13). While the extraordinary ordeals of Abraham and Job necessitate resignation and belief, the demanding nature of Christianity necessitates voluntary resignation and belief. Kierkegaard thus suggests that the extreme cases of Judaism anticipate the normal situation of Christian existence.

The first part of the double movement of faith (i.e., resignation) seems to belong to immanent (natural) religiousness, although voluntary resignation requires Christian faith for Kierkegaard. However, the second part of the double movement belongs exclusively to transcendent (revealed) religiousness based on divine grace. Thus, it is shared by Judaism *and* Christianity. What sets Christianity apart from Judaism, however, is neither divine revelation nor divine assistance, but the ability to resign without being (actually) put through an ordeal as Job and Abraham were. Indeed, Christianity sees our whole life as an ordeal or examination, whereas Judaism believes that true happiness can be realized in this world since an ordeal is something that passes (SKS 4, 131, 115–16 / FT, 56, 19–20; SKS 12, 183 / PC, 183; SKS 20, 392, NB5:48 / KJN 4, 392–3).

Specifically, Judaism interprets the highest good as this-worldly, whereas Christianity sees this life as an ordeal that prepares for the realization of the highest good in the afterlife. For Christianity, the highest good cannot be completely realized in human history, due to sin, normative conflict, and problems with uniting believers in a true church. As a result, it can only be realized eschatologically (Fremstedal 2014a: chs. 4–9).

CHAPTER 12

Faith Beyond Reason: Suprarationalism and Antirationalism

Introduction

The controversy over faith and reason is the longest-standing controversy in the Kierkegaard literature. It started in 1850 and is still ongoing.[1] Interpretations of Kierkegaard can be divided into those that are irrationalist, antirationalist, and suprarationalist. *Irrationalists* claim that faith is irrational in some decisive respect. *Antirationalists*, by contrast, claim that faith and reason oppose each other, without any logical contradiction or irrationality (Carr 1996; Buben 2013). Antirationalists think there is a deep hostility and antagonism between faith and reason that cannot be overcome by faith. The latter is denied by *suprarationalists*, who maintain that faith is above mere reason, not against it. None of these interpretations normally distinguish between reason and understanding or between faith and belief (cf. Helms 2017; Westphal 2018).

Suprarationalism is a fairly orthodox view, while irrationalism and antirationalism may both be considered part of Kierkegaard's contribution to theology and philosophy. However, the irrationalist reading is most widespread among nonspecialists (cf. McKinnon 1980: 126). Specialists, by contrast, tend to favor either suprarationalism or antirationalism. Those who defend Kierkegaard, or sympathize with him, tend to favor suprarationalism, while critics often rely on irrationalism.

Against the Irrationalist Reading

The irrationalist reading of Kierkegaard typically assumes that Kierkegaard endorses belief in something known to be *logically impossible* (Buben 2013: 319). Typically, the paradox of the incarnation is taken to involve a formal

[1] See the references below and Nielsen 1849; Eiríksson 1850; Koch 2004: chs. 10–12; Tullberg 2006: 12–15, 19–33, 46–54, 73–83.

contradiction, since the God-man is simultaneously finite and infinite, temporal and eternal (Hannay 1993: 106–8; Knappe 2004: 128).

First, this reading is weakened by the fact that Kierkegaard himself tries – and largely succeeds in – *refuting* it in his 1850 reply to Eiríksson (Pap. X–6, B68–B82 / JP 1, 9–12; JP 6, 6598–6601). As we saw in the previous chapter, Eiríksson (1850) introduced and developed the irrationalist reading. Unfortunately, the secondary literature largely overlooks Kierkegaard's critique of this reading since it is obscure and unfamiliar to most readers. Still, those who take the time to read Eiríksson's lengthy critique of Kierkegaard and the latter's response will be almost forced to admit that he *denies* that he is an irrationalist, opting for suprarationalism instead. Specifically, faith is above reason, since supernatural revelation cannot be discovered by mere reason (or derived from reason alone); nor can it become completely transparent and clear to mere reason.

Second, it is often claimed that Kierkegaard's Christology involves endorsing a formal, logical contradiction. But Kierkegaard clearly holds that the incarnation "contains no self-contradiction [*Selvmodsigelse*]" (SKS 23, 137, NB16:60 / KJN 7, 139; cf. SKS 4, 298 / PF, 101). Further, it hardly clear if this is supposedly a specific problem with Kierkegaard's Christology or if it is a more general problem with Christology. The irrationalist reading must *either* show that Christology generally involves irrationality *or* that Kierkegaard has a particular irrationalist Christology. The former would be quite demanding.[2] And the latter seems untrue, since Kierkegaard's Christology seems orthodox (i.e., Nicene-Chalcedonian-Athanasian).[3] But even if Kierkegaard's Christology were irrational, Kierkegaardians could avoid irrationality by adopting a less problematic Christology.

Third, the irrationalist reading cannot explain why Kierkegaard thinks that there is only one true path for all human beings, namely Christianity (see Carr 1996: 238–9). As should become clear, it is absolutely not the case that *any irrational or passionate belief* would do for Kierkegaard. Therefore, he contrasts genuine paradoxes and absurdities with ordinary nonsense (as seen in the previous chapter). Kierkegaard thus draws a distinction that irrationalists overlook. Although some specific paradoxes are vital for religious existence, these should nevertheless be resolved by the believer.

[2] For the logical coherence of the incarnation, as stated in the Chalcedonian Creed, see, e.g., Bøhn 2013.

[3] Still, specialists discuss whether Kierkegaard favors kenotic or krypsis Christology; see Law 2013; Schulz 2015: 116–7; cf. Thomas 1980: 199–200; Gouwens 1996: 168–72; Deuser 1998; Bubbio 2014: 104–16.

These paradoxes cannot be replaced by other paradoxes or irrational beliefs, as the irrationalist reading would have to assume. It is absolutely not the case that any instance of irrational belief would do, as irrationalists must assume (Carr 1996: 239; cf. Eiríksson 1850: 11–16). As we saw, religious belief cannot be motivated by irrationality as such, since any irrationality would then suffice for motivating it. If that were the case, there is hardly anything religious about believing something irrational. And it does not make sense to believe something just because it is irrational. Neither can irrationality be the cause or basis of genuine faith; if this were the case, faith would neither be genuine nor true. Indeed, faith based on irrationality is superstition (Eiríksson 1850: 16).

Fourth, the irrationalist reading seems to destroy Christianity as a doctrinal religion (Emmanuel 1996: 42). Brand Blanshard writes:

> To ... reduce truth to a passionate commitment of feeling and will, would not save Christianity; on the contrary, it would largely destroy it. For it implies that there are no common truths for Christians to accept, no common principle by which their lives may be guided, indeed no common Deity for them to contemplate and worship. The Kierkegaardian subjectivity would dissolve things away into a set of processes in individual minds where there would be as many Christians as there were persons to exercise their "inwardness" and passion. (1968: 15–16)

But passionate belief need not imply anything irrational or a-rational since emotions and passion have *cognitive* content for Kierkegaard (Furtak 2005: 45–7); Kierkegaard does not reduce truth to passionate commitment. Instead, he thinks that both passionate commitment and common dogmas are needed (cf. Evans 1999: 209–10; Law 2015). As we saw (in Chapter 9), wholehearted faith must believe in the true God. Indeed, faith seems based on the epistemic concern to grasp truth of "vital existential importance" (Bishop 2016: Part VII).

Finally, reason (as a faculty) plays a decisive *negative* role (see Emmanuel 1996: 35, 145; Czakó 2015: 283). Put in Kant's terms, reason "den[ies] *knowledge* in order to make room for *faith*" (B xxx). Indeed, faith is not even possible unless reason judges that sufficient epistemic evidence is lacking (cf. SKS 4, 281 / PF, 83; SKS 7, 36, 187 / CUP1, 29, 203; SKS 27, 487, Papir 408 / KJN 11.2, 188–9; Pap. X–6, B79 / JP 1, 10). Kierkegaard's repeated references to Kant, and Socratic ignorance that is aware of its own ignorance, clearly support this point (see Chapter 10). Kierkegaard writes: "Hamann rightly says: As 'Law' annuls 'grace,' so does 'to Comprehend' annul 'to believe.' This is my thesis" (SKS 22, 375, NB14:51 / KJN 6, 380; cf.

SKS 27, 150, Papir 185 / KJN 11.1, 154). This passage refers to the following claim by Hamann:

> Our reason is therefore just what Paul calls the law – and the command of reason is holy, righteous, and good; but it is given ... to convince us of the opposite: how unreasonable our reason is, and that our errors should increase by it, just as sin increased through the law.[4]

Just as the Mosaic law makes possible sin (for Paul), our reason makes possible Socratic ignorance (for Hamann, Kant, and Kierkegaard). For it is reason that recognizes something as a paradox or absurdity that it cannot think or understand (Michalson 1985: 83; Czakó 2015: 283). Reason limits itself since it knows that it cannot know the paradox. This limit is a limit that reason itself can identify and assent to; it is not an arbitrary limit imposed from outside by a nonrational authority (Evans 1999: 211–16). Indeed, a "boundary" that "is not dialectical" involves "superstition and narrow-mindedness" (SKS 7, 41n / CUP1, 35n). A dialectical boundary, by contrast, can be recognized by reason itself (a broadly Kantian point). Indeed,

> the believing Christian ... uses the understanding – [precisely] in order to see that he believes against the understanding. Therefore he cannot believe nonsense ... because the understanding will penetratingly perceive that it is nonsense and hinder him in believing it. (SKS 7, 516 / CUP1, 568)

We have seen (in Chapters 4–11) that the understanding can criticize problematic forms of religion. Emmanuel therefore points out that Kierkegaard thus

> recognizes that there must be some rational procedure for distinguishing between genuine and spurious claims to revelation ... even though we are not in a position to judge revelation, we can and must be able to determine the conditions under which the term *revelation* has a coherent use in the Christian context. (1996: 145, 147)

Against irrationalism (and antirationalism and fideism), I contend that Kierkegaard allows rational assessment and *critique of religion* on both practical and theoretical grounds, based on standards that are both external and internal to Christian faith. This allows him to criticize superstition, false prophets, idolatry, and religious nonsense. Indeed, we have seen (in Chapters 4–8) that he criticizes religious immorality in general and religious egoism and violence in particular. Specifically, he attacks bitter

[4] Hamann, *Briefwechsel*, ed. Walther Ziesemer, vol. 1, 355–6 translated in Betz 2007: 315.

mockery, poisonous distrust, cold callousness, accusations, and condemnations of other people (Chapter 8). Moreover, he repeatedly attacks those who either objectify faith or lack personal, moral commitment (Chapters 2–3, 8–9). Finally, he attacks self-contradictions and intellectual confusion more generally (cf. Chapters 7–11). Clearly, much of this critique does *not* require Christian faith.

Still, for Kierkegaard the problem is not so much to judge the doctrinal content of revelation, as to determine how it enters the world by a divine revelation (SKS 15, 216–26 / BA, 176–87; more on this later). However, the irrationalist reading cannot account for the fact that reason plays a role here, even if it is a negative one (Carr 1996: 239). Nor can it account for Kierkegaard's reliance on Socrates and Kant here. Neither can it account for the fact that Kierkegaard claims that the truth of Christianity is based on an objective, historical reality (which he interprets in realistic metaphysical and theological terms), not on irrationality (cf. SKS 15, 273 / BA, 117–18; Carr 1996: 238–9; Evans 2006b: 40). Indeed, Kierkegaard is explicit that "[o]nly once has Governance [*Styrelsen*] intervened omnipotently: in [Christ]" (SKS 26, 341, NB34:29 / KJN 10, 349).

Still, one variant of the irrationalist reading only claims that Kierkegaard endorses an *arbitrary* choice between alternatives that cannot be justified rationally (Buben 2013: 319). Typically, the transition from one life-view to another involves a blind leap of faith that cannot be justified rationally. However, the latter involves a genuine problem that is found not only in the Kierkegaard literature. Anyone who believes that different normative domains – or noninstrumental values – (e.g., morality and prudence) diverge and conflict faces the same problem. But this is not so much a problem of irrationality as a problem of normative pluralism or value pluralism (cf. Chang 1997a; Bader 2015). It arises once we introduce diverging and conflicting types of normativity (or value). Without global standards, we therefore face problems of *incommensurability and incomparability* that allows or even favors (nondeductive) leaps between different standards.[5]

To avoid this problem, we can either opt for normative monism (e.g., that anything but moral virtue is indifferent, as the Stoics claimed), or a weak form of pluralism that prevents normative conflict completely (e.g., by arguing that prudence may diverge from but never conflict with

[5] Cf. Joseph Raz's "quasi-existentialist view," according to which reason provides "rationally eligible options" while the will simply chooses one of them by plumping for one over the other; cf. Chang 1997b: 10.

morality; see Bader 2015). However, Kierkegaard's category of the leap differs from both of these without involving relativism. It neither presupposes objectionable irrationalism nor arbitrariness, since the standard one leaps from collapses *internally*, while the new standard holds up: a leap is practically *necessary* in order to avoid despair. As we have seen, the transition from aesthetic amoralism to ethics is justified on these grounds. Religious conversions are more difficult, but even here Kierkegaard claims that only Christianity allows a wholehearted identity. If true, that would in principle allow practical reasons for religious belief that could justify religious conversions. Conversions or leaps are therefore not objectionable, irrational, or arbitrary, although normative pluralism remains controversial in contemporary philosophy (as does normative monism).

Kierkegaard's Suprarationalism

In 1842–43, Kierkegaard uses Leibniz to clarify his own view of faith and (mere) reason (as a cognitive faculty):

> What I usually express by saying that Christianity consists in paradox, philosophy in mediation, Leibniz expresses by distinguishing between what is above reason and what is against reason. Faith is *above* reason. By reason he understands ... a linking together of truths, a conclusion from causes. Faith therefore cannot be proved, demonstrated, comprehended, for the link which makes a linking together possible is missing, and what else does this say than it is a paradox ... nothing else should be said of the paradox and the unreasonableness of Christianity than that it is the first form [i.e., above reason]. (SKS 19, 390–1, Not13:23 / KJN 3, 388)

Kierkegaard distinguishes between the paradoxical truths of (supernatural) revelation and the truths of (mere) reason, associating the latter with Hegelian mediation. This passage clearly indicates that Christian faith is *above* reason, not against it, since the supernatural (as such) transcends the boundaries of mere reason. Indeed, faith ventures beyond – not against – epistemic evidence, something that makes it suprarational (cf. Bishop 2016: Part VII). Kierkegaard is then a suprarationalist, not an irrationalist (Jackson 1987: 78–82; Løkke and Waaler 2009: 55–9). Richard McCombs comments:

> Kierkegaard seems to say that faith is nonrational or suprarational but not irrational. His explanation for his claim that faith is non-rational is that Christianity "*cannot be proved, demonstrated, comprehended.*" But to say that faith is nonrational because Christianity cannot be demonstrated is to hold faith and Christianity to a very high standard of rationality. One might have

> thought that a way of life can be rational in some sense even if its basis cannot be demonstrated. Otherwise few or no people would have a rational way of life. (2013: 14)

The fact that religious belief is not rational in one sense does not prevent it from being rational in some other sense (cf. Emmanuel 1996: ch. 3; Helms 2017). Still, Kierkegaard is explicit that divine revelation "surpasses human understanding" (SKS 15, 109 / BA, 23). Although it is possible to understand its doctrinal and cognitive *content*, we cannot understand but only believe *that* it entered the world through a supernatural revelation (SKS 15, 216–26 / BA, 176–87). Even if the propositional content could be grasped and assessed rationally, the same does not hold for how it was revealed supernaturally. Therefore, we cannot know if Adler had a revelation, but we can still discuss its alleged content and criticize Adler's confused account of it. Indeed, speculation can prevent nonsense by examining the content of faith (*Speculationen kan controllere Troen*; see SKS 23, 69, NB15:97 / KJN 7, 67). Clearly, the doctrinal and propositional content of faith is subject to *rational* assessment, even if some of it is based on Christian grounds. Here Kierkegaard presupposes a conception of revelation known as "propositional revelation" (cf. Wahlberg 2020: Part 1.11).

However, the incarnation is not a propositional doctrine that can be separated from God's *presence* and *self-revelation* in Christ (SKS 4, 258, 264 / PF, 55, 62). In this case, there is no neat distinction between form and content. The message and its delivery (or revelation) cannot be neatly separated, since God's teaching is a performative utterance where he enacts the love he speaks of by his very presence (Stokes 2015: 49, referencing Glenn). It thus seems that Kierkegaard is concerned with divine presence and self-revelation, not just with doctrine. Although propositional doctrine can be understood, divine presence (as such) cannot. As Mats Wahlberg points out:

> [I]n modern theology, "propositional" accounts of revelation are often said to have given way to a focus on divine "self-revelation". The locus of revelation is not propositions but events, and its content is not a body of truths about God, but "the living God" revealing himself in his actions toward man. (2020: Part 1.11, quoting John Hick towards the end of the quote)

Still, God's self-revelation cannot be separated entirely from propositional revelation:

> God could not reveal himself without simultaneously revealing (making knowable) some propositions about himself. Propositions must figure in the

> content of . . . both propositional and manifestational revelations [where the latter refer to revelations in which God manifests some reality, including his own self-revelation]. (Wahlberg 2020: Part 1.11)

In any case, whether revelation is given or not is beyond mere reason as a faculty for Kierkegaard (cf. Helms 2020: 3). Reason cannot decide *a priori* whether something exists or not, and supernatural revelation cannot be verified empirically either (see Chapter 10). Still, this does not imply that revelation is impossible. Although the supernatural and the infinite (as such) are inaccessible to reason, it is nevertheless possible to represent them *symbolically* for practical purposes. But we will see that such symbols involve regulative ideas that transcend particular concepts, while still belonging to reason as a faculty. Faith cannot become completely transparent and clear to reason, albeit *reason is still determined to honor faith.* Kierkegaard explains his view by quoting Hugh of St. Victor approvingly:

> "With respect to the things that surpass reason, faith is in fact not really supported by any reason, because reason does not comprehend what faith believes; but nevertheless here there is also a something through which reason becomes determined or is determined as honoring the faith that it nonetheless is incapable of grasping fully."
>
> This is what I have explained (e.g. in *Concluding Postscript*): that not every absurdity is the absurd or the paradox. The activity of reason is precisely to know the paradox negatively – but no more than that. (SKS 23, 23, NB15:25 / KJN 7, 20)

However, we will see indications later that reason does more than knowing the paradox negatively, since even faith involves some rationality and understanding that is not merely negative. In any case, there is very strong textual evidence for suprarationalism. This 1850 passage supports it, just like the 1842–43 passage quoted above and the 1850 reply to Eiríksson examined in the previous chapter (see also SKS 15, 109 / BA, 23). Among the published writings, *Philosophical Fragments* supports suprarationalism (cf. SKS 4, 261–4 / PF, 59–62). The latter is not only claimed by suprarationalists like Evans (1999: ch. 11) but even by antirationalists like Carr (1996: 241).

Specifically, *Fragments* claims that the understanding is sublated by faith, just as self-love is sublated by love of another (SKS 4, 249, 252 / PF, 44, 47–8). Self-love is both negated and confirmed when it is recontextualized, or *aufgehoben*, by love of another. As egoistic or self-serving, love is negated (or dethroned), although it is transformed and preserved as unselfish love for the other. Similarly, mere understanding is *both* negated *and* confirmed by religious faith. It is denied insofar as it cannot understand divine revelation and the divine as such. But it is confirmed (even by faith) as *valid*, including when it limits itself by becoming aware of its own ignorance in religious matters. Faith never suspends reason (as such), although reason cannot grasp faith perfectly either. Like egoism, mere reason is *aufgehoben* when it goes from being self-grounding and absolute to being a part of a larger whole (cf. Westphal 2018: 371). Antirationalism and irrationalism can at best explain why it is negated or denied. But they cannot explain why it is confirmed and *preserved by faith*, as suprarationalism can.

Moreover, the signed writings do not speak of the absurdity of faith as the pseudonymous writings do (cf. Carr 1996: 240; McKinnon 1998: 76–9). Conflict between faith and reason is not unavoidable since faith overcomes offense. And as we have seen, reason plays a crucial negative role for Kierkegaard. Finally, Kierkegaard claims that reason is determined to honor faith without perfect conceptual understanding of it (SKS 23, 23–4, NB15:25 / KJN 7, 20–1). In the 1850 passage (on Hugh) quoted above, Kierkegaard writes:

> [I]f one utterly abolishes "faith" and lets the entire sphere disappear, then reason becomes conceited [*indbildsk*] and perhaps concludes that ergo the paradox is nonsense . . . [P]eople have a twaddling and conceited concept of human reason, especially in our times, when one never thinks of a thinker, a reasonable hum[an] being [*et fornuftig Msk*], but of pure reason and the like, which do not exist at all, inasmuch as there is no one, be he a professor or whatever, who is pure reason. (SKS 23, 23–4, NB15:25 / KJN 7, 20–1)

Reason without faith becomes conceited, since it can get exaggerated ideas about itself, by disrespecting its limits and finitude. *Faith here seems beneficial for reason* since reason without faith can transcend its own limits (e.g., by involving fanaticism). In addition, we will see that faith itself must involve understanding.[6] But then *reason seems strengthened by faith*, which contradicts both irrationalism and antirationalism.

In the quote above, Kierkegaard continues by saying that our time has a conceited and twaddling concept of human reason. Specifically, he attacks the concept of pure reason on the grounds that no one is perfectly rational (SKS 23, 24, NB15:25 / KJN 7, 21);[7] however, Kantians could

[6] Emmanuel (1996: 59) says that reason honors faith by accepting that revelation points the way to a higher truth.

[7] Kierkegaard could be influenced by Hamann's attack on Kant's "pure reason" here; see Betz 2007: 306.

object that the human potential for rationality does not entail any perfect development of rationality in individuals. Kierkegaard seems to take rationality to be finite, fallible, and conditioned historically and socially (Westphal 1991: 22, 97; cf. Emmanuel 1996: 49, 58). But it is far from clear that reason as such must be sinful (see Helms 2017).

Antirationalism as a Corrective against Rationalism

The suprarationalist reading is supported by many scholars (e.g., Jackson 1987; Evans 2006b: chs. 7–11; Czakó 2015). It represents perhaps *the* most authoritative interpretation of Kierkegaard, although it is challenged by the antirationalist reading developed and defended by Karen Carr (1996) and Adam Buben (2013).[8] Antirationalism claims the following:

1. There is a deep antagonism, hostility, and animosity between faith and reason that is unavoidable.
2. Reason cannot see things as they are concerning faith. As a result, reason cannot be used to pursue religious truth. Any attempt to use reason to assist faith is a mistake, since faith lies beyond reason.
3. Still, faith is *a*-rational, not irrational.
4. Finally, religious belief is constrained by something external to human subjectivity (e.g., divine revelation).

This reading does have some clear textual support. Indeed, it seems to capture the pre-Christian perspective quite well, since it focuses on how the natural man perceives Christ and the *imitatio Christi* as a provocation and scandal. Whereas the suprarationalist reading is supported by writings that describe faith from the Christian perspective, the antirationalist reading fits writings that describe and problematize it from the perspective of nonbelievers.[9] Specifically, it fits de silentio and Climacus, not Kierkegaard. Unlike Kierkegaard, Climacus goes to the extreme of saying that *faith crucifies the understanding* (SKS 7, 545, cf. 508, 513 / CUP1, 600, cf. 559, 564). Still, even Climacus admits that faith is a "happy passion [*lykkelige Lidenskab*]" (SKS 4, 261 / PF, 59) in which there is a happy

[8] See also Söderquist 2019: 236n1.

[9] Buben 2013: 325 refers to SKS 11, 268, which claims that faith is humanly speaking blind and against reason. However, this passage mainly contrasts believers with pharisees and publicans. Kierkegaard is therefore saying that faith is blind to many of the things that concern pharisees and publicans, and that it therefore seems opposed to their reason.

encounter between faith and reason without any self-contradiction (SKS 4, 253, 298 / PF, 47, 101).

However, Carr (1996) and Buben (2013) could be right that Kierkegaard's polemics against Christendom involve antirationalism. For antirationalism works as a valuable *corrective* against complacent theological speculation and the Christian establishment. Indeed, Kierkegaard himself suggests that his criticism of Danish Lutheranism and speculation represents exactly such a corrective (SKS 21, 296–7, NB10:76 / KJN 5, 307; SKS 25, 51–2, NB26:47 / KJN 9, 49; SKS 25, 279, NB28:82 / KJN 9, 281). At least, he is explicit that he recognizes the following correctives as valid or justified:

1. The Socratic emphasis on human ignorance is a corrective against the excesses of alleged speculative, scientific knowledge in philosophy and theology associated with right-Hegelianism (SKS 22, 224, NB12:134 / KJN 6, 225). Likewise, the claim that not everything can be explained is a corrective against the exaggerations of German philosophy (SKS 18, 217, JJ:239 / KJN 2, 199).
2. His own authorship is a corrective against the Danish establishment (notably Bishop Mynster and Martensen) and Christendom (SKS 22, 194–5, NB12:97 / KJN 6, 194; SKS 24, 74, NB21:122 / KJN 8, 70; cf. Horn 2007: 220).[10]

Although he is not explicit, Kierkegaard seems to also *use antirationalism to counteract* the use of *speculation* and science in religious matters. He therefore seems to counteract right-Hegelian theology not only with Socrates and Kantianism but also with Hamann and Jacobi. Like Hamann and Jacobi, he may appeal to a view that is seemingly irrational, fideist, or antirationalist in order to counteract exaggerated rationalism and speculation in religious matters.[11] When he writes from the non-Christian perspective, he therefore stresses the *discontinuity* and *incongruity* between natural and revealed standards by depicting Christian revelation as something absurd that offends natural man. Still, I contend that this approach is

[10] In addition, (3) the emphasis on inwardness is a corrective against overemphasis on outwardness, while the emphasis on suffering and martyrdom is a corrective against exaggerated inwardness (cf. SKS 22, 241, NB12:162 / KJN 6, 243; SKS 23, 435, NB20:74 / KJN 7, 443; SKS 24, 368, NB24:78 / KJN 8, 373; SKS K26, 243). Finally (4), Protestantism is a corrective against Catholicism (SKS 14, 173; SKS 22, 367).

[11] Indeed, Eiríksson reports that "Kierkegaard once admitted as much to me in a private conversation, after I had expressed my opposition to his conception of faith as 'by virtue of the absurd,' that he had indeed pushed the point to extremes [*stillet det vel meget paa Spidsen*]." Eiríksson 1866: 102n translated in Schreiber 2019: 283.

best viewed as a *corrective* against those who pushed the opposite approach, namely that reason and revelation are continuous and in harmony (e.g., Christendom, including Kantians, Martensen, and liberal theologians). The problem with the latter approach is that it removes the very possibility of *offense*. It thereby removes the very *condition of possibility* for genuine faith since the very alterity of revelation disappears. To counteract it, *Practice in Christianity* stresses the alterity of revelation and how it invites offense (SKS 12, 107 / PC, 99). Kierkegaard thus insists that revelation and reason are heterogeneous and that Christianity differs from Christendom (cf. Bohlin 1944: 168n14). He writes:

> When Christianity came into the world, it did not itself need to point out (even though it did so) that it was contending with human reason, because the world discovered this easily enough. But now, now when Christianity for centuries has lived in protracted association with human reason, now when a fallen Christianity (just like those fallen angels who married mortal women) has married human reason, now when Christianity and reason have a *Du* relationship – now Christianity must above all itself pay attention to the obstacle. (SKS 9, 189 / WL, 199)

Kierkegaard admits, however, that by its very nature, a corrective tends to be extreme and may seem paradoxical and overly harsh (SKS 22, 208, NB12:115 / KJN 6, 209; SKS 13, 25 / PV, 18). Specifically, correctives are necessarily one-sided since they counteract one extreme by being extreme in an opposite direction. If one complains about this one-sidedness, one can only say that it is easy enough to "add the other side" again, but then the corrective "ceases to be the corrective and becomes itself the established order" instead (SKS 22, 194, NB12:97 / KJN 6, 194). Kierkegaard thereby indirectly *admits* that his critique of speculation and the establishment is one-sided. Indeed, he (Climacus) writes:

> Honor be to speculative thought [*Speculationen*], praised be everyone who is truly [*i Sandhed*] occupied with it. To deny the value of speculative thought ... would, in my eyes, be to prostitute oneself and would be especially foolish for one whose life in large part and at its humble best is devoted to its service, and especially foolish for one who admires the Greeks. (SKS 7, 59 / CUP1, 55–6)

Theoria and speculation are worthy endeavors, although *praxis* has priority ultimately. We may then conclude as follows: First, the antirationalist reading is right to emphasize the category of the offense. Still, Kierkegaard is clear that the believer overcomes both offense and absurdity insofar as he believes. Indeed, faith is described (even by Climacus) as "that happy passion" in which "the understanding and the paradox happily encounter each other in the moment" (SKS 4, 261, cf. 257, 263 / PF, 59, cf. 54, 61). This entails a happy encounter between faith and understanding that overcomes offense, absurdity, and contradictions (SKS 4, 253, 298 / PF, 47, 101). The opposition between faith and reason is therefore *contingent and avoidable*, not necessary or inescapable as antirationalists assume (although Carr [2019: 374] responds that a happy meeting between faith and reason is unusual). Indeed, we have seen Kierkegaard suggesting that faith is *beneficial* for reason (SKS 23, 24, NB15:25 / KJN 7, 20–1), something that clearly undermines antirationalism.

Second, antirationalists are right that the believer lapses back into offense if he stops believing. Offense is always possible, since faith never becomes a permanent possession that cannot be lost. Therefore, the *tension* between faith and reason remains (as the antirationalists insist), although it can nevertheless be *lessened over time.* Despite the demanding nature of Christian faith, Kierkegaard assumes that we can make progress towards Christian ideals by gradually changing our second natures. Even though "faith always remains a struggle," it is still the case that "faith may arguably [*kan nu vel*] become *second nature*" (SKS 4, 293, 304 / PF, 96, 108, modified transl.). "The possibility of offense" is therefore not constant "like the pull of gravity" (pace Carr 1996: 249). We can cultivate and improve our natures, but perfection is never reached (Stern 2012: 197–8, 217–18).

Third, the possibility of offense is *contingent on sin* (which Carr [1996] seems to admit). But in order to maintain the opposition between reason and faith, the antirationalist reading must presuppose an implausibly strong form of original sin in which it is utterly impossible to overcome both sin and offense. However, Kierkegaard does not accept total depravity (genuine guilt-consciousness, for instance, is possible independently of divine revelation and divine assistance). Specifically, human sinfulness does not prevent cognition of truth. Even Carr admits this:

> [E]ven on the Christian model, there is a sense in which the learner [believer] knows at least part of the truth of which he is ignorant; Climacus emphasizes that the ignorance is a product of an ongoing act of will on the learner's part, an act of will for which he is both responsible and culpable. We can only make sense of this act of will if, on some level, the individual knows the truth from which he is fleeing. That is, the individual, in order to flee the truth, must antecedently know what the truth is, otherwise he could not be said to be willing the flight. (2019: 367)

It seems clear, however, that believers can overcome sin by accepting divine grace (see Chapters 5–11). Still, we are absolutely different from God insofar as we are (unrepentant) sinners, although creation and Creator are still akin (SKS 4, 251–2 / PF, 47–8). We are related or kindred to God (SKS 16, 86–7 / PV, 106), and even resemble him insofar as we love our neighbor (SKS 9, 69–70 / WL, 62–3). Yet, there is an infinite qualitative difference between God and us in the sense that God is capable of everything, while we are capable of nothing without his grace (SKS 21, 235, NB9:59 / KJN 5, 244). But the acceptance of divine grace makes it possible to overcome both sin and offense, which sets faith and reason in opposition to one another. Yet sin is only finally defeated eschatologically.

Fourth, Kierkegaard maintains that divine revelation never becomes completely transparent and clear to us (SKS 27, 297, Papir 306 / KJN 11.2, 8). But it does not follow that it is equally obscure to believers and nonbelievers; it can be less obscure to believers than to nonbelievers.

Fifth, it is unclear how faith can sacrifice reason as assumed by antirationalism. One problem for the antirationalist is to account for the conversion to Christianity, another is to account for life after conversion. Both require not just reflection and motivation but also *reasoning and normativity*, although some of it is specifically Christian (cf. Helms 2020: 8–13). However, the antirationalist reading can hardly account for this since it does not leave sufficient room for normative and explanatory reasoning in ethico-religious contexts.

Since it takes faith to be a-rational, antirationalism does not allow rational assessment and critique of faith. Faith then seems *beyond rational critique* – but that is neither Kierkegaard's view nor a very promising one. As indicated above, neither doctrine nor passion is a-rational since both have cognitive content. Like irrational faith, a-rational faith would seem to undermine Christianity as a doctrinal religion. In the words of Blanshard (1968: 15), it would imply "that there are no common truths for Christians to accept, no common principle by which their lives may be guided, indeed no common Deity for them to contemplate and worship."

Finally, the antirationalist reading relies on an overly *narrow notion of reason.* Buben (2013: 324), notably, contrasts faith with evidence that seems exclusively theoretical and epistemic. Söderquist (2019: 230, 236n) similarly contrasts faith and reason, taking the latter in a narrow sense that requires objective arguments instead of subjective arguments. But as we saw in the discussion of the God-postulate (in Chapters 9–10), Kierkegaard here follows Kant in aligning *the subjective with the practical and the objective with the theoretical* (SKS 7, 183n / CUP1, 200n). Unlike knowledge, faith is *not* objective in the sense of having an objective ground in epistemic evidence. But it is nevertheless objective in the broad sense of being intersubjectively *valid* and communicable. By limiting rationality to theoretical, objective concerns, the antirationalist reading overlooks the decisive role played by practical reasoning. Söderquist (2019: 230), for example, admits that he limits reasons to "objective arguments that will appeal to and satisfy the understanding." Similarly, fideist and irrationalist readings often overlook the extensive use of practical *and* epistemic reasoning in Kierkegaard's writings.[12]

To a large extent, the problem here is to clarify the role of the understanding (*Forstanden*) within Kierkegaard's account of faith. I contend that it *typically* involves the following elements (although Kierkegaard's use of it and its cognates is context sensitive):

1. It represents a natural human *faculty* (or cognitive function), elsewhere described as *reason* (although commentators use "reason" more often than Kierkegaard does; see Helms 2017).
2. It is *finite* and cannot therefore cognize the infinite, supernatural, supersensual, unconditioned, absolute, and divine as such.
3. It involves a *naturalism* that excludes reference to the supernatural and eschatology (Davenport 2008a: 196–233; Fremstedal 2014a: 97 and ch. 7; Westphal 2014: 91).
4. It is *discursive* rather than intuitive and reflective rather than immediate in its operations (cf. Chapter 11).
5. It involves a rational capacity for *calculation* and manipulation.
6. It only allows risks and sacrifices that are likely to pay off. It is therefore highly concerned with probability and *pro et contra* reasoning (SKS 12, 104, 124 / PC, 96, 116).
7. It does not represent moral rationality, but *prudential and instrumental* rationality that is informed by experience (cf. the hypothetical imperatives in Chapter 4). It is therefore *not* concerned with unconditional ethico-religious imperatives (SKS 16, 206 / JFY, 156–7), but with something that holds only to some extent or on some condition (typically self-interest).
8. It therefore serves only relative ends, not the highest good (SKS 12, 123 / PC, 116).
9. It does not represent pure reason but rather a *social* enterprise that is *historically* conditioned (cf. Westphal 1991: 22, 97; Emmanuel 1996: 49; Betz 2007: 306; Fremstedal 2014a: 97).

[12] For these types of reasoning, see Purkarthofer 2009; Fox-Muraton 2018 and 2019a.

10. It is concerned with what is *humanly possible*, not what is divinely possible. Specifically, it is concerned with practical possibility (and probability) in which an agent contributes to the realization of an end by acting. Mere metaphysical (or divine) possibility is ruled out.
11. It seems to involve a form of *evidentialism* concerning belief, according to which strong beliefs require strong evidence, whereas weak beliefs require weak evidence (Fremstedal 2020b: 82).
12. Insofar as it is considered self-sufficient and absolute, it tends towards self-deification that is *sinful* and corrupted, since it separates man from God (see Blanshard 1968: 12; Westphal 1991: 22, 97; 2018; Emmanuel 1996: 58; Betz 2007: 306).
13. Still, it can avoid these problems (##5–12) by limiting itself and allowing faith.

Faith is not opposed to rationality as such, but there *is* a *contingent* opposition between faith and self-sufficient reason (Helms 2017: 476–9). However, Kierkegaard thinks that it is *dialectics*, not the understanding, that deals with reasons for religious belief and the acceptance of divine authority (SKS 7, 31–2n / CUP1, 24n; SKS 18, 212, JJ:225 / KJN 2, 195).[13] Indeed, reasons that justify religious belief seem possible if rationality limits itself (#13), rejects self-sufficiency, naturalism, evidentialism, and egoistic striving for relative ends, while allowing divine assistance to realize the highest good (cf. ##3, 5–8, 10–12). To allow reasons for belief, dialectics must then differ from the understanding by including the following elements (that depart from the list above in several respects):

3*. It must reject naturalism (and allow eschatology and the supernatural).
5*. It cannot be based merely on calculation and manipulation, or
6*. on probability and profitability alone.
7*. It must include moral rationality, and
8*. serve the highest good.
10*. It must allow metaphysical and divine possibilities as well as
11*. pragmatism concerning belief.

Still, both the understanding and dialectics (1) represent reason as a natural human faculty, which is (2) finite, (4) discursive, and (9) a social and historical enterprise. But dialectics cannot be entirely corrupted by sin. Rather, it takes a broadly Kantian form (more on this later).

[13] For Kierkegaard's use of dialectics and examinational (*peirastike*) arguments, see Purkarthofer 2009.

Still, in 1851 Kierkegaard objects to attempts to provide reasons for faith:

> The priest says that one must give reasons in order to get people to accept [Christianity]; it is an accommodation, but it is necessary . . . Take a closer look and you will see that "the priest" has even more reasons than those he cites . . . He has, in fact, the reason that he wants to get along well with peop[le] who might perhaps become angry if he represented [Christianity] more truthfully. He has the reason that it is his living and that he must take care to speak in such a way that the congregation does not stint in its offerings. In short, he has the reason that he himself is mired in the same worldliness as the congregation. (SKS 24, 413, NB24:140 / KJN 8, 419)

Here Kierkegaard objects to attempts to justify Christianity as motivated by worldly reasons. This is objectionable since there would not be anything specifically Christian left if Christianity is justified entirely in worldly and pagan terms.

While Kierkegaard might object to non-Christian reasons for faith, it does not follow that reason giving generally relativizes the unconditioned. Rather, the unconditioned is supported by reasons that are *unconditional and overriding*. Kantian ethics, for instance, is not undermined by categorical reasons that trump all other reasons and concerns. It therefore seems that the problem is not with reasons as such but only some particular reasons. Specifically, the problem is with *pro tanto* and *prima facie* reasons (since these reasons are defeatable) as well as reasons that are not categorical but rather *hypothetical* or instrumental. Even an overriding hypothetical reason could therefore be contrasted with unconditional or absolute reasons that are overriding. In one passage, Kierkegaard almost concedes this, since he contrasts "an infinite 'why'" with finite reasons (SKS 12, 126–7 / PC, 120), saying that Christianity is "not commensurable with any finite wherefore" (SKS 12, 75 / PC, 62). This suggests that there are *absolute reasons*.

Nevertheless, Kierkegaard claims that "the understanding comes to a standstill at the absolute" (SKS 12, 126 / PC, 120). He holds that "[r]easons cannot be given for something unconditioned; at the most, reasons can be given for the fact that reasons cannot be given" (SKS 24, 386, NB24:107 / KJN 8, 392). He argues that reasons make the unconditioned into something conditioned (SKS 24, 382–3, NB24:101 / KJN 8, 387). One gives reasons for the unconditioned that not only relates it to something else but even conditions it on something else (SKS 25, 66, NB26:61 / KJN 9, 63–4).

However, it is hardly clear why it is impossible to give reasons for something unconditioned. The explanation could be that Kierkegaard uses reason and understanding in a *narrow* sense that excludes overriding categorical reasons. It is exactly for this reason that he claims that reasonableness (*Forstandighet*) rebels against what holds unconditionally, suggesting that it is conditioned by egoistic prudential concerns that contradict categorical obligations (SKS 16, 206–7 / JFY, 157). Moreover, he contrasts human standards with the unconditioned, since he thinks the former is concerned with something that only holds to some extent or on some condition (typically self-interest; cf. SKS 12, 40–1, 71–2 / PC, 26, 59–60).

In addition, he contrasts ordinary reasoning, which justifies arguments and provides reasons, with a Kantian *dialectics* of reason. As we saw (in Chapter 10), reason in its dialectical use seeks the unconditioned for everything conditioned in order to make the chain of conditions complete (A307/B364). But due to its finitude, reason fails to reach the unconditioned as such, since it lies beyond the boundaries of reason. Therefore, it seems impossible to give reasons for it, as Kierkegaard insists (SKS 24, 386, NB24:107 / KJN 8, 392).

Here commentators agree that *Philosophical Fragments* seems influenced by Kant (Westphal 1991: 113; Green 1992: 77–8; Evans 1999: 222–4; Verheyden 2000: 157; Tjønneland 2004: 88–95; Pinkard 2010: 348). *Fragments* and *Postscript* both claim that the highest passion of the understanding lies in dialectically transcending its limit by becoming faith, although worship of the Absolute (or unconditioned) does not belong to dialectics (SKS 4, 242–53 / PF, 37–47; SKS 7, 444–5 / CUP1, 490–1). However, dialectics does not only provide anomalies that prepare the ground for faith. It even includes reasons for religious belief and reasons for accepting religious authority (SKS 7, 31–2n / CUP1, 24n; SKS 18, 212, JJ:225 / KJN 2, 195). As such, it represents a form of rationality that is not only ignored by antirationalism but also something not entirely corrupted by sin.

Except for his concept of dialectics, Kierkegaard's conceptions of reason and philosophy are *narrow* compared to those of Kant and Hegel (Bubbio 2014: 93; Fremstedal 2014a: 97–8, 150). Typically, he contrasts the divine unconditioned, which reveals itself supernaturally, with human reasoning (SKS 25, 29–30, NB26:22 / KJN 9, 26–7). The contrast is then not only between the *infinite* God and *finite* reason but also between *supernatural* revelation and mere *reason*, something that is a traditional contrast in Christian theology and philosophy.

Faith Seeking Understanding?

However, does Kierkegaard break with the Augustinian idea of "faith seeking understanding [*fides quaerens intellectum*]" and with Anselm's phrase "I believe so that I may understand [*credo ut intelligam*]"? In 1851, he states:

> Faith cannot be comprehended [*begribes*]; at the most, it can be comprehended that it cannot be comprehended, so also: Reasons cannot be given for something unconditioned; at the most, reasons can be given for the fact that reasons cannot be given. (SKS 24, 386, NB24:107 / KJN 8, 392; cf. SKS 11, 210 / SUD, 98)

Lee C. Barrett comments:

> Kierkegaard focused on the [Anselmian] phrase's apparent implication that understanding should be the fulfillment or *telos* of faith, and therefore condemned it as a precursor of speculative idealism's sublation of faith. Kierkegaard became suspicious of any language suggesting that religious pathos should be transmuted into a science. By 1849 Kierkegaard was explicitly rejecting the notion that believing involves a drive toward comprehension and dismissed the putative ability to comprehend faith's objects as a vain imagination. Instead of comprehension, faith involves will and obedience . . . Faith does not involve any sort of seeing, but operates against reason . . . He accused the Alexandrian theologians and Augustine of developing the definition of faith in an unfortunate Platonic direction by associating it with intellectual insight. (2008: 172–3)

But faith that does *not* seek understanding may involve *blind* assent that believes without questioning. As such, it neither seeks speculative knowledge nor practical wisdom. Rather, it seems indifferent to truth and may revel in mystification and obscurantism. Indeed, unquestioning faith can easily slip into superstition, fanaticism, self-indulgence, and idolatry (Migliore 2014: 2–9). John Bishop explains:

> The theist traditions hold a deep fear of idolatry – of giving one's "ultimate concern" . . . to an object unworthy of it. The desire to be assured of entitlement to faith is thus not merely externally imposed by commitment to philosophical critical values: it is a demand internal to the integrity of theistic faith itself. Arguably, believers must even take seriously the possibility that the God they have been worshipping is not, after all, the true God. (2016: Part IV, quoting Paul Tillich)

To avoid these problems, Kierkegaard – and his defenders – cannot dismiss understanding or a rational examination of faith. Instead, they must distinguish between an understanding that is *appropriate* for faith and one that is not. In 1843, Kierkegaard (de silentio) writes:

> Even if someone were able to transpose the whole content of faith into conceptual form [*Begrebets Form*], it does not follow that he has

> comprehended [*begrebet*] faith, comprehended how he entered into it or how it entered into him. (SKS 4, 103 / FT, 7)

However, this is a critique of Hegelian attempts to sublate faith into knowledge (see Horn 2007: 220). As Mark Wrathall explains:

> His target is anyone who, like Hegel . . . "cannot rest satisfied with the plain pictures of faith, but rather [feels] duty bound to proceed to thought – at first, to reflective understanding, but ultimately to conceptual thought."[14]

Again, Kierkegaard describes his own emphasis on human ignorance as a corrective against the excesses of speculative knowledge in philosophy and theology (SKS 18, 217, JJ:239 / KJN 2, 199; SKS 22, 224, NB12:134 / KJN 6, 225). Famously, he denies that the content of faith can be transposed into *conceptual* (*begrebslig*) form or comprehended conceptually (Czakó 2015: 284–5). Specifically, he criticizes Hegelian attempts to replace the religious *Vorstellungen* (picture thinking) with philosophical *Begriffen* (concepts), since the latter cannot represent faith adequately. But this only implies that religious language and its images cannot be replaced entirely by philosophical concepts and knowledge. Furthermore, even if thought and philosophy understand the propositional content of revelation, it cannot understand how it entered the world by a revelation (SKS 15, 216–26 / BA, 176–87).

The reason for this is hardly clear. As we saw in connection with the incarnation, Kierkegaard seems concerned not just with doctrine but also with the manifestation of *divine presence*, understood as a reality, not just a representation of it. John Bishop points out that "[p]ropositional articulations of what is revealed may still be essential, but they need to be accepted as at a remove from the object of revelation itself, and therefore as limited" (2016: Part v). Thus, the reality of divine presence (and God's self-revelation) cannot be exhausted propositionally or conceptually. In addition, faith involves trust (*fiducia*) in God that makes a practical commitment (cf. SKS 21, 240, NB 9:66 / KJN 5, 250). And this trust cannot be comprehensively understood either since it is not just a propositional attitude (Bernier 2015: 166; cf. Bishop 2016: Part vi).

Like *negative* theology, Kierkegaard emphasizes divine transcendence and hiddenness, seeing adequate conceptual knowledge of God as impossible (Law 1993; Czakó 2015: 288), at least from a theoretical perspective.

[14] Wrathall 2019: 249–50 referencing G. W. F. Hegel (1986) *Enzyklopädie der philosophischen Wissenschaften im Grundrisse: Dritter Teil: Die Philosophie des Geises* [3rd ed., 1830], in *Werke*, Frankfurt am Main: Suhrkamp, vol. x, §564.

Like Kant, he assumes that the general concepts of reason fail to fully capture the specific, concrete, intuitive, and imaginative content of faith. Like aesthetic experience, faith thus transcends existing concepts since no determinate concept can be quite adequate for it.

Still, faith is guided by reason in its regulative use (Helms 2020: 3–13). As noted in Chapter 10, Kierkegaard follows Kant in taking religious language (like aesthetic experience) to be symbolic, allegoric, and metaphoric. Like Kant, he interprets religious symbols (both notions and narratives) as visible representations of transcendent ideas that lie beyond the limits of our understanding. Religious symbols and images are then transitional forms that mediate between transcendent ideas and experience. These ideas are transcendent since experience can never provide an object that would represent them adequately. Nor can these ideas be captured fully by determinate concepts. Still, these transcendent or invisible ideas are represented and symbolized by something visible that we grasp (Tjønneland 2004: 84–96; Bubbio 2014: 31–8, 87–114).

These symbols do not represent theoretical knowledge or general concepts, but they still grasp something imperfectly for *practical* purposes. This practical understanding allows faith to make sense of our striving through the use of different metaphors, symbols, and ideas. A regulative use of the idea of God, notably, makes use of God as an ideal that we can approximate only asymptotically. It does not concern what God is in himself, but what he is *for us* existentially. Specifically, Kierkegaard relies on a practical use of the God-idea when he interprets human selfhood as an endless striving towards an endpoint of completion that cannot be reached completely (cf. Pattison 1997; Verstrynge 2004; Bubbio 2014: ch. 4; Dalferth 2015: 75). Christian ethics in particular is based on imitation of Christ as a regulative ideal.[15] Thus *For Self-Examination* emphasizes that scripture should be understood *practically* as a guide to Christian life, not as an object of theoretical study.

But as Wrathall (2019: 244) notes, "belief" is ambiguous since it either refers to "a practical stance of trust or reliance" or "a cognitive state or attitude of holding-to-be true." It can either be taken in a practical sense as a disposition to *act* or in a theoretical sense of assenting to *doctrine*. But even the former requires practical understanding that involves our cognitive powers. Faith must therefore engage reason, even if it cannot be derived from mere reason. Instead of suspending reason, it thus involves the faculty of reason, in its practical and regulative use, which strives

[15] Indeed, even Kant uses Christ to symbolize moral perfection (R 6:65n). Cf. Bubbio 2014: 35.

towards new and deeper understanding and seeks to harmonize actuality with ideality (principles, concepts, or ideas; see Helms 2020: 6).

Wrathall (2019: 248) suggests that Christian faith may be considered "a kind of [practical] expertise," involving "the ability to respond skillfully, fluidly, and appropriately to the needs of others in a Christ-like manner" without

> worry[ing] about our inability to offer a coherent discursive account of the God-man who is the paradigm and focus of the practice of faith. We need not worry about this, because skillful expertise by its nature resists discursive articulation. (2019: 248)

Christian faith cannot be entirely incomprehensible or blind if we are to live according to it. We must be able to respond positively "to the needs of others in a Christ-like manner" (2019: 248). This requires moral *vision* that sees the neighbor and is perceptive to his needs as Christ was (Ferreira 2001: 102–3, 115). Indeed, Kierkegaard writes:

> Indeed, no gaze is as sharp-sighted as that of faith, and yet faith, humanly speaking, is blind; reason, understanding, is, humanly speaking, sighted, but faith is against the understanding. (SKS 11, 268 / WA, 132)

Eleanor Helms (2017: 482) points out that "both reason *and* faith are described as a kind of sight" here. Faith in particular involves a "transformative vision" that reorients the sight of the agent, presumably by changing the perspective from what is humanly possible to what is divinely possible. Instead of contemplating abstract, noncommittal possibilities, faith uses moral imagination to recognize and anticipate possibilities as tasks to be realized (Helms 2017: 482–6; cf. Stokes 2010: 85).

Faith therefore represents a *practical understanding* of one's situation and tasks that sees the neighbor and his needs. It is decisive, however, that "the eye of faith" involves not only intellect but also volition (SKS 27, 302–3, Papir 306 / KJN 11.2, 14; Helms 2017: 482–3). Faith is not merely an intellectual matter, since it requires a will to *obedience* and worship that transcends mere thinking (SKS 20, 222, NB2:209 / KJN 4, 221; cf. SKS 4, 281, 242–53 / PF, 83, 37–47; SKS 7, 444–5 / CUP1, 490–1; SKS 23, 69, NB15:97 / KJN 7, 67). Presumably, it requires an unconditional will to trust and imitate Christ that overcomes sin and offense (cf. SKS 21, 240, NB 9:66 / KJN 5, 250).

By seeing the neighbor, Christian faith therefore involves a practical understanding, or seeing of truth, based on revelation. David Law points out that

> Kierkegaard does not reject doctrine, but aims to shake people out of complacently accepting Christianity as *only* a doctrine and not as a way of life that demands self-sacrifice and renunciation (*SKS* 22, 95, NB11:160 / *KJN* 6, 91), and for which the genuine believer should be prepared to *suffer*. (2015: 258)

Faith can be *described and presented*, but not penetrated conceptually (Schreiber 2018: 115). Indeed, Kierkegaard's descriptions and interpretations of it would make little sense, unless this were the case. These descriptions involve theoretical accounts of practical questions, just like moral philosophy theorizes over morality. In part, this account seems conceptual, although religious *Vorstellungen* are not reduced to, or replaced by, philosophical concepts (cf. SKS 15, 216–26 / BA, 176–87). Still, a propositional articulation of the content of faith, which allows dogmatics, seems possible to a considerable extent.

Conclusion: Against Blind Faith

Instead of denying all understanding, Kierkegaard denies that we can ever exhaust, solve or comprehend the *mystery* of God and his revelation (Emmanuel 1996: 146). Specifically, he denies that we can comprehend the incarnation (SKS 12, 89 / PC, 77). Revelation therefore remains partially *opaque and impenetrable*. It never becomes completely transparent and clear to existing human beings. Therefore, God is not only revealed but also hidden, even in revelation (SKS 27, 297, Papir 306 / KJN 11.2, 8). István Czakó comments:

> [T]he God of Abraham does not appear as that of reason, or as absolute Spirit, but as *Deus absconditus* (the hidden god), whose *absconditas* is conceded *sub contrario* (under the opposite) of the paradox and the absurd. (2015: 286)

Schulz comments that "in Christ[,] God actualizes his omnipotence . . . in the guise of weakness and complete powerlessness" (2015: 116). Indeed, Kierkegaard writes that Christ "constrains himself entirely from intervening omnipotently" (SKS 26, 340, NB34:29 / KJN 10, 349). John Betz comments:

> For Hamann and Kierkegaard, however, the challenge was not simply to bring reason to acknowledge historical revelation but to find revelation where it would least expect it, that is to say, *sub contrario*: the eternal God

> in time, the infinite God in a virgin's womb, the omnipotent God on a cross. (2007: 324)

But revelation is less obscure to believers than to nonbelievers (cf. SKS 23, 23, NB15:25 / KJN 7, 20–1; Barrett 2021: Part II). For the believer must understand the practical importance of faith to live as a Christian. Indeed, even Kierkegaard (the pseudonym H. H.) concedes this:

> Although a revelation is the paradoxical fact that passes [*overgaaer*] human understanding, one can still understand this much, which also has manifested itself everywhere: that a person is called by a revelation to go out in the world, to proclaim the Word, to act and to suffer, is called to the unceasingly active life as the Lord's messenger. (SKS 11, 109–10 / WA, 106; cf. SKS 8, 365 / UD, 268)

Faith as a doxastic venture beyond epistemic evidence seems performed out of epistemic concern to grasp truth of "vital existential importance" (Bishop 2016: Part VII). Although it cannot be understood perfectly, faith can nevertheless be comprehended imperfectly, symbolically, and practically. As such, it is still guided by reason as a faculty since reason must seek new understanding (Helms 2020: 3–13). Thus, faith cannot abolish reasoning or dialectics (SKS 7, 31–2n / CUP1, 24n). Like others, believers need valid reasons for believing and acting (SKS 18, 212, JJ:225 / KJN 2, 195; SKS 15, 182, 207 / BA, 59). And the doctrinal and propositional content of faith is subject to rational assessment, although we cannot understand how something is revealed supernaturally (SKS 15, 216–26 / BA, 176–87; SKS 23, 69, NB15:97 / KJN 7, 67).

CHAPTER 13

The Ethics of Belief: Fideism and Pragmatism

Evidentialism and Nonevidentialism: The Ethics of Belief

The ethics of belief concerns epistemic and practical normativity governing the formation, maintenance, and relinquishment of beliefs (Chignell 2018). Although it concerns belief in general, the ethics of belief is particularly important to religious belief. Peter Forrest (2017) therefore notes that "[c]ontemporary epistemology of religion may conveniently be treated as a debate over whether evidentialism applies to religious beliefs, or whether we should instead adopt a more permissive epistemology."

Unfortunately, Kierkegaard scholars rarely discuss the ethics of belief.[1] Kierkegaard is normally seen as a fideist, although Emmanuel (1996) reads him as a pragmatist instead. Both fideism and pragmatism dismiss strict evidentialism concerning belief, which is based on W. K. Clifford's principles (Chignell 2018: Part I.1):

> [Synchronic Principle:] [I]t is wrong always, everywhere, and for anyone to believe anything on insufficient evidence. (Clifford 1876–77: 295)
>
> [Diachronic Principle:] It is wrong always, everywhere, and for anyone to ignore evidence that is relevant to his beliefs, or to dismiss relevant evidence in a facile way. (Van Inwagen 1996: 145)

Nonevidentialism, by contrast, is the view that not all rational or justified belief requires sufficient epistemic evidence (or that we know we have such evidence). However, nonevidentialists can form beliefs based either on

1. normative practical reasons, or
2. conservatism concerning belief, or
3. fideism concerning belief.[2]

[1] For an exception, see McDaniel 2020: 436–9.

[2] Chignell 2018: Part VI. I follow Booth (2016) and Chignell (2018) in distinguishing between fideism and pragmatism concerning belief, although fideism is often taken in a *wide* sense that is not clearly

(1) Pragmatism (practical nonevidentialism) offers normative practical reasons for belief in cases where evidence is insufficient. (2) Conservatism, by contrast, thinks that one is justified in believing something if one in fact does believe it, or it seems true, as long as the belief in question is not defeated or overridden. Finally, (3) fideism appeals to a self-constituting leap of faith instead. Anthony Booth explains:

> Fideism, is commonly associated with S[ø]ren Kierkegaard ... Fideism contends that certain beliefs may be made rational – that is, can be justified – when they are the products of *faith*. Paradigmatically, belief in God is considered justified on this basis – but the Fideist need not restrict her domain solely to religious beliefs. What is important to her is that the belief be held in an act of self-constitution rendered possible by our radical human freedom, in a "leap of faith". (2016: 7)

Fideism seems to involve a *sui generis* justification of belief that is neither based on reasons nor on conservative considerations (cf. Wahlberg 2020: Part II.IV). Indeed, neither (2) conservatism nor (3) fideism tries to justify belief by offering reasons. Evidentialism and pragmatism, by contrast, both offer *reasons for belief*, although they disagree over whether the reasons are exclusively epistemic (evidentialism) or whether normative practical reasons are also allowed (pragmatism).

Practical nonevidentialism is known as *pragmatism* concerning belief, since it was developed by American pragmatists (especially William James 1956). But *practical nonevidentialism* concerning belief seems more accurate, since it is a view held by many (e.g., Kant) who are not American pragmatists (cf. Chignell 2018: Part VI). This view is not committed to American pragmatism in general or Pierce, James, or Dewey in particular. It only holds that belief is justified by both practical and epistemic reasons. Still, pragmatism regarding belief is often used because the practical reasons that support nonevidentialist belief often involve pragmatic arguments for belief (see Jordan 2018). Such arguments simply aim to show that we have practical reasons for belief without epistemic evidence. These reasons count in favor of managing our beliefs so that our beliefs become rational. As shorthand, such belief will be referred to as "practical belief."[3]

delimited from pragmatism. See Evans 2006b: 175–82; Carroll 2008; Helms 2013: 445; Amesbury 2017.

[3] To simplify the discussion of the ethics of belief somewhat, I have largely abstracted from whether our actual beliefs result from reasoning or not, since this is a contingent psychological issue separate from the question of whether such reasoning is good. To some extent, I have also abstracted from whether or not beliefs can be willed, either directly or indirectly. Although Kierkegaard is often

Arguments for evidentialism indicate that it is *epistemically* rational only to believe on sufficient evidence. But these arguments do not preclude that practical belief is rational in some other respect (cf. McCormick 2015: ch. 3; Reisner 2018). Indeed, such belief could be supported by practical reasons if pragmatism is allowed. Practical belief could therefore be rational practically, although it is not warranted epistemically. However, pragmatists deny that practical belief is irrational in any respect, holding practical belief to be rational all-things-considered.[4]

Recently, the very concept of fideism has become increasingly controversial since it is usually used pejoratively and anachronistically to criticize views that contrast faith and reason in highly different ways (see Carroll 2008; Bernier 2015: 160; Amesbury 2017: Part II.I). Although Pascal, Kierkegaard, James, and Wittgenstein are often used as standard representatives of fideism, these readings are all contested – in part because fideism is not always distinguished from pragmatism and conservatism (or even suprarationalism, antirationalism, and irrationalism). Fideist readings of Kierkegaard, notably, often take fideism in a *wide* sense that include pragmatism and suprarationalism (Evans 2006b; Amesbury 2017: Part II.II.II). But even if fideism were an acceptable position, it still makes sense to explore and develop a nonfideist reconstruction of Kierkegaard that allows reasons for belief.

Kierkegaard: Fideist or Pragmatist?

In modern philosophy, evidentialism is the dominant view, whereas pragmatism is a minority view (Chignell 2018: Part IV.I). Still, Kierkegaard was familiar with pragmatism from Pascal, Kant, I. H. Fichte, and Poul M. Møller. His student notes from Martensen's lectures, notably, shows familiarity with Kant's moral argument for the existence of God and immortality (SKS 19, 141–3, Not4:12 / KJN 3, 140–2), and his writing on immortality is influenced by Møller (Stewart 2015a: 140–1). Møller argues that the alternative to belief in immortality is a practical absurdity that involves suicide or nihilism (1842: 162, 164, 176, 210). He offers practical

associated with doxastic voluntarism, I have indicated (in Chapter 10) that he does *not* think that beliefs can be willed, at least not directly.

4 Cf. Emmanuel 1996: 50–60. *Ecumenicists* admit both epistemic and practical reasons for belief since we are both epistemic and practical agents. Although practical belief is not justified epistemically, it is nevertheless practically rational (or perhaps even rational all-things-considered). Cf. Reisner 2018.

reasons for belief in immortality by arguing that it avoids this absurdity and makes possible meaning and unity in life.[5]

Clearly, Kierkegaard is concerned with the ethics of (religious) belief (Emmanuel 1996: 57). In 1838, he insists that we are morally responsible not only for our actions but also for our beliefs and our intellectual views (SKS 17:271–2, DD:180 / KJN 1, 262). In 1849, he points to a distinction between acting by faith and acting according to the understanding:

> The absurd . . . is quite simply that I, a rational being [*Fornuft-Væsen*], must act in a situation in which my understanding, my reflection, says to me: You can just as well do the one thing as do the other – that is, when my understanding and my reflection say to me, You cannot act – but where I nevertheless must act . . . Thus the absurd, or acting by virtue of the absurd, is acting in faith [*Troen*], trusting in God. (SKS 21, 240, NB 9:66 / KJN 5, 250)

Here the absurd and faith concern a situation that requires action that is not supported by our reflection or understanding. Thus, action and faith are practically necessary yet theoretically unsupported or impossible (since evidence is lacking). Kierkegaard then goes on to contrast action with reflection and epistemic considerations:

> Nothing is more impossible and self-contradictory than to act (infinitely – decisively) by virtue of reflection. The person who says that he has done so merely reveals either that he possesses no reflection (for the reflection that does not possess a counter-possibility for every possibility is not reflection, which is of course doubleness), or he does not know what it means to act. (SKS 21, 240–1, NB 9:66 / KJN 5, 250)

Clearly, religious belief is motivated by practical or existential concerns, something that is recognized even by the antirationalist. Referring to Kierkegaard's analysis of despair, Söderquist (2019: 230) therefore writes that "Christianity is meant to be a cure for a spiritual illness and it is on these terms it must be judged and understood." For Kierkegaard, religion concerns the moral task of cultivating a wholehearted self that overcomes despair. However, he contrasts morality with intellectual, epistemic issues as follows:

> In the New Testament, faith is not an intellectual category but an ethical category designating the relation of personality betw[een] God and

[5] Møller is influenced by I. H. Fichte (see Koch 2004: 261). Møller's pragmatic argument for immortality is similar to Kant's postulate of immortality as developed by I. H. Fichte. Indeed, Møller (1842: 247–9) attributes it to the latter's *Die Idee der Persönlichkeit und der Individuellen Fortdauer* (1834), a work Kierkegaard read and spoke approvingly of (SKS 17, 41–2, AA:22 / KJN 1, 35–6). For I. H. Fichte's (minimal) influence on Kierkegaard, see Rosenau 2007: 60–1. For Pascal's influence on Kierkegaard, see Landkildehus 2009.

> a hum[an] being. Therefore faith is required (as an expression of devotion) – to believe against reason, to believe even though one cannot see (entirely a category of personality and the ethical). (SKS 27, 616, Papir 486 / KJN 11.2, 318, 320)

Here believing against reason need not amount to more than belief that is not based on epistemic evidence and intellectual considerations. Indeed, Kierkegaard continues by criticizing intellectualist interpretations of Christian belief that seek understanding and knowledge (SKS 27, 616, Papir 486 / KJN 11.2, 320), something we discussed in the previous chapter.

It is uncontroversial that Kierkegaard is not an evidentialist who tries to justify belief by pointing to sufficient epistemic evidence. Indeed, he is clear that we cannot possibly have sufficient epistemic evidence for – or against – religious belief. As seen (in Chapters 8–10), his approach here is broadly Kantian, since he views human cognition as finite and limited, denying that we can have knowledge of the infinite, supersensual, and supernatural as such. But it is less clear which variant of nonevidentialism Kierkegaard favors, whether it is fideism, pragmatism, or conservatism. The fideist reading is clearly the *dominant* reading, whereas the pragmatist reading is largely neglected (and the conservatist reading seems virtually nonexistent).[6]

A reading inspired by Gadamer could lead to the view of Kierkegaard as a *conservative* regarding belief. Specifically, prejudices, in the sense of *prejudgments,* are a necessary condition for human understanding and cannot be illegitimate even if not based on evidence. Hermeneutically, one can therefore be a conservative regarding beliefs that represent necessary prejudgments. Such prejudgments are inescapable by representing the facticity of our understanding. Here the pseudonym Climacus is explicit that he starts to philosophize by using inherited traditional ideas (SKS 15, 24 / JC, 125).[7] Still, the question of justification – or normativity – enters the picture when judgments can be revised and criticized. A change of beliefs is therefore only possible against the background of prejudgments that entail conservatism. For we can only revise and criticize some – not all – of our beliefs simultaneously.

Kierkegaard is not a conservative who thinks that ethical and religious beliefs are justified just by virtue of the fact that they are already believed.

[6] For pragmatism, see Emmanuel 1996: 50–60. For fideism, see Evans 2006b: 175–205; Helms 2013; Booth 2016: 7; Amesbury 2017. Note that Helms discusses the fideist reading without defending it. For nonevidentialism (particularly concerning trust and love), see Lippitt 2013: 139–40.

[7] Again, I am indebted to a reviewer.

Quite the opposite, he lauds Socrates for breaking with traditional beliefs and holds that Christianity must break with paganism, Judaism, and the inauthentic and complacent faith of bourgeois Christendom. Christian belief must therefore be acquired through a personal conversion that seems to require normative reasoning that breaks with traditional ideas (more on this later). The question then is whether Kierkegaard is *a fideist or a pragmatist* concerning religious belief? Does he and the pseudonyms offer practical reasons for religious belief or not?

One problem with a fideist reading is that it does not offer reasons that could justify belief, except for a leap of faith. Worse still, it seems impossible to criticize beliefs rationally. For fideism, beliefs cannot be subject to independent *rational assessment.*[8] Nor are they something that can be changed rationally as a result of reasoning independent of faith. Rather, beliefs rely on a self-constituting leap of faith. Beliefs then seem to have a *noncognitive* or a-rational status, involving "passionate commitment of feeling and will," implying that "there are no common truths for Christians to accept . . . [and] no common Deity" (Blanshard 1968: 15). But again, this is *not* Kierkegaard's view. For him, the doctrinal content of religious belief is *subject to rational assessment* (SKS 15, 216–26 / BA, 176–87; SKS 23, 69, NB15:97 / KJN 7, 67). Unlike fideism and irrationalism, he grants reason the ability to distinguish between nonsense and faith. As we have seen (in Chapters 4–12), he allows critique of religious beliefs, based on standards that are both natural and Christian.

Pragmatism Concerning Religious Belief

Indeed, Kierkegaard and his pseudonyms seem to *offer practical reasons* for religious belief. We have seen that Söderquist (2019: 230) points out Christianity "must be judged and understood" as "a cure for a spiritual illness." In light of this, consider the following passage from *Fear and Trembling*:

> If a human being did not have an eternal consciousness, if underlying [*til Grund for*] everything there were only a wild, fermenting power [*Magt*] that writhing in dark [*dunkle*] passions produced everything . . . if a vast, never appeased emptiness hid beneath everything, what would life be then but

[8] Hasker 1995: 294; cf. Carroll 2008: 3. Evans (2006b: 203–4) contests this, holding some – not all – variants of fideism to be subject to rational assessment. This makes sense since he takes fideism in a wide sense, which includes pragmatism and Kantianism. Still, he thinks that fideist belief lies beyond the limits of reason. But how could reason then assess something outside its limits?

> despair? If such were the situation, if there were no sacred bond that knit humankind together, if one generation emerged after another like forest foliage . . . how empty and devoid of consolation would life be! But precisely for that reason it is not so. (SKS 4, 112 / FT, 15)

This cryptic passage anticipates a key claim from *Concluding Unscientific Postscript* and *The Sickness unto Death*, namely that the *alternative to faith is despair*. Whereas the *Postscript* describes faith as self-defense against despair (SKS 7, 183n / CUP1, 200n), *The Sickness unto Death* claims that only faith avoids despair consistently (SKS 11, 195–6 / SUD, 81). It is therefore clear that the alternative to faith is rejected since it involves despair.

Note, however, that the passage quoted above speaks explicitly of a "reason" why it is not the case that life is "empty and devoid of consolation" and nothing but "despair." This reason for this is not theoretic or epistemic but normative practical. Specifically, the *hypothetical* scenario (indicated by the initial "[i]f"), in which life is "empty and devoid of consolation," is ruled out as being absurd, since it involves despair. This is a practical *reductio*, which rejects a hypothetical nonreligious view on practical grounds.

Although this is not a developed pragmatic argument, it still sketches a practical reason for religious belief. The idea is that we have practical reason to prefer a religious scenario involving consolation over (a non-religious scenario involving) emptiness and despair. For that reason, we must assume an "eternal consciousness" and "sacred bond that knit[s] humankind together" as well as what is (later) described as an "eternal divine order" and "the world of spirit" (SKS 4, 123–4 / FT, 27). The latter is interpreted as the world where "only the one who works gets bread" (SKS 4, 123 / FT, 27), something that refers to a moral world – the highest good – in which virtue causes happiness. This world also seems associated with a "sacred bond" that "knit[s] humankind together" (SKS 4, 112 / FT, 15), something which may be read as the kingdom of God.

Elsewhere, Kierkegaard himself speaks explicitly about an *argument* for religious belief. Specifically, *Christian Discourses* sketches a "new argument for immortality." It is presented as follows in Kierkegaard's *Journals*:

> There will be the resurrection of the dead, of both the righteous and the unrighteous. Rejoice, you are not to ask for three demonstrations – it is certain enough that you are immortal – it is absolutely certain – because you must come up for judgment. This is a new argument [*Argument*] for immortality. (SKS 20, 289, NB4:5 / CD, 378; cf. SKS 4, 439–42, 451–3 / CA, 139–41, 151–4; SKS 7, 153–73 / CUP1, 165–88; SKS 10, 211–21 / CD, 202–13)

This is not a theoretic argument involving demonstrations (the reference to three demonstrations here alludes to C. F. Göschel's three proofs for the immortality of the soul; see SKS K20, 299). Instead, it is a pragmatic argument concerned with moral justice (SKS 10, 221, 214 / CD, 212–13, 205; SKS K10, 190; SKS 20, 289, NB4:5 / KJN 4, 289). The idea is that immortality involves an eternity in which the just or righteous are separated from the unjust or unrighteous (SKS 10, 216 / CD, 208). In a discussion of moral duty, Kierkegaard writes:

> There ought not to be discussion about immortality, whether there is an immortality, but about what my immortality requires of me, about my enormous responsibility in my being immortal. (SKS 10, 214 / CD, 205)

Kierkegaard claims that "it is absolutely certain" "that you are immortal" (SKS 20, 289, NB4:5 / CD, 378) . But the certainty is not epistemic but moral since we have moral reason to believe in justice. The very same is the case with the passage just quoted from *Fear and Trembling* as well as the God-postulate in the *Postscript.*[9] Kierkegaard then suggests that we do have moral reason to believe in justice by assuming that "both the righteous and the unrighteous" will be resurrected so that justice is done. In *Christian Discourses*, he writes:

> Just as Christianity demonstrates, precisely from all the disapprobation [*Miskjendelse*] and persecution and wrong the truth must suffer, that justice must exist (what a marvelous way of drawing conclusions!), so also in the extremity of hardship, when it squeezes most terribly, there is this conclusion, this *ergo*: *ergo*, there is an eternity to hope for. (SKS 10, 122 / CD, 111)

The idea seems to be that the injustice of the world cannot be accepted morally, so that we have moral reasons to postulate justice, or a moral order. Elsewhere he writes:

> The Apostle Paul declares (1 Corinthians 15:19), "If we hope only for this life, we are the most miserable [*Elendigste*] of all." This is indeed the case, because if there were no eternal happiness in a life to come, the person who for Christ's sake renounces all of the world's goods and bears all its evil would be deceived, dreadfully deceived. If there were no eternal happiness in the life to come, it seems to me that just out of compassion for a person like that it must come into existence. (SKS 8, 329 / UD, 228; cf. SKS 7, 355 / CUP1, 389)

[9] "God is indeed a postulate, but not in the [pointless] sense in which it is ordinarily taken. Instead, it becomes clear that this is the only way an existing person enters into a relationship with God: when the dialectical contradiction brings passion to despair and assists him in grasping God with 'the category of despair' (faith), so that the postulate, far from being the arbitrary, is in fact *necessary* defense, self-defense; in this way God is not a postulate, but the existing person's postulation of God is – a necessity" (SKS 7, 183n / CUP1, 200n, slightly modified transl.).

A similar point is made in 1842:

> [W]hat would be frightful would not be that I would suffer the punishment I deserved because I had done wrong, but what would be frightful would be if I or any pers[on] could be capable of doing wrong and there would be no one who punished it; and indeed what would be frightful would not be for me to awaken in anguish and horror, deceived in my heart, but rather that I or any pers[on] could deceive his heart in such a way that there would no longer be any power capable of awakening it . . . I will beseech you, O God, if I have acted wrongly, that your judgment will not grant me peace until I have realized my error; for what is important to me is not that I escape from your judgment, but that truth might prevail . . . I want to know it distinctly and clearly, whether in later times it will be to my shame – indeed, to my horror – or to my joy and reassurance [*Beroligelse*]. (SKS 18, 309–10, JJ:508 / KJN 2, 284–5)

Here and elsewhere, Kierkegaard is concerned with moral justice. As we saw, he writes: "The best proof that there is a just governance is to say: 'I will believe it, come what may'" (SKS 18, 296, JJ:469 / KJN 2, 273). Indeed, he goes as far as saying that we must will the existence of a loving God, unless we are to lose everything (SKS 8, 364–5 / UD, 268).

In 1854, he makes it clear that arguments to the effect that "this can only lead to despair . . . therefore . . . it cannot be so" are based on "the human," not on Christian revelation (SKS 25, 476, NB30:112 / KJN 9, 482–3). Clearly, such practical *reductio* arguments rely on mere reason, not supernatural revelation. If successful, they show that religious belief is rational since the alternatives collapse. It then seems possible to justify a religious conversion rationally if a conversion is necessary to avoid despair. Thus, the pragmatist reading seems supported. But even an *abductive* argument could suffice if religion offers a better explanation, which is less absurd, than competing views (cf. Rudd 2001: 144–5). For practical absurdities (such as despair) seem to come in degrees (see Skirbekk 1994: 49–72).

Natural Religion and Theology

It is often denied that Kierkegaard uses natural theology (see Czakó 2015: 288; Carr 2019: 365–6). But he (and Climacus) is clear that Christian faith *presupposes* immanent (or Socratic) religiousness (SKS 4, 258 / PF, 55; SKS 7, 505–21 / CUP1, 555–73; cf. Pap. V, B40:11 / JP 3, 3606).[10] Christianity

[10] See also Chapter 11 on infinite resignation as part of natural religion. Despite Kierkegaard's polemics against Eiríksson, he does not object against Eiríksson's interpretation of immanent religiousness as natural religion (1850: 152–8).

thus presupposes natural religion, just as Christian theology presupposes natural theology (Fabro 1962: 190–1).

Like Kant, Kierkegaard rejects theoretical approaches to natural theology. For both thinkers, the limits of human cognition exclude epistemic evidence of the divine (as such). But religious belief on practical grounds is nevertheless possible. As we have seen (in Chapters 10 and 12), God can be symbolized for practical purposes, even if he is hidden and transcendent, lying beyond conceptual knowledge. God can then be seen as a regulative ideal we can approximate asymptotically through endless striving (see Bubbio 2014: ch. 4).

In the *Postscript*, immanent religiousness involves a moral interpretation of natural religion that emphasizes guilt-consciousness and suffering (SKS 7, 392–504 / CUP1, 431–555). Specifically, morality is so demanding that it inevitably results in a moral gap between our moral obligations and our natural capabilities. Non-Christian ethics prepares for Christian ethics by emphasizing this gap, which involves despair or double-mindedness – a fundamentally split between ideals and reality (see Chapters 5–12). The basic argument here can be reconstructed as follows:

1. Wholeheartedness, or a coherent personal identity, requires unconditional moral commitment (Davenport 2012; Rudd 2012).
2. Still, morality is so demanding that it leads to the moral gap between our obligations and our natural capabilities as finite beings with moral character flaws (Quinn 1998; Evans 2006a: 49–50, 82–3; Hare 2002b; Stern 2012: 206, 246).
3. Overcoming the moral gap requires divine assistance.
4. We have moral reason to believe in divine assistance, since it is necessary for overcoming the moral gap. Without it, we would be double-minded, unable to reconcile ideals and reality, obligations and capabilities.

Clearly, the leap to Christian faith is motivated by the collapse and despair of pre-Christian views. As such, it undoubtedly results from *practical deliberation* and practical reasoning. Therefore, Kierkegaard maintains that we must reflect ourselves out of paganism, although the conversion to Christianity requires volition, not just cognition (SKS 16, 72 / PV, 93).

Indeed, Kierkegaard indicates that dialectics deals with justificatory reasons for religious belief that accepts divine authority. In 1844, he writes:

> [T]he dialectical begins with asking how it is that one submits to this authority, whether or not one can understand for oneself why one has

> chosen it, whether it is a contingency [*et Tilfælde* – an accident]; for in that case, the authority is not authority, not even for the believer when he himself is aware that it is a contingency. (SKS 18, 212, JJ:225 / KJN 2, 195)

In 1846, he (Climacus) comments:

> The dialectical ... cannot be excluded ... [F]or a long time it was deemed possible to exclude dialectics from faith by saying that its conviction was upheld by virtue of authority. Then if someone wanted to question the believer ... he would turn the matter this way: I am not able and should not be able to account for it, because I rest in a confidence in others, in the authority of the saints [*de Helliges*], etc. This is an illusion, because dialectics merely turns and asks ... about what authority is then and why he now regards these as authorities. Consequently, it speaks dialectically with him ... about *the faith* he has *in them*. (SKS 7, 31–2n / CUP1, 24n)

The last quote does not attack the authority of saints or Catholicism, since the latter is not discussed (see SKS 7, 41 / CUP1, 34). Instead, it critiques appeals to religious authority that fail to account for reasons that justify belief. Indeed, such appeals to nonrational authority are deemed illusory. And attempts to limit dialectical reasoning by imposing external limits that cannot be recognized by reason itself are criticized for "superstition and narrow-mindedness" (SKS 7, 41n, 50 / CUP1, 35n, 44). The impulse (*Trang*) to exclude dialectics, in order to find a firm footing, is described as only an impulse towards a superstitious fixed point (*overtroisk Holdningspunkt*; see SKS 7, 50 / CUP1, 44). To avoid such superstition and narrow-mindedness, we must do justice to dialectics, by letting it have its due (SKS 7, 35 / CUP1, 28):

> Even the most certain of all, a revelation, *eo ipso* becomes dialectical when I am to appropriate it ... As soon as I take away the dialectical, I am superstitious and defraud God of the moment's strenuous acquisition of what was once acquired. It is, however, far more comfortable to be objective and superstitious, boasting about it and proclaiming thoughtlessness. (SKS 7, 41n / CUP1, 34–5n)

To deny the value of speculation and theoretical thinking would be like prostituting oneself intellectually (SKS 7, 59 / CUP1, 55–6). Presumably, it is like intellectual prostitution insofar as one follows an external power instead of thinking for oneself. Anyway, these points support pragmatism rather than fideism since belief seems supported by practical reasons. But they do *not* abolish divine authority as such. Instead, the point is that the acceptance of faith and divine authority can be supported by nonarbitrary normative reasons (SKS 18, 212, JJ:225 / KJN 2, 195). Faith could therefore be justified rationally. But this presupposes that we have normative reasons to acknowledge the need for divine assistance (to overcome the moral gap) and that Christianity can therefore be taken to solve a pre-Christian problem.[11]

Concluding Discussion

There is a fundamental *tension* between pragmatism concerning religious belief and theological suprarationalism, although Kierkegaard is committed to both (see Emmanuel 1996: 44–60). The former sees belief as justified by normative practical reasons, but the latter see it as at least partially above mere reason as a natural human faculty. But how is this even possible? The point seems to be that we have practical reasons for believing in something that at least partially transcends unaided reason by being opaque and impenetrable. Kant, for instance, takes freedom to be mysterious while insisting that we nevertheless have reason to believe in it. We may not know how something is possible or how it works, but it can be practically necessary, rational, and true all the same. That something lies beyond the limits of our reason in its theoretical use certainly does not mean that we should deny it or that it cannot be true or practically necessary. Thus, reason limits itself, making room for faith and accepting that it does not and cannot understand human freedom or God. Yet it has reason to postulate both.

Kierkegaard, similarly, suggests that we have reason to – or must – accept that there is something that we do not understand. He therefore writes that "if thinking is permitted to decide something because it cannot grasp it, then Christianity is lost" (SKS 20, 222, NB2:209 / KJN 4, 221). Thus, Kierkegaard combines the suprarationalist view that the mysteries of faith are above reason with a pragmatist view concerning the justification of belief.[12] However, he goes beyond Kant by not only relying on suprarationalism but also on supernatural revelation. In this respect, he comes closer to Møller and I. H. Fichte than Kant (Fremstedal 2014a: chs. 6–8).

[11] See Hare 2002b (on the moral gap); Helms 2017: 476 (on recognizing the need for revelation).

[12] Bishop (2016: Part VII) argues that a defense of the broadly Kierkegaardian idea of faith as a doxastic venture implies suprarationalism *and* nonevidentialism (describing the latter as fideism in a wide sense, which seems to include pragmatism). Specifically, faith is a venture beyond epistemic evidence performed out of epistemic concern to grasp truth of "vital existential importance." Similarly, Jordan (2018: Part III) suggests that "James's argument is not just a pragmatic argument, but also an epistemic argument, since he is arguing that one of the pragmatic benefits is a more reliable access to reality."

Christian faith cannot be rational by being derived from mere reason as a human faculty, since supernatural revelation diverges from our reason due to its alterity. But it can nevertheless be rational by being supported by normative practical reasons (i.e., by overcoming the moral gap through divine assistance). Although Christianity solves pagan problems (and can be justified pragmatically), it cannot be reduced to natural categories since it has its own perspective and language. Still, we may recognize that divine assistance could bridge the moral gap without revelation (Hare 2002b). If given, such assistance could be supported by reasons, since it fills a natural need and overcomes despair. Without revelation, it therefore seems *hypothetically* or conditionally rational.

Kierkegaard seems to take revelation in a realist sense as an objective fact. But he maintains that revelation can only be recognized *within* the perspective of faith (SKS 19, 126, 129–30, Not4:3, Not4:5 / KJN 3, 125–9); it cannot be dealt with adequately by nonbelievers (or by reasons external to faith). Therefore, he writes: "There is only one proof for the truth of [Christianity]: the inner proof, argumentum *spiritus sancti* [the witness or testimony of the Holy Spirit]" (SKS 22, 108, NB11:179 / KJN 6, 105). Any other proof or reason is but preliminary, removing hindrances to faith (SKS 22, 108–9, NB11:179 / KJN 6, 105–6).

This theological circularity resembles *fideism* since Christian belief seems justified by constituting itself supernaturally. However, it is not based on a blind leap of faith but on divine revelation *and* sin-consciousness, where the latter is the condition of possibility (*Troens Betingelse*) for receiving revelation (SKS 4, 222, 269–70, 290–301 / PF, 13, 68–70, 93–104). Only sin-consciousness therefore provides a decisive reason (*Grund*) for faith (SKS 21, 163, NB8:39 / KJN 5, 170). But this consciousness is given supernaturally, just as revelation is (SKS 11, 197 / SUD, 83; SKS 23, 100, NB16:6 / KJN 7, 100). Strictly speaking, revelation is therefore *not* epistemically self-authenticating since it requires sin-consciousness as the condition of faith (*Troens Betingelse*), as that which allows for the reception and recognition of revelation as such. Without it, revelation cannot be authenticated. Therefore, Kierkegaard does not accept a fideist *sui generis* justification of revelation, unless sin-consciousness is added.[13]

But even this claim must be qualified, however. For sin-consciousness and the conversion to Christianity must be prepared and motivated by pre-Christian guilt-consciousness and despair. As we have seen (in

[13] For such fideist *sui generis* justifications of revelation often associated with Kierkegaard and Barth, see Wahlberg 2020: Part II.IV.

Chapter 5), the conversion to Christianity requires an "anguished conscience," one aware of personal moral failure (SKS 20, 69, NB:79 / KJN 4, 68; SKS 21, 285, NB10:55 / KJN 5, 296). Moreover, even Christian despair *reiterates* human despair by identifying it as sin before God (as seen in Chapter 1). Instead of recognizing sin as sin, pagans interpret it in terms of despair, moral guilt, and evil (cf. SKS 7, 483–5 / CUP1, 532–4). Still, pagan consciousness of despair, guilt, and evil *does* prepare for sin-consciousness and faith. Indeed, the content of human and Christian despair overlaps greatly, so that the Christian claims in Part II of *The Sickness unto Death* are supported by the reasons holding independent of faith spelled out in Part I of *The Sickness unto Death*. Specifically, valid critiques of pagan despair hold also for Christian despair.

It then seems that the fideist element in Kierkegaard concerns the *form* of revelation rather than its doctrinal *content*. It concerns divine presence and performative speech-acts rather than propositional or doctrinal content. The former is *above* reason and can only be believed, not understood. But the latter may nevertheless be assessed rationally by philosophy (SKS 15, 216–26 / BA, 176–87; SKS 23, 69, NB15:97 / KJN 7, 67). Indeed, it seems possible for it to be *justified* rationally by practical reasons. Kierkegaard then seems to be a *pragmatist concerning the content of belief yet a fideist concerning its revelatory form*. Still, this is hardly dangerous or irrational since the propositional content of belief can be assessed rationally.

One worry, however, is that, Kierkegaard does not offer a detailed and clear account of how revelation differs from ordinary experiences or ordinary thinking (although revelation may have a unique power to transform moral agents; see Barrett 2021). Another worry is that he introduces religious content that is more specific and orthodox than what pragmatism requires or perhaps even supports. But we have seen that he prefers a moral reading of religious texts, not a literal or historical-critical one (cf. Bayer 2007: 161–8). However, it is not perfectly clear how the whole of scripture could be read morally, although its different elements may nevertheless belong to a larger narrative with practical import.

Still, a strict pragmatist reading is perhaps best viewed as the development of Kierkegaard's view along Kantian or pragmatist lines. At best, it can explain why religious belief is necessary, although it may not take orthodox and conservative theological views too literally. To make religion rational, it must probably tone down some of Kierkegaard's theological views by developing a rational construction that would presumably be reminiscent of Kant's moral theology or pragmatic variants of analytic theology (or analytic philosophy of religion). A Kantian reading, for instance, would change the theological views somewhat when it comes to both Christology and the doctrine of sin. However, the pragmatist reading of Kierkegaard is not developed in much detail unfortunately, so it is probably too early to pass any final judgment on this matter.[14]

Both here and elsewhere, Kierkegaard may be considered a transitional figure. He combines fideism with pragmatism concerning religious belief, and he has one leg in classical German philosophy and another in existentialism. Still, he is neither an irrationalist nor a subjectivist concerning beliefs or values. Nor does he let religion override morality. Rather, he moralizes religion by identifying the good with the divine.

[14] The most detailed discussion is still Emmanuel (1996: 50–60), who devotes less than one chapter to it.

Conclusion

Summary and Remaining Issues

By building on earlier scholarship, the present book tries to change the picture of Kierkegaard somewhat, arguing that his views are often more defensible and relevant than often thought.

Like recent work on fideism, Chapter 13 argues that the concept of fideism is problematic insofar as it is used in a pejorative and anachronistic manner to attack views that contrast faith and reason in very different ways (see Carroll 2008; Amesbury 2017). The influential fideist reading of Kierkegaard particularly ignores pragmatist elements in his thinking that are decisive for assessing how religious belief is supported by practical reasons. The Kierkegaard literature often takes fideism in a *wide* sense that is not clearly distinguished from nonevidentialism in general, or pragmatism or conservatism concerning belief in particular. Nor is Kierkegaard's alleged fideism clearly distinguished from suprarationalism, antirationalism, and irrationalism, since all these views contrast faith and reason in different ways (see Chapter 12). As a result, Kierkegaard's position is far from clear in the secondary literature.

Fideism in a more precise or narrow sense relies on a self-constituting *leap of faith*, not epistemic evidence, practical reasons, or conservative considerations (Booth 2016: 6–9; Chignell 2018). Like Emmanuel (1996), Chapter 13 argues that Kierkegaard is not a fideist in this sense, since he offers practical reasons for belief like *pragmatists* concerning belief do. Indeed, these reasons justify the content of belief or faith, making it *rational* (something that may surely seem like a highly unKierkegaardian view).

In his neglected reply to Eiríksson (1850), Kierkegaard insists that Christian faith is not irrational since it overcomes both absurdity and offense (see Chapter 11). Yet faith remains *above* reason as a natural faculty since divine revelation can neither be derived from mere reason (as a faculty) nor discovered by reason alone. Nor can it become completely transparent and clear to mere reason (Chapters 11–12). But even if faith remains *above* reason in this sense, as suprarationalism maintains, it is still the case that it can be comprehended imperfectly, symbolically, and practically. As such, faith must be guided by reason as a faculty that seeks new understanding (Helms 2020: 3–13). Indeed, faith can neither abolish reasoning nor dialectics since we need reasons both for beliefs and actions (Chapters 12–13).[1]

Like Kant, Kierkegaard justifies religious faith on practical and subjective grounds, denying that there is objective, epistemic evidence for or against faith (Chapters 9–10). Whereas Kant argues that faith is morally necessary (if we are to think consistently), Kierkegaard argues that it is necessary for wholeheartedness. Indeed, in *Concluding Unscientific Postscript* the latter approach allows a subjective justification of faith closely associated with *subjective truth*. Although this subjective justification does not have an objective basis in epistemic evidence, it nevertheless seems supported by practical reasons that are objective or at least intersubjectively valid. Thus, I have argued that the much-discussed subjective justification of faith need neither entail subjectivism nor fideism.

Indeed, Chapter 9 shows that even alternative accounts of subjective truth rule out objectionable subjectivism. A straightforward reading of subjective truth takes it to concern subjective *appropriation* of objective truth. On this reading, truth becomes subjective insofar as an individual appropriates objective truth by identifying with it and by acting upon it. This clearly presupposes truth that is independent of the agent's response to it, at least to a significant extent.

On the other hand, Watts (2018) interprets subjective truth as an adverbial *truth theory*, according to which living truly requires self-coincidence or wholeheartedness. But there are nevertheless clear *objective, formal* constraints on wholeheartedness that rule out relativism and subjectivism (see Chapter 9). Specifically, wholeheartedness, or being true to oneself, requires unconditional moral commitment that unifies facticity and freedom. Indeed, it even seems to require the Christian virtues of faith,

[1] However, Kierkegaard's concept of dialectics deserves more scholarly attention, since it seems to represent a form of rationality that transcends the understanding (*Forstanden*) by allowing pragmatic arguments (see Chapter 13). In this connection, Kierkegaard's positive use of natural (immanent) religion and natural theology deserves special attention. More generally, there is need for scholarly work that moves beyond Kierkegaard's polemics against those who (allegedly) confuse faith and knowledge. Denying understanding is not sufficient, since one must consider the type of understanding and rationality that is appropriate for faith – otherwise faith seems blind and indifferent to truth (see Chapter 12).

hope, and charity for Kierkegaard. Thus, even if we interpret subjective truth as a truth theory, it still does not involve subjectivism or relativism. Still, this adverbial truth theory is relatively unexplored and deserves more discussion before final judgment is passed on it.

In any case, ethico-religious wholeheartedness is not only central to subjective truth but also to the controversial concept of hidden *inwardness*. Chapter 8 argues that "hidden inwardness" neither involves a hidden, private domain nor "negative outwardness" (Mulder 2000: 317). Instead, it involves a wholehearted moral character expressing itself in words and deeds. For Kierkegaard, these expressions are secondary, while character is primary since it underlies and constrains different expressions.[2]

Chapters 6–7 discuss the relation between morality and religion by focusing on Abraham's sacrifice of Isaac – a special case that has been discussed extensively by philosophers and theologians. It is argued that – despite appearances – Kierkegaard does not try to justify murder on religious grounds. Instead, he consistently interprets religion in moral terms, suggesting that God never intended or required the sacrifice of Isaac. Indeed, for Kierkegaard religion does not compete with ethics but it entails and *supports* ethics. As a Christian Platonist, he not only accepts moral realism but also *identifies* moral goodness with the divine. Although Kierkegaard clearly takes non-Christian ethics as a preparation for Christian ethics, it is still not perfectly clear if their content is identical or not.

Chapters 4–5 show that Kierkegaard consistently attacks eudaimonism, which tries to justify ethics and faith prudentially. Like Kant, he assumes conflict between morality and prudence, insisting that morality should be pursued for its own sake. For both thinkers, neither morality nor faith are but means towards happiness or salvation. Still, personal happiness represents a genuine good that even morality must presuppose, although morality has priority over prudence.[3]

[2] However, Kierkegaard's anticonsequentialism deserves more scrutiny (as does his interpretation of impartiality and universalism in ethics more generally). Even if he does *not* see consequentialism as an ethical theory, he could perhaps still allow consequentialist considerations outside of ethics proper. But with the exception of his 1854–55 attack on the Danish state church, Kierkegaard is not known for advocating political and social reform. Still, he seems to leave conceptual room for such reform, even if he does not develop it much theoretically. At least, his theory is based on a moral fundament and *normative* social ontology in which we should take responsibility for our traditional (conventional) identity by criticizing it and transcending it. As such, the theory seems to allow for political and social reform, at least in principle. Still, Kierkegaard's actual contribution to political theory seems negative rather than positive; and politics tends to play an unclear normative role in his theory (see Tilley 2015; Fremstedal 2020c: 304–6).

[3] Even though I have argued at length for substantial conceptual overlap between the views of Kant and Kierkegaard, it is still the case that Kant's historical influence on Kierkegaard remains largely

However, Kierkegaard's noneudaimonism makes justifications of morality demanding, since it cannot justify morality prudentially. Still, Chapters 2–3 show that Kierkegaard develops an original answer to the "why be moral?" question. Specifically, he argues that amoralism is incoherent, since coherent selfhood requires full commitment that presupposes morality. Such commitment avoids incompatible projects and provides unity to our lives by being a metaproject that coordinates, shapes, and unifies all other projects.

Clearly, Kierkegaard's interrelated accounts of ethics, religion, and truth all rest on his account of wholehearted selfhood. This account has attracted significant attention, particularly within discussions of personal identity, hierarchical agency, and existentialism. Although it has been central to the reception of Kierkegaard in continental philosophy (and theology), it has also received significant attention within anglophone philosophy, which shows its relevance for ongoing debates on selfhood, ethics, and religion.[4]

This book has offered a broadly Kantian reading of Kierkegaard that focuses on the task of establishing coherent or unified selfhood. However, I do not think that a coherent or unified self can remove (motivational and normative) *tension* between morality and prudence, or even tension between Christian revelation and natural standards. Certainly, Kierkegaard is not a monist concerning value or normativity, which thinks that only one thing matters. Full moral commitment, notably, does not rule out other concerns, norms, or reasons. For morality not only allows self-interest but it even seems to presuppose it, since we could not choose morality only for its own sake, unless it differs from prudence (see Chapter 4; cf. Fremstedal 2014a: ch. 4 and 2018: 4–5). And Christian revelation, on the other hand, builds on and reinterprets pre-Christian, natural standards. Therefore, the tension between different standards remains.[5]

obscure (Green 2011: ch. 5; Fremstedal 2014a: ch. 11). And there is need for more scholarly work on Kierkegaard's relations to both Herder and Fichte, both historically and conceptually.

[4] Despite the massive literature on Kierkegaard's account of selfhood, there is very little work on Kierkegaard's action theory. This is surprising since he seems to interpret selfhood in terms of hierarchical agency (see Chapter 1). And Kierkegaard's relation to constitutivism, which tries to derive morality from agency, is underexplored. And quite independent of this, there is very little systematic work on value theory, normative pluralism, and the meaning of life in Kierkegaard studies.

[5] This is quite complex since there is not only tension between Christian revelation and natural standards but also tension between Judaism and Christianity. Although Kierkegaard's journals (his *Nachlaß*) does include anti-Semitic views (see Tudvad 2010), I nevertheless hope to have indicated (in Chapter 11) that his judgment of Judaism is not entirely negative, since Judaism represents a genuine form of revealed religion. Still, Kierkegaard does assume that Judaism is *superseded* by Christianity (Blattberg 2020: 65). In any case, he hardly offers a detailed and clear account of how (Jewish and Christian) revelation differs from ordinary experiences or ordinary thinking.

But this does not mean that Kierkegaard is a pluralist (or relativist) who denies unity or coherence concerning selfhood. Rather, he is a *pluramonist* who combines plurality with unity and coherence (Blattberg 2020). This is an attractive, complex, and difficult position. It is similar – but not identical – to the coherent Kantian value dualism of Bader (2015). The latter avoids an incoherent dualism of practical reason by limiting and conditioning prudence on morality. Although morality and prudence represent heterogeneous normative domains, the hypothetical imperative of prudence is limited by the categorical imperative of morality, something both Kant and Kierkegaard hold (see Chapter 4). As a result, we avoid a dualism of practical reason, which demands both that we seek personal happiness and that we sacrifice it for the sake of morality (cf. Fremstedal 2018: 6). But instead of denying normative conflict (as Bader 2015 does), Kierkegaard assumes that morality overrides prudence by having lexical *priority*. This is a complex position that certainly deserves more scholarly attention. Particularly the connection that Kierkegaard draws between morality, religion, and wholeheartedness is controversial and provocative, although it should nevertheless be taken as seriously as contemporary attempts to justify ethics and religion.

References

Ad. [pseudonymous reviewer] (1793) "Kritik der Volksmoral für Prediger, nach K. Grundsätzen bearbeitet, von J. P. L. Snell," *Neue allgemeine deutsche Bibliothek* 29(5): 551–60.

Adams, Robert M. (1987) *The Virtue of Faith and Other Essays in Philosophical Theology*, Oxford: Oxford University Press.

(2006) *A Theory of Virtue: Excellence in Being for the Good*, Oxford: Oxford University Press.

(2016) "Human Autonomy and Theological Ethics," *European Journal for Philosophy of Religion* 8(3): 3–20.

Allison, Henry E. (1995) *Kant's Theory of Freedom*, Cambridge: Cambridge University Press, 146–52.

Amesbury, Richard (2017) "Fideism," in Edward Zalta (ed.), *The Stanford Encyclopedia of Philosophy*, accessed February 4, 2021, https://plato.stanford.edu/archives/fall2017/entries/fideism/.

Annas, Julia (1993) *The Morality of Happiness*, Oxford: Oxford University Press.

Anscombe, Gertrude E. M. (1958) "Modern Moral Philosophy," *Philosophy* 33: 1–16.

Assiter, Alison (2009) *Kierkegaard, Metaphysics and Political Theory: Unfinished Selves*, London: Continuum (Continuum Studies in Philosophy).

Augustine (1998) *The City of God Against the Pagans*, Cambridge: Cambridge University Press (Cambridge Texts in the History of Political Thought).

Bader, Ralf M. (2015) "Kantian Axiology and the Dualism of Practical Reason," in Iwan Hirose and Jonas Olson (eds.), *The Oxford Handbook of Value Theory*, Oxford: Oxford University Press, 175–201.

Balle, Nicholai E. (1791) *Lærebog i den Evangelisk-Christelige Religion, indrettet til Brug i de danske Skoler*, Copenhagen: Schultz.

Barrett, Lee C. (2008) "Anselm of Canterbury: The Ambivalent Legacy of Faith Seeking Understanding," in Jon Stewart (ed.), *Kierkegaard and the Patristic and Medieval Traditions*, Aldershot: Ashgate (Kierkegaard Research: Sources, Reception and Resources, vol. IV), 167–81.

(2021) "Kierkegaard's Understanding of Revelation and Its Influence," in Balázs M. Mezei, Francesca A. Murphy, and Kenneth Oakes (eds.), *The Oxford Handbook of Divine Revelation*, Oxford: Oxford University Press, 275–91.

Bayer, Oswald (2007) *Theology the Lutheran Way*, translated by Jeffrey Silcock and Mark Mattes, Grand Rapids, MI: Eerdmans.

Behler, Ernst (1997) "Kierkegaard's *The Concept of Irony* with Constant Reference to Romanticism," in Niels Jørgen Cappelørn and Jon Stewart (eds.), *Kierkegaard Revisited*, Berlin: de Gruyter (Kierkegaard Studies, Monograph Series, vol. I), 13–33.

Beiser, Frederick C. (1987) *The Fate of Reason: German Philosophy from Kant to Fichte*, Cambridge, MA: Harvard University Press.

(2006) "Moral Faith and the Highest Good," in Paul Guyer (ed.), *The Cambridge Companion to Kant and Modern Philosophy*, Cambridge: Cambridge University Press (Cambridge Companions), 588–629.

Bernier, Mark (2015) *The Task of Hope in Kierkegaard*, Oxford: Oxford University Press.

Betz, John R. (2007) "Hamann before Kierkegaard: A Systematic Theological Oversight," *Pro Ecclesia* 16: 299–333.

(2012) *After Enlightenment: The Post-Secular Vision of J. G. Hamann*, Oxford: Wiley-Blackwell.

Bishop, John (2016) "Faith," in Edward Zalta (ed.), *The Stanford Encyclopedia of Philosophy*, accessed February 4, 2021, https://plato.stanford.edu/archives/win2016/entries/faith/.

Blanshard, Brand (1968) "Kierkegaard on Faith," *Personalist* 49: 5–23.

Blattberg, Charles (2020) "Kierkegaard's Deep Diversity: The One and the Many," in Melissa Fox-Muraton (ed.), *Kierkegaard and Issues in Contemporary Ethics*, Berlin: de Gruyter (Kierkegaard Studies, Monograph Series, vol. XLI), 51–68.

Bohlin, Torsten (1944) *Kierkegaard Tro och andra Kierkegaardstudier*, Stockholm: Svenska Kyrkans Diakonistyrelse.

Bøhn, Einar Duenger (2013) "The Logic of the Incarnation," in Andrew Schumann (ed.), *Logic in Orthodox Christian Thinking*, Heusenstamm: Ontos Verlag, 104–21.

Bohrer, Karl Heinz (1989) *Die Kritik der Romantik: Der Verdacht der Philosophie gegen die literarische Moderne*, Frankfurt am Main: Suhrkamp.

Boldt, Joachim (2006) *Kierkegaards "Furcht und Zittern" als Bild seines ethischen Erkenntnisbegriffs*, Berlin: de Gruyter (Kierkegaard Studies, Monograph Series, vol. XIII).

Booth, Anthony R. (2016) *Islamic Philosophy and the Ethics of Belief*, London: Palgrave Macmillan.

Brandes, Georg (1877) *Søren Kierkegaard: En Kritisk Fremstilling i Grundrids*, Copenhagen: Gyldendal.

Breazeale, Daniel and Günter Zöller (2005) "Introduction," in Johann Gottlieb Fichte, *The System of Ethics: According to the Principles of the Wissenschaftslehre*, Cambridge: Cambridge University Press (Cambridge Texts in the History of Philosophy), vii–xxxiii.

Bubbio, Paolo Diego (2014) *Sacrifice in the Post-Kantian Tradition: Perspectivism, Intersubjectivity, and Recognition*, Albany, NY: State University of New York Press (SUNY Series in Contemporary Continental Philosophy).

Buben, Adam (2013) "Neither Irrationalist Nor Apologist: Revising Faith and Reason in Kierkegaard," *Philosophy Compass* 8: 318–26.

Buber, Martin (2002) *Between Man and Man*, London: Routledge.

Buss, Sarah (1999) "What Practical Reasoning Must Be If We Act for Our Own Reasons," *Australasian Journal of Philosophy* 77: 399–421.

Carr, Karen (1996) "The Offense of Reason and the Passion of Faith: Kierkegaard and Anti-Rationalism," *Faith and Philosophy* 13: 236–51.

(2019) "Christian Epistemology and the Anthropology of Sin: Kierkegaard on Natural Theology and the Concept of 'Offense'," in Patrick Stokes, Eleanor Helms, and Adam Buben (eds.), *The Kierkegaardian Mind*, London: Routledge (Routledge Philosophical Minds), 365–76.

Carroll, Tomas (2008) "The Traditions of Fideism," *Religious Studies* 44: 1–22.

Caswell, Matthew (2007) "Kant on the Diabolic Will: A Neglected Alternative?," *Kantian Review* 12: 147–57.

Chang, Ruth (ed.), (1997a) *Incommensurability, Incomparability, and Practical Reason*, London: Harvard University Press.

(1997b) "Introduction," in Ruth Chang (ed.), *Incommensurability, Incomparability, and Practical Reason*, London: Harvard University Press, 1–34.

Chignell, Andrew (2007) "Belief in Kant," *The Philosophical Review* 116: 323–60.

(2018) "The Ethics of Belief," in Edward Zalta (ed.), *The Stanford Encyclopedia of Philosophy*, accessed February 4, 2021, https://plato.stanford.edu/archives/spr2018/entries/ethics-belief.

Clark, Justin (2016) "Eudaimonistic Virtue Ethics and Self-Effacement," *The Journal of Value Inquiry* 50: 507–24.

Clifford, William (1876–77) "The Ethics of Belief," *Contemporary Review* 29: 289–309.

Cohen, Andrew J. (2008) "Existentialist Voluntarism as a Source of Normativity," *Philosophical Papers* 37: 89–129.

Collins, James (1967) *The Emergence of Philosophy of Religion*, New Haven, CT: Yale University Press.

Compaijen, Rob (2018) *Kierkegaard, MacIntyre, Williams, and the Internal Point of View*, New York: Palgrave Macmillan.

Czakó, István (2015) "Rethinking Religion Existentially: New Approaches to Classical Problems of Religious Philosophy in Kierkegaard," in Jon Stewart (ed.), *A Companion to Kierkegaard*, Oxford: Wiley-Blackwell (Blackwell Companions to Philosophy, vol. LVIII), 281–94.

Dalferth, Ingolf (2015) "The Middle Term: Kierkegaard and the Contemporary Debate about Explanatory Theism," *Kierkegaard Studies Yearbook* 20: 69–90.

Das, Ramon (2017) "Virtue Ethics and Right Action: A Critique," in Lorraine Besser-Jones and Michael Slote (eds.), *The Routledge Companion to Virtue Ethics*, London: Routledge (Routledge Philosophy Companions), 331–43.

Davenport, John (2007) *Will as Commitment and Resolve: An Existential Account of Creativity, Love, Virtue, and Happiness*, New York: Fordham University Press.

(2008a) "Faith as Eschatological Trust in *Fear and Trembling*," in Edward Mooney (ed.), *Ethics, Love, and Faith in Kierkegaard*, Indianapolis: Indiana University Press, 196–233, 265–74.

(2008b) "Kierkegaard's *Postscript* in light of *Fear and Trembling*: Eschatological Faith," *Revista Portuguesa de Filosofia* 64: 879–908.

(2012) *Narrative Identity, Autonomy, and Mortality: From Frankfurt and MacIntyre to Kierkegaard*, London: Routledge.

(2013) "Selfhood and Spirit," in John Lippitt and George Pattison (eds.), *The Oxford Handbook of Kierkegaard*, Oxford: Oxford University Press, 230–51.

(2017) "The Esthetic Validity of Marriage: Romantic Marriage as a Model for Ethical Will: In Defense of Judge Wilhelm," in Hermann Deuser and Markus Kleinert (eds.), *Søren Kierkegaard: Entweder– Oder*, Berlin: de Gruyter, 169–92.

Despland, Michel (1973) *Kant on History and Religion*, Montreal: McGill-Queen's University Press.

Deuser, Hermann (1998) "Religious Dialectics and Christology," in Alastair Hannay and Gordon Marino (eds.), *The Cambridge Companion to Kierkegaard*, Cambridge: Cambridge University Press (Cambridge Companions), 376–96.

Di Giovanni, George and Paolo Livieri (2018) "Friedrich Heinrich Jacobi," in Edward Zalta (ed.), *The Stanford Encyclopedia of Philosophy*, accessed February 4, 2021, https://plato.stanford.edu/archives/win2018/entries/friedrich-jacobi.

Dorrien, Gary (2012) *Kantian Reason and Hegelian Spirit: The Idealistic Logic of Modern Theology*, Oxford: Wiley-Blackwell.

Dorsey, Dale (2016) *The Limits of Moral Authority*, Oxford: Oxford University Press.

Dreyfus, Hubert (2008) "Kierkegaard on the Self," in Edward Mooney (ed.), *Ethics, Love, and Faith in Kierkegaard*, Bloomington: Indiana University Press, 11–23, 246–7.

Driver, Julia (2017) "The Consequentialist Critique of Virtue Ethics," in Lorraine Besser-Jones and Michael Slote (eds.), *The Routledge Companion to Virtue Ethics*, London: Routledge (Routledge Philosophy Companions), 321–9.

Düsing, Klaus (1973) "Die Rezeption der Kantischen Postulatenlehre in den frühen philosophischen Entwürfen Schellings und Hegels," *Hegel-Studien* 9: 53–90.

Eiríksson, Magnús (1846) *Tro, Overtro og Vantro, i deres Forhold til Fornuft og Forstand, samt til hinanden indbyrdes*, Copenhagen: H. C. Klein.

[Theophilus Nicolaus] (1850) *Er Troen et Paradox og "i Kraft af det Absurde"? et Spørgsmaal foranlediget ved "Frygt og Bæven, af Johannes de silentio", Besvaret ved Hjelp af en Troes-Ridders fortrolige Meddelelser, til fælles Opbyggelse for Jøder, Christne og Muhamedanere, af bemeldte Troes-Ridders Broder*, Copenhagen: Chr. Steen & Søn.

(1866) *Gud og Reformatoren: En religiøs Idee. Samt nogle Bemærkninger om de kirkelige Tilstande, Dr. S. Kierkegaard og Forfatteren*, Copenhagen: J. H. Schubothe.

Emmanuel, Steven (1996) *Kierkegaard and the Concept of Revelation*, Albany, NY: State University of New York Press.

Evans, Charles S. (1982) *Subjectivity and Religious Belief: An Historical, Critical Study*, Washington, DC: University Press of America.

(1999) *Kierkegaard's* Fragments *and* Postscript*: The Religious Philosophy of Johannes Climacus*, New York: Humanity Books.

(2006a) *Kierkegaard's Ethics of Love: Divine Commands and Moral Obligations*, Oxford: Oxford University Press.

(2006b) *Kierkegaard on Faith and the Self: Collected Essays*, Waco, TX: Baylor University Press.

(2009) *Kierkegaard: An Introduction*, Cambridge: Cambridge University Press.

(2010) *Natural Signs and Knowledge of God: A New Look at Theistic Arguments*, Oxford: Oxford University Press.

(2012) "Faith and Reason in Kierkegaard's *Concluding Unscientific Postscript*," in Rick Anthony Furtak (ed.), *Kierkegaard's* Concluding Unscientific Postscript*: A Critical Guide*, Cambridge: Cambridge University Press (Cambridge Critical Guides), 204–18.

(2014) *God and Moral Obligation*, Oxford: Oxford University Press.

(2015) "Can an Admirer of Silentio's Abraham Consistently Believe That Child Sacrifice Is Forbidden?," in Daniel Conway (ed.), *Kierkegaard's* Fear and Trembling*: A Critical Guide*, Cambridge: Cambridge University Press (Cambridge Critical Guides), 61–78.

Evans, Charles S. and Robert C. Roberts (2013) "Ethics," in John Lippitt and George Pattison (ed.), *The Oxford Handbook of Kierkegaard*, Oxford: Oxford University Press, 211–29.

Evans, Charles S. and Sylvia Walsh (2006) "Introduction," in Kierkegaard, *Fear and Trembling*, edited by C. S. Evans and Sylvia Walsh, Cambridge: Cambridge University Press (Cambridge Texts in the History of Philosophy), vi–xxx.

Fabro, Cornelio (1962) "Faith and Reason in Kierkegaard's Dialectic," in Howard A. Johnson and Niels Thulstrup (eds.), *A Kierkegaard Critique: An International Selection of Essays Interpreting Kierkegaard*, New York: Harper, 156–206.

Fahrenbach, Helmut (1968) *Kierkegaards existenzdialektische Ethik*, Frankfurt am Main: Klosterman.

Ferreira, M. Jamie (1998) "Faith and the Kierkegaardian Leap," in Alastair Hannay and Gordon Marino (eds.), *The Cambridge Companion to Kierkegaard*, Cambridge: Cambridge University Press (Cambridge Companions), 207–34.

(2001) *Love's Grateful Striving: A Commentary on Kierkegaard's* Works of Love, Oxford: Oxford University Press.

(2009) *Kierkegaard*, Oxford: Wiley-Blackwell.

Fichte, Johann Gottlieb (2005) *The System of Ethics: According to the Principles of the Wissenschaftslehre*, translated by Daniel Breazeale and Günter Zöller, Cambridge: Cambridge University Press (Cambridge Texts in the History of Philosophy).

Firestone, Chris L. and Nathan Jacobs (2008) *In Defense of Kant's* Religion, Indianapolis: Indiana University Press.

Formosa, Paul (2009) "Kant on the Limits of Human Evil," *Journal of Philosophical Research* 34: 189–214.

Forrest, Peter (2017) "The Epistemology of Religion," in Edward Zalta (ed.), *The Stanford Encyclopedia of Philosophy*, accessed February 4, 2021, https://plato.stanford.edu/archives/sum2017/entries/religion-epistemology.

Forschner, Maximilian (1992) "Das Ideal des moralischen Glaubens. Religionsphilosophie in Kants Reflexionen," in Friedo Ricken and François Marty (eds.), *Kant über Religion*, Berlin: Kohlhammer, 83–99.

Fossheim, Hallvard (2015) "Aristotle on Virtuous Questioning of Morality," in Beatrix Himmelmann and Robert B. Louden (eds.), *Why Be Moral?*, Berlin: de Gruyter, 65–80.

Fox-Muraton, Melissa (2012) "Election or the Individual? Levinas on Kierkegaard's Challenges to Judaism," *Kierkegaard Studies Yearbook* 17: 367–86.

(2018) "There Is No Teleological Suspension of the Ethical: Kierkegaard's Logic against Religious Justification and Moral Exceptionalism," *Kierkegaard Studies Yearbook* 23: 3–32.

(2019a) "Logic, Language, and Existential Knowledge," in Patrick Stokes, Eleanor Helms, and Adam Buben (eds.), *The Kierkegaardian Mind*, London: Routledge (Routledge Philosophical Minds), 397–408.

(2019b) "Existence Philosophy as a Humanism?," *Kierkegaard Studies Yearbook* 24: 345–73.

Frankfurt, Harry (2004) *The Reasons of Love*, Princeton: Princeton University Press.

Fremstedal, Roe (2006) "Forfekter Kierkegaard fundamentalisme i *Frygt og Bæven*?," *Norsk teologisk tidsskrift* 107: 84–108.

(2008) "Universalisme, fundamentalisme og Abraham i *Frygt og Bæven* – et svar til Mjaaland," *Norsk teologisk tidsskrift* 109: 159–80.

(2014a) *Kierkegaard and Kant on Radical Evil and the Highest Good: Virtue, Happiness, and the Kingdom of God*, Basingstoke, UK: Palgrave Macmillan.

(2014b) "Double Movement," in Steven Emmanuel, William McDonald, and Jon Stewart (eds.), *Kierkegaard's Concepts: Classicism to Enthusiasm*, Farnham, UK: Ashgate (Kierkegaard Research: Sources, Reception and Resources, vol. XV, tome II), 187–94.

(2015a) "Kierkegaard's Use of German Philosophy: Leibniz to Fichte," in Jon Stewart (ed.), *A Companion to Kierkegaard*, Oxford: Wiley-Blackwell (Blackwell Companions to Philosophy, vol. LVIII), 36–49.

(2015b) "Kierkegaard's Views on Normative Ethics, Moral Agency, and Metaethics," in Jon Stewart (ed.), *A Companion to Kierkegaard*, Oxford: Wiley-Blackwell (Blackwell Companions to Philosophy, vol. LVIII), 113–25.

(2015c) "Why Be Moral? A Kierkegaardian Approach," in Beatrix Himmelmann and Robert B. Louden (eds.), *Why Be Moral?*, Berlin: de Gruyter 2015, 173–97.

(2017) "Eiríksson's Critique of Kierkegaard and Kierkegaard's (Drafted) Response: Religious Faith, Absurdity, and Rationality," in Gerhard Schreiber and Jon Stewart (eds.), *Magnús Eiríksson: A Forgotten Contemporary of Kierkegaard*, Copenhagen: Museum Tusculanum Press (Danish Golden Age Studies, vol. X), 145–66.

(2018) "Morality and Prudence: A Case for Substantial Overlap and Limited Conflict," *Journal of Value Inquiry* 52: 1–16.

(2019a) "Kierkegaard's Post-Kantian Approach to Anthropology and Selfhood," in Patrick Stokes, Eleanor Helms, and Adam Buben (eds.), *The Kierkegaardian Mind*, London: Routledge (Routledge Philosophical Minds), 319–30.

(2019b) "Demonic Despair under the Guise of the Good? Kierkegaard and Anscombe vs. Velleman," *Inquiry: An Interdisciplinary Journal of Philosophy*, 1–21, DOI:10.1080/0020174X.2019.1610047.

(2019c) "Hidden Inwardness and 'Subjectivity Is Truth': Kant and Kierkegaard on Moral Psychology and Religious Pragmatism," in Lee C. Barrett and Peter Sajda (eds.), *Kierkegaard in Context: A Festschrift for Jon Stewart*, Macon, GA: Mercer University Press (Mercer Kierkegaard Series), 112–29.

(2020a) "Kant and Existentialism: Inescapable Freedom and Self-Deception," in Jon Stewart (ed.), *The Palgrave Handbook of German Idealism and Existentialism*, Basingstoke, UK: Palgrave Macmillan (Palgrave Handbooks in German Idealism), 51–75.

(2020b) "Kierkegaard on Hope as Essential to Selfhood," in Titus Stahl and Claudia Blöser (eds.), *The Moral Psychology of Hope: An Introduction*, Lanham, MD: Rowman & Littlefield International (The Moral Psychology of the Emotions), 75–92.

(2020c) "Søren Kierkegaard's Critique of Eudaimonism and Autonomy," in Douglas Moggach, Nadine Mooren, and Michael Quante (eds.), *Perfektionismus der Autonomie*, Munich: Wilhelm Fink (HegelForum, Studien), 291–308.

Fremstedal, Roe and Timothy P. Jackson (2015) "Salvation/Eternal Happiness," in Steven Emmanuel, William McDonald, and Jon Stewart (eds.), *Kierkegaard's Concepts: Salvation to Writing*, Farnham, UK: Ashgate (Kierkegaard Research: Sources, Reception and Resources, vol. XV, tome VI), 1–8.

Furtak, Rick Anthony (2005) *Wisdom in Love: Kierkegaard and the Ancient Quest for Emotional Integrity*, Notre Dame: University of Notre Dame Press.

(2012) "The Kierkegaardian Ideal of 'Essential Knowing' and the Scandal of Modern Philosophy," in Rick Anthony Furtak (ed.), *Kierkegaard's*

Concluding Unscientific Postscript: *A Critical Guide*, Cambridge: Cambridge University Press (Cambridge Critical Guides), 87–110.
Gava, Gabriele and Robert Stern (eds.) (2017) *Pragmatism, Kant, and Transcendental Philosophy*, London: Routledge (Routledge Studies in Nineteenth-Century Philosophy).
Geach, Peter (1979) *The Virtues: The Stanton Lectures 1973–4*, Cambridge: Cambridge University Press.
Glenn, John D., Jr. (1997) "'A Highest Good ... An Eternal Happiness': The Human Telos in Kierkegaard's *Concluding Unscientific Postscript*," in Robert L. Perkins (ed.), *Concluding Unscientific Postscript to "Philosophical Fragments,"* Macon, GA: Mercer University Press (International Kierkegaard Commentary, vol. XII), 247–62.
Gouwens, David J. (1996) *Kierkegaard as a Religious Thinker*, Cambridge: Cambridge University Press.
Green, Ronald M. (1988) *Religion and Moral Reason: A New Method for Comparative Study*, Oxford: Oxford University Press.
(1992) *Kierkegaard and Kant: The Hidden Debt*, Albany, NY: State University of New York Press.
(1994) "Kierkegaard's *Philosophical Fragments*: A Kantian Commentary," in Robert L. Perkins (ed.), *Philosophical Fragments and Johannes Climacus*, Macon, GA: Mercer University Press (International Kierkegaard Commentary, vol. VII), 169–202.
(2011) *Kant and Kierkegaard on Time and Eternity*, Macon, GA: Mercer University Press.
Grøn, Arne (1995) "Kierkegaards forudsætning," *Dansk teologisk tidsskrift* 58: 267–90.
(1997) *Subjektivitet og negativitet: Kierkegaard*, Copenhagen: Gyldendal.
Habermas, Jürgen (2019) *Auch eine Geschichte der Philosophie*, 2 vols., Frankfurt am Main: Suhrkamp.
Hannay, Alastair (1993) *Kierkegaard*, 2nd ed., London: Routledge (The Argument of the Philosophers).
(2006) *Kierkegaard and Philosophy: Selected Essays*, London: Routledge.
(2009) "Note on the Translation," in Søren Kierkegaard, *Concluding Unscientific Postscript to the Philosophical Crumbs*, edited and translated by Alastair Hannay, Cambridge: Cambridge University Press (Cambridge Texts in the History of Philosophy), xxxvii–xl.
Harbsmeier, Eberhard (1999) "Der Begriff der Innerlichkeit bei Søren Kierkegaard," *Kierkegaardiana* 20: 31–50.
Hare, John E. (2001) *God's Call: Moral Realism, God's Commands and Human Autonomy*, Grand Rapids, MI: Eerdmans.
(2002a) *Why Bother Being Good?*, Downers Grove, IL: InterVarsity Press.
(2002b) *The Moral Gap: Kantian Ethics, Human Limits, and God's Assistance*, Oxford: Clarendon Press.
Hasker, William (1995) "Evidentialism," in Robert Audi (ed.), *Cambridge Dictionary of Philosophy*, Cambridge: Cambridge University Press, 294.

Hatfield, Gary (2005) "The History of Philosophy as Philosophy," in Tom Sorell and Graham A. J. Rogers (eds.), *Analytic Philosophy and History of Philosophy*, Oxford: Clarendon Press, 83–128.

Haybron, Daniel (2010) *The Pursuit of Unhappiness: The Elusive Psychology of Well-Being*, Oxford: Oxford University Press.

Hegel, Georg W. F. (1991a) *Elements of the Philosophy of Right*, translated by Hugh B. Nisbet, Cambridge: Cambridge University Press (Cambridge Texts in the History of Political Thought).

(1991b) *The Encyclopedia Logic: Part One of the Encyclopedia of the Philosophical Sciences with the Zusätze*, translated by Theodore F. Geraets, Wallis A. Suchting, and Henry S. Harris, Indianapolis: Hackett.

(1991c) *Enzyklopädie der philosophischen Wissenschaften im Grundrisse*, 3rd ed. (1830), Hamburg: Meiner.

Helms, Eleanor (2013) "The Objectivity of Faith: Kierkegaard's Critique of Fideism," *Res Philosophica* 90: 439–60.

(2017) "On Climacus's 'Against Reason' Thesis: A Challenge to Westphal," *Faith and Philosophy* 34: 471–88.

(2020) "Hope and the Chaos of Imagination in Kant and Kierkegaard," *History of European Ideas*, 1–14, DOI:10.1080/01916599.2020.1799556.

Henrich, Dieter (1957–58) "Hutchinson und Kant," *Kant-Studien* 49: 49–69.

(2008) *Between Kant and Hegel: Lectures on German Idealism*, Cambridge, MA: Harvard University Press.

Hills, Allison (2010) *The Beloved Self: Morality and the Challenge from Egoism*, Oxford: Oxford University Press.

Hoeltzel, Steven (2020) "Fichte and Existentialism: Freedom and Finitude, Self-Positing and Striving," in Jon Stewart (ed.), *The Palgrave Handbook of German Idealism and Existentialism*, Basingstoke, UK: Palgrave Macmillan (Palgrave Handbooks in German Idealism), 77–101.

Høffding, Harald (1909) *Danske Filosofer*, Copenhagen: Gyldendal.

Holm, Søren (1967) *Filosofien i Norden før 1900*, Copenhagen: Munksgaard.

Honenberger, Phillip (ed.), (2015) *Naturalism and Philosophical Anthropology: Nature, Life, and the Human between Transcendental and Empirical Perspectives*, Basingstoke, UK: Palgrave Macmillan.

Horn, Christoph (2014) *Nichtideale Normativität: Ein neuer Blick auf Kants politische Philosophie*, Frankfurt am Main: Suhrkamp.

Horn, Robert L. (2007) *Positivity and Dialectic: A Study of the Theological Method of Hans Lassen Martensen*, Copenhagen: Reitzel (Danish Golden Age Studies, vol. 11).

Hösle, Vittorio (1992) "Kan Abraham reddes? Og: kan Søren Kierkegaard reddes? Et hegelsk oppgjør med 'Frygt og Bæven'," *Norsk filosofisk tidsskrift* 27: 1–26.

Howland, Jacob (2012) "Lessing and Socrates in Kierkegaard's *Postscript*," in Rick Anthony Furtak (ed.), *Kierkegaard's* Concluding Unscientific Postscript*: A Critical Guide*, Cambridge: Cambridge University Press (Cambridge Critical Guides), 111–31.

Hühn, Lore and Philip Schwab (2013) "Kierkegaard and German Idealism," in John Lippitt and George Pattison (eds.), *The Oxford Handbook of Kierkegaard*, Oxford: Oxford University Press, 62–93.

Hursthouse, Rosalind (2013) "Virtue Ethics," in Edward Zalta (ed.), *The Stanford Encyclopedia of Philosophy*, accessed February 4, 2021, http://plato.stanford.edu/archives/fall2013/entries/ethics-virtue.

Inwagen, Peter van (1996) "It is Wrong, Everywhere, Always, and for Anyone, to Believe Anything upon Insufficient Evidence," in Jeff Jordan and Daniel Howard-Snyder (eds.), *Faith, Freedom and Rationality*, Lanham, MD: Rowman and Littlefield, 137–53.

Irwin, Terence (1996) "Kant's Criticism of Eudaemonism," in Stephen Engstrom and Jennifer Whiting (eds.), *Aristotle, Kant, and the Stoics: Rethinking Happiness and Duty*, Cambridge: Cambridge University Press, 63–101.

(2011) *The Development of Ethics: A Historical and Critical Study*, 3 vols., Oxford: Oxford University Press.

Jackson, Timothy P. (1987) "Kierkegaard's Metatheology," *Faith and Philosophy* 4: 71–85.

(1998) "Arminian Edification: Kierkegaard on Grace and Free Will," in Alastair Hannay and Gordon Marino (eds.), *The Cambridge Companion to Kierkegaard*, Cambridge: Cambridge University Press (Cambridge Companions), 235–56.

(2010) *Love Disconsoled: Meditations on Christian Charity*, Cambridge: Cambridge University Press.

(2014) "The Relevance of God: A Reply to Ronald Dworkin," *The Journal of Law and Religion* 29: 535–46.

(2017) "*Agape* and Virtue Ethics," in Lorraine Besser-Jones and Michael Slote (eds.), *The Routledge Companion to Virtue Ethics*, London: Routledge (Routledge Philosophy Companions), 283–303.

Jacobi, Friedrich Heinrich (2005 [1785]) "Recollections of Conversations with Lessing in July and August 1780," in Gotthold E. Lessing, *Philosophical and Theological Writings*, edited and translated by Hugh B. Nisbet, Cambridge: Cambridge University Press (Cambridge Texts in the History of Philosophy), 241–56.

James, David (2011) "The 'Self-Positing' Self in Kierkegaard's *The Sickness unto Death*," *The European Legacy* 16: 587–98.

James, William (1956 [1897]) *The Will to Believe and Other Essays in Popular Philosophy*, New York: Dover.

Johansen, Kjell Eyvind (1988) *Begrepet* Gjentagelse *hos Søren Kierkegaard*, Oslo: Solum.

(2002) "*Fear and Trembling* – the Problem of Justification," *British Journal for the History of Philosophy* 10: 261–70.

Jordan, Jeff (2018) "Pragmatic Arguments and Belief in God," in Edward Zalta (ed.), *The Stanford Encyclopedia of Philosophy*, accessed February 4, 2021, https://plato.stanford.edu/archives/spr2018/entries/pragmatic-belief-god.

Kangas, David J. (2007) "J.G. Fichte: From Transcendental Ego to Existence," in Jon Stewart (ed.), *Kierkegaard and His German Contemporaries: Philosophy*, Aldershot, UK: Ashgate (Kierkegaard Research: Sources, Reception and Resources, vol. VI, tome I), 67–95.

Katsafanas, Paul (2015) *Agency and the Foundation of Ethics: Nietzschean Constitutivism*, Oxford: Oxford University Press.

(2018) "Constitutivism about Practical Reasons," in Daniel Star (ed.), *The Oxford Handbook of Reasons and Normativity*, Oxford: Oxford University Press, 367–91.

Kekes, John (2013) "Meaning and Narratives," in Beatrix Himmelmann (ed.), *On Meaning in Life*, Berlin: de Gruyter, 65–82.

Kisiel, Theodore (2008) "On the Genesis of Heidegger's Formally Indicative Hermeneutics of Facticity," in François Raffoul and Eric Sean Nelson (eds.), *Rethinking Facticity*, Albany, NY: State University of New York Press, 41–68.

Knappe, Ulrich (2004) *Theory and Practice in Kant and Kierkegaard*, Berlin: de Gruyter (Kierkegaard Studies, Monograph Series, vol. IX).

Koch, Carl H. (2003) *Dansk oplysningsfilosofi 1700–1800*, Copenhagen: Gyldendal (Den danske filosofis historie, vol. III).

(2004) *Den danske idealisme 1800–1880*, Copenhagen: Gyldendal (Den danske filosofis historie, vol. IV).

Korsgaard, Christine (1996a) *The Sources of Normativity*, edited by Onora O'Neill, Cambridge: Cambridge University Press.

(1996b) *Creating the Kingdom of Ends*, Cambridge: Cambridge University Press.

(2013) *Self-Constitution: Action, Identity, and Integrity*, Oxford: Oxford University Press.

Kosch, Michelle (2006a) *Freedom and Reason in Kant, Schelling, and Kierkegaard*, Oxford: Oxford University Press.

(2006b) "Kierkegaard's Ethicist: Fichte's Role in Kierkegaard's Construction of the Ethical Standpoint," *Archiv für Geschichte der Philosophie* 88: 261–95.

(2015a) "Fichtean Kantianism in Nineteenth-Century Ethics," *Journal of the History of Philosophy* 53: 111–32.

(2015b) "The Ethical Context of *Either/Or*," *Konturen* 7: 84–101.

(2018) *Fichte's Ethics*, Oxford: Oxford University Press.

Krishek, Sharon (2009) *Kierkegaard on Faith and Love*, Cambridge: Cambridge University Press (Modern European Philosophy).

Kuehn, Manfred (2001) *Kant: A Biography*, Cambridge: Cambridge University Press.

Kyselo, Miriam (2020) "More Than Our Body: Minimal and Enactive Selfhood in Global Paralysis," *Neuroethics* 13: 203–20.

Landau, Iddo (2015) "The 'Why Be Moral?' Question and the Meaning of Life," in Beatrix Himmelmann and Robert B. Louden (eds.), *Why Be Moral?*, Berlin: de Gruyter, 159–71.

Landkildehus, Søren (2009) "Kierkegaard and Pascal as Kindred Spirits in the Fight against Christendom," in Jon Stewart (ed.), *Kierkegaard and the Renaissance and Modern Traditions: Philosophy*, Farnham, UK: Ashgate (Kierkegaard Research: Sources, Reception and Resources, vol. v, tome i), 129–46.

Law, David (1993) *Kierkegaard as Negative Theologian*, Oxford: Clarendon Press.

(2013) *Kierkegaard's Kenotic Christology*, Oxford: Oxford University Press.

(2015) "Kierkegaard as Existentialist Dogmatician: Kierkegaard on Systematic Theology, Doctrine and Dogmatics," in Jon Stewart (ed.), *A Companion to Kierkegaard*, Oxford: Wiley-Blackwell (Blackwell Companions to Philosophy, vol. lviii), 253–68.

Leffler, Olof (2016) "The Foundations of Agency – and Ethics?," *Philosophia* (Ramat-Gan) 44: 547–63.

Lessing, Gotthold E. (1777) *Über den Beweis des Geistes und der Kraft: An den Herrn Director Schumann, zu Hannover*, Braunschweig: [Buchhandlung des Waisenhauses].

(2005) *Philosophical and Theological Writings*, edited and translated by Hugh B. Nisbet, Cambridge: Cambridge University Press (Cambridge Texts in the History of Philosophy).

Lippitt, John (2000) *Humour and Irony in Kierkegaard's Thought*, Basingstoke, UK: Palgrave Macmillan.

(2013) *Kierkegaard and the Problem of Self-Love*, Cambridge: Cambridge University Press.

Løkke, Håvard (2010) "*Nicomachean Ethics*: Ignorance and Relationships," Jon Stewart and Katalin Nun (eds.), *Kierkegaard and the Greek World: Aristotle and Other Greek Authors*, Farnham, UK: Ashgate (Kierkegaard Research: Sources, Reception and Resources, vol. ii, tome ii), 47–58.

Løkke, Håvard and Arild Waaler (2009) "Gottfried Wilhelm Leibniz: Traces of Kierkegaard's Reading of the *Theodicy*," in Jon Stewart (ed.), *Kierkegaard and the Renaissance and Modern Traditions: Philosophy*, Farnham, UK: Ashgate (Kierkegaard Research: Sources, Reception and Resources, vol. v, tome i), 51–76.

Louden, Robert B. (2002) *Kant's Impure Ethics: From Rational Beings to Human Beings*, Oxford: Oxford University Press.

(2011) *Kant's Human Being: Essays on His Theory of Human Nature*, Oxford: Oxford University Press.

(2015a) "Why Be Moral? A New Answer to an Old Question," in Beatrix Himmelmann and Robert B. Louden (eds.), *Why Be Moral?*, Berlin: de Gruyter, 45–64.

(2015b) "The End of All Human Action/The Final Object of All My Conduct: Aristotle and Kant on the Highest Good," in Joachim Aufderheide and Ralf Bader (eds.), *The Highest Good in Aristotle and Kant*, Oxford: Oxford University Press, 112–28.

Lübcke, Poul (1991) "An Analytic Interpretation of Kierkegaard as a Moral Philosopher," *Kierkegaardiana* 15: 93–103.

(2006) "Kierkegaard's Concept of Revelation," in Gesche Linde, Richard Purkarthofer, Heiko Schulz, and Peter Steinacker (eds.), *Theologie zwischen Pragmatismus und Existenzdenken*, Marburg: Elwert, 405–14.

Malantschuk, Gregor (1968) *Dialektik og Eksistens hos Søren Kierkegaard*, Copenhagen: Reitzel.

(1978) *Fra Individ til den Enkelte: Problemer omkring Friheden og det etiske hos Søren Kierkegaard*, Copenhagen: Reitzel.

Manis, Zachary (2006) "Virtues, Divine Commands, and the Debt of Creation," Ph.D. dissertation, Baylor University.

(2009a) "Kierkegaard and Divine-Command Theory: Replies to Quinn and Evans," *Religious Studies* 45: 289–307.

(2009b) "Foundations for a Kierkegaardian Account of Moral Obligation," *Southwest Philosophy Review* 25: 71–81.

Marina, Jacqueline (2000) "Making Sense of Kant's Highest Good," *Kant-Studien* 91: 329–55.

Marquard, Odo (1971) "Anthropologie," in Joachim Ritter (ed.), *Historische Wörterbuch der Philosophie*, vol. 1, Basel: Schwabe, 362–74.

Marshall, Ronald F. (2013) *Kierkegaard for the Church: Essays and Sermons*, Eugene, OR: Wipf & Stock.

Martens, Paul (2015) "H.H.: A Guerrilla Writer after Theologians . . . and More," in Katalin Nun and Jon Stewart (eds.), *Kierkegaard's Pseudonyms*, Farnham, UK: Ashgate (Kierkegaard Research: Sources, Reception and Resources, vol. XVII), 89–96.

Martin, Mike K. (2012) *Happiness and the Good Life*, Oxford: Oxford University Press.

McCombs, Richard (2013) *The Paradoxical Rationality of Søren Kierkegaard*, Bloomington: Indiana University Press.

McCormick, Miriam (2015) *Believing against the Evidence: Agency and the Ethics of Belief*, London: Routledge.

McDaniel, Kris (2020) "Teleological Suspensions in *Fear and Trembling*," *Philosophy and Phenomenological Research* 100: 425–51.

McKinnon, Alastair (1980) "Irrational," in Niels Thulstrup and Maria Mikulová Thulstrup (eds.), *Concepts and Alternatives in Kierkegaard*, Copenhagen: Reitzel (Biblioteca Kierkegaardiana, vol. III), 126–7.

(1998) "Kierkegaard's Conceptual Confusion," *Kierkegaardiana* 20: 71–82.

Mendham, Matthew (2007) "Eudaimonia and Agape in MacIntyre and Kierkegaard's *Works of Love*," *Journal of Religious Ethics* 35: 591–625.

Michalson, Gordon E., Jr. (1985) *Lessing's "Ugly Ditch": A Study of Theology and History*, University Park, PA and London: The Pennsylvania State University Press.

Migliore, Daniel L. (2014) *Faith Seeking Understanding: An Introduction to Christian Theology*, 3rd ed., Grand Rapids, MI: Eerdmans.

Mill, John Stuart (1969) *Essays on Ethics, Religion, and Society*, edited by John M. Robson, vol. X of *The Collected Works of John Stuart Mill*, London: Routledge and Kegan Paul.

Millay, Thomas J. (2015) "Petrus Minor: A Lowly and Insignificant Ministering Critic," in Katalin Nun and Jon Stewart (eds.), *Kierkegaard's Pseudonyms*,

Farnham, UK: Ashgate (Kierkegaard Research: Sources, Reception and Resources, vol. XVII), 215–21.

Mjaaland, Marius (2007) "Funderinger over Abrahams offer: Fundamentalisme, mysterium og teleologisk suspensjon i Kierkegaards *Frygt og Bæven*," *Norsk teologisk tidsskrift* 108: 116–43.

Møller, Poul M. (1842) "Tanker over Muelighheden af Beviser for Menneskets Udødelighed, med Hensyn til den nyeste derhen hørende Literatur," vol. II of *Efterladte Skrifter*, Copenhagen: Bianco Lund, 158–272.

Mooney, Edward (2012) "From the Garden of the Dead: Climacus on Intrapersonal Inwardness," in Rick Anthony Furtak (ed.), *Kierkegaard's* Concluding Unscientific Postscript*: A Critical Guide*, Cambridge: Cambridge University Press (Cambridge Critical Guides), 64–86.

Morgan, Seiriol (2005) "The Missing Formal Proof of Humanity's Radical Evil in Kant's *Religion*," *The Philosophical Review* 114: 63–114.

Mulder, Jack, Jr. (2002) "Re-Radicalizing Kierkegaard: An Alternative to Religiousness C in Light of an Investigation into the Teleological Suspension of the Ethical," *Continental Philosophy Review* 35: 303–24.

Mulligan, Kevin (2010) "Emotions and Values," in Peter Goldie (ed.), *The Oxford Handbook of Philosophy of Emotion*, Oxford: Oxford University Press, 475–500.

Nason, Shannon (2012) "Contingency, Necessity, and Causation in Kierkegaard's Theory of Change," *British Journal for the History of Philosophy* 20: 141–62.

Neiman, Susan (1997) *The Unity of Reason: Rereading Kant*, Oxford: Oxford University Press.

Nielsen, Rasmus (1849) *Mag. Kierkegaards "Johannes Climacus" og Dr. H. Martensens "Christelige Dogmatik": En undersøgende Anmeldelse*, Copenhagen: Reitzel.

Olivares-Bøgeskov, Benjamin (2014) "Happiness," in Steven Emmanuel, William McDonald, and Jon Stewart (eds.), *Kierkegaard's Concepts: Envy to Incognito*, Farnham, UK: Ashgate (Kierkegaard Research: Sources, Reception and Resources, vol. XV, tome III), 137–44.

Orth, Ernst W. (1997) "Philosophical Anthropology," in Lester Embree, Elisabeth A. Behnke, David Carr et al. (eds.), *Encyclopedia of Phenomenology*, London: Kluwer, 522–5.

Osborn, Eric (1987) *Tertullian: First Theologian of the West*, Cambridge: Cambridge University Press.

Palmquist, Stephen R. (1992) "Does Kant Reduce Religion to Morality?," *Kant-Studien* 83: 129–48.

(2016) "The Paradox of Inwardness in Kant and Kierkegaard: Ronald Green's Legacy in Philosophy of Religion," *Journal of Religious Ethics* 44: 738–51.

Parfit, Derek (2013) *On What Matters*, 2 vols., Oxford: Oxford University Press.

Pattison, George (1997) "'Before God' as a Regulative Concept," *Kierkegaard Studies Yearbook* 2: 70–84.

(2002) *Kierkegaard's Upbuilding Discourses: Philosophy, Theology, Literature*, London: Routledge.

Piety, Marilyn G. (2010) *Ways of Knowing: Kierkegaard's Pluralist Epistemology*, Waco, TX: Baylor University Press.

(2017) "Kierkegaard on Nature and Miracles: A Reply to Hampson," accessed February 1, 2018, https://pietyonkierkegaard.com/tag/kierkegaard-on-kant/.

Pinkard, Terry (2001) *Hegel: A Biography*, Cambridge: Cambridge University Press.

(2010) *German Philosophy 1760–1860: The Legacy of Idealism*, Cambridge: Cambridge University Press.

Purkarthofer, Richard (2009) "Some Remarks on Kierkegaard's Method of Indirect Proof in *The Book on Adler*," in Roman Kralik, Abrahim Khan, Peter Sajda, Jamie Turnbull, Andrew J. Burgess (eds.), *Kierkegaard and the Nineteenth Century Religious Crisis in Europe*, Toronto: Kierkegaard Circle (Acta Kierkegaardiana, vol. IV), 251–9.

Quinn, Philip L. (1996) "The Divine Command Ethics in Kierkegaard's *Works of Love*," in Jeff Jordan and Daniel Howard-Snyder (eds.), *Faith, Freedom, and Rationality*, Lanham, MD: Rowman and Littlefield, 29–44.

(1998) "Kierkegaard's Christian Ethics," in Alastair Hannay and Gordon D. Marino (eds.), *The Cambridge Companion to Kierkegaard*, Cambridge: Cambridge University Press (Cambridge Companions), 349–75.

(2006) *Essays in the Philosophy of Religion*, Oxford: Oxford University Press.

Rapic, Smail (2007) *Ethische Selbstverständigung: Kierkegaards Auseinandersetzung mit der Ethik Kants und der Rechtsphilosophie Hegels*, Berlin: de Gruyter (Kierkegaard Studies, Monograph Series, vol. XVI).

Rapp, Gottlob Christian (1791) *Ueber die Untauglichkeit des Prinzips der allgemeinen und eigenen Glückseligkeit zum Grundgesetze der Sittlichkeit*, Jena: Nauke.

Rasmussen, Anders Moe (2009) "Friedrich Heinrich Jacobi: Two Theories of the Leap," in Jon Stewart (ed.), *Kierkegaard and the Renaissance and Modern Traditions: Philosophy*, Aldershot, UK: Ashgate (Kierkegaard Research: Sources, Reception and Resources, vol. V, tome I), 33–49.

Reisner, Andrew (2018) "Pragmatic Reasons for Belief," in Daniel Star (ed.), *The Oxford Handbook of Reasons and Normativity*, Oxford University Press, 705–28.

Ricoeur, Paul (1998) "Philosophy after Kierkegaard," in Jonathan Chamberlain and Jane Ree (eds.), *Kierkegaard: A Critical Reader*, Oxford: Blackwell, 9–25.

Roberts, Robert C. (2008) "Kierkegaard and Ethical Theory," in Edward Mooney (ed.), *Ethics, Love, and Faith in Kierkegaard*, Bloomington: Indiana University Press, 72–92, 256–7.

Rocca, Ettore (2002) "If Abraham Is Not a Human Being," *Kierkegaard Studies Yearbook* 7: 247–58.

Rosenau, Hartmut (2007) "I.H. Fichte: Philosophy as the Most Cheerful Form of Service to God," in Jon Stewart (ed.), *Kierkegaard and His German Contemporaries: Philosophy*, Aldershot, UK: Ashgate (Kierkegaard Research: Sources, Reception and Resources, vol. VI, tome I), 49–66.

Rudd, Anthony (2001) "Reason in Ethics: MacIntyre and Kierkegaard," in John Davenport and Anthony Rudd (eds.), *Kierkegaard after MacIntyre: Essays on Freedom, Narrative, and Virtue*, Chicago: Open Court, 131–50.

(2005) *Kierkegaard and the Limits of the Ethical*, Oxford: Clarendon Press.

(2012) *Self, Value, and Narrative: A Kierkegaardian Approach*, Oxford: Oxford University Press.

Šajda, Peter (2009) "François de Salignac de la Mothe-Fénelon: Clearing the Way for *The Sickness unto Death*," in Jon Stewart (ed.), *Kierkegaard and the Renaissance and Modern Traditions: Theology*, Farnham, UK: Ashgate (Kierkegaard Research: Sources, Reception and Resources, vol. V, tome II), 129–48.

Schaber, Peter (2015) "Why Be Moral: A Meaningful Question?," in Beatrix Himmelmann and Robert B. Louden (eds.), *Why Be Moral?*, Berlin: de Gruyter, 31–41.

Schmitt, Carl (2007) *The Concept of the Political: Expanded Edition*, translated by Georg Schwab, Chicago: University of Chicago Press.

Schopenhauer, Arthur (1969) *The World as Will and Representation*, translated by Eric F. J. Payne, 2 vols., New York: Dover.

Schreiber Gerhard (2009) "Magnús Eiríksson: An Opponent of Martensen and an Unwelcome Ally of Kierkegaard," in Jon Stewart (ed.), *Kierkegaard and His Danish Contemporaries: Theology*, Aldershot, UK: Ashgate (Kierkegaard Research: Sources, Reception and Resources, vol. VII, tome II), 49–94.

(2018) *Happy Passion: Studies in Kierkegaard's Theory of Faith*, Berlin: Peter Lang (Theologisch-Philosophische Beiträge zu Gegenwartsfragen).

(2019) "Passage to Divinity: Magnús Eiríksson on the Rationality of Faith," in Gerhard Schreiber (ed.), *Interesse am Anderen: Interdisziplinäre Beiträge zum Verhältnis von Religion und Rationalität. Für Heiko Schulz zum 60. Geburtstag*, Berlin: de Gruyter (Theologische Bibliothek Töpelmann, vol. CLXXXVII), 259–83.

Schulz, Heiko (2015) "O2 Can Do? Kierkegaard and the Debate on Divine Omnipotence," *Kierkegaard Studies Yearbook* 20: 91–125.

Schwarz, Gerhard (2004) *Est Deus in nobis: Die Identität von Gott und reiner praktischer Vernunft in Immanuel Kants "Kritik der praktischen Vernunft,"* Berlin: Verlag TU.

Silber, John (1963) "The Importance of the Highest Good in Kant's Ethics," *Ethics* 73: 179–97.

Sinnott-Armstrong, Walter (2019) "Practical Moral Skepticism," in Edward Zalta (ed.), *The Stanford Encyclopedia of Philosophy*, accessed March 8, 2021, https://plato.stanford.edu/entries/skepticism-moral/supplement.html.

Skirbekk, Gunnar (1994) *Rationality and Modernity: Essays in Philosophical Pragmatics*, Oslo: Scandinavian University Press.

Skorupski, John (2012) *The Domain of Reasons*, Oxford: Oxford University Press.

Snell, Johann P. (1793) *Kritik der Volksmoral für Prediger: Nach Kantischen Grundsätzen bearbeitet*, Frankfurt am Main: Pech.

Söderquist, Kent B. (2019) "On Faith and Reason(s): Kierkegaard's Logic of Conviction," in Patrick Stokes, Eleanor Helms, and Adam Buben (eds.), *The Kierkegaardian Mind*, London: Routledge (Routledge Philosophical Minds), 227–38.

Søltoft, Pia (2000) *Svimmelhedens etik – om forholdet mellem den enkelte og den andre hos Buber, Lévinas og især Kierkegaard*, Copenhagen: Gad.

Stan, Leo (2011) "Slavoj Žižek: Mirroring the Absent God," in Jon Stewart (ed.), *Kierkegaard's Influence on the Social Sciences*, Aldershot, UK: Ashgate (Kierkegaard Research: Sources, Reception and Resources, vol. XIII), 297–321.

(2017) *Selfhood and Otherness in Kierkegaard's Authorship: A Heterological Investigation*, Lanham, MD: Lexington.

Stern, Robert (2012) *Understanding Moral Obligation: Kant, Hegel, Kierkegaard*, Cambridge: Cambridge University Press (Modern European Philosophy).

(2017) "Round Kant or Through Him? On James's Arguments for Freedom, and Their Relation to Kant's," in Gabriele Gava and Robert Stern (eds.), *Pragmatism, Kant, and Transcendental Philosophy*, London: Routledge (Routledge Studies in Nineteenth-Century Philosophy), 152–76.

Stewart, Jon (2003) *Kierkegaard's Relations to Hegel Reconsidered*, Cambridge: Cambridge University Press (Modern European Philosophy).

(2007) *A History of Hegelianism in Golden Age Denmark: The Martensen Period: 1837–1842*, Copenhagen: Reitzel (Danish Golden Age Studies, vol. III, tome II).

(ed.), (2009) *Kierkegaard's International Reception: Northern and Western Europe*, Farnham, UK: Ashgate (Kierkegaard Research: Sources, Reception and Resources, vol. VIII, tome I).

(2010) *Idealism and Existentialism: Hegel and Twentieth-Century European Philosophy*, London: Continuum.

(2015a) "Poul Martin Møller and the Danish Debate about Immorality in the Wake of Hegel's Philosophy," *Estudios Kierkegaardianos. Revista de filosofía* 1: 115–46.

(2015b) *Søren Kierkegaard: Subjectivity, Irony and the Crisis of Modernity*, Oxford: Oxford University Press.

Stilling, Peter Michael (1850) *Om den indbilte Forsoning af Tro og – Viden med særligt Hensyn til Prof. Martensens "christelige Dogmatik." Kritisk-polemisk Afhandling*, Copenhagen: Reitzel, accessed October 21, 2021, www.kb.dk/e-mat/dod/110308009OOB.pdf.

Stokes, Patrick (2010) *Kierkegaard's Mirrors: Interest, Self, and Moral Vision*, Basingstoke, UK: Palgrave Macmillan.

(2015) *The Naked Self: Kierkegaard and Personal Identity*, Oxford: Oxford University Press.

(2019) "Consciousness, Self, and Reflection," in Patrick Stokes, Eleanor Helms, and Adam Buben (eds.), *The Kierkegaardian Mind*, London: Routledge (Routledge Philosophical Minds), 269–80.

Stolzenberg, Jürgen (2010) "Moralisches und religiöses Selbstbewusstsein bei Fichte und im Blick auf Søren Kierkegaard," in Jürgen Stolzenberg and Smail Rapic (eds.), *Kierkegaard und Fichte: Praktische und religiöse Subjektivität*, Berlin: de Gruyter (Kierkegaard Studies, Monograph Series, vol. xxii), 1–21.

Taylor, Charles (1985) *Human Agency and Language: Philosophical Papers 1*, Cambridge: Cambridge University Press.

Tenenbaum, Sergio (2021) "The Guise of the Good," in Ruth Chang and Kurt Sylvan (eds.), *The Routledge Handbook of Practical Reasons*, London: Routledge, 226–36.

Tennemann, Wilhelm G. (1798–1819) *Geschichte der Philosophie*, 11 vols., Leipzig: Barth.

Theunissen, Michael (1991) *Negative Theologie der Zeit*, Frankfurt am Main: Suhrkamp.

(2005) *Kierkegaard's Concept of Despair*, translated by Barbara Harshav and Helmut Illbruck, Princeton: Princeton University Press.

Thomas, John H. (1980) "Paradox," in Niels Thulstrup and Maria Mikulová Thulstrup (eds.), *Concepts and Alternatives in Kierkegaard*, Copenhagen: Reitzel (Biblioteca Kierkegaardiana, vol. III), 192–219.

Thompson, Curtis (2009) "Gotthold Ephraim Lessing: Appropriating the Testimony of a Theological Naturalist," in Jon Stewart (ed.), *Kierkegaard and the Renaissance and Modern Traditions: Philosophy*, Farnham, UK: Ashgate (Kierkegaard Research: Sources, Reception and Resources, vol. V, tome I), 77–112.

Thuborg, Anders (1951) *Den Kantiske periode i dansk filosofi, 1790–1800*, Copenhagen: Gyldendal.

Tilley, Michael (2015) "Prolegomena for Thinking of Kierkegaard as a Social and Political Philosopher," in Jon Stewart (ed.), *A Companion to Kierkegaard*, Oxford: Wiley-Blackwell (Blackwell Companions to Philosophy, vol. LVIII), 480–9.

Timmermann, Jens (2013) "Divine Existence and Moral Motivation," in Stefano Bacin, Alfredo Ferrarin, Claudio La Rocca, and Margit Ruffing (eds.), *Kant und die Philosophie in weltbürgerlicher Absicht*, vol. 1, Berlin: de Gruyter, 669–78.

Tjønneland, Eivind (2004) *Ironie als Symphom: Eine kritische Auseinandersetzung mit Søren Kierkegaards* Über den Begriff der Ironie, Bern: Peter Lang (Texte und Untersuchungen zur Germanistik und Skandinavistik, vol. LIV).

Toner, Christoph (2017) "Virtue Ethics and Egoism," in Lorraine Besser-Jones and Michael Slote (eds.), *The Routledge Companion to Virtue Ethics*, London: Routledge (Routledge Philosophy Companions), 345–57.

Tudvad, Peter (2010) *Stadier på antisemitismens vej: Søren Kierkegaard og jøderne*, Copenhagen: Rosinante.

(2013) "Henrik Pontoppidan: Inspiration and Hesitation," in Jon Stewart (ed.), *Kierkegaard's Influence on Literature and Criticism: Denmark*, Aldershot, UK: Ashgate (Kierkegaard Research: Sources, Reception and Resources, vol. XII, tome II), 137–65.

Tullberg, Steen (2006) *Søren Kierkegaard i Danmark: En receptionshistorie*, Copenhagen: Reitzel.

Verheyden, Jack (2000) "The Ethical and the Religious as Law and Gospel," in Dewi Z. Phillips and Timothy Tessin (eds.), *Kant and Kierkegaard on*

Religion, Basingstoke, UK: Macmillan and New York: St. Martin's Press (Claremont Studies in the Philosophy of Religion), 153–77.

Verstrynge, Karl (2004) "The Perfection of the Kierkegaardian Self in Regulative Perspective," *Kierkegaard Studies Yearbook* 9: 473–95.

Vos, Pieter H. (2016) "'A Human Being's Highest Perfection': The Grammar and Vocabulary of Virtue in Kierkegaard's Upbuilding Discourses," *Faith and Philosophy* 33: 311–32.

Wahlberg, Mats (2020) "Divine Revelation," in Edward Zalta (ed.), *The Stanford Encyclopedia of Philosophy*, accessed March 19, 2021, https://plato.stanford.edu/archives/fall2020/entries/divine-revelation/.

Walker, Jeremy (1972) *To Will One Thing: Reflections on Kierkegaard's* Purity of Heart, Montreal: McGill-Queen's University Press.

Watts, Daniel (2018) "Kierkegaard on Truth: One or Many?," *Mind* 127: 197–223.

Webb, Carson (2017) "Kierkegaard's Critique of Eudaimonism: A Reassessment," *Journal of Religious Ethics* 45: 437–62.

Wedgewood, Ralph (2008) "Butler on Virtue, Self-Interest, and Human Nature," in Paul Bloomfield (ed.), *Morality and Self-Interest*, Oxford: Oxford University Press, 177–204.

Welz, Claudia (2008) *Love's Transcendence and the Problem of Theodicy*, Tübingen: Mohr Siebeck (Religion in Philosophy and Theology, vol. xxx).

(2013) "Kierkegaard and Phenomenology," in John Lippitt and George Pattison (eds.), *The Oxford Handbook of Kierkegaard*, Oxford: Oxford University Press, 440–63.

(2016) *Humanity in God's Image: An Interdisciplinary Exploration*, Oxford: Oxford University Press.

(2019) "Conscience, Self-Deception, and the Question of Authenticity in Kierkegaard," in Patrick Stokes, Eleanor Helms, and Adam Buben (eds.), *The Kierkegaardian Mind*, London: Routledge (Routledge Philosophical Minds), 281–92.

Westphal, Merold (1991) *Kierkegaard's Critique of Reason and Society*, University Park, PA: Pennsylvania State University Press.

(1996) *Becoming a Self: A Reading of Kierkegaard's* Concluding Unscientific Postscript, West Lafayette, IN: Purdue University Press.

(1998) "Kierkegaard and Hegel," in Alastair Hannay and Gordon Marino (eds.), *The Cambridge Companion to Kierkegaard*, Cambridge: Cambridge University Press (Cambridge Companions), 101–24.

(2012) "Climacus on Subjectivity and the System," in Rick Anthony Furtak (ed.), *Kierkegaard's* Concluding Unscientific Postscript*: A Critical Guide*, Cambridge: Cambridge University Press (Cambridge Critical Guides), 132–48.

(2014) *Kierkegaard's Concept of Faith*, Grand Rapids, MI: Eerdmans (Kierkegaard as a Christian Thinker).

(2018) "Reply to Eleanor Helms on Faith versus Reason in Kierkegaard," *Faith and Philosophy* 35: 367–72.

Wietzke, Walter (2011) "Kierkegaard's Constitutivism: Agency, the Stages of Existence and the Issue of Motivation," *Kierkegaard Studies Yearbook* 16: 411–32.
Williams, Bernard (2004) *Truth and Truthfulness: An Essay in Genealogy*, Princeton: Princeton University Press.
Wimmer, Reiner (1990) *Kants kritische Religionsphilosophie*, Berlin: de Gruyter (Kantstudien-Ergänzungshefte, vol. CXXIV).
Winkel Holm, Isak (1998) *Tanken i Billedet: Søren Kierkegaards poetik*, Copenhagen: Gyldendal.
Wisdo, David (1987) "Kierkegaard and Euthyphro," *Philosophy* 62: 221–6.
Wood, Allen (1970) *Kant's Moral Religion*, Ithaca, NY: Cornell University Press.
(2000) "Religion, Ethical Community and the Struggle against Evil," *Faith and Philosophy* 17: 498–511.
(2016) *Fichte's Ethical Thought*, Oxford: Oxford University Press.
(2019) "Evil in Classic German Philosophy: Selfhood, Deception and Despair," in Andrew Chignell (ed.), *Evil: A History*, Oxford: Oxford University Press (Oxford Philosophical Concepts), 322–49.
Wrathall, Mark A. (2019) "Coming to an Understanding with the Paradox," in Patrick Stokes, Eleanor Helms, and Adam Buben (eds.), *The Kierkegaardian Mind*, London: Routledge (Routledge Philosophical Minds), 239–53.
Wyller, Egil A. (1999) *Mellom Dürer og Kierkegaard: Moderne europeisk åndsliv*, Oslo: Andresen og Butenschøn and Spartacus (Henologisk skriftserie, vol. XI).
Zammito, John H. (2002) *Kant, Herder, and the Birth of Anthropology*, Chicago: The University of Chicago Press.
Zimmerman, Michael (2015) "Value and Normativity," in Iwao Hirose and Jonas Olson (eds.), *The Oxford Handbook of Value Theory*, Oxford: Oxford University Press, 13–28.
Zyl, Liezl van (2017) "Eudaimonistic Virtue Ethics," in Lorraine Besser-Jones and Michael Slote (eds.), *The Routledge Companion to Virtue Ethics*, London: Routledge (Routledge Philosophy Companions), 183–96.

Index

For EU product safety concerns, contact us at Calle de José Abascal, 56–1°, 28003 Madrid, Spain or eugpsr@cambridge.org.

www.ingramcontent.com/pod-product-compliance
Ingram Content Group UK Ltd.
Pitfield, Milton Keynes, MK11 3LW, UK
UKHW020356140625
459647UK00020B/2512

* 9 7 8 1 0 0 9 0 7 4 7 3 5 *